D1216828

ETHOLOGICAL STUDIES OF
CHILD BEHAVIOUR

ETHOLOGICAL STUDIES OF CHILD BEHAVIOUR

Edited by

N. BLURTON JONES

Department of Growth and Development,
Institute of Child Health, University of London

CAMBRIDGE

AT THE UNIVERSITY PRESS

1972

Published by the Syndics of the Cambridge University Press

Bentley House, 200 Euston Road, London NW1 2DB

American Branch: 32 East 57th Street, New York, N.Y.10022

© Cambridge University Press 1972

Library of Congress Catalogue Card Number: 70–160102

ISBN: 0 521 08260 9

Printed in Great Britain

by The Eastern Press, Ltd., London and Reading

155.4

J 78e

158932

CONTENTS

CONTENTS

COMPARATIVE STUDIES

FOREWORD BY
PROFESSOR N. TINBERGEN, F.R.S.

It is a pleasure to introduce this collection of ethological studies of children, edited by Dr N. G. Blurton Jones. As an animal ethologist of standing who has, since obtaining his doctorate, spent a number of years applying ethological methods to the study of child behaviour, he was the obvious man to take the initiative for bringing to the attention of child psychologists these examples of the ways in which ethologists study behaviour.

As I was reading the variety of studies on which the book reports (many of which I had until recently been following only from a distance), I was increasingly reminded of the early days of animal ethology, and I felt that what is now just beginning to happen in human ethology is reminiscent of what occurred in the later 'twenties and early 'thirties to the science of animal behaviour; a new type of research worker is busy building the foundations of a science, by returning, with renewed attention and interest in detail, to the basic task of observation and description of the natural phenomena that have to be understood. I call this ' building ' because, with due respect to human psychology in its widest sense, I consider that it is not yet really a science.

When, well over thirty years ago, a small group of zoologists began to revive the study of animal behaviour, they looked in vain for guidance from the psychological literature. The earlier writings of Lashley and Watson were helpful, and so was the work initiated by Yerkes and his co-workers, but their work soon became part of a trend toward concentration on laboratory-oriented and experimental research on essentially human problems, which was to lead to the preoccupation with too few phenomena and too few methods, and to theoretical weaknesses that have characterised psychology for a long time. The zoologists, being acquainted with the bewildering variety of behavioural systems that were so obviously typical of separate species, felt the need for recording and classifying all these behaviour repertoires. The pioneering studies of Konrad Lorenz stimulated work on what were then called ' ethograms ' – monographs on the behaviour of a variety of animal species, at first mainly descriptive, but gradually incorporating a growing body of interpretations and hypotheses. Thus the science of animal Ethology was born, which, whatever its initial shortcomings, has been, to use the words of Huxley, like a ' breath of fresh air ', and has no doubt been largely responsible for a more biologically oriented approach in other behavioural sciences. It also has itself profited from its interaction with those sister disciplines.

As Ethology grew up, claims began to be made, first diffidently and vaguely, later with increasing confidence, that animal Ethology would one day become important to the study of human behaviour. These claims made at first little impact, partly because ethologists could not provide hard evidence, partly because human psychologists and psychopathologists were not interested. The first psychopathologist who really applied the modern ethological approach to human studies, and who drew the attention of his colleagues to Ethology was John Bowlby, whose work on the effects of mother deprivation on subsequent social behaviour in Man has acted as an important catalyst.

Recently, the application of Ethology to the study of Man has been given worldwide publicity by Konrad Lorenz's *On Aggression* and Desmond Morris' *The Naked Ape*. As I have pointed out elsewhere, these books, while in many respects of great importance, have had two undesirable effects. On the one hand, they have led to an uncritical acceptance of their bold but not sufficiently substantiated extrapolations to Man – an attitude which Callan has recently called ' ethologism '. On the other hand, professional students of human behaviour have, in rejecting some of Lorenz's and Morris' claims, thrown away the baby with the bathwater, and so the Ethology of Man finds itself at the moment in a false position: over-acclaimed by many, shrugged off by others.

But in the meantime, Ethology has begun to invade the human sciences in a less spectacular, but in the long run perhaps more influential way. Rather than extrapolating interpretations from animals to Man, a growing number of young ethologists have themselves begun to collect factual information about Man's behaviour, using ethological methods. These ethologists are by no means all zoologists; they come in part from psychological, psychopathological and anthropological training centres. But what they all have in common with the early animal ethologists is that they are beginning to construct a human ' ethogram '. Working thirty years later than the early animal ethologists, they are naturally doing so with more sophistication. But also, like the ethologists, they did not need much time to discover that the descriptive/interpretative task is much more formidable than initially envisaged. If ethologists who have devoted a lifetime to the study of one species, or group of species, now feel that they have not done more than make a good start, it is not surprising that the handful of ethologists who are reporting here on their first few years of research on children cannot claim more than that they are scratching the surface of an enormous field; nor will they deny the tentative, searching nature of much of their work. At the same time they can justifiably claim that even this little scratching has produced a surprising amount of information of the greatest interest. Being less assertive than we were thirty years ago, Dr Blurton Jones makes this point quietly and persistently rather than shouting it from the rooftops, but the message is clear enough: it is on the one hand surprising how much is being discovered which so far has simply been ignored by the professional psychologists; on the other hand it is clear that this simple, careful observation of normal children is going to be a very demanding task indeed. But it will give a wider scope and more purpose to human studies. And, no less important: by gradually building up an ethogram of our species, work such as is represented here will provide the yardstick by which behavioural pathology can be measured. The words of Sir Peter Medawar could well have been taken as a motto: ' . . . it is not informative to study variations of behaviour unless we know beforehand the norm from which the variants depart '. The research effort that will be needed to provide us with this knowledge of the behavioural ' norm ' will have to become an important task for medical research, and it is clear that ethologists will have an important part to play in this effort.

ACKNOWLEDGEMENTS

In the organisation of this book I have above all to thank the contributors for their enthusiasm and patience. For long-suffering typing and secretarial assistance I wish to thank Miss Jane Forrest, who besides typing my own manuscripts also retyped those of some other contributors, and for similar help at typing bottlenecks we both wish to thank Miss Gillian Meek. For maintaining, caring for and entertaining a constant ready supply of healthy, normal children attending our playgroup I am very much indebted to Miss Susan Drysdale. For contriving the circumstances that brought the idea of the book into being, and turned the idea into reality, the editor and the contributors must thank Dr A. Ambrose, Dr P. M. Driver and Dr A. Winter. I also wish to thank my wife Jill for bearing with the agonies of producing a book which authors and editors always mention but never anticipate.

Acknowledgements on a broader scale are also appropriate at this juncture. The development of ethological studies of human behaviour owes a great deal to several people who have gained too little of the credit. Dr M. R. A. Chance gathered together a vigorous group at Birmingham among whom Ewan Grant's work is best known. The Birmingham group is represented here by Brannigan and Humphries. My own part in this field is due to a series of fortunate coincidences, beginning with a chance discussion in Oxford in 1960 with Eileen Molony and John Burton of the B.B.C. Natural History Unit, while I was a research student working on bird behaviour under Professor N. Tinbergen. Miss Molony suggested that ethologists should look at human behaviour, and overcame my initial objections with the suggestion that nursery school provided the obvious and ideal setting in which to start. Mrs Kate Lee of the College of Further Education in Oxford provided further encouragement to start the research and arranged access to suitable facilities. The work immediately got off to a good start although several interruptions followed, until I moved to Professor Tanner's department at the Institute of Child Health. His decision to seek out an ethologist and give him the chance to study development of behaviour in children (while at the same time continuing work on animals) was at that date a brave piece of scientific management and prediction. I hope that this book and the steadily growing number of ethological studies of human behaviour will reward his remarkable foresight. Linked with this has been the most encouraging, and essential, financial support from the Nuffield Foundation grant to Professor Tanner. The Foundation has also supported other contributors to the book and these indications of their interest in this work have been an encouragement in the often uphill struggle to convey the justification for our approach to others in related disciplines.

N. B. J.

INTRODUCTION

1

CHARACTERISTICS OF ETHOLOGICAL STUDIES OF HUMAN BEHAVIOUR

N. BLURTON JONES*

SUMMARY

This chapter outlines the author's view of those characteristics of ethology which may be of practical importance, particularly in child development research. It starts from the origins of ethology in zoology and the division of questions about behaviour into questions of (1) causation (2) development (3) survival value (4) phylogeny. The book and this introductory chapter concentrate on applications of methods of studying causation, particularly in interactions between individuals, to the study of child behaviour. The numerous popular books relating ethology to human behaviour are rather undisciplined attempts at discussing the phylogeny of human behaviour, which, whatever they claim, have little to say about causation or development.

Ethological methods are held to be partly characterised by emphasis on a preliminary descriptive and observational phase, use of large numbers of anatomically described items of behaviour as the raw data, a distrust of large preselected and untested categories of behaviour. They are contrasted with the use of rating scales and interviews as ways of assessing child behaviour. There is a brief discussion of class and cultural differences and the commonly held but erroneous view that ethologists are looking for human innate behaviour. It is also argued that the use of numerous variables in fairly rigorous analyses will not mask the presence of fine individual differences.

Introduction

There has been a welcome trend in recent years towards closer relationships between previously separated branches of the behavioural sciences. One part of this movement has been a convergence of the interests and methods of developmental psychologists and of ethologists. This convergence has occurred in several ways and this book concerns itself with one of these: the direct application of ethological methods in studies of human behaviour. There have been other points of contact such as: (1) use of animal studies as a source of hypotheses, thoroughly summarised by Ambrose (1968); (2) increasing use of more empirical and ' objective ' measures of social behaviour, e.g. studies of gaze direction in adult interactions by Argyle

* Department of Growth and Development, Institute of Child Health, University of London.

(1967) and others, in studies of the child in the first year by Kagan and Lewis (1965) and in studies of older children by Hutt and Ounsted (1963, 1966), Hutt and Hutt (1970) and others; (3) the use of an evolutionary framework, and of recent data on the processes of ontogeny of behaviour, to form a theory of the child's attachment to its mother more directly testable than previous theories (Bowlby, 1969; Ainsworth, 1970); and (4) relatively speculative accounts of the 'taxonomic position' of human behaviour, e.g. Morris (1967), which impinge on the more serious field of human evolution studied by anthropologists, e.g. Lee and DeVore (1968), Jolly (1970).

My original aim in organising this book was to make available in one volume some examples of recent work where methods used in studying behaviour of animals (especially social behaviour) had been directly applied in studies of human behaviour. I hoped that this would enable readers from the other behavioural sciences to see some of the things that this particular aspect of ethology has to offer. It has been very evident that many of the interested people outside ethology have found it hard to locate summaries of recent work or views in ethology, and consequently are pre-occupied with using or criticising theories long ago discarded by ethologists. They have also found it hard to see which aspects of ethological method are applicable to human behaviour or why this may sometimes be useful. Some have also been put off the scent by the spate of popular books purporting to give authoritative ethological accounts of vital aspects of human behaviour.

Despite the availability of excellent textbooks like Manning (1967), Marler and Hamilton (1967), and Hinde (1966), 'ethological' still makes too many people in related disciplines think of discarded concepts like 'innateness', 'displacement activity', or 'spontaneity' of behaviour; of superficial comparisons with other animals, or of specialised areas like imprinting, territory and dominance. This is unfortunate, not only because these are outdated or limited specialised topics, but also because it neglects the wider and more fundamental issues of theory and methodology (described for example by Tinbergen, 1963, 1969).

Ethological theory has diminished at a rate that some find alarming. But the process was active and a great deal of clarification of methodology resulted from the criticisms by Lehrman (1953) and Hinde (1956, 1959) of early ethological theory. Some of us feel that theories in the behavioural sciences have more often concealed ignorance than explained facts, others feel that a 'new wave' of theory is called for. But one or two basic issues seem to be undisputed, yet to some extent still peculiar to ethology, for instance (1) emphasis on the use of a large variety of simple observable features of behaviour as the raw data; (2) emphasis on description and a hypothesis-generating, natural history phase as the starting point of a study; (3) a distrust of major categories of behaviour whose meaning and reality

4

have not been made clear; (4) belief in the usefulness of an evolutionary framework for determining which kinds of questions need to be asked about behaviour.

The traditional divisions of the behavioural and human sciences are probably impossible to maintain on the basis of subject matter. But workers originating from different traditional disciplines usually bring useful differences in attitude and approach into the field. It is my hope that this will prove no less true of ethologists, who originate from zoology. In this introductory chapter I wish to summarise what I see to be the characteristics of ethology. Most ethologists would shrink from defining ethology and even if they are called ethologists by others, many would scarcely know how to decide whether to apply the classification to themselves. This introduction is consequently a highly personal view of the characteristics of ethology and its potential role in the study of human behaviour. Many other ethologists would disagree with my emphasis of some points rather than others, and some might even find that, although what I say is not very original, it was new to them. Many of the contributors to this book give their own evaluations of ethology in their own papers. Some general discussion of the relationship between ethology and psychology, and some actual studies, have already been published, for example: Ambrose (1968), Ainsworth (1970), Berg (1966), Blurton Jones (1967), Callan (1970), Clancy and McBride (1969), Clark, Wyon and Richards (1970), Crook (1970), Eibl-Eibesfeldt (1968, 1970), Esser et al. (1965), Esser (1968), Foss (1961–9), Freedman (1967), Grant (1965, 1968, 1969), Kaufman (1960), McGrew (1969), Rheingold and Eckerman (1970), Siegel (1960), and Zegans (1967).

Meetings of previously isolated disciplines, while usually fruitful, also often produce hostile reactions from those who cling to the traditional camps. The reader may locate a few hostile remarks in the papers in this book. But the contributors hope that their provocative comments may result in thought and cooperation more than entrenchment. Unfortunately there has often been a tendency for ethologists to take up an arrogant attitude towards psychology. This attitude has sometimes been based on ignorance of the wide range of activities of psychologists, sometimes on the difference in the aspects of behaviour in which they are interested, and only rarely and to a very small extent has it been based on the advantages given by a training in biology and evolution. It is therefore pleasant to be able to report that the contributors to this book are of such mixed academic backgrounds as to be immune to any charges of purely sectarian arrogance. Their undergraduate training ranges from physics, zoology, physical anthropology, to psychology. Their postgraduate experience ranges from invertebrate genetics to psychotherapy. The majority have worked at both ends of these scales, although most either graduated in zoology or spent a long time working with zoologists, and all are intentionally applying an ethological approach to human behaviour. But, simply because the subject matter of psychology is all around us and has for long been investigated, the suggestion that ethological methods can contribute to psychology must imply criticism of the methods of psychologists who have worked on the same topics. Thus some rivalry and competitive responses seem to be inescapable. It also follows that I will be able to illustrate most easily some of the points that I wish to make by criticising established methods. But it should not be forgotten that the use of ethological methods on humans is still in its infancy and that they are usually more time-consuming, and are often more intrusive on the subject than are traditional psychological methods.

The implications of the zoological origin of ethology

Ethology has grown from the traditional discipline of zoology. This means that ethologists have tried explicitly to treat behaviour in the way that a zoologist treats any other feature of an animal. This results in a number of differences between their approach and those prevalent in the other behavioural sciences. My account of the characteristics of the ethological approach relies very much on the writings of Professor Niko Tinbergen. His views as expressed in the early chapters of *The Study of Instinct* (1951), the introduction to his comparative paper on gull displays (1959) and in his celebration essay for Konrad Lorenz 'On the aims and methods of ethology' (1963) are exactly those that I would like to express.

Since ethology draws its methods and subjects of study from general zoology it can be easily classified into studies of causation (physiology), development (embryology), survival value (ecology), and comparative studies (taxonomy and comparative anatomy). These are of course linked around an interest in the evolution of both the form and the behaviour of an animal. An interest in evolution coordinates these disciplines and makes zoology a unified subject. In practice ethologists move freely across these fields, and across anatomy and behaviour. For instance behavioural studies of *Tupaia* led Martin (1968a) into revisions of the taxonomy of mammals using a great deal of anatomical as well as behavioural data (Martin, 1968b). Studies of the behaviour of Black-headed gulls towards their predators led Kruuk (1964) (see also Tinbergen, 1965) to conclusions about interacting selection pressures in animal ecology. A comparable reflection of the unity of biology is rarely found in behavioural sciences perhaps because of the belief that man is an exception to the rules that cover the rest of the animal kingdom. A notable exception is the work of the anthropologists and archaeologists who contributed to Lee and DeVore (1968) which I find provides convincing examples of the interrelationship of all features of human behaviour and biology. Similar examples are provided in the present volume by the papers of Konner and of Richards and Bernal.

Many of the studies described in this book derive not from this general view of ethology, which might well provide a useful framework for a genuinely biological view of human behaviour but more specifically from methods developed for studying interactions between animals and for studying the causation of behaviour, predominantly social behaviour. The details of the rationale of these methods are described by Tinbergen (1959) in relation to the motivation of behaviour of one individual in complex motivational states. Their extension to studies of interaction between animals, based on earlier work described in Tinbergen (1953) is described by Altmann (1962, 1965) and by Hinde and Atkinson (1970).

When one transfers this zoology-based methodology to studying human behaviour one comes up against the belief that man is completely unique among animals. This is well known as an argument (in my view fallacious) against comparative studies which cover human behaviour. But it is conceivable that it could also be used to argue that even the methods of investigating the behaviour of animals are inevitably not applicable to human behaviour. It is probable that there are large areas of human behaviour, such as language, which are not readily investigated by these methods, and it remains to be seen just where this sets the limits to the use of ethological methods in studying human interactions. There may be other areas of psychology, if not behaviour, which could not be studied in this way either in man or animals, such as features of conscious experience.

It seems unnecessary and too time-consuming to review the evidence that man is an animal, though a unique one just as is any other animal. It may be worth commenting that the most eager proponents of ' man is the only animal which . . .' statements are those who know least about animals. One may hope that by now enough heads have fallen in this particular game (culture, kinship, tool-making, food-sharing, and now perhaps language) for people to be learning not to play it.

The really important points here are that (a) most biologists think it unreasonable to isolate man from other animals and assume that it is reasonable to expect some behavioural as well as anatomical and physiological continuity, (b) we may discover that ethological methods have limited usefulness, and that methods that are no less scientific in a general sense demonstrate this to be so by providing better explanations of behaviour, and (c) we may discover that there are limits to the usefulness of the scientific method in its broadest sense. It is my view that we are unlikely to make these discoveries if we do not try, and that these possibilities do not excuse us from attempting to investigate human behaviour by any form of scientific method, including the specialised methods of ethology.

Kinds of question about behaviour

A major feature of the zoological approach to behaviour is the division made by Tinbergen in 1951 of questions about behaviour into four different categories. He argues that when we ask 'why does this animal behave in this way?' we may mean four different things by 'why'. (1) We may be asking 'what made it do it now?', in other words 'what is the immediate causal control of this behaviour?'. (2) We may mean 'how did this individual grow up to be an animal who responds that way?', in other words we may be asking questions about development and learning. (3) We may mean 'what use is this to the animal? Why do these animals do this sort of thing? What do they get from it?', in other words 'what is the survival value for the behaviour?' (4) We may mean 'why does this kind of animal solve this problem of survival in this particular way?' and here the answer is often a reflection of the evolutionary origins of this particular kind of animal. It uses a mammalian solution to the problem rather than an avian solution for instance, the earlier adaptations of their ancestors having set limits to the possible later adaptations. For example, a tool-using bird like the Galapagos Woodpecker Finch has to hold its tool in its beak, whereas a mammal whose forelimbs have not specialised into wings or similarly unpliable locomotor organs can hold it in its hands (many birds could use their feet for this sort of thing and some do for example in string-pulling tests (Vince, 1956)).

This division into four kinds of question simplifies many features of studying behaviour and avoids much confusion, particularly between proximate and ultimate causes and between features of learning (development) and features of motivation (causation). It should also prevent confusion of adaptation and evolution with development, but seldom has (see Ch. 12). Richards (pers. comm.) regards failure to appreciate this as one reason for the stubborn persistence of nature–nurture arguments in research on animal behaviour.

Many of the contributions to this volume are concerned ultimately with development of behaviour, but most of them are still at the stage of investigating the causal organisation of behaviour and of interactions between individuals. Subsequent studies of development will be all the more fruitful because of this. The developmental question is 'what are the changes in the organisation of behaviour as the individual grows?' rather than questions of how this individual acquires the behaviour of an adult.

Very little space in the book is taken up with considerations of survival value of behaviour, but this question is in the back of the minds of several contributors. For example Konner is interested in observing development of behaviour among hunter–gatherer people because this is the way of life which contains the selection pressures which brought about the major structural changes in human physique and brain anatomy. Therefore this is the situation most likely to show us directly the survival value of aspects of child behaviour and development. The discussions in the volume edited by his teachers, Lee and DeVore (1968), indicate how rapidly discussion of almost any feature of early man leads to unsolved ecological questions.

But having survival value at the back of our minds is, as Bowlby (1969) also argued, quite an advantage in studying development. It may be easier to investigate a piece of behaviour when one knows what it is designed to do, and certainly to know this gives one a goal for one's analyses of causation or development. One wishes to answer the question ' how does the animal's behaviour help it to solve this problem of survival? ' But also consideration of natural selection and familiarity with development of a diversity of animals reminds one of a point that Konner makes very clearly, that behaviour of a child must be adapted towards survival as a child, as well as towards acquisition of information. A child is not just a half-formed adult.

Nonetheless, studies of survival value and of phylogeny are notable sections of ethological method which hardly appear in our book at all. This is partly intentional. Most of us started our studies feeling that direct observation of many measures in uncontrolled situations had been fruitful with animals and should be tried on humans. The editor's selection was aimed at this kind of study. The omission is also partly because studies of survival value and phylogeny depend on a sufficient description of the behaviour of the species and most of us feel that this is lacking. However, the attempt to study survival value and phylogeny is one of the best ways of showing up the important gaps in our knowledge. Studies of causation and ontogeny benefit greatly from concurrent studies on effects of behaviour and survival value as well as phylogeny. A good example of the benefit of a phylogenetic outlook can be seen in McGrew's chapter where he discusses the distribution of hostile, investigative and friendly responses to individuals introduced to a group. He then proceeds to a detailed study of this in children, after which further comparative discussion points out the need to allow for age changes in comparative surveys, and therefore the need for more data both on humans and on other primates of varying ages. This heuristic result is in notable contrast to recent popular books which give the impression that everything necessary is now fully known. These books of course are the nearest thing to a predominantly phylogenetic treatment of human behaviour. It is my view that they do this, not only too dogmatically, without explaining their methods, but also much less well than their authors are capable of, and less well than the more direct studies of current (mainly American) archaeologists and anthropologists. However, proper use of the comparative method may be the only way of determining what relevance, if any, studies of primate behaviour have for human behaviour beyond their use in putting up hypotheses to test on humans, and in developing methods. However, since no serious work has yet been done in this field we may be excused from omitting (apart from Ch. 5 and part of Ch. 13) this very classical ethological method from the book. Chapter 12 where I attempt a comparative survey of certain limited aspects of mammalian child-rearing practices is thus completely different from the other chapters. It is intended to illustrate this one part of ethological method – the comparative method. In fact I embarked on this study partly from the wish to try to find out what, if anything, could be properly done in this field. Firstly I had a feeling that many of us too uncritically assumed that human babies must have always been treated in the same way as the young of other higher primates, and secondly a feeling that there must be something valid along the lines of comparing man and his fellow animals, even if Lorenz (1966), Morris (1967, 1969) and Ardrey (1961, 1967) had not succeeded in showing convincingly what it was.

NATURAL HISTORY AND DESCRIPTION

The origins of ethology in zoology have produced other characteristic features of ethology. One of these is an emphasis on the preliminary observational descriptive phase of any scientific investigation. This is in marked contrast to much of psychology, perhaps because psychology has tried to model itself on the physical sciences. The physical sciences have developed excellent methods for investigating relatively small systems but the biological sciences (and those parts of psychology that have remained aloof from the belief in an exclusively experimental approach) have developed methods for investigating the very large complex systems with which they are normally confronted.

The observational phase has been humorously decried as 'trawling for facts'. And indeed there is dispute within developmental and social psychology between those who work at the survey end of the scale and those whose work is predominantly experimental. This dispute would seem unnecessary to most ethologists. The distinction between science and non-science is not seen by zoologists as coincident with the distinction between observation and experiment, and zoologists (including the contributors to this volume at various stages in their careers) use both techniques. It would be quite wrong to think that ethology is non-experimental. But to ethologists and to many other zoologists observation and description must form the first part of any study. This should give rise to hypotheses, which may be (and perhaps to be really interesting ought to be) only testable in experiments. In this connection it should be noted that when zoologists talk of experiments they do not mean the same as many people in psychology or medicine mean. They do not mean 'working with animals rather than people'. They do not mean 'working indoors rather than outdoors'. Many experiments can be done in the field, in an animal or a person's natural environment. Nor does a zoologist describe as an experiment a controlled test or systematic measurement. Psychological tests are in no way experimental. An experiment normally consists of some controlled modification of the situation where the modified and the unmodified situation are compared for their effects on the animal in order to disprove one of a pair of hypotheses. Whether these are done on animals or people or indoors or outdoors is quite irrelevant.

CHARACTERISTICS OF ETHOLOGICAL STUDIES

The advantages of a thorough and leisurely descriptive phase of an investigation are several. The observational phase of a study establishes what there is to explain in real life occurrences, and it generates new hypotheses at a high rate as it goes along. The hypotheses that result are also likely to be somewhere nearer the mark than hypotheses that result from armchair speculation, textbook reading or traditional theory. Thus a long observational phase may, in fact, save time on experimental tests of very unrealistic hypotheses. An experiment merely chooses between two hypotheses, it does not prove the correctness of either or exclude many of the other possible hypotheses that it was not specifically designed to test. Nor does an experiment determine whether the tested effects play an important role in the occurrence of the phenomenon during real life. It is interesting that Connolly and Elliot moved towards the observational kind of study from experimental studies, finding a need for a broader view of what children do with their hands in real life, rather than relying on the literature on how children solve preselected problems. Early studies such as Halverson's (1932) purported to concern the 'natural history' of hand use but they always picked on arbitrary restricted test situations rather than having the courage to risk a genuine 'natural history' which would give information on the variety of hand movements and their relationship to various situations.

The kind of 'unbiased, aimless' observation with which ethologists like to say they begin a study is often held to be an impossibility. It is argued that the large number of observables which are recorded reduces inter-observer reliability (which is a good argument for the more extensive use of film). More importantly it is argued that while the treatment of the observables may be relatively unbiased their selection is subject to bias (although equally often one receives the incompatible accusation that one is recording 'indiscriminately'). The surprising agreement between the independently devised catalogues of behaviour of contributors to this book suggests either some basic reality to these categories or a very uniform set of biases. But in any case the use of these observables (a) gives greater replicability and (b) provides at worst a new set of biases which may be useful, and (c) allows a very wide variety of explicit treatment of the data which, in the use of rating scales and recording of larger predetermined categories, is implicit and untested. By being explicit these analyses are rendered more fashion- and culture-free than analyses using the orthodox techniques. In practice an ethologist probably looks for observables which (a) are repeated in the same form, (b) look as if they affect other individuals and (c) look as if they are responses to other individuals. There is discussion (albeit inconclusive) of the process by which items of animal behaviour are selected in Altmann (1962, 1965), Andrew (1956 and in press) and Blurton Jones (1968 and in press).

Probably during the preliminary 'sit and watch' phase of a study, ethologists build up a habit of quite considerable selectivity about what they record. They unconsciously discard movements that they feel to be unrelated to social interactions or other major events, like a change of weight distribution in a gust of wind, or a brief scratch which may happen at any time. Often they come to the view that some of these insignificant events were, after all, not so insignificant, such as yawning in many higher primates which turns out to be closely related to social situations in individuals at the top of the peck order. Besides the simple ability to see well and quickly, to concentrate and yet to keep responsive to events in the periphery, the ability to develop this sort of selectivity and to notice correlations is presumably part of what we mean by being 'a good observer'. Practical experience, usually in the field, of both good and bad observers is one of the factors predisposing ethologists to scepticism over too great a reliance on inter-observer reliability as a way of evaluating the reality of items to be recorded. The rare bird that two experts spot and identify as it flies past (and which they collect the next day) is made no less real by the fact that ten other observers didn't notice it or couldn't identify it.

In practice ethologists sometimes describe behaviour in terms of the effects that it has, which often very quickly produces circular arguments and has other equally serious objections against it. More often they attempt a more straightforward anatomical description of the form of the movement. But there is still room for selection influenced by hidden assumptions. This means that there is some possibility of choosing behaviour items so that they confirm a hypothesis which is ostensibly under test. However, the description of these items makes it possible for subsequent workers to test this possibility, since they can tell what was actually recorded and then attempt to see what was left out. This has occurred in ethology, for instance in the studies by Andrew (1956) on displays of birds, and on displays and calls of primates (Andrew, 1963 and in press), and following this to a limited extent in studies of human facial expressions by Blurton Jones and Konner (1971) and Blurton Jones (in press). Andrew has pointed out that students of displays in birds and primates have often ignored the occurrence of components of the display patterns in non-social situations. He argues that this may give important information about their causation in the social situation, with radical effects on conclusions about causation of behaviour. The fact that there is this sort of uncertainty about selection of the raw materials of ethological study does not to my mind mean that we are entitled to revert to the infinitely greater uncertainty of untested intuitive major categorisations of behaviour and treat these as having as much reality as categorisations checked against observables.

An incidental result of careful description is the potential replicability of ethological studies. A worker in another laboratory on a different continent can, we claim, read the account of one ethologist and know exactly what behaviour to look for, and can therefore repeat earlier studies. This is unfortunately not true of most so-called observational studies of children. Until recently behaviour was never described in terms of what the observer saw, but in terms much more of what he thought it meant, or in terms with an intermediate status but of equal vagueness. The early observational studies reported on frequencies of ' aggression ', or frequencies of ' affiliative behaviour ' but, for example, there is no way to tell what occurrences Green (1933) recorded as ' quarrels '. These sorts of categories are still in use in some quarters today, but how does one tell what one observer called aggression or what another called affiliativeness?

Even where contributors to this volume classify behaviour in an arbitrary way, their descriptions of behaviour still allow replications of their studies. This is not true of child studies which use rating techniques, or interview techniques. In interviews, even if the questions are recorded, the treatment of the answers remains unrecorded or undefinable. The tedious and space-consuming descriptions in the papers in this volume are completely essential. We should however, aim in future at some uniformity in descriptions, simply for convenience and economy. The stress on description and hence replicability in ethology may account for the neglect of inter-observer (within laboratory) reliability testing which has characterised the work of ethologists on animals and, to a lesser extent, on man. Intense concern for inter-observer reliability testing is fairly characteristic of social and developmental psychology and may have had its origins in the non-replicable nature of the measures that were being attempted (possibly related to the non-operational nature of the concepts being gauged by the measures).

The ethologist's reliance on replication of studies may also have been encouraged by the assumption that the behaviour of animals did not vary greatly within a species. With the recent increase in descriptions of apparent inter-troop differences in various primate species (see Crook, 1970 for summary and references) this assumption can no longer be relied upon. However, inter-observer reliability testing is not a very useful solution to this problem. One team of observers may agree together but disagree with an isolated team, and even if the teams train together before a field study they may diverge during the study. The best solutions are either the one that has been adopted where the students of the two differing populations visit each other's study areas, or the more generous use of permanent records like film and videotape. The same things apply to studying class, culture and area differences in human behaviour. Ideally the same team should work in both areas, or else each of two teams should use film as their raw data so that it is then available for inter-observer tests with the other team. The problem is increased by the propensity of some cultures to change. The same problem can arise in a longitudinal study where observers may come and go during the study and where even those who stay with it from start to finish may be expected to change their criteria or their alertness as the study proceeds. Here the use of film and tape is the only solution, with observers processing film from children of all ages.

There is a hidden assumption in ethology that observations should take precedence over theories, not only to the extent that the results of an experiment determine which of two hypotheses is discarded, but also that theories should be formed after a large collection of observations have been made and should not simply be inherited from textbooks or everyday folk views of behaviour, or be allowed to become an article of faith, in the way that the (otherwise fundamental and important) theories of psychoanalysis have been allowed to do. This assumption is part of the reason for the ethologist's stress on the descriptive phase of science and for the insistence that theories or even any remark about behaviour should immediately allow one to answer the perennial but essential question; ' how do you tell if that is so or not? ' This is the meaning of ' operationalism ' as used by ethologists. It is my belief that this is healthily near to its original meaning. I have recently seen uses that seem much less operational. An insistence on operationalism at every stage, an infinite progression of ' how do you tell? ' questions, seems to me to be an essential for any attempt at a scientific approach to behaviour. For example it is not enough for one to say that one can tell operationally when a subject feels x or y because one's definition is that he says he feels x or y, without going on to say how one decides which statements count as descriptions of x and not of y. It is sad that a rigorous operational approach has been lacking until very recently in so much of social and developmental psychology and in many studies of motivation.

STUDIES OF INTERACTIONS

The aspects of ethological method that are of most obvious immediate use, for instance to students of child development, are those concerning the study of causation and of interactions between individuals. In studying interactions between animals the distinction made by ethologists between causation and between effects of behaviour (leading to its survival value) and the distinction of these from the history of the behaviour during development, make it clear that one must distinguish between what makes an animal perform a piece of behaviour and what effect this behaviour has on another animal. Thus there are two meanings of a piece of social behaviour and it is a topic for investigation as to how far and by what means these two meanings are related to each other in real life. In other words ' how is it that behaviour is set off at such times as to have the effects on other animals that it does have? ' This question is of major importance in dealing with pieces of behaviour, the main function of which appears to be changing the behaviour of other animals. This topic is discussed in detail by Brannigan and Humphries in their chapter on non-verbal communication. The short-term analysis of interactions has been explored extensively by Altmann (1962, 1965) in his studies of rhesus monkey behaviour. In his 1965 paper he describes and discusses the relevant statistical treatment for analysing the sequences of behaviour and investigating the way the behaviour of one animal may be found to affect the behaviour of another, either immediately afterwards or at different durations afterwards. Several contemporary workers on social behaviour of children are aiming to analyse sequences of behaviour to this extent but so far none have overcome fully the practical problems of getting programs written for computers that have big enough memories to analyse fairly long sequences of behaviour.

The separation of causes and effects becomes even more difficult and important when one attempts to analyse long chains of interactions thoroughly, for example in studying the development of the interactions between a mother and her offspring, whether she be a bird, a monkey or a person. The studies of development of mother–infant interaction in monkeys by Hinde and Spencer-Booth (1967, 1968) at Cambridge and by Jensen *et al.* in Seattle (Jensen, Bobbitt and Gordon, 1967, 1968*a, b*) had as their main aim finding out how the behaviour of the mother affects the baby and how the behaviour of the baby affects the mother. Often there appear to be long reciprocal chains of these effects. The method employed by Jensen consists of careful observation of mother and of infant and comparison of these observations in two situations. Hinde's studies consist of detailed analysis of the behaviour of mother to child and child to mother with careful measures of mother behaviour which are independent of child behaviour, and measures of child behaviour which are independent of mother behaviour. These studies acted as a model for some of the sections of the chapter by Blurton Jones and Leach where we attempt to look at relationships between maternal responsiveness and child behaviour. It is essential when doing this to have measures which measure responsiveness and not really the child's requests. It seems impossible to tell whether ratings of maternal response would take this into account or not. It seems to me equally possible, either that they take it into account as well and as effectively as the most careful calculation, or alternatively that the rater responds almost entirely to the child's requests for responses from the mother.

The papers on mother–infant interaction in this book illustrate most clearly the amount of information needed to discern effects of one individual on another. Richards and Bernal show the need for use in one study of data from many levels, from pharmacological to sociological. Not only is their study unique in including data at all these levels but it is also (and consequently) one of the few to be showing any clear differences between breast-fed and bottle-fed babies, though these appear at this stage not to be results of the different methods of feeding. Blurton Jones and Leach illustrate the importance of caution in using large categories of behaviour like 'attachment' and show the amount of behavioural detail needed to separate even short-term effects of child on mother or mother on child. They are led to criticise the current unitary theories of 'attachment' and to commend a fresh look at the ways a number of pieces of 'child to mother behaviour' vary and are controlled. Leach's paper also provides a very explicit account of how one such study of this topic was carried out. It should be of great use to anyone starting this kind of work. Anderson's paper, covering a little-studied age group, provides probably the most 'new discoveries' of any, and shows very well how much can be gained from a genuinely 'natural history' study. Anderson's analysis of the ineffectiveness of various possible stimuli for departure from or return to the mother, and his demonstration that waving by toddlers signals the onset of interaction rather than farewell, are valuable examples of causal analysis and provide results which are unexpected by psychologists and mothers alike. His hitherto unpublished finding that small children can maintain proximity to a stationary but not a moving mother has already been quoted widely.

STUDIES OF DEVELOPMENT

Ethological studies of development of behaviour are less well developed than other subjects, probably because of the long obsession with a sharp innate versus learned dichotomy. But some important points have arisen, in addition to the growth of a proper attitude to processes of development. I have already mentioned how an interest in survival value leads to examining the adaptations of the child to survival as a child. There is also an influence of familiarity with the diversity of animal childhoods which leads one not to expect a single mechanism of behavioural development or a simple process of 'building an adult'. This is part of an expectation that all aspects of behaviour will show a diversity of underlying mechanisms. To a zoologist, whose training consists of becoming familiar with the extraordinary diversity of the animal kingdom and the amazing range of solutions to the problems of survival, it would be very surprising indeed if a general theory or explanation of behaviour could ever be obtained. Any such grand theory would have to be so vague as to explain very little. Similarly zoologists may be more prepared to find mechanisms and performances which initially defy explanation. Many a psychologist has criticised statements about the innateness of behaviour, not on the grounds that all behaviour has a developmental history which consists of an interaction between genes and environment (as does any other feature of an animal), but on the grounds that it is inconceivable that so much information could be built into a brain without interaction between the behaviour and the environment. Many zoologists have become resigned to finding natural selection capable of producing almost any achievement. It may also be worth pointing out that developmental psychology has, even with animals, largely used techniques inappropriate to investigating internal factors in development. The work of neuro-embryologists such as Hamburger (1968), who use the appropriate methods, has been too widely neglected.

There are several aspects of development in which the techniques already developed by psychologists are better than anything ethologists have attempted. An instance is the use of statistical analysis of individual variations during longitudinal studies. As has often happened in the past ethologists will learn a lot from the statistical sophistication of psychologists in this field. The question of the identity of systems of behaviour across ages (Is behaviour A at age 1 really 'the same' as behaviour A at age 2? Is behaviour B a mature replacement of C?) has been tackled more seriously by psychologists, e.g. Lewis (1967), than by any ethologist.

CATEGORISATION AND MULTIPLE MEASURES

There is one basic and simple but very important habit that ethologists have developed in studies of causation which should be of use in social and developmental psychology. When faced with a big word denoting a kind of behaviour or process, like 'aggression', 'attachment', 'anxiety', or 'socialisation', ethologists have the habit of asking themselves 'what do we mean by this?', 'how do we know when we see it?' 'is it one thing or more than one, or nothing at all?' This habit is just basic 'operationalism' but in ethology its origins were in the study of motivation or causation. When looking at an animal and getting the impression that it was 'aggressive' it was easy to realise that this term really referred to what it felt like to be angry or to hate. It is also easy to see that we had never known, and would never have any way of knowing, what it felt like to be an animal in the way that we think we know what it is like to be another person. There is no way of telling whether an animal feels the same as we do. So if 'aggressive' was to have any meaning it must refer to behaviour. It could mean for instance 'likely to attack or fight'. 'Attack' and 'fight' could in turn be defined simply as certain motor patterns, e.g. in a bird pecking another individual or hitting it with the wings (though complications arose when we realised that some of these motor patterns could occur in what appeared to be other contexts). Other 'aggressive' behaviour would have to be behaviour for which we could find evidence that it shared causal factors with attack. When an ethologist uses a word like 'aggressive' he is using it as a label for such behaviour, and he should and usually does only apply this label after gathering the evidence, a point missed for example by some reviewers of Grant (1965) and Lorenz (1966).

Several methods, some non-experimental; statistical, circumstantial, correlational methods and some experimental; controlling the situation, were worked out for gathering this evidence (see Tinbergen, 1959; Tugendhat,

1960; Blurton Jones, 1960, 1968). These techniques have been found adequate even for working out details of complicated situations of conflicting motivation (Blurton Jones, 1968; and Tinbergen and Tinbergen, in press). The success in analysing these complex aspects of motivation leads the ethologist to a growing faith in the possibility of operational definitions of important concepts about behaviour and therefore in the likelihood that overt behaviour is not just a number of superficial externals, but is the key to any basic understanding of behaviour.

In this volume only the most elementary uses are made of these techniques. For instance we have looked at the ways various movements vary together in time, in sequence, from individual to individual, and between the sexes. But these techniques are basic to current topics such as 'attachment', as well as the less topical but perennial topic of 'aggression'. What is 'attachment'? Does it really summarise some set of causal or developmental factors which are a set because they all affect the same group of behaviour patterns? Alternatively does it refer to effects of behaviour? In which case, it does not necessarily say anything about causation. And if it does refer to effects, how are these behaviour patterns caused, how does the causal system produce this common effect?

If the possible 'measures' of 'attachment' do not in fact co-vary and measure the same 'thing' then there is no future in looking for causes of 'attachment' in this global sense. Relationships between cause A and behaviour A will be obscured by lumping that behaviour with behaviour patterns B and C which vary independently of A. Basically the same argument has been rightly raised by critics of Lorenz (1966). Ambition, war, status-seeking, defence of property, defence of space, hostility to strangers and violent crime have all been lumped as 'aggression'. This may or may not be justified but the evidence has seldom been sought. This point is covered again in several of the papers in this volume and I have to rely on these to strengthen the preliminary argument presented here. For instance Brannigan and Humphries' introduction to the study of facial expressions and their part in social behaviour considers this point in practice, drawing ultimately on the classical studies of bird displays described by Tinbergen (1959). It raises basic theoretical points like the distinction between questions of causation, of function and of development and shows the importance of starting with a thorough descriptive study. It is an excellent paper with which to introduce the reader to these aspects of ethological methods. The paper by Connolly and Smith (Ch. 3) gives a valuable review of earlier observational studies of children and points out how the modern studies differ from these. After that my own chapter on categories of child–child interaction concentrates on the derivation of larger categories from the data rather than from theory and the question of dimensions or kinds of behaviour. For instance, is there any use in looking for background causes of 'aggression' if one's measures of 'aggression' confuse two causally quite different kinds of behaviour? Possible relationships will more likely be obscured than revealed. But this analysis is only a first step to understanding in more detail and with more precision how this behaviour is organised.

The point discussed above is very simple. But it is often very hard to communicate, perhaps because it turns the usual processes upside down. It has for long been customary to start with a concept such as 'aggression' or 'attachment' and then look for a 'good' measure of it. For instance Wright (1960) reviewing observational studies of child behaviour cites the following terms, as all used quite uncritically: 'anger, outbreaks of fear, jealousy, conformity, competitive behaviour, seeking affection, friendly approaches, seeking recognition, sociability'. These and other more obscure but no more scientific terms are still in use today. My argument requires a reversal of this process and for this reason is not often understood. The traditional view is defended with a number of well-worn axioms like: 'you can't measure everything' (who says you have to, and anyway why not try?), 'counting movements is like counting the leaves on a tree' (actually a useful thing to do in several circumstances), 'we are not interested in superficial behaviour but in the psychologically meaningful variables' (how are these to be determined?).

This inversion has further implications for those not fully in agreement with the mechanistic approach to behaviour, and I think it is this, rather than any difference in training or academic thoroughness, which accounts for this difference between psychology and ethology. This inversion implies that there are no 'psychologically meaningful variables' other than those derived from the data (these can nonetheless be very high level concepts, or complex models). This would appear to me to be an unassailable position if one's goal is a scientific study of behaviour but there are workers who prefer to determine what is meaningful either from pre-existing theory, or from introspection or intuition. Intuition will be discussed later but introspection is rendered unreliable by the individual variation whose extensiveness would be most enthusiastically argued by the same people. Introspection may still be a very fruitful source of theories but these are no substitute for data, and introspection is not operational evidence for or against the theories that it produces. If on the other hand one refers by 'psychologically meaningful' to aspects of conscious experience my criticism may be escaped. But it remains to be shown (a) how subjects' reports can be evaluated and (b) how conscious experience is related to behaviour.

The view that I have expressed about the need to validate major categories of behaviour, plus the common finding that a piece of behaviour often has a variety of causal factors (differentiated in the last resort by their differing effects on other behaviour), leads to caution over trying to use single measures of behaviour in any test (a conclusion also reached by developmental psychologists such as Lewis, 1967). Only if one uses a number of measures can one keep any check on what one is actually measuring or, in other words, what the experimental variable affects and how it does it. For example, ethological studies of children closely resemble studies proposed for kinesics (e.g. Birdwhistell, 1963) and proxemics (e.g. Hall, 1959, 1963) in their emphasis on direct observation and on recording clearly defined features of behaviour. However, probably partly because children are easier to observe than adults, most of the contributors to this volume would feel it unnecessary as well as undesirable to segregate the study of gestures and posture from the study of spacing and from other aspects of behaviour. We like the interest in everyday life and in well-defined observables but are unhappy to see gesture and spacing unrelated when, for example, Argyle and Dean (1965) have demonstrated a link between spacing and visual behaviour.

The view that all the interesting things about behaviour are to be derived from data about observable behaviour commits the ethologist to a very long-term programme of analysis of the details of form, sequencing and other features of organisation of behaviour. This is a constant process of translating our ' intuition ' or ' social perception ' into explicit observation and description, which then enables us to test our original intuition and perhaps construct better models of behavioural mechanisms. What do we see that tells us that this time he wasn't ' really ' joking, or that he was feigning friendliness? Brannigan and Humphries in their studies of facial expression have gone as far as any workers towards answering this kind of question. An unexplored part of this field, that still sets us briefly despairing of an explicit description of behaviour when we respond but don't notice the cues that made us respond, is the non-verbal aspect of speech. Also, few of us have looked in sufficient detail at the temporal organisation of behaviour. For instance Leach differentiates *offer* from *show* (Ch. 10) although the arm positions are often the same in these two patterns but she is not sure how she does it (she combines them anyway in her analyses). Perhaps the child looks at different things in the two patterns, they certainly say apparently different things, but more likely the impression also comes from the sequence of behaviour, and from the reaction of the child to the reaction of others to its initial movement. Unless we pay attention to this sort of detail we will soon have exploited our techniques up to a false limit. It is sometimes said that observations of observable behaviour miss the ' flavour ' or ' colour ' of an event. This is really just another way of saying that one chose to record too many of the wrong things and not enough of the subtle social signals that have just been discussed.

One may realistically argue that if our intuition is so far ahead there is no point in trying to describe these things explicitly. There are two answers to this. One is the practical one that in the case of individuals whose communication is not functioning properly one cannot tell exactly how it is failing without a systematic study, nor can one help them to correct it without being able to pinpoint the fault. The other is the academic argument that since we are attempting some sort of systematic study of social behaviour we cannot simply express opinions or interpretations which we are unable to back up with evidence which we can describe to other people. Our intuition is also likely to be an idiosyncratic reflection of our culture and personality. An explicit description is at least to a greater extent independent of these two variables.

It could be one task of ethologists working on human behaviour to take words like depression, distress, sulking, sorrow, negativism, and attempt to clarify their meaning in terms of the control of overt behaviour, in much the same way as Hinde (1954) translated ' mood ' as ' changes in responsiveness '. This often requires looking at very many items of behaviour at the same time. For example, crying is commonly accompanied by slumped body position and sitting down or leaning on someone. These occasions might correspond to times when people use ' sorrow ', ' distress ' or ' depression ' rather than the other terms. Sulking can imply either a reduced responsiveness or hostile response to friendly behaviour. Negativism may include frequent use of aggressive ' no ' and ' won't ' verbalisations, best defined by the physical, non-verbal properties of the sound, eventually leading to crying if the situation does not abate. These are simple examples treated rather hastily but there may be more important ones worthy of study like the use of the word ' rejection ' in describing responses of a child to its mother, or vice versa. It is hoped that by examining the meaning of terms like this which are actually used in developmental psychology ethologists may be able to help put the subject onto a firmer basis. They may help make what many would call a very ' soft ' science (and which some of these consequently and very foolishly ignore) slightly ' harder '. Conversely, ethologists must be prepared to deal with concepts like fantasy and pretence and with occurrences such as one child inside the ' Wendy-house ' shouting to another ' you can't come in here ' then ' pretending ' to turn a (non-existent) key in the door (how much ' pretend ' behaviour consists of actions performed without the object usually involved in them or with a substitute object?). We may take courage against misconceptions of the problems posed by dramatic ' pretend ' play from the observation of Gardner and Gardner (in press) of a young chimpanzee ' pretending ' to inject itself with a nail after evading an injection earlier in the day.

It may be that examining overt behaviour can contribute to the study of children's dramatic play. The overt behaviour involved in dramatic play divides into three types: rough and tumble play, social exchange of objects, imitation of adult activities. The imitation of adult activities (often with parental mannerisms superimposed) sometimes combines with rough and tumble (e.g. games of police cars) or social exchange (e.g. shops, offices). It seems sensible to argue that some of the reinforcement, or some of the causal factors of these activities are involved in dramatic play. There is of course the added factor of the dramatisation, the naming and definition and adoption of rules for the game. The attractiveness of the definitions and rules may nonetheless partly depend on how far they fit the tendency to do rough and tumble play, to exchange objects, and to imitate adults.

It may be that the natural history approach and consideration of survival value can help if applied not only to social behaviour but also to the more manipulative, intellectual seeming kinds of play. Connolly and Elliot have gone a considerable way towards this in their study of painting (Ch. 13) and more could be done on other aspects of manipulative behaviour and use of play objects and materials. Children's great readiness to examine and then to do things with objects after ceasing to examine them (Hutt, 1967) may be quite as significantly human as the acquisition of language, though there seems to be little data from other primates on time spent handling non-food objects. It would certainly be useful to find out more about what determines the precise choice of play material, particularly in view of present day ' informal ' primary school teaching methods, where increased ability to guide and exploit the naturally occurring interests might be welcome. Examining individual variations and looking for relationships of specific occupations to other kinds of behaviour may help. For example, I have the impression that painting is often used by mothers and teachers as a way of getting the child busy if it is hesitant about leaving its mother, and it may acquire particular meaning from this. Different occupations may be chosen depending on the amount of social interaction they involve. As described above, dramatic games, often involving large construction work or use of objects as weapons incorporate many rough and tumble play actions. The problem of the two-way interaction of sociability and occupations was raised by Clark, Wyon and Richards (1970) and is being investigated by Leach (pers. comm.).

Criticisms of established methods

Two particular established techniques can be taken to illustrate some of the criticisms an ethologist would level at some of his colleagues in developmental psychology, which in turn serves to illustrate the characteristics of at least one ethologist's approach. The first that I will discuss is the use of ratings of behaviour on pre-arranged scales.

CRITICISMS OF RATING SCALES FOR OBSERVED BEHAVIOUR

Critical discussion of rating scales usually concerns the number of divisions necessary (the more divisions, the higher the correlations between observers' scores incidentally), inter-observer agreement within one laboratory, the need to avoid halo effects and sometimes the difficulty of validating the scale.

The first point which occurs to me about rating scales concerns the source of the dimensions on which children are rated. The source is too often either a previous author, or the current author's imagination, or a major psychological theory into whose framework the subjects are about to be fitted. The biggest surprise to ethologists is that these dimensions are so seldom empirically derived, as in some personality questionnaire factor analysis studies. One only has to look at a few rating scales to see that they often include more than one empirical dimension in the same scale. This is true both when one relates them to the existing studies of observable defined behaviour (which show or suggest independent relationships, e.g. between amount of fighting and position in peck order, between friendliness and timidity) and when one asks a perceptive and experienced teacher or mother (not trained in theory) to rate a group of children on a feature such as sociability, or aggressiveness.

The other major problems with rating scales concern validation and normality. Normality is used in two explicit senses and one implicit sense in child psychology but which of these is in mind is seldom specified (a fourth, evolutionary, one is theoretically possible but would be culturally unacceptable, e.g. it may well be normal for a child to refuse to leave mother on her initiative, and be normal to sleep with the mother). One, the most useful, is the empirically derived statistical mean for the population under study. Another is the theoretical healthy ideal which unfortunately merges into cultural ideals. The implicit sense is healthy in the sense of seldom being complained about. It will always be wrong to use the word ' normal ' in the descriptions of the scale. This may give a classification which depends entirely on the culture of the rater (including his theoretical sympathies) and it makes it impossible to derive statistical normality from the results. Either way it gives no data of any validity outside the culture and era of the investigator, standardisation will be suspect if not actually impossible.

Validation implies relating the scoring system to some other scores of the same aspects of behaviour. The only reasonable validations appear to be those on aptitude tests for career selection. Validation of rating scales of children's behaviour can only be matched to adult feelings or attitudes to the children, or to the kind of data on behaviour found in the contributions to this volume. On the latter criterion few if any rating scales would show any validity.

<h2 style="text-align:center">CRITICISM OF INTERVIEWS AS A MEANS OF FINDING OUT ABOUT CHILD BEHAVIOUR</h2>

Much child development research is done by interviewing the mother rather than by studying children. The better studies using these techniques appear to get round most of the problems of leading questions and embarrassment (see Newson and Newson, 1963 for differences in answers to familiar psychologist interviewers and to visitors from the local health authority) and in some cases provide immense amounts of valuable data about the subjective life of mothers and their problems and aims in child rearing (e.g.

Newson and Newson, 1963, 1968). As regards information about what the mothers actually do and signal to their children and what the children actually do, the interview is of much more limited value. Presumably the accuracy of reporting some kinds of events will be greater than others. A mother may or may not recall her child's behaviour, she may or may not wish to report these to the interviewer. In addition, as Richards and Bernal argue (Ch. 7), she is unlikely to recall sufficient detail with sufficient accuracy to allow investigation of interactions between herself and her child. Her answers may also provide problems of interpretation. Newson and Newson (1963) very fruitfully go into the reasons mothers give for not breast feeding their babies and discuss the various possible interpretations, moving from the superficial 'practical' answers 'my milk was too thin' (see Ch. 12) to the more obviously emotional answers 'I don't know why, but I just can't, I feel a sort of disgust for it'. However, there are no explicit rules for deciding when a mother has given the 'real' answer (even supposing there is such a thing as a real answer), or when she has answered at all the relevant levels, or even how one decides that 'I didn't want to be tied' or 'my milk was too thin' really mean something else.

Psychoanalysis started this problem of levels of interpretation with its technique of investigating the symbolism of patients' statements or accounts of their dreams. Psychoanalysis gave some pointers about methods of interpretation (which requires a much larger amount of material than is usually gathered in interviews of mothers) linguists of course also investigate this problem, e.g. Bierwisch (1970). But the determination of meaning remains a problem whatever use is made of interview data. Because verbal information by virtue of the nature of language commonly consists of unique statements, no simple solution as with the more limited motor behaviour can be adopted. The same applies to any use of verbal content in direct studies of children. It would obviously be wrong to say one must exclude verbal information from studies of child behaviour. But it is equally wrong to assume that anyone's stated reason for doing something is necessarily the only reason or the 'real' reason. In addition to the considerations resulting from psychoanalysis, the 'meaning' of a verbal remark can be affected by non-verbal aspects of speech. Thus some statements can be interpreted differently depending on whether they are heard and seen, heard on tape, or read in transcription.

If a mother says to her child 'you are always wandering off' this is at one level a simple statement about the child's behaviour but it can also be a simple request to stay nearby, or an encouragement and approval, or a hostile criticism or various combinations of these. Which of these we interpret it as depends on the context, on our feelings about this mother and observations of her on other occasions and on the intonation and other non-verbal components of the utterance. Ethological analysis of non-verbal communication like that of Grant (1968) and Brannigan and Humphries in

Chapter 2 in this volume can help to elucidate these meanings. In fact as Mahl (1967) indicates and as Schneck (1967) shows in a paper on blushing in interviews, some psychoanalysts already use non-verbal behaviour but usually in a less systematic way than ethologists could help them achieve.

When the child's or mother's reports of their own behaviour differ (e.g. McCord and McCord, 1961, Fazio, 1969, Reynolds, pers. comm.) from their observed behaviour a number of interesting questions arise. What are the differences between individuals whose verbal reports agree with their behaviour and those that do not? Why, beyond the possibilities of trying to impress the observer more in one than the other, do they differ and which if any is the 'real' answer? This implies that interview data is important information but that it must not be mistaken for information about what behaviour the subjects actually show. One might contrast the sophisticated use of interview data about mothers and babies by Robson and Moss (in press) and by Richards and Bernal (Ch. 7) with that in many studies purporting to be about the behaviour of mothers and children.

Proponents of interviewing have defended interviewing by attacking direct observation on the following grounds:

(1) the observer only sees a small and possibly unrepresentative part of the child's and mother's life,

(2) if the observer is concealed this usually means the subjects are at a special establishment where they may be putting on their best behaviour,

(3) if the observer is in view he may likewise affect the behaviour, particularly of the mothers.

These are fair criticisms of many observational studies (but, for example, 2 and 3 do not apply to Anderson's study and 1 and 2 do not apply to Konner's) but they do not amount to a defence of the use of interviews for obtaining information about behaviour. The presence of an observer can be tested (see Connolly and Smith, Ch. 6) for effects on children. Differences in behaviour of mothers observed by a visible observer, and one behind a one-way screen could be investigated, even though neither can be considered a 'natural' situation. Some aspects of these problems of novelty of the setting are covered in McGrew's chapter (Ch. 5). Our impression with the mothers in Leach's study is that, particularly with those attending the psychiatrist, we go through the same process of familiarisation and relaxation as interviewers go through. We also gained the tantalising impression that we could identify very early the mothers who later turned out to have been putting on their best behaviour. Unfortunately, we have not been able to identify what cues we saw or heard that give us this impression.

A conspicuous feature of the works in this book is that they all concern children, and this may appear to imply that our approach is of no help in studying adult behaviour, where language is even more important. The historical reason is that we all felt that children were easier to study, partly because they were easily available and partly bcause they do talk less and act out more than adults. But how limited are we by the problems involved in dealing with language, and by the assumed greater complexity of adults? I feel that we do not know because we often haven't tried. But this self-criticism is also inaccurate. Leach, and Richards and Bernal in this volume and Esser *et al.* (1965), Grant (1968) and Eibl-Eibesfeldt (1968) have all worked on adults with some success. I think that the distraction of anthropocentrism is the major part of the problem of studying adults. Language may be less of an obstacle than we suppose.

CLASS AND CULTURAL DIFFERENCES

One criticism that has sometimes been made of ethological studies of human behaviour (even though so few have yet been published) is that we ignore possible class and culture differences. This criticism is worth discussing because it reveals a mistaken view of our aims. It was assumed that we hoped that observations in one nursery school would be typical of the entire species *Homo sapiens*. Because of the kinds of behaviour we look for (having been trained in looking at species differences and species-specific behaviour) it is highly likely that some of what we have been recording is human species-specific behaviour. But none of us have claimed to have proved this (see Blurton Jones, 1967, p. 362, where I disclaim it and also make the point that using observable constant motor patterns in studies of causation does not imply anything about the development of these patterns – following Tinbergen, 1951, rather than Lorenz, 1950 or 1966).

Even if this was our aim we would not attempt to achieve it without using cross-cultural and cross-racial data. Such data is slowly accumulating (e.g. Eibl-Eibesfeldt, 1968, Konner, this volume Ch. 11, for cross-cultural data) and supports the obvious suggestion that there is a large repertoire of motor patterns which are the same throughout the species. But to show that their organisation, or their effects, are the same in all or many cultures, races, classes, is a later, more interesting stage in which the variations are just as interesting as the constancies, though again Eibl-Eibesfeldt (1968) and Ekman, Sorenson and Friesen (1969) and Konner have made a start at looking at the constancies in this kind of measure. It also remains to be seen whether relationships like the correlations shown in Blurton Jones and Leach's chapter within a narrow class range between individual differences in maternal behaviour and child behaviour, apply also across classes and 'explain' some class differences. Ainsworth (1969) and Schaffer and Emerson (1964) have found the same apparent relationship between responsiveness of mother and attachment of child in two different races in three widely different cultures. And one might wish to regard Konner's study as evidence showing that this also applies cross-culturally. Certainly we assume that some constant relationships can be found, even if they have to be more complex than that example, e.g. rules of the way the relationship of maternal responsiveness to the child's attachment changes. Otherwise there are indeed no rules and no explanations of human behaviour. Perhaps this implies an assumption that class and culture have their effects on the individual through the behaviour of other individuals, like parents, siblings, and peers. The rigid separation of sociology from psychology seems to deny this assumption. I cannot argue this point beyond saying that I anyway find this separation highly artificial, and that I cannot regard class differences as explanations of behavioural differences (a valuable model is the study of the relationship between class, maternal height, smoking in pregnancy, and low birth weight, (Butler, Alberman and Goldstein, 1969)). But the separation of sociology from psychology anyway relies on assumptions about development of behaviour (e.g. the ways in which 'roles', however they are to be identified, are acquired).

If ethologists so readily accept the possibility of some kinds of class–culture differences, why have we nonetheless gone in for detailed studies on small, single-class, single-culture samples? The answer is that we believe that such detailed data is far more worth comparing than the more general data so far available. For example, children in different social classes may be expected to have different 'attitudes' to strange adults from those in Connolly and Smith's study, and different 'attitudes' to joining a playgroup from the children in McGrew's study. But while frequencies of, for example, auto-manipulation might be less in children of some classes when joining a play-group, I would expect automanipulation, being stationary, looking, glancing, and walking, to perform in the same way relative to each other as they do in McGrew's study. Thus a profile of frequencies of various behaviour items on a child's first day could show large class differences but the underlying relationships might be the same. One then needs to explain how class affects 'unease' or 'social immaturity'; for instance by differences in the number of peers the child meets. If the relationships differ one knows the problem is different, one needs to ask why growing up in different classes changes the organisation of 'settling-in' behaviour. This cannot be done unless one first elucidates the organisation of 'settling-in' behaviour. The value of cross-cultural studies like those of Eibl-Eibesfeldt, which look for 'universals' at the 'low' level of motor patterns, seems to me to lie as much in the opportunity they give for more precise description of differences between populations as in any evidence they may provide about mechanisms of development of these motor patterns. Examination of cross-cultural differences is a most important source of information about development (e.g. see Whiting, 1963).

A goal of describing the behaviour of 'pre-cultural' man would be quite unbiological. No such creature existed, whether called man or ape, and certainly it would not be of any relevance to the 'formative years' in the evolution of *Homo* during which his brain developed most markedly (at least in size), and did so reciprocally with his cultural development. Man's material culture has exerted selection pressures on his hands and his brain. The cultural variations in behaviour of mammals and birds are now so well documented as to preclude any sensible division of ethology from sociology or anthropology across a culture–no culture border. The division of biological from cultural evolution seems to be yet another exaggerated dichotomy. Describing the species-specific behaviour of *Homo sapiens* is not a matter of peeling off the cultural crust but either seeking out the ranges of variation in behaviour, or finding the general rules which underlie the variation of behaviour within this range. This has of course been an aim of many schools of anthropology from Freud and Malinowski up to contemporary followers of Levi-Strauss and in the sphere of child development (Whiting, 1963). There are also, however, schools of thought in anthropology and sociology which appear to argue against the possibility of any general rules of human behaviour.

Conclusion

It is risky to look into the future and say what role I expect to see ethological methods play in social and developmental psychology. But we all know that exposing one's ideas to disproof is part of the job of being a scientist. I think that the differences in the methods employed by ethologists and by psychologists are going to get smaller and smaller. There is already very little difference between the way Gewirtz and Gewirtz (1969), Ainsworth and Bell (1970, and in press) or Rheingold and Eckerman (1970) investigate mother-child relationships and the way any of the contributors to this book would do it. On the whole I think ethological methods, being so time-consuming, will be of more use in research than for example in practical diagnosis or treatment, though present indications are that I may be being too modest.

In general I feel that ethological methods give the traditionally 'soft sciences' of child development and social behaviour a useful opportunity to make themselves a little 'harder' without at the same time getting as narrow-minded as could result from too successful an imitation of the physical sciences. I think that ethologists can usefully set themselves the task of repeating important studies such as the developmental studies of Sears, Rau and Alpert (1965), Schaffer and Emerson (1964), Ainsworth (1969), and the cross-cultural studies of the Whitings and others (e.g. Whiting, 1963) with the expectation of providing confirmation for findings that are of central importance to child psychology. Of course one cannot exclude the possibility that such detailed studies might revise our ideas and give us new insight into child development. If the criticisms of orthodox method are as important in practice as they are in theory, then this is highly likely.

Rigour in a science often threatens to bring inflexibility and oversimplification with it. But our use of large numbers of small observable items of behaviour as a starting point for analysis allows the description of a very much wider range of organisations of behaviour than does for instance a series of rating scales. In fact Leach found that her data showed up the individual differences between 'problem children' so well as to make general comparisons with the controls very difficult. Consequently I see in the 'hardening' process no necessary danger of losing the sensitivity and the readiness to deal with complexity and individual variation which developmental psychology has justifiably cultivated.

REFERENCES

Ainsworth, M. D. S. (1969). Attachment and exploratory behaviour of one-year-olds in a strange situation. In *Determinants of infant behaviour*, vol. 4. Ed. B. M. Foss. London: Methuen.

Ainsworth, M. D. S. (1970). Object relations, dependency, and attachment: A theoretical review of the infant–mother relationship. *Child Develop.* **40**, 969–1026.

Ainsworth, M. D. S. and Bell, S. M. (1970). Attachment, exploration and separation: illustrated by the behaviour of one-year-olds in a strange situation. *Child Develop.* **41**, 49–67.

Ainsworth, M. D. S. and Bell, S. M. (in press). Infant crying and maternal responsiveness: reinforcement reassessed. *Science, N.Y.*

Altmann, S. A. (1962). A field study of the sociobiology of rhesus monkeys, *Macaca mulatta. Ann. N.Y. Acad. Sci.* **102**, 338–435.

Altmann, S. A. (1965). Sociobiology of rhesus monkeys. II: Stochastics of social communication. *J. theor. Biol.* **8**, 490–522.

Ambrose, A. (1968). The Comparative Approach to Early Child Development: The Data of Ethology. In *Foundations of Child Psychiatry*. Ed. E. Miller. London: Pergamon.

Andrew, R. J. (1956). Some remarks on behaviour in conflict situations, with special reference to *Emberiza* spp. *Br. J. Anim. Behav.* **4**, 41–5.

Andrew, R. J. (1963). The origin and evolution of the calls and facial expressions of the Primates. *Behaviour* **20**, 1–109.

Andrew, R. J. (in press). The information available in mammal displays. In *Non-verbal Communication*. Ed. R. A. Hinde. London: Cambridge University Press.

Ardrey, R. (1961). *African Genesis*. London: Collins.

Ardrey, R. (1967). *The territorial imperative*. London: Collins.

Argyle, M. (1967). *The Psychology of Interpersonal Behaviour*. Harmondsworth: Penguin Books.

Argyle, M. and Dean, J. (1965). Eye contact, distance and affiliation. *Sociometry* **28**, 289–304.

Berg, I. (1966). A Note on Observations of Young Children with Their Mothers in a Child Psychiatric Clinic. *J. Child Psychol. Psychiat.* **7**, 69–73.

Bierwisch, M. (1970). Semantics. In *New Horizons in Linguistics*. Ed. J. Lyons. Harmondsworth: Penguin Books.

Birdwhistell, R. L. (1963). The Kinesic level in the investigation of Emotions. In *Expression of the Emotions in Man*. Ed. P. H. Knapp. New York: International University Press.

Blurton Jones, N. G. (1960). Experiments on the causation of the threat postures of Canada Geese. *Wildfowl Trust 11th Ann. Report 1958–9*, 46–52.

Blurton Jones, N. G. (1967). An ethological study of some aspects of social behaviour of children in nursery school. In *Primate Ethology*. Ed. D. Morris. London: Weidenfeld and Nicolson.

Blurton Jones, N. G. (1968). Observations and Experiments on the causation of threat displays of the Great Tit *Parus major*. *Anim. Behav. Monog.* **1**, 75–158.

Blurton Jones, N. G. (in press). Criteria for use in describing facial expressions of children. *Hum. Biol.*

Blurton Jones, N. G. and Konner, M. J. (1971). An experiment on eyebrow-raising and visual searching in children. *J. Child Psychol. Psychiat.* **11**, 233–40.

Bowlby, J. (1969). *Attachment and Loss*, vol. 1. *Attachment*. London: Hogarth Press.

Butler, N. R., Alberman, Eva D. and Goldstein, H. (1969). Maternal factors affecting duration of pregnancy, birthweight and foetal growth. In *Perinatal Problems*. Ed. N. R. Butler and Eva D. Alberman. Edinburgh and London: Livingstone.

Callan, H. (1970). *Ethology and Society*. London: Oxford University Press.

Clancy, H. and McBride, G. (1969). The autistic process and its treatment. *J. Child Psychol. Psychiat.* **10**, 233–44.

Clark, A. H., Wyon, S. M. and Richards, M. P. M. (1970). Free-play in nursery school children. *J. Child Psychol. Psychiat.* **10**, 205–16.

Crook, J. H. (1970). Social organisation and the environment: aspects of contemporary social ethology. *Anim. Behav.* **18**, 197–209.

Eibl-Eibesfeldt, I. (1968). Zur ethologie des menschlichen Grussverhaltens. *Z. Tierpsychol.* **25**, 727–44.

Eibl-Eibesfeldt, I. (1970). *Ethology: the biology of Behaviour*. New York: Holt Rinehart and Winston.

Ekman, P., Sorenson, E. R. and Friesen, W. V. (1969). Pan-cultural elements in facial displays of emotion. *Science, N.Y.* **164**, 86–8.

Esser, A. H. (1968). Dominance hierarchy and clinical course of psychiatrically hospitalised boys. *Child Develop.* **38**, 147–57.

Esser, A. H., Chamberlain, A. S., Chapple, E. D. and Kline, N. S. (1965). Territoriality of patients on a research ward. In *Recent advances in biological psychiatry* **7**. Ed. J. Wortis. New York: Plenum.

Fazio, A. F. (1969). Verbal and Overt-behavioural assessment of a specific fear. *J. Consult. Clin. Psychol.* **33**, 705–9.

Foss, B. M. (ed.) (1961–9). *Determinants of Infant Behaviour*, vols. 1–4. London: Methuen.

Freedman, D. G. (1967). A biological view of man's social behaviour. In *Social Behaviour from Fish to Man*. Ed. W. Etkin. Chicago and London: Univ. of Chicago Press.

Gardner, B. T. and Gardner, R. A. (in press). Two-way communication with an infant Chimpanzee. In *Behaviour of Non-human Primates 3*. Ed. A. M. Schrier, H. F. Harlow and F. Stollnitz. New York: Academic Press.

Gewirtz, H. B. and Gewirtz, J. L. (1969). Caretaking settings, background events and behaviour differences in four Israeli Child-rearing environments: some preliminary trends. In *Determinants of Infant Behaviour*, vol. 4. Ed. B. M. Foss. London: Methuen.

Grant, E. C. (1965). The contribution of ethology to child psychiatry. In *Modern Perspectives in Child Psychiatry*. Ed. J. G. Howell. Edinburgh: Oliver and Boyd.

Grant, E. C. (1968). An ethological description of non-verbal behaviour during interviews. *Br. J. Med. Psychol.* **41**, 177–83.

Grant, E. C. (1969). Human facial Expression. *Man* **4**, 525–36.

Green, E. H. (1933). Group play and quarrelling among pre-school children. *Child Develop.* **4**, 302–7.

Hall, E. T. (1959). *The silent language.* New York: Doubleday Anchor.

Hall, E. T. (1963). A system for the notation of proxemic behaviour. *Amer. Anthrop.* **65**, 1003–26.

Halverson, H. M. (1932). A further study of grasping. *J. genet. Psychol.* **7**, 34–63.

Hamburger, V. (1968). Emergence of Nervous Coordination. Origins of Integrated Behaviour. *Developmental Biology Suppl.* **2**, 251–71.

Hinde, R. A. (1954). Changes in Responsiveness to a constant stimulus. *Brit. J. Anim. Behav.* **2**, 41–55.

Hinde, R. A. (1956). Ethological models and the concept of ' drive '. *Brit. J. Philos. Sci.* **6**, 321–31.

Hinde, R. A. (1959). Unitary drives. *Anim. Behav.* **7**, 130–41.

Hinde, R. A. (1966). *Animal Behaviour.* London and New York: McGraw-Hill.

Hinde, R. A. and Atkinson, S. (1970). Assessing the roles of social partners in maintaining mutual proximity, as exemplified by mother–infant relations in rhesus monkeys. *Anim. Behav.* **18**, 169–76.

Hinde, R. A. and Spencer-Booth, Y. (1967). The behaviour of socially living rhesus monkeys in their first two and a half years. *Anim. Behav.* **15**, 69–196.

Hinde, R. A. and Spencer-Booth, Y. (1968). Review lecture. The study of mother–infant interactions in captive group-living rhesus monkeys. *Proc. Roy. Soc. B.* **169**, 177–201.

Hutt, C. (1967). Temporal effects on response decrement and stimulus satiation in exploration. *Br. J. Psychol.* **58**, 365–73.

Hutt, C. and Ounsted, C. (1963). A method for the study of children's behaviour. *Develop. Med. & Child Neurol.* **5**, 253.

Hutt, C. and Ounsted, C. (1966). The biological significance of gaze aversion with particular reference to the syndrome of infantile autism. *Beh. Sci.* **11**, 346–56.

Hutt, S. J. and Hutt, C. (1970). *Direct observation and Measurement of Behaviour.* Springfield, Ill.: Charles C. Thomas.

Jensen, G. D., Bobbitt, R. A. and Gordon, B. N. (1967). Sex differences in social interaction between infant monkeys and their mothers. *Recent adv. biol. Psychiat.* **9**, 283–93. Ed. J. Wortis. New York: Plenum.

Jensen, G. D., Bobbitt, R. A. and Gordon, B. N. (1968a). Effects of environment on the relationship between mother and infant Pigtailed monkeys (*M. nemestrina*). *J. Comp. and Physiol. Psych.* **66**, 259–63.

Jensen, G. D., Bobbitt, R. A. and Gordon, B. N. (1968b). Sex differences in the development of independence of infant monkeys. *Behaviour* **30**, 1–14.

Jolly, C. (1970). The seed-eaters: a new model of hominid differentiation based on a baboon analogy. *Man* (n.s.) **5**, 1–26.

Kagan, J. and Lewis, M. (1965). Studies of attention in the Human Infant. *Merril–Palmer Quart.* **11**, 95–122.

Kaufman, I. C. (1960). Symposium on psychoanalysis III. *Int. J. Psychoanal.* **41**, 318–26.

Kruuk, H. (1964). Predators and Anti-predator behaviour of the Black-headed Gull (*Larus ridibundus*). *Behaviour Suppl.* **11**, 1–129.

Lee, R. B. and DeVore, I. (eds.) (1968). *Man the Hunter.* Chicago: Aldine.

Lehrman, D. (1953). A critique of Konrad Lorenz's theory of instinctive behaviour. *Quart. Rev. Biol.* **28**, 337–63.

Lewis, M. (1967). The meaning of a response, or why researchers in infant behaviour should be oriental metaphysicians. *Merril–Palmer Quart.* **13**, 7–18.

Lorenz, K. (1950). The Comparative Method in Studying innate behaviour patterns. *Symp. Soc. exp. Biol.* **4**, 221–68.

Lorenz, K. (1966). *On Aggression.* London: Methuen.

Mahl, G. F. (1967). Some clinical observations on non-verbal behaviour in interviews. *J. Nerv. Mental Dis.* **144**, 492–505.

Manning, A. (1967). *An Introduction to Animal Behaviour.* London: Arnold.

Marler, P. and Hamilton, W. J. (1967). *Mechanisms of Animal Behaviour.* New York: Wiley.

Martin, R. D. (1968a). Reproduction and Ontogeny in tree-shrews (*Tupaia belangeri*), with reference to their general behaviour and taxonomic relationships. *Z. Tierpsychol.* **25**, 409–95 and 505–32.

Martin, R. D. (1968b). Towards a new definition of primates. *Man* (n.s.) **3**, 337–401.

Morris, D. (1967). *The Naked Ape.* London: Jonathan Cape.

Morris, D. (1969). *The Human Zoo.* London: Jonathan Cape.

McCord, Joan and McCord, W. (1961). Cultural stereotypes and the validity of interviews for research in child development. *Child Develop.* **32**, 171–85.

McGrew, W. (1969). An Ethological Study of Agonistic Behaviour in preschool Children. *Proc. Second Internat. Congr. Primatol., Atlanta* **1**, 149–59. Basel and New York: Karger.

Newson, J. and Newson, E. (1963). *Infant Care in an Urban Community.* London: Allen and Unwin.

Newson, J. and Newson, E. (1968). *Four years old in an Urban Community.* London: Allen and Unwin.

Rheingold, H. L. and Eckerman, C. O. (1970). The infant separates himself from his mother. *Science, N.Y.* **168**, 78–83.

Robson, K. S. and Moss, H. A. (in press). Patterns and Determinants of Maternal Attachment. *J. Pediat.*

Schaffer, H. R. and Emerson, P. E. (1964). The development of social attachments in infancy. *Monog. Soc. Res. Child Develop.* **29**, 3 (serial no. 94).

Schneck, J. M. (1967). Blushing and unconscious hostility. *Diseases of the Nervous System* **28**, 679.

Sears, R. R., Rau, L. and Alpert, R. (1965). *Identification and Child Rearing.* Stanford: Stanford University Press.

Siegel, A. E. (1969). Current issues in Research on early development. *Hum. Dev.* **12**, 86–92.

Tinbergen, N. (1951). *The Study of Instinct.* London: Oxford University Press.

Tinbergen, N. (1953). *Social Behaviour in Animals.* London: Methuen.

Tinbergen, N. (1959). Comparative studies of the behaviour of gulls (Laridae): a progress report. *Behaviour* **15**, 1–70.

Tinbergen, N. (1963). On the aims and methods of ethology. *Z. Tierpsychol.* **20**, 410–33.

Tinbergen, N. (1965). Behaviour and Natural Selection. In *Ideas in Modern Biology* 521–42. Ed. J. A. Moore, New York: Doubleday.

Tinbergen, N. (1969). Ethology. In *Scientific Thought 1900–1960*. Ed. R. Harré, Oxford: Clarendon Press.

Tinbergen, N. and Tinbergen, E. A. (in press). Social interactions in normal and autistic children – an ethological study. *Z. Tierpsychol.*

Tugendhat, B. (1960). The disturbed feeding behaviour of the three-spined stickle-back. I. Electric shock is administered in the food area. *Behaviour* **16**, 159–87.

Vince, M. A. (1956). String-pulling in birds. I. Individual differences in wild adult great tits. *Br. J. Anim. Behav.* **4**, 111–16.

Whiting, B. B. (ed.) (1963). *Six cultures: studies of child rearing.* New York: Wiley.

Wright, H. F. (1960). Observational Child Study. In *Handbook of Research Methods in Child Development.* Ed. P. H. Mussen, New York: Wiley.

Zegans, L. C. (1967). An appraisal of ethological contributions to psychiatric theory and research. *Amer. J. Psychiat.* **124**, 729–39.

CHILD—CHILD INTERACTIONS

2

HUMAN NON-VERBAL BEHAVIOUR, A MEANS OF COMMUNICATION

CHRISTOPHER R. BRANNIGAN *

AND

DAVID A. HUMPHRIES †

SUMMARY

This chapter deals with the use made of facial expressions and body gestures in human communication, as a signalling system optionally independent of speech, and on other occasions influencing and itself modified by speech.

Facial expressions have been the subject of earlier experimental research, much of which suffered from inadequate description of the expressive patterns themselves and insufficient attention to the natural circumstances in which such patterns are normally shown. Recent studies, particularly by ethologists, have partly overcome these deficiencies by tending to concentrate on descriptive analysis of behaviour in ' natural situations ' such as children's playgroups. The methods of observation available and on the findings from direct observational studies are discussed, including the forms and significance of some of the common units of expression, such as smiles, frowns, and units seen in aggressive and defensive situations. Some common pitfalls in the description and interpretation of human expression are illustrated.

An agreed terminology is urgently needed, the problem being complicated by the various levels of detail at which description of expressions is possible. As a tentative contribution towards a standard terminology, an Appendix is included, defining 136 units.

Since recent studies have demonstrated that there are important pan-cultural factors in the forms and recognition of facial signalling it is suggested that further research on the development of expression from birth onwards is needed to reveal the ways in which learning may influence the forms, usage and recognition of expressions. Finally the relevance of non-verbal communication in psychiatry is briefly discussed.

It is a well-known fact of everyday life that the smiles, frowns, gestures and other non-verbal behaviours of our acquaintances provide useful cues about their moment to moment attitudes to ourselves or others. Much of their non-verbal behaviour is generally accepted to be a means of communication.

* Charles Burns Child Psychiatric Clinic, Birmingham and Department of Psychiatry, University of Birmingham.
† Department of Biological Sciences, University of Aston in Birmingham.

However, the scientific study of this everyday fact is still in its infancy, despite the ubiquity of the phenomenon and despite the obvious practical advantages to be gained from its scientific understanding, for example in child psychiatry, education, management and the visual arts.

The scientific study of human communication has been concentrated almost exclusively on linguistic systems (Cherry, 1957; Lenneberg, 1967), and knowledge and theoretical interpretations of non-verbal, non-linguistic communication have been derived mainly from studies on other animal species using an ethological approach described by Tinbergen (1948) and Lorenz (1950). Man's behavioural flexibility and his possession of language are sufficient reasons for pausing to consider whether it is valid to apply directly these ethological methods developed on other species. Likewise, the effectiveness of these methods and the established evolutionary relationship between man and other species are also sufficient cause for reluctance in accepting as adequate the more circumscribed psychological and psychiatric approaches used for example by Honkavaara (1961), Osgood (1966) and Scheflen (1963). Indeed, research on the nature and signal value of human non-verbal behaviour, particularly gesture and facial expression, has been carried out not only by ethologists, psychologists and psychiatrists, but also by sociologists, anthropologists and telecommunications researchers; not surprisingly there has been a diversity of methods of study and a variety of theoretical interpretations. We shall therefore begin by considering the biological background to human non-verbal communication, and will then discuss methodology.

The organisation and coherence of a social group in any species, including man, depends on an interchange of information between its members. This information is concerned with the integration, into the organised social group, of successive changes in each individual's behaviour and spatial positioning. It is in this connection that we here use the term ' communication '; an act of communication occurs when certain attributes of an individual (usually behavioural attributes) appearing in specific situations are, via their effect on the sense organs of another individual, capable of altering that individual's future behaviour.

In some species scents or other chemical signals are most important in transmitting the necessary information, in others acoustic or visual signals predominate. In man the vocal signalling system is obviously supreme and the complexity and information-carrying capacity of human language far exceed that of acoustic systems in other species (Cherry, 1957). However, vocal language is probably a recent evolutionary acquisition for it is shown by none of our closest primate relatives (although a recent report (Gardner and Gardner, 1969) suggests that individual chimpanzees may possess at least the potential to learn a non-vocal linguistic communication system). Before our separation from the evolutionary line leading to the present-day great apes it is probable that our ancestors relied on social signalling systems similar to those found in the modern higher primates, systems using body posture, facial expression, gesture, movement relative to another individual, scent and non-linguistic sound (Marler, 1965). Modern man has not lost the ability to acquire information from the non-verbal attributes of his conspecifics, and the changes induced in an individual's behaviour by his perception of a smile, frown or tears in a social partner are, subjectively, well known. Indeed we may regard the evolution of the capacity for verbal language as having occurred within the context of this more primitive signalling system. This context is likely to have affected the nature of speech just as linguistic capacity has affected human non-verbal signalling (Humphries, 1970). In man therefore we are not dealing with a primitive non-verbal visual signalling system as a phenomenon entirely separate from linguistic communication; conceptually the two systems can be isolated but in practice they often form a functional whole. This is an important point. Since non-verbal signals can be used semi-linguistically during conversation (Humphries, 1970) it is evident that the uncritical application of ethological methods and interpretations derived from other species would be inadequate if not misleading.

Non-verbal signalling can be studied most clearly and separately in young children up to 4 years of age, before language has become the predominant method of communication. This is particularly true in child–child interactions. During a four-year study in a Birmingham nursery school we found that although 3- and 4-year-old children used speech fairly freely to communicate with adults, they used it infrequently – usually as brief imperatives – during group play, relying instead on gestures, facial expressions and intention movements to integrate their activities. This is one reason why the development of ethological studies on human communication behaviour has been concentrated on the under fives (e.g. Grant, 1965a; Blurton Jones, 1967; McGrew, 1969; Brannigan and Humphries, 1969), or has found special application where verbal communication has largely broken down, as in the study of adult schizophrenics by Grant (1965b) and the ethologically based operant conditioning procedure developed by Currie and Brannigan (1970) for autistic children.

The ethological approach, as seen in the present volume, was essentially formulated in the pioneering work of Darwin (1872) which remains an important source of ideas and information concerning human non-verbal expression. Darwin described expressions seen in suffering, sobbing, anxiety, bad temper, sulking, surprise, fear and horror, and many others, and considered their evolutionary origins in relation to then current physiological and anatomical knowledge. Darwin's meticulous attention to the description of the forms of the expressions themselves – a central part of the ethological approach – was not followed in many subsequent psychologically orientated studies. Some of these studies centred on the judgement of ' meaning ', relying mainly on samples of expression photographically isolated from the social context (Schlosberg, 1954; Honkavaara, 1961) and aiming at agreement between independent judges rather than validation of what the judges agreed about.

The method of photographic isolation of expressions is in any case valid only if the basic descriptions and definitions of the original expressions have been correctly made, so that the photographic isolate does not merely represent an unidentifiable fragment of a unit normally identified by changing in a specific manner over a definite period, like a nod or wink. The isolation of an expression from its general context can also be a dubious procedure; it is certainly not the way in which we learn to derive meaning from phonemes, for which context is all-important. Marler (1965) has pointed out that even in other higher primates the response to a social signal (and therefore presumably its ' meaning ') depends on the latter's context in the general situation and in the envelope of other accompanying signals. It is not surprising that studies based on the judgement of still photographs have generally yielded disappointing results. A notable exception is the success of the cross-cultural study made by Ekman, Sorenson and Friesen (1969) in which the photographs were selected on the basis of a thorough descriptive analysis of expressions guided by Tomkins' theory of personality (1962, 1963).

An insufficient descriptive analysis of expressions, particularly in relation to naturally occurring situations is perhaps again the reason for the failure of the experimental situational approach. This was used by Landis (1929) who recorded the expressions of subjects undergoing what were intended to be experimentally specified experiences, for example as a result of receiving an electric shock, or looking at a photograph of a nude. Landis found great variation of expressions in each situation and concluded that there were therefore unlikely to be standard ' meanings ' for each expression. It may be argued however that although the situations were standard, the subjects' experiences were not, since these depended on the initial states of the subjects, which could not be standardised for the experiment.

The lack, in many studies, of a sufficiently accurate description of the expressive movements themselves may be partly explained by the apparent complexity of human expressions, and by man's ability to alter details of expression at will. Given a complex and highly flexible set of actions it may well have seemed unprofitable to try to reveal by description some kind of systematic order in the form of expressions, although Darwin (1872) had already shown the validity of this approach. It is also notoriously difficult to be objective about the behaviour of one's own species and the natural tendency is to judge the subjective impression made by the expression, rather than recording the details of the expression itself. A group of eighteen university students we asked to describe verbally the eyebrow movements which would accompany an aggressive blow gave very diverse answers; yet when shown a series of four simple diagrams of a face, each with a different eyebrow position, they were almost unanimous in picking out the correct aggressive frown. This illustrates the natural tendency and ability of man to infer the mood accompanying an expression rather than describing or remembering the objective details of the movements of the parts of the face or body.

We comment that in order scientifically to explain any phenomenon it is first necessary to describe it thoroughly, accurately and objectively. Tinbergen (1951) has emphasised the importance of adequate initial description of behaviour, to provide a sound basis for subsequent interpretations. Variability and complexity have not prevented progress in other areas of science, and several independent studies now confirm that the variability and complexity of child expression and gesture are based on a large number of repeatable units of regular form. This finding together with the success of the same ethological approach in elucidating communicatory processes in other species is sufficient evidence of its value.

The comparative evolutionary approach begun by Darwin (1871, 1872) is another prominent feature of ethology and useful insights into human communication may well be obtained from comparative studies on our closest primate relatives (Andrew, 1963, 1964; Bastian, 1965; Van Hooff, 1962). But it must be emphasised that data derived from species other than man can be used only to *suggest* hypotheses which may be worth applying to man for testing by critical observations. In the absence of critical evidence derived from observing man such hypotheses are no more than intelligent guesses. There is a danger in human ethology, as in some other branches of the science of man, that interesting, but untested, hypotheses may gain the status of accepted theory. Callan (1970) has coined the term ' ethologism ' as a label for the present vogue (Ardrey, 1967; Morris, 1967) for uncritically invoking the findings from ethological studies of other species as necessary and sufficient explanations for large aspects of human social life. Theory based on superficial analogies between species has always impeded biological understanding, and at the present time little has been achieved towards providing the necessary validation of comparative interpretations of the behaviour of man in relation to that of other animals. We conclude that a valid ethology of man must be based primarily on data derived from man, and not on data obtained from fish, birds or other primates.

Accepting that exact description of the observed pattern of behaviour is to form the starting point of a study on human non-verbal communication, how is this description to be achieved? One of the most powerful descriptive procedures in science is the analysis of a phenomenon into its basic units. So we may ask on what criteria units can be distinguished and defined in human non-verbal behaviour. We may also consider whether such particulate description is valid.

Behaviour can be analysed into units on four kinds of criteria – *phenomenological*, a unit being all items of behaviour which take the same form;

or *functional*, all items serving the same kind of consequence (a special case of this is all items serving the same biological function); or *situational*, items occurring in the same situation; or *causal*, items sharing common causal factors. The units we obtain and the patterns they form will differ according to which criterion is used, and for this reason it is important that the chosen type of criterion should be used consistently.

The most striking advances in understanding animal communication have arisen on the basis of an initial phenomenological description of behaviour, and this is the approach which we, and others, have adopted for human behaviour. It differs from the inferential description which is commonly used by laymen; thus behaviours which may be functionally similar in that they serve some destructive purpose are commonly described by the same term 'aggressive', yet a number of quite different patterns of behaviour are lumped together by this procedure, in which observation is directly translated into an inferred mood rather than being stated explicitly as an objective description of the behaviour. The recognition and definition of the whole range of units is a lengthy process, requiring observations in many situations. Human ethology is still mainly in this descriptive stage and little experimental work has been done.

There has been good agreement on units defined in largely independent studies (Blurton Jones, 1967; McGrew, 1969; Grant, 1969; Brannigan and Humphries, 1969; Krebs, pers. comm.). This can be seen in the present volume. But it is also evident from published reports and privately circulated checklists that differences have arisen due, not to errors in observation, but to the various levels of description adopted. For example the large unit 'rough and tumble play' (Blurton Jones, 1967) can be broken down into smaller constituent units like those used by McGrew (1969) in his study of agonistic behaviour. He considers 'Gross behaviour' as fourteen elements including *hug, body oppose, shrug, fall*, whilst locomotion is divided into eight categories including *run, walk, chase* and *flee*. To these are added twenty-one facial elements and seventeen limb elements. Of McGrew's sixty elements one can confidently expect all but two, *yawn* and *digit suck*, to occur commonly during 'rough and tumble play'.

The level of description is of major importance in determining the data, and depends on two major factors; the purpose of the study and the facilities and subjects available. For example, the frequent changes in position of freely playing children render it very difficult to obtain long complete records of the sequence of changes in fine details of facial expressions; accordingly 'large' units have generally been used to describe the play of pre-school children (Blurton Jones, 1967; Clark, Wyon and Richards, 1969). Grant (1965b, 1968) was able to use a finer level of description for seated adults, and has shown that many of the same units of expression occur in freely playing nursery school children (Grant, 1969). Analysis into similar small units was found to be necessary by Currie and Brannigan (1970) in

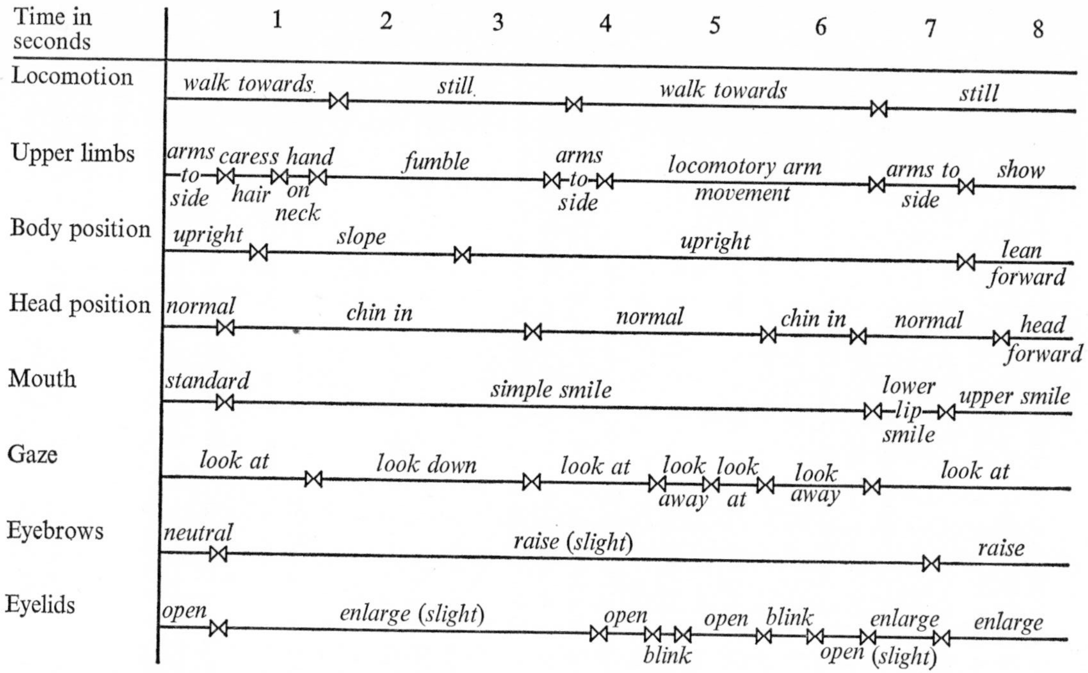

Fig. 2·1. Composite diagram of observed behaviour during approaches by pre-school children, showing an object to an observer. At this level of analysis simultaneous sequences can be seen to occur in seven body regions. An approximate time scale is indicated.

training social communication in an autistic child. At an even finer level of description Blurton Jones (in press) has attempted to relate facial expressions to the action of individual muscles; at this level the limitations of unassisted direct observation indicate that special recording facilities and some degree of control over the subject's movements may become critical for reliability.

The information-processing capacity of the unaided observer becomes critical too in attempts to handle large numbers of different units occurring in rapid sequence. Grant (1969) has defined 118 items of non-verbal behaviour, more than half arising from the face, and this list is not complete. These units have different durations and may overlap in complex ways in sequence (see Fig. 2·1). Grant's (1968) method of summarising stochastically the non-verbal behaviour in interviews by treating it as a simple sequence of thirty or so units in the classical manner of Baerends and Baerends-van Roon (1950) can now be seen to be an over-simplification of the problem. The unaided observer can handle limited aspects of the subject's behaviour but video-recording facilities are preferable where reliable complete accounts are required.

At this point we may conveniently introduce examples of the units of facial expression, some of which we shall later discuss in detail. A list of the units, with definitions, is given in the Appendix.

Smiles are characterised by an upward and outward movement of the mouth corners, and may be classified into various categories (Fig. 2·2) according to the degree and form of mouth opening and tooth exposure

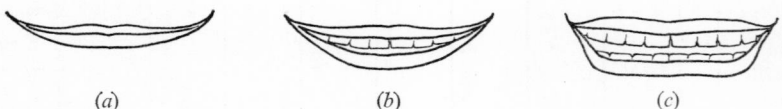

(a) (b) (c)

Fig. 2·2. Three common smiles: (a) *simple smile*, (b) *upper smile*, (c) *broad smile*.

(Brannigan and Humphries, 1969). Each type of smile tends to occur in its own characteristic situations, although some overlap occurs. Thus *upper smile* is usually combined with eye to eye gaze contact between individuals, whereas *broad smile* is not, although it is the commonest smile in children's play, particularly in rough and tumble play. Gaze contact acquired during a *broad smile* usually results in an immediate switch in form to *upper smile* by an upward movement of the lower lip to cover the lower set of teeth. Display of the lower set of teeth is the main feature of the aggressively threatening unit *intention bite* described by Grant (1969); it seems likely that the covering of the lower teeth during smiles involving gaze contact functions to eliminate any possibility of the signal being interpreted as aggressive.

The two smiles in which the lips are not parted also tend to occur in rather different situations. The *simple smile* is seen mainly when the individual is not actively participating in social interactions, for example when playing alone with toys, though it also occurs in social interactions apparently as a low intensity form of open mouthed smiles, particularly the *upper smile*. The *compressed smile* (Fig. 2·4*f*) resembles the *simple smile*, except for compression and thinning of the lips and in general less upward movement of the mouth corners. It occurs in situations in which a response is being suppressed, as where it is socially unacceptable to laugh outright at teacher's misfortune in tripping over, or where a verbal reply is being politely suppressed.

The appearance of the eye region can be seen to change regularly in relation to changes of mouth shape. *Broad* and *upper smiles* are normally seen in association with an even and symmetrical elevation of the eyebrows, *raise* (Fig. 2·3*c*). We see *raise* with *upper smile* when the child greets his parents, or when two friends meet; we see *raise* with *broad smile* when an individual is suddenly and pleasantly surprised, and accompanying laughing during rough and tumble play. The eyebrows are not always raised during laughter, which particularly in adults may be seen in association with closed, or almost closed, eyes, and a wrinkling of the bridge of the nose with the eyebrows pulled slightly down and in. These methods of emphasising or suppressing the signal value of the eyes suggest that the interpretation of the meaning of a smile is closely affected by signals from the eye region. These will also include wrinkling of the eye corners as a consequence of the lifting of the mouth corners, and in *upper smile* a swelling of a small pouch under each eye (Grant, 1969). The pouch is not under voluntary control, and its presence affords a means of confirming that an *upper smile* is genuine, not false. During conversation or play a person may quickly raise and lower the eyebrows as in *raise*; this is *flash* (Fig. 2·3*d*). *Flash* appears to serve various functions, firstly it can indicate special emphasis by the speaker on a particular word or phrase. Secondly, *flash* is frequently seen in the listener, possibly as a device for indicating continued attention. In these circumstances *flash* is often combined with head *nod*.

The existence of a relationship between units arising from the mouth region and the eye region can also be seen in the frowns. By describing a fairly common sequence of behaviour in pre-school children we will illustrate how the different forms of the frowns are again closely related to specific kinds of social situation. The child is ' happily ' playing, with a smile and slightly raised eyebrows, when another child comes to take from him his toy. The intruder has his eyebrows drawn down, particularly at the inner ends, *angry frown* (Fig. 2·3*a*), his lips are tensed and pushed forwards, *lips forward*, the head and often the chin are thrust forward, *threat, chin out*. The child whose toy is being taken may unwillingly yield to this threat, in which case the eyebrows are drawn down at their outer ends to produce *sad frown*,

(Fig. 2·3*b*), the mouth corners are drawn back and down, *mouth corners down*, and the child may then begin to cry, opening the mouth more widely, *square mouth*. If this performance is rewarded by a teacher coming to see what is going on the crying child maintains the same slope of eyebrows as for *sad frown* but raises them, *sad raise* (Fig. 2·3*e*). This unit is commonly seen when an adult patient tells his psychiatrist about his troubles, or when singers are rendering an emotional song. In children the set of units described

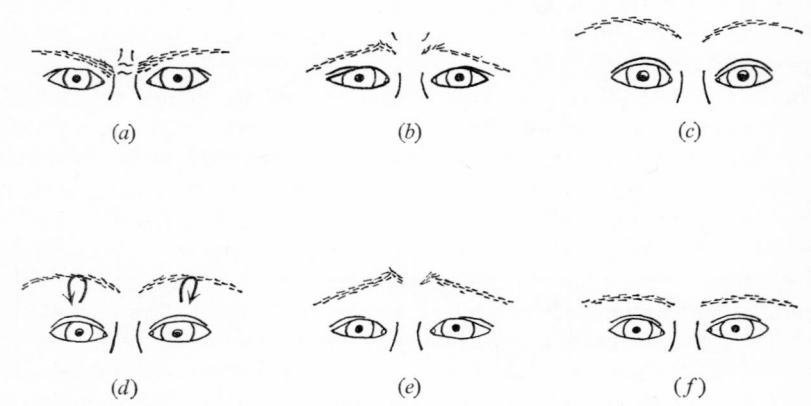

Fig. 2·3. Eyebrow units: (*a*) *angry frown*, (*b*) *sad frown*, (*c*) *raise*, (*d*) *flash*, (*e*) *sad raise*, (*f*) *neutral*.

above readily elicits an ' " Ahh! what's the matter? " response ' from adults and other children, and functions to attract attention to a distressful situation.

Having broken down non-verbal behaviour into a series of observable and precisely defined units (see Appendix), we may enquire how many of the units serve as signals. We have already commented on the effect of the expression of a crying child on adult behaviour; an act which has signal value can be recognised because in at least some circumstances its occurrence changes the behaviour of another individual. Thus in order to determine what is a signal we must be sufficiently familiar with the behaviour of the reactor to be able to predict confidently that it would have been different if the signal had not been given. In much ethological work, including that on non-human primates, this criterion is seldom used to demonstrate clearly that supposed signals do in fact have signal value. Instead the criterion is used semi-intuitively and the observational evidence which leads to the conclusion that an act is a signal seldom appears in print. Thus Marler (1965), while pointing out that the main approach in research on primate communication is to describe and classify signals, admits that in few species do we have detailed knowledge of the response evoked by these signals. This is *not* to say that we should reject judgements which are unaccompanied by a mass of explicit supporting evidence. Experienced ethologists develop an ability to recognise items of behaviour which have signal value; this is often recognition by analogy, when a piece of behaviour is assumed to have signal value because it shares certain general characteristics with acts known to be signals in other species or situations, e.g. it is conspicuous, it is restricted to a particular social context, has little obvious non-signal function, and perhaps shows typical intensity.

Wherever possible the evidence supporting judgements should be stated explicitly, and where it is not we should refrain from building further hypotheses on an untested basis. We should also be careful not to expect a clear separation of behaviours into signal and non-signal categories. There is no reason for not taking as our starting point all those features of behaviour which can be perceived by a conspecific, even those items which have obvious non-signal functions, like walking, standing, and eating, for many features of organisms have more than one function.

In studying the non-verbal signals of our own species we are both at an advantage and at a disadvantage; our subjective reaction often indicates immediately that a given act or posture has signal value, but we find it exceedingly difficult to become sufficiently detached and objective to gather clear objective evidence concerning this signal value. Many ethological phenomena which are prominent in man were first noted in other animals because it is so difficult to become a detached objective observer of human behaviour; examples include redirection and displacement activities, and releasers (Tinbergen, 1951), and cut-off acts (Chance, 1962). In man, therefore, it is both easier to judge what has signal value, and harder to avoid being misled by (*a*) current popular misconceptions about the significance of certain expressions, and (*b*) current word usage in relation to expressions, and (*c*) popular modes of thinking about our own behaviour. We can briefly illustrate these pitfalls.

'Red with rage' is a common phrase, yet although reddening of the face frequently occurs in agonistic interactions between children it has been found both by Blurton Jones (1967) and in our own nursery school studies to be characteristic of the defeated child, not the victor. Similarly the everyday use of single words like 'frown' or 'smile' to lump together a number of objectively quite distinct patterns (see Appendix) can prejudice the observer against making the necessary separate definitions. Again, the term 'crying' covers at least two distinct patterns, one characterised by sobs, *tears, sad frown, mouth corners back*, or *oblong mouth*, and *facial reddening*, and the other distinguished by *angry frown* and few or no tears. Both patterns tend to be hidden by the hands over the face, and are found in adults as well as children. The provision of criteria for distinguishing between these patterns is useful in adult group psychotherapy where the first pattern may be interpreted as signifying a patient's genuine distress, and the second pattern as revealing an attempt at group manipulation. As a final example we take the word 'aggression', which in normal usage tends to imply that all behaviours which are labelled aggressive form a coherent group sharing common causal factors. The units regularly associated with *beat* – an open handed blow delivered against another child – are *lips forward, thrust,* and *angry frown.* A blow delivered from the *arm over face* posture (Grant, 1969) is not associated with these units but with *oblong mouth, chin in, sad frown,* and *evade;* this pattern occurs when a defeated child still under attack cannot or will not escape by moving away. It also occurs in schizophrenic adults when their territory (e.g. a favourite chair) is threatened. The two patterns of expression accompanying the two kinds of blow are quite different which suggests that the causation of the blows may also be different in kind. The use of the term 'aggression' as an explanatory label is therefore likely to be misleading. This was well illustrated when we were shown an adult schizophrenic who was a problem patient; she was lying in a crouched position, chin tucked in, hands covering the head, with an intense *sad frown* and *mouth corners back,* all unequivocal signs of escape motivation (Grant, 1965*b*, 1969; Brannigan and Humphries, 1969). The psychiatrist assured us that the behaviour was aggressive on the grounds that it was destructive of his attempts at therapy! We see here that confusion of 'functional' with 'causal' definition can lead to the lumping of very different forms of behaviour into what is uncritically assumed to be a single causal category.

The term 'signal value', leads to the question 'signals of what?'. Darwin (1872) answered the question with the title of his book *The Expression of the Emotions in Man and Animals,* suggesting that expressions are signals of inner emotions. But the term 'emotion' is vague, and in terms of observables it is difficult to separate from the behaviour patterns themselves. The biological function of an activity can be defined in terms of selective advantage, in which case the biological function of signals is to modify a reactor's behaviour so that this behaviour will mesh more adaptively with the future behaviour of the actor. Signals should then be regarded as giving information about future likely behaviour and to signal how another person's previous behaviour has been received. To the extent that future likely behaviour correlates with subjectively experienced emotional states, signals may well indicate particular emotions. But in terms of natural selection, as well as ethological objectivity, it is the signal itself and the ensuing behaviour of the actor and reactor which alone are of primary importance. Ultimately if we are to talk of signal value in a quantitative, objective way, we suggest that it will be necessary to classify signals not in terms of their supposed emotional causation but in terms of those behavioural relationships which will under certain stated conditions invariably follow the signal. Thus our understanding of the form and behavioural context of a signal is likely to be advanced far more by discovering that it has an appeasement function (i.e. reduces the probability or intensity of a reactor's attack in a given type of situation) than by attempting by sleight of words to convert its stochastic connection with overt escape into a conjectured intensity of ' escape motivation ' or ' fear '. Motivational analysis is more appropriately used in attempts to reveal features of causal processes.

The motivational approach is also misleading in tending to type each signal with a specific emotional context. This is by no means true. *Angry frown* can be observed, though varying in degree, in several contexts some of which appear unconnected with the emotion of anger; it occurs in identical form as the frown of concentration and the frown of puzzlement. The inclusion of the motivational term ' angry ' in the name of the unit is to be taken as an aid to remembering the unit's name, and nothing to do with its objective definition. The units could have been assigned numbers or nonsense syllables rather than descriptive labels, but this would make it harder to learn and to use skilfully the full list. A danger in using motivationally descriptive labels for units is that if the observer infers that his subject is, for instance, angry, this may unconsciously distort his perceptions of the units to fit the expected schema (Abercrombie, 1969).

The particulate description of expressive behaviour, in which each unit is labelled with a type definition can easily lead to errors of oversimplification. Two points in particular arise in this connection.

First, although some units of expression, like an eyebrow *flash,* tend to adhere to their type form on all occasions, many like a *simple smile* or an *angry frown* occur in various degrees – they show any intensity from being barely perceptible to the maximum movement possible. Subjectively, every change in intensity appears to modify the signal value. In some instances the typological approach has led to the isolation of the extreme ends of a continuously graded series. For example, in agonistic interactions, pre-school children frequently adopt a *beating posture* in which the hand is raised as if preparing for a blow as described for *beat* earlier. Grant (1969) describes this as two distinct postures, an *offensive beating posture* and a *defensive beating posture*. We have pointed out (Brannigan and Humphries, 1969) that the defensive and offensive beating postures are merely extreme points joined by a range of intermediates, and we suggested that the ambivalent and variable nature of the posture is essential to its signal function in indicating the state of balance between aggressive and escape tendencies.

Second, as Marler (1965) has pointed out, primates, more than any other group of animals, tend to combine several independently varying signalling elements to create new composite signals. This interstitial openness (Bastian, 1965) of the non-verbal signalling system is a prominent feature in man. Smiling, for example, while usually unequivocal may on occasion be combined in an appeasing manner with signal elements normally indicating threat, doubt/aversion, or refusal to respond. The addition of threat is achieved by a tendency to square the mouth corners and to expose the lower teeth and to bring these teeth forward in opposition to the upper teeth. The resulting *oblong smile* (Fig. 2·4*b*) may be regarded as a combination of an *upper smile* (Fig. 2·2*b*) – the usual smile used in human greeting (Brannigan and Humphries, 1969) – with *oblong mouth* (Fig. 2·4*a*) (Grant, 1969), an ambivalent element seen in nursery school children who are about equally likely to flee or attack. In the nursery school situation oblong smiles have often been followed by ' exploratory ' attacks on the authors.

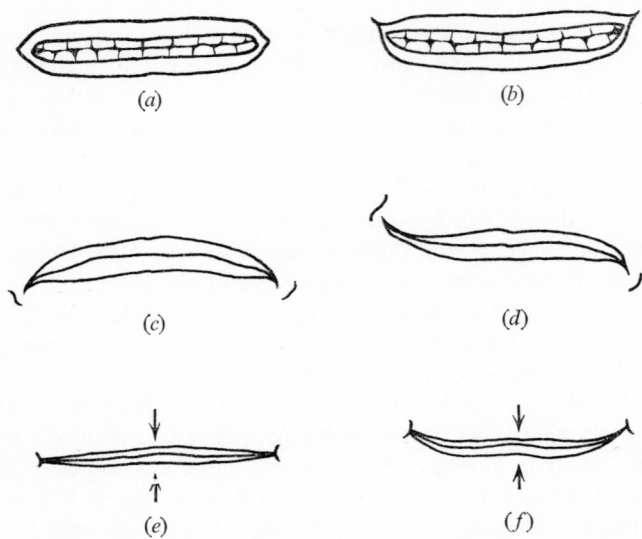

Fig. 2·4. Interactions in the form of units: (*a*) *oblong mouth*, (*b*) *oblong smile*, (*c*) *mouth corners down*, (*d*) *wry smile*, (*e*) *tight lips*, (*f*) *compressed smile*.

Mouth corners down (Fig. 2·4*c*), an expression commonly used to indicate doubt or aversion, may be combined with a *simple smile* (Fig. 2·2*a*) to produce a new expression *wry smile* (Fig. 2·4*d*) with a unique signal value. Similarly *tight lips* (Fig. 2·4*e*), indicating that an individual is *not* responding verbally, may combine with *simple smile* to produce *compressed smile* (Fig. 2·4*f*).

In the *wry smile* the bilateral symmetry seen in most expressions is sacrificed to achieve a combination of movements which would otherwise be impossible. Asymmetry is necessary too in the combination of *angry frown* (Fig. 2·3*a*) with *raise* (Fig. 2·3*c*) an expression commonly used to express strong rather disapproving doubt about some statement or action, but not outright aggressive disapproval, or mere surprised attention which symmetrical *angry frown* or symmetrical *raise* alone would indicate in the same situation.

That almost all elements of facial expression are bilaterally symmetrical is itself worthy of comment, since there would seem to be a rich potential for subtle modification of signal value by combinations of different move-ments of the same facial structure on the two sides. It seems likely that such an asymmetrical system would be readily open to misinterpretation when social partners are not directly facing each other. Combinations of elements are consequently symmetrical and involve different (though sometimes subtly different) aspects of facial structure.

Fig. 2·5. (a) (b) eye region and mouth region both indicate affect states, (c) (d) overall impression of affect alters when *mouth corners down* is combined with different frowns, (e) (f) antithesis of smile and mouth corners down.

The redundancy due to facial symmetry is added to by at least partial duplication of signal value in different expressive regions. We would con-fidently expect the reader to be able to recognise the 'mood' or 'affect state' in Figs. 2·5a and b even when either the mouth region or eye region is covered. However, signals in a given region are not purely concerned with restatements of those in other regions, they also modify the overall signal value as illustrated in Fig. 2·5c and d where *mouth corners down* is modified in different ways by *angry frown* and *sad frown*.

Darwin (1872) noted that opposite states of mind are often reflected by opposite movements. This principle of antithesis, which minimises ambiguity of signal, can be easily illustrated in the units of facial expression. By changing the smile's upward curve, we obtain an opposite impression of mood (Fig. 2·5e and f). The *angry frown* and *sad frown* are likewise antithetic (Fig. 2·3a and b), as is the lowering of brows in *angry frown* compared with the raised eyebrows accompanying an *upper smile* (Figs. 2·3a and c).

Darwin (1872) concluded that the chief expressive actions exhibited by man are innate, and do not have to be learned by the individual. Other authorities have maintained that facial displays are socially learned and therefore show extreme individual and cultural variation (Klineberg, 1940). The nature–nurture controversy has in the past fruitlessly engaged many ethologists and psychologists and it would be a pity if it became an all-absorbing issue in non-verbal communication. Nevertheless the possible existence of genetically programmed components (i.e. components highly resistant to environmentally induced variation) in the motor or perceptional aspects of non-verbal communication is fundamental to any attempt to understand how the individual acquires his abilities as sender and receiver. Little work has been done on this aspect and definitive statements are impossible. However we will briefly review the relevant evidence.

The finding of Ekman, Sorenson and Friesen (1969) that adults in widely different and geographically separated cultures show significant agreement in their judgements of the signal value of photographs of certain facial expressions strongly supports the view that genetically inherited information provides at least certain constant reference points around which a similar basic pattern of expressions can develop in different cultures. This does not deny the possibility of culturally learned differences in some details. Ekman *et al.* presented photographs to members of various races and cultural groups with the intention that the observers should categorise the photographs into pre-selected groups. They report that their literate and preliterate groups significantly chose the predicted emotion for the photographs, although there was higher agreement for literate than preliterate groups. Agreement was best in the affect category ' happy '; a photograph categorised ' happy ' by 97% of a sample of people in the U.S.A. was also said to be happy by 92% of a sample of preliterate natives of Borneo. Agreement for disgust–contempt was much poorer, and although it was over 80% in the three literate cultures of Japan, Brazil and the U.S.A., the expression was predominantly confused with ' sadness ' and ' happy ' in the small Borneo sample (fifteen people). In so far as the photographed face is, for racial reasons, of a structure unfamiliar to some observers, and since language differences mean that the verbal labels for the categories are not strictly equivalent between different cultures, some apparent cultural differences are likely to be generated by the method itself. The latter point is illustrated in Ekman, Sorenson, and Friesen's study, in the Fore culture of New Guinea where sharp differences in judgement of ' surprise ' and ' sadness ' were obtained depending on whether the affect categories were described in Pidgin or in the Fore language. The general cross-cultural agreement obtained is all the more significant in the light of these methodological inaccuracies.

Ekman *et al.* (1969) concluded that the pan-cultural element in facial displays of emotion is the association between facial muscular movements and discrete primary emotions. While agreeing that the study shows that certain important patterns of facial expression are used in similar circumstances in different cultures, and that this strongly suggests a genetically inherited component common to different races, we are less sure of the value of associating this component with supposed discrete primary emotions. These emotions cannot be defined in terms of observables independent of the expressions with which they are supposed to be linked, and we must therefore beware of tautology. As much confusion as light is thrown onto the study of non-verbal communication by talking in terms of ' primary affects ', at least until such time as these can be defined neuro-physiologically. Little cross-cultural work has yet been done by direct observation and recording of the expressive units, though Eibl-Eibesfeldt (1966) has described basic similarities in greeting and flirting in several cultures.

Inherited components which in each individual would lead to the development of a common species-characteristic pattern of facial expression might be involved perceptually – linking perceived expression with appropriate response, or might determine the patterns of facial muscular contraction, or might link these patterns with specific motivational states.

Many facial units such as *mouth corners back, angry frown, raise,* and *sad frown* can be seen during the first day after birth, when there is no possibility of them being learned by imitation, because for several days after birth an infant cannot visually resolve the features of its parent's face (Fantz, 1961). These units are therefore probably innate, though this leaves unresolved the problem of whether the infant at first employs them consistently in relation to its motivational state or social circumstances.

In this connection Freedman (1964) has described the smiling response (*upper smile*) of blind infants and found it similar in form and usage to that of sighted children. Eibl-Eibesfeldt (1968) has confirmed this finding which he regards as proof that smiling is ' a fixed action pattern '. While other studies (e.g. Ambrose, 1960) suggest that this conclusion is correct, the argument of course is unjustified since the operant learning of pieces of behaviour is well known, and there is no evidence to refute the possibility that units of expression are maintained, partly shaped, and assigned specific contexts in the behavioural repertoire by operant learning occurring naturally

53

in the child–parent relationship. We have evidence that at least some expressive units can be conditioned into a child's behavioural repertoire (Currie and Brannigan, 1970). When the greeting sequence, to approach, *look at,* and *smile,* had been operantly conditioned in an autistic child, there was without additional deliberate conditioning a further rapid development of various facial expressions and gestures, such as *angry frown, threat, chin out* and *beat,* in relevant situations. This latter phenomenon indicates that the expressions were not learnt at this stage; they presumably formed part of a complex of communicative expressions, which was either innate or had been first learned and then, as autism developed, suppressed.

Ambrose (1960, 1961) studying the smiling response in human infancy, concluded that smiling is an ' innate ' pattern which during the first five weeks after birth may be elicited by unspecific moderate or intense stimulation. The eliciting stimuli gradually became more specific until after five weeks of age human eyes are the main feature triggering the response. The connection between this sensory input and the smiling pattern Ambrose considered to be due to a releasing mechanism which although innate is modified by learning of the classical conditioning type. He also discussed how changes in response strength may be explained in terms of operant conditioning and habituation. Thus both motor and perceptual antecedents of smiling show an innate basis modified by learning in such a way as to change the intensity and usage of the response. However, the course of this learning during the first few months depends on such general features of the parent–infant interaction that it is likely to be a constant across all human cultures. An expression which is pan-cultural is therefore not necessarily devoid of learned components though it must at some point be set on a specific course of development by genetic information. This genetic information need not be concerned with facial communication as such, thus Ekman and Friesen (1969a) speculate (as an alternative to the theory of Tomkins) that in each individual facial displays might be developmentally based on constants in the human equipment involved in performing rudimentary activities like rejection of a bad taste or smell, biting, or control of blood flow in the eye region.

Ethology, particularly human ethology, has a practical potential which has not yet come to fruition. In considering its applications in communication we will deal with the psychiatric field, of which we have had several years' experience. Psychiatric diagnosis, and most therapeutic procedures, depend on a two way process of communication between psychiatrist and patient. While concentrating mainly on the analysis of verbal communication, most psychiatrists are well acquainted with the passage of non-verbal cues, but are not trained in analysing or interpreting them. Consequently a great deal of information is lost or misinterpreted.

During a two year study of non-verbal communication in an adult psychotherapeutic group one of us (D. A. H.) found that ethologically identified units of expression and gesture can be of great use to the therapist when the patient is blocking at the verbal level. This phenomenon has been called ' leakage ' by Ekman and Friesen (1969*b*) and defined as betrayal of information which the individual has consciously tried to withhold. Freud (1905) has commented that ' if his lips are silent, he chatters with his finger-tips; betrayal oozes out of every pore '. We can illustrate the psychiatric value of understanding leakage by two examples from the psychotherapeutic group. Mrs A was an anxiety neurotic, with whom little progress had been made since joining the group. During a talk between the psychiatrist and Mr Y concerning holding a baby in his hands, she showed the following behaviour sequence – momentary *sneer*, then *look down, hang, foot rock*, then *fumble* (with fingers). *Sneer* is seen during aggressive rejection of persons or objects, and subsequent questioning based on this cue revealed that Mrs A's problems centred on her fear of childbirth.

Mr X when involved in group discussion on another patient's homosexuality placed his hand on the back of his neck (*hand to neck*) when saying the word ' homosexual '. In a subsequent meeting further questions based on this cue revealed that problems of homosexuality were central to Mr X's neurosis. *Hand to neck* is a defensive cue derived from the *beating posture* of the pre-school child, the transition occurring at the age of about 5 years when the *beating posture* as an obvious preparation for physical violence becomes inappropriate to the largely verbally resolved conflicts of the older child and adult. The misbehaving child, however, is likely to discover that both *beating posture* and *beat* are still retained in its mother's repertoire. In instances where an adult is suddenly put on the defensive a momentary *beating posture* may precede *hand to neck*.

In the therapeutic group many other expressive units may ' leak ' verbally suppressed information, either when the patient is speaking, or when merely listening to a discussion between other members of the group. Leakage is closely related to deception; we have already mentioned that falsified *upper smiles* are not accompanied by the relevant changes in the eye region and that manipulative crying can be distinguished by the position of the eyebrows. It is obviously useful for the therapist to be able to distinguish these.

The depressed patient awaiting discharge is, as Ekman and Friesen (1969*b*) point out, likely to act as much more confident and happy than he actually feels. Objective, quantitative analysis of the repertoire of expressive units in standard interview situations could give measures assisting in the evaluation of recovery to ' normal '; Grant (1968) has shown that the non-verbal repertoire of patients in mental hospitals is severely restricted and that the restriction is greater in more severe illness. By observing psychiatric interviews and tape-recording the non-verbal units shown by the patient we have found that the repertoire increases as therapy progresses towards eventual discharge. Brannigan (1970) has indicated how the ethological assessment of the behavioural repertoire of mentally ill children could be used both in designing therapeutic procedures and assessing progress. Cues from non-verbal behaviour become particularly valuable in patients who lack or have partially lost the power of coherent speech; many psychotics and very young children fall into this category.

Non-verbal cues can only become a reliable tool in general psychiatry, and other fields, on the basis of an objective description of the units, and a scientific analysis of their signal functions. As we have attempted to show, this research has only just begun.

APPENDIX

A CONTRIBUTION TO A LIST OF THE UNITS OF NON-VERBAL BEHAVIOUR WITH DEFINITIONS

The following terms and definitions form part of the list used by the authors. We have included those units which are most probably concerned in inter-personal communication, and have generally omitted units which are vocalisations, or primarily locomotory, or which describe the various kinds of resting or sitting postures, or sighing and swallowing, although according to the social situation these latter units also often have signal value. We have commented on the units and definitions published by other authors only where necessary to avoid the confusion of different terminology or to clarify definitions.

UNITS IN THE MOUTH REGION

1. Simple smile – Lips together but not compressed, drawn up and out at the corners. This unit includes both *simple smile* and *wide smile* defined by Grant (1969).

2. Upper smile – The mouth corners are drawn up and out, remaining pointed, the lips parting to reveal some of the upper set of teeth, but not the lower.

3. Broad smile – Similar to *upper smile*, but the lower lip is pulled down to reveal some of the lower teeth. The vocalisations of laughter are often associated with this smile, but can occur in most other forms of smiling.

4. Compressed smile – As *simple smile*, but lips compressed and tending to be turned slightly into the mouth.

5. Wry smile – An asymmetrical smile in which the lips remain closed. One side of the face adopts the form seen in *mouth corners down* while the other side adopts the form seen in a *grin* or in *simple smile*.

6. Oblong smile – Lower jaw pushed out so that the incisor teeth are directly opposed and usually in contact, both upper and lower sets being exposed, and the mouth corners are drawn up and out tending to be rounded not pointed.

7. Lip-in smile – Similar to *upper smile*, with the lower lip drawn in between the teeth but not bitten.

8. Play face – The mouth is widely opened as in *open mouth,* and the mouth corners tend to move out and up, producing the pointed appearance characteristic of smiles. The teeth are mainly or entirely hidden by the lips.

9. Grin – As *simple smile,* but involving one side of the mouth only.

10. Open grin – General appearance rather as in *upper smile,* but instead of being passively lifted from the mouth corners the top lip is actively raised as in *sneer* and is slightly out-turned. Often on one side only, but may be symmetrical.

Intermediates (*false smile*) between symmetrical *open grin* and *upper smile* are seen in attempts to mimic an *upper smile*.

11. *Mouth corners tremble* – The corners of the mouth tremble laterally. Often associated with sad crying, just prior to tears.

12. *Mouth corners back* – The corners of the mouth are drawn well back but not lifted, the lips remaining together.

13. *Squared mouth* – Lips opened widely and drawn back to give the mouth a rather squared appearance.

14. *Mouth corners out* – As in *mouth corners back*, but the lips are parted. Teeth visible but not displayed so obviously as in *oblong mouth*. *Oblong mouth* of Grant (1969) includes both this unit and the next.

15. *Oblong mouth* – As in *mouth corners out* but the lower jaw is pushed forwards so that the upper and lower incisors are displayed meeting in opposition. The mouth corners tend to be roundly squared, not pointed.

16. *Intention bite* – As *oblong mouth* but the lower jaw is jutted pushing the lower set of teeth as far forward as possible and they are broadly displayed by lowering the lip. The upper incisors are hidden by the upper lip.

17. *Lip up* – As *sneer* but a fleeting movement not held even briefly at the extreme position.

18. *Sneer* – The upper lip on one or both sides is lifted, more to the side of the centre than near the mouth corners, and the raised position is held for one or more seconds.

19. *Bite lip* – The upper or lower lip is gripped between the teeth. When the mouth is closed this cannot be directly seen, but can be inferred from slight jaw movements and an inward movement of part of a lip. Equivalent to *chew lips* (McGrew, Ch. 5).

20. *Tight lips* – The lips are pressed tightly together but are not appreciably turned into the mouth and the distance between the mouth corners is not appreciably shortened. This definition is more specific than that used by Grant (1969) which does not differentiate *lips in*.

21. *Lips in* – The lips are pressed together and turned into the mouth.

22. *Lower lip out* – The lower lip is pushed up over the upper then curled forward and out.

23. *Point* – Both lips are protruded and though held together are full, not compressed. There is less movement of the mouth corners towards the centre than in *purse*.

24. *Purse* – The mouth corners are pulled in towards the centre, and the lips tightly compressed and pushed forwards.

25. *Small mouth* – The mouth corners move in towards the centre but without noticeable compression or protrusion of the lips.

26. *Twist mouth* – An asymmetrical unit in which the lips are pressed together and slightly protruded centrally, one corner of the mouth being brought in towards the mid-line, the other corner being drawn back.

27. *Lips forward* – The lips are parted, mainly in the centre, and protruded. The corners of the mouth tend to be pointed and are not squared and sometimes move a little towards the mid-line.

28. *Open mouth* – The mouth is opened widely, but the teeth are not shown, except occasionally the tips. The mouth corners are not drawn back and up as in a smile, but remain in the neutral position.

29. *Spit* – Action of spitting.

30. *Kiss* – The lips are moved forwards, and touch, part of the same or another person (specify).

31. Intention speak – The mouth suddenly opens in a context where speech might be expected, but no words issue.

32. Chew – Variable chewing movements of the jaws. Not always associated with material in the mouth.

33. Tongue between lips – Just the tip of the tongue protrudes between, and is gripped by, the lips.

34. Tongue out – The tongue is well protruded beyond the lips. This includes sticking out the tongue at another person, and the protrusion of the tongue sometimes seen during ' excited play ' or during ' delighted surprise '.

35. Lick – The tongue moves forward and its tip briefly touches the parted lips.

36. Mouth corners down – The corners of the mouth are drawn down, the lips do not pout forward and are usually closed but occasionally may be slightly apart.

37. Scowl. – A unit combining *mouth corners down* and *lower lip out,* the chin usually acquiring a crumpled appearance.

38. Lower lip tremble – Up and down trembling movement of the lower lip, which may occur during *lower lip out, scowl* or *mouth corners out.*

39. Yawn – The mouth opens widely, roundly and fairly slowly, closing more swiftly. A swelling of the throat is usually visible, accompanied by a deep breath and often closing of the eyes and lowering of the brows.

40. Basic mouth – Lips in a resting position. This varies from individual to individual and the lips may or may not be parted.

UNITS INVOLVING THE EYEBROWS

41. Raise – One or both eyebrows are raised and are held, at least briefly, in the raised position. They are not drawn in towards the mid-line and are not tilted.

42. Flash – A swift raising of the eyebrows which is not held, the brows returning immediately to the neutral position.

43. Angry frown – The eyebrows are lowered mainly in the midline towards the nose, tending to draw together. *Puzzled frown,* distinguished by Grant (1969) is a less intense form of *angry frown* in which the lowering of the brows is minimal.

44. Sad frown – The inner ends of the eyebrows have kinked and slightly lifted and the outer ends are lowered.

45. Sad raise – The eyebrows are raised sloping as in sad frown.

46. Low frown – The eyebrows are drawn low against the upper eyelids and show no clear tilting outwards or inwards.

The individual's eyebrows in their usual resting position are termed *neutral.* This position may vary somewhat from person to person.

UNITS INVOLVING THE EYELIDS AND EYE SURROUNDINGS

47. Shut – The eyelids close and remain shut for about a second or longer, before opening again. (In a normal blink there is no noticeable pause in the closed position.) Equivalent to *eyes closed* (Grant, 1969).

48. Blink – A burst of rapid blinking. (Single, isolated blinks are not included.)

49. Narrow eyes – Both upper and lower eyelids draw partly together, narrowing the area of eyeball visible. The eye region appears tense. This unit may or may not be held in the narrowed position for several seconds.

50. Droop – The upper eyelid falls so that the eyeball is almost, but not quite, covered. The lower lid does not move, and the eye region appears relaxed.

51. Wink – As *shut* but for one eye only, the other eye usually looking at another person.

52. Stare – The eyelids are held wide open, exposing a greater area of eyeball than in the usual *open* position. This unit is equivalent to that termed *eyes open* (Grant, 1969) and is not the same as his unit *stare*.

53. Widen – As *stare*, but the widening of the eyes is momentary. Relates to *stare* rather as *flash* relates to *raise*.

54. Pouch – A small area of skin immediately beneath each eye swells. The swelling is not coincident with ' tiredness pouches ', being above these, and cannot be properly produced by merely screwing up the face.

55. Tears – Excess moisture in the eyes.

56. Open – The usual position of the lids when the eyes are open.

UNITS OF GAZE DIRECTION
These definitions depend primarily on the eye movements of gaze direction and on the subject of gaze, not on head movement.

57. Look at – Gaze directed at another person. Specify the part, e.g. look at the face, the body, the legs.

58. Look away – Gaze directed away from the other person.

59. Look down – Gaze directed at own person. This definition is different from that given by Grant (1969).

60. Look up – The gaze is suddenly directed upwards, then usually more slowly returns to a level or downward direction. The suddenness of the unit makes it quite distinct from *look away* in an upward direction.

61. Look around – The gaze continually wanders, but otherwise as *look away*.

ADDITIONAL FACIAL UNITS
62. Grimace – The eyes are partially or completely closed, with the skin on the bridge of the nose and around the eyes wrinkled. The corners of the mouth are drawn out and slightly down, the lips parting to reveal the upper set of teeth. May be more exaggerated on one side of the face.

63. Screwface – The skin on the bridge of the nose is wrinkled by an upward movement of the skin immediately to the sides of the nose and by a slight downward movement of the brows. The eyes are partially closed, with wrinkling beneath them. The upper lip lifts and may partly expose the upper teeth but this movement is achieved in a different way to that of *sneer*. Probably equivalent to *wrinkle* (Grant, 1968) and *pucker face* (McGrew, Ch. 5).

64. Flare – Widening of the nostrils.

65. Twitch – A tic-like twitching in the upper cheek region.

66. Sweat – Beads of sweat appear on the skin.

67. Facial reddening – A reddening of the facial skin from its normal colour.

68. Blanch – A paling of the facial skin from its normal colour.

69. Smooth face – The cheeks flatten into harder-looking planes; no special expression of mouth or eyes but there is an impression of tenseness of the facial muscles.

70. Normal face – No special expression present but face not slack as in sleep.

UNITS DEFINED BY HEAD MOVEMENT
71. Threat – The head jerks sharply forward, remaining level, towards the other person. Usually accompanied by *look at*.

72. Head forward – The head is held in a forward position like that at the end of *threat*. Not necessarily preceded by *threat* as the forward movement of the head is often gradual not sudden.

73. Chin out – The head is tilted, pushing the chin forward and stretching the throat.

74. Head to side – The head is tilted to the side. Equivalent to *head tilt* (Mc-Grew, Ch. 5).

75. Head movement – A burst of varied movements of the head, not described by the definitions of other units.

76. Jerk – The head abruptly jerks up and to one side and may move the hair.

77. Nod – Affirmative gesture. Repetitive, rhythmic, dorso-ventral tilting of the head.

78. Shake – Negative gesture. Oscillatory partial rotation of the head on the neck.

79. Bob – The head quickly moves once up and down, like a short inverted nod.

80. Chin in – The chin is tucked tightly against the throat, the head tilting forward without being thrust forward.

81. Hang – The head is tilted forward fully until the gaze is directed almost vertically down.

82. Head rock – An antero-posterior rocking of the head and neck, distinguished from nodding by its orientation, the involvement of the neck and its slower rhythm.

83. Evade – A sharp head, or head and shoulder, movement away from the other person.

84. Level – Head in a level, neutral position.

UNITS FORMED BY THE HANDS AND ARMS
85. Shrug – A fairly sudden raising of both shoulders.

86. Sit on hands – Sitting on the fingers of one or both hands.

The following five units are each to be qualified by the object and person of their activity, e.g. *scratch arm self* or *pick jacket interviewer*.

87. Scratch – The finger nails are used to scrape, usually repetitively, at skin, hair or clothes.

88. Caress – Stroking movements made mainly by the finger pads – not the extreme tips and nails – against the skin, hair or clothes. The rate of repetition is slower than in *scratch* and *rub*.

89. Rub – Similar to *scratch* but the nails are not used. Almost any part of the hand or fingers may be used.

90. Pick – The thumb and forefinger are used as if (or actually) to pick something from the skin, hair or clothes.

91. Adjust – One or both hands are used manipulatively to alter the position of clothing or hair.

92. Fumble – A twisting and turning movement of the fingers of each hand with those of the other. Similar fumbling often occurs with a ring, tie, hair etc. and the object of the activity is then specified, e.g. *fumble ring*.

93. Tap – A repetitive rhythmic movement of the fingers, tapping or jerking in sequence.

94. Hand flutter – Hand or hands with fingers outstretched, palms facing the actor, normally in front of the eyes, the fingers being shaken rapidly by an oscillating partial rotation of the wrist and forearm.

95. Digit suck – Finger(s) or thumb in mouth.

96. Mouth – The fingers rest against the lips, but do not touch the teeth.

97. Cup – The hand is brought up sharply and cupped over the mouth.

98. Teeth – The tips or sides of the fingers are pressed hard against, but not between, the teeth.

99. Cover eyes – The hand is cupped to cover the eyes, the palm turned towards the face.

100. Face – The fingers, and usually the palm too, rest against the face (excluding the mouth). The palm is not directed towards the other person.

101. Finger face – One or more fingers are extended with their tips touching the face, the palm not touching the face and tending to be turned towards the other person.

102. Offensive beating posture – The arm is raised with the elbow out to the side, and the hand some inches to one side of the head. The hand is usually rather to the front of the ear, with the palm foremost, fingers extended or loosely flexed.

103. Defensive beating posture – This differs from the offensive beating posture in that the raised hand is close to the ear or side of the head, the fingers often touching the hair or skin. The hand tends to be further back and is not lifted so high. This definition differs from that given by Grant (1969).

Intermediate positions between this and the preceding posture often occur, and are referred to as *beating posture*.

104. Beat – The hand is brought from the *beating posture* position sharply into contact with another person.

105. Incomplete beat – As *beat,* but delivered out of range or with minimal movement and force. This unit is often preceded by *defensive beating posture.*

106. Hand on neck – The palm of the hand is placed on the neck.

107. Arm over face – One or both arms are raised and crooked over the head, palms facing the head.

108. Clap – The palms of both hands are brought together sharply.

109. Pound – A sharp blow by one hand against the other immobile hand or against an object such as a table.

110. Push gesture – A steady but fairly rapid movement of the hands outward from the actor, palms facing directly away from the body.

111. Demonstrate – A movement of arm, hand or fingers used to describe the direction, shape, size or other qualities of that which is being talked about.

112. Show – The arm, with an object in the hand, is extended towards another person.

113. Gesture – Variable movements of arm, hand or fingers, usually during conversation, not covered by other gestural unit definitions. It is possible to break *demonstrate* and *gesture* into many subunits, defined by the speed, orientation and extent of the movements.

114. Flat gesture – The hand is opened flat, palm facing the ground, then moved sharply a short distance diagonally forward and sideways parallel to the ground. The elbow points to the side.

115. Palms up – The hands are held to the front of the body then the wrists are rotated to bring the palms uppermost. Sometimes accompanies *shrug.*

116. Akimbo – Hand on hip, the bent elbow pointing laterally away from the body.

117. Fold – Forearms in contact with each other along their whole length, held horizontally across the chest.

118. Fist – One hand grips itself, the fingers curled tightly into the palm.

119. Link – The two hands clasp each other without great force.

120. Grasp – The two hands clasp each other very tightly; white or red marks may be visible on the skin.

121. Hands behind back – The hands are placed behind the back, usually with *link.*

122. Hold – One or both hands grip some object (specified).

123. Punch – Hand as in *fist,* arm extended sharply to deliver a blow.

124. Touch – Hand lightly placed on object or person (specify).
125. Single – The hands are separate, immobile and not covered by the definition of any other unit.

LOWER LIMB UNITS
There are many units defined by movements of the lower limbs, such as the various kinds of locomotion, sitting and standing. However the lower limbs become particularly expressive when the individual is seated in a chair and they are freed from locomotory requirements. The following are some of the common units to be seen in a seated person.
126. Cross legs – Legs crossed at knee level or ankle level.
127. Shuffle – Irregular movements of the foot against the floor.
Also seen when standing.
128. Tap foot – A fairly regular tapping of the sole of the foot against the floor.
129. Leg tremor – A rapid trembling of the whole leg particularly noticeable at the knee, the foot tapping against the floor much faster than in *tap foot*.
130. Foot – Movement of the foot, when free of the floor, irregularly around the ankle joint.
131. Foot rock – A regular up and down movement of the foot when free of the floor.
132. Circle – A circling motion of the foot around the ankle joint, often involving the whole lower leg in movement.
133. Swing – A to and fro swinging of a crossed leg. Other units whose names are self explanatory are *feet back, feet forward, feet apart, feet together, knees together, knees apart*.

TRUNK UNITS
Many of the units which fall under this heading are self explanatory and we shall not define them here (see Grant, 1969); they include, *lean forward, lean back*, the variable movements seen in getting comfortable (*settle*), the *to–fro rock* and *side rock* movements seen particularly in psychotics, and other units. In the three units defined below the trunk is involved as one component of a complex posture.
134. Slope – A composite unit of *chin in, lean back,* and *hands behind back*. Occasionally the hands *link* in front of the waist.
135. Crouch – The legs are flexed and the body is bent forward so that the forehead is close to the knees. The shoulders are drawn forward, and the chin is tucked tightly into the neck. The arms may cover the head.
136. Hunch – Intermediate between *chin in* and *crouch*, in which the shoulders are drawn forward and the back is rounded.

REFERENCES

Abercrombie, M. L. J. (1969). *The Anatomy of Judgment*. Harmondsworth: Penguin Books.
Ambrose, J. A. (1960). The smiling and related responses in early human infancy: an experimental and theoretical study of their course and significance. *University of London, Ph.D. thesis*.
Ambrose, J. A. (1961). The development of the smiling response in early infancy. In *Determinants of Infant Behaviour*, vol. 1. Ed. B. M. Foss, London: Methuen.

Andrew, R. J. (1963). The origin and evolution of the calls and facial expressions of the Primates. *Behaviour* **20**, 1–109.

Andrew, R. J. (1964). The displays of the primates. In *Evolutionary and Genetic biology of Primates*, vol. 2. Ed. J. Buettner-Janusch, London: Academic Press.

Ardrey, R. (1967). *The territorial imperative*. London: Collins.

Baerends, G. P. and Baerends-van Roon, J. M. (1950). An introduction to the ethology of cichlid fishes. *Behaviour, suppl. 1.*

Bastian, J. R. (1965). Primate signalling systems and human languages. In *Primate Behavior*. Ed. I. DeVore, New York: Holt Rinehart and Winston.

Blurton Jones, N. G. (1967). An ethological study of some aspects of social behaviour of children in nursery school. In *Primate Ethology*. Ed. D. Morris, London: Weidenfeld and Nicolson.

Blurton Jones, N. G. (in press). Criteria for use in describing Facial Expressions of Children. *Hum. Biol.*

Brannigan, C. R. (1970). Ethological analysis of behaviour as an aid to therapy. Paper given at British Psychological Society Conference, Southampton 1970. *Bull. B.P.S. 23* **79**, 139.

Brannigan, C. R. and Humphries, D. A. (1969). I see what you mean. *New Scientist* **42**, 406–8.

Callan, H. M. (1970). *Ethology and Society*. London: Oxford University Press.

Chance, M. R. A. (1962). An interpretation of some agonistic postures: the role of 'cut off' acts and postures. *Symp. Zool. Soc. Lond.* **8**, 71–89.

Cherry, C. (1957). *On Human Communication*. New York: Wiley.

Clark, A. H., Wyon, S. M. and Richards, M. P. M. (1969). Free-play in nursery school children. *J. Child Psychol. Psychiat.* **10**, 205–16.

Currie, K. H., and Brannigan, C. R. (1970). Behavioural analysis and modification with an autistic child. In *Behaviour Studies in Psychiatry*. Ed. S. J. Hutt and C. Hutt, Oxford: Pergamon.

Darwin, C. R. (1871). *The descent of man and selection in relation to sex*. London: Murray.

Darwin, C. R. (1872). *The expression of emotions in man and animals*. London: Murray.

Eibl-Eibesfeldt, I. (1966). Ethologie, die Biologie des Verhaltens. In *Handbk. d. Biologie 6*. Ed. Gessner, Frankfurt: Akad. Verlagsges.

Eibl-Eibesfeldt, I. (1968). Ethological perspectives on primate studies. In *Primates: studies in adaptation and variability*. Ed. P. Jay, London: Holt, Rinehart and Winston.

Ekman, P., Sorenson, E. R. and Friesen, W. V. (1969). Pan-cultural elements in facial displays of emotion. *Science, N.Y.* **164**, 86–8.

Ekman, P. and Friesen, W. V. (1969a). The repertoire of non-verbal behavior – categories, origins, usage and coding. *Semiotica* **1**, 49–97.

Ekman, P. and Friesen, W. V. (1969b). Non-verbal leakage and clues to deception. *Psychiatry* **32**, 88–106.

Fantz, R. L. (1961). The origin of form perception. *Sci. Amer.* **204**, 66–72.

Freedman, D. G. (1964). Smiling in blind infants and the issue of innate versus acquired. *J. Child Psychol. Psychiat.* **5**, 171–84.

Freud, S. (1905). Fragment of an analysis of a case of hysteria. *Collected papers, vol. 3*. London: Basic Books 1959.

Gardner, R. A. and Gardner, B. T. (1969). Teaching sign language to a chimpanzee. *Science, N.Y.* **165**, 664.

Grant, E. C. (1965a). The contribution of ethology to child psychiatry. In *Modern perspectives in child psychiatry*. Ed. J. G. Howell, Edinburgh: Oliver and Boyd.

Grant, E. C. (1965b). An ethological description of some schizophrenic patterns of behaviour. *Proc. Leeds Symposium on Behavioural Disorders*. Dagenham: May and Baker.

Grant, E. C. (1968). An ethological description of non-verbal behaviour during interviews. *Br. J. Med. Psychol.* **41**, 177–84.

Grant, E. C. (1969). Human facial expression. *Man* **4**, 525–36.

Honkavaara, S. (1961). The psychology of expression. *Br. J. Psychol. Monogr. Suppl.* **32**.

Humphries, D. A. (1970). Ethology and linguistic communication. *Technology and Society* **6**, 27–33.

Klineberg, O. (1940). *Social psychology*. New York: Holt.

Landis, C. (1929). The interpretation of facial expression of emotion. *J. genet. Psychol.* **2**, 59–70.

Lenneberg, (1967). *Biological foundations of language*. New York: Wiley.

Lorenz, K. (1950). The comparative method in studying innate behaviour patterns. *Sym. Soc. exp. Biol.* **4**, 221–68.

Marler, P. (1965). Communication in monkeys and apes. In *Primate Behavior*. Ed. I. DeVore, New York: Holt Rinehart and Winston.

McGrew, W. C. (1969). An ethological study of agonistic behaviour in pre-school children. *Proc. Second Internat. Congr. Primatol, Atlanta, G.A. 1968*, vol. 1. Ed. C. R. Carpenter, Basel and New York: Karger.

Morris, D. (1967). *The naked ape*. London: Jonathan Cape.

Osgood, C. E. (1966). Dimensionality of the semantic space for communicating via facial expressions. *Scand. J. Psychol.* **7**, 1–30.

Scheflen, A. E. (1963). The significance of posture in communication systems. *Psychiat.* **26**, 316–31.

Schlosberg, H. (1954). Three dimensions of emotion. *Psych. Rev.* **61**, 81–8.

Tinbergen, N. (1948). Social releasers and the experimental method required for their study. *Wilson Bull.* **60**, 6–51.

Tinbergen, N. (1951). *The study of instinct*. London: Oxford University Press.

Tomkins, S. S. (1962). *The positive affects. Affect, imagery, consciousness 1*. New York: Springer.

Tomkins, S. S. (1963). *The negative affects. Affect, imagery, consciousness 2*. New York: Springer.

Van Hooff, J. A. R. A. M. (1962). Facial expressions in higher primates. *Symp. zool. Soc. Lond.* **8**, 97–125.

3

PATTERNS OF PLAY AND SOCIAL INTERACTION IN PRE-SCHOOL CHILDREN

PETER K. SMITH AND KEVIN CONNOLLY *

SUMMARY

Recent developments in ethology have had considerable influence on studies of human and especially child behaviour. Earlier observational work on pre-school children dating largely from the 1930s is reviewed in the light of these developments and some of its weaknesses discussed. The problems of units of behaviour, levels of analysis, sampling techniques, reliability and methods of data analysis are discussed. An extensive set of behavioural categories is defined. The results of a time-sampling study (in which these categories were used) of free-play in three day nurseries is outlined. Twelve five-minute samples of behaviour were taken for each of forty children. The mean frequency of occurrence of the various behaviours, inter-observer agreements and split-half reliabilities were computed. The effects of various factors on the behaviour of the children in the nursery situation were discussed. Determinants of behaviour examined in this way include particular day nursery, age, sex, presence or absence of a father in the home, length of nursery experience, whether activity indoors or outdoors, time of day (morning or afternoon). Significant findings related to these variables are summarised. Some of the more interesting findings relating to vocalisations, social participation, physical activity, rough and tumble play and sucking are considered in more detail.

It is also possible to define personality differences in terms of the data collected from direct observations. The main dimensions of individual differences in the forty children were established by the use of principal component analyses on the inter-correlations between frequencies of the different behaviours. Reliability was checked by split-half analyses and validity by a comparison with a re-analysis of data published by Arrington in 1931. The main reliable dimensions are: one of social maturity (with equal loadings for age and for nursery experience), and one relating to the kind of play engaged in (with or without toys or apparatus). The latter dimension is probably sex-linked. Further developments of this approach are outlined.

Introduction

It has been argued by some that any scientific discipline must in the course of its development go through a stage of fact gathering before an experimental analysis of specific hypotheses may be profitably attempted. It has also often been suggested that psychology leapt prematurely to experimental analysis, with rather artificial laboratory experiments designed to investigate limited

* Department of Psychology, University of Sheffield.

aspects of behaviour within narrow confines, neglecting description and the patient accumulation of basic facts about animal and human behaviour. This has been blamed on the undue reverence paid by early psychology to the established methods of contemporary physical sciences.

The fact that ethology and animal psychology have, until recently, been virtually separate disciplines, gives some credence to this point of view. The distinction between ' observation ', or the recording of observed events, and ' experiment ', or the testing of hypotheses, is of course a relative one since any observations we make do in themselves involve inferences or hypotheses about what is important and what is not important to record. Hypotheses are also likely to lie latent in the treatment of observational data after they have been collected. Nevertheless, it may be conceded that some kinds of ' observation-experiment ' make fewer assumptions, or alternatively exclude fewer possible hypotheses from emerging than others. In the early stages of a science, these studies are likely to be more fruitful than those which are designed to test only one or two hypotheses and hence implicitly exclude almost all others.

Thus in the earlier work in animal psychology the more observational kinds of research, such as Kohler's work on insight in chimpanzees or that of Lorenz on imprinting, seem in the long run to have more permanent interest than the narrower experimental approach, such as Hull's investigations of maze learning in the rat. Even so, observational studies of animal behaviour were far from exhaustive, either of behaviours or species, as the post-war blossoming of ethology indicates. Although much current ethological work is now more experimental in character a great deal of descriptive work remains to be done.

The current influence of ethology on psychology has led to renewed emphasis on the importance of description in human as well as animal research. Relatively little work of this kind has been done on human adults, although when it has (e.g. Esser, 1965; Grant, 1968) the results have been interesting and worth while. Much of the research resulting from, or influenced by, this cross-fertilisation of disciplines has been done on pre-school children and newborn infants. This probably reflects the comparative ease of observing these subjects in fairly standard surroundings, the usually small disturbing effect of the observer and the assumption that the behaviour observed is relatively simple compared to that of adults.

In the case of work with young children however, it is far from correct to say that psychology bypassed the fact-gathering stage. A great deal of work of just this kind was carried out, mostly in the United States, beginning in the 1920s and reaching a peak in the 1930s (Brackbill, 1967). This upsurge of investigation declined in the 1940s being gradually superseded by more ' experimental ' researches such as characterise much of the present child psychology journals. This would seem to be a classic example of experiment following observation, and the relevance of more ' observational ' work at the present time on infants and neonates might well be questioned. It seems appropriate, therefore, to discuss some of the work done in this period, and attempt an assessment of its relevance to present-day research and its completeness in giving an account of '*Homo sapiens infans*'. The account is concerned primarily with the work done on pre-school children (2–5 years), though much is also applicable to the work on the newborn.

Earlier research

Much of the work carried out during the 1920s and through into the 1940s was reported in the following journals and serial publications: *Child Development, Pedagogical Seminary (Journal of Genetic Psychology* after 1927), *Genetic Psychology Monographs, Journal of Experimental Education, University of Iowa Studies of Child Welfare,* and *Studies from the University of Toronto Child Development Service*. The period 1925 to 1940 was especially fertile.

The relevant kinds of article may be divided into five categories, though with some overlap, which also reflect very roughly the sequential development of research interests during the period:

(1) Physical development. Anthropometric measurements, growth curves, motor coordination, performance on simple skills.

(2) Intellectual development. Performance on mental tests; development of academic, linguistic and musical abilities.

(3) Behaviour problems and adjustments. Eating, sleeping and toilet habits; training procedures. Development of responsibility. Parental attitudes; effects of foster homes.

(4) Social development. Age, sex and class differences. Social contacts, choice of companions, types of toys used, attention span, teacher-child contacts, cooperation and competition, sympathetic behaviour, leadership, laughter and crying, talkativeness. Effects of nursery experience. Stable individual differences from teachers' ratings or direct observation.

(5) Critiques of observational methodology; reviews.

The ensuing discussion will be concerned with (4) and (5) only.

TYPES AND UNITS OF BEHAVIOUR

As a broad generalisation it appears that the studies on social behaviour emerged from (*a*) a realisation that physical and intellectual measurements provided an incomplete picture of a child's development, and (*b*) a concern with behaviour difficulties such as temper tantrums, withdrawal, etc. (see for example, Marston, 1925).

Because of its origins, much of the work on social behaviour was useful in a fairly immediate sense, suggesting norms for development, the kinds of behaviour difficulties which might be expected and how they might be dealt with. Often however, this lessens its relevance by a more scientific criterion; the observational categories used may to a great extent reflect the preconceptions of nursery school teachers as to what is important. Berne and Kelly (1934) for example, have as their six categories: *obeys, disobeys, interest in group, cooperates, sociable, kind,* and Hattwick (1937) has categories such as *hard to reason with, ignores requests, leaves tasks incomplete, rushes into danger, jealous, misrepresents facts.* These examples while selected, are not atypical. Such categorisations now seem unsatisfactory in two ways. Firstly, many kinds of potentially interesting behaviours are excluded. Secondly, the categories used are often of a highly complex type, already assuming the motivational structure of the behaviour, and open to some variety of interpretation by different observers. Hypotheses which might emerge from a wider range of categories, or finer categories, are excluded.

The latter criticism is relevant even with respect to more ' objective ' categories which were sometimes used such as *stays near adult, smiles,* or *screams.* It was usually implicit in the gathering and treatment of data of this kind (in the prevalent use of correlation coefficients for example) that the categories used represented *unitary* concepts, in the sense of having similar causal antecedents and consequences. However, an ethologically oriented investigator may question whether behaviours such as *obeys,* or even *smiles* are unitary. They could be broken down into smaller components, and subsequent temporal analysis might yield different and more motivationally valid large-scale categories. Such categories might be more precisely defined and more amenable to comparison across different studies and indeed across different cultures.

An example of such a composite behaviour category ignored in the 1930s seems to be the ' rough and tumble ' play behaviour described by Harlow and Harlow (1965) for young rhesus monkeys (*Macaca mulatta*) and Blurton Jones (1967) for human children. The only relevant description in the earlier literature is provided by Hattwick (1937), where among other sex differences it is mentioned that it is more common for boys to ' laugh, squeal and jump around excessively '. It is important to note that Blurton Jones described the separate components of rough and tumble play and showed that they tended to occur together, hence justifying the composite category.

Detailed descriptions of facial expressions and bodily postures represent a degree of analysis rather finer than was usually attempted in the 1930s, though Landis and Hunt (1936) and Gilmer (1933) are exceptions to this. Undoubtedly, the influence of ethology in the direction of making interspecies comparisons has been important here, perhaps because such expressions and postures have more obvious significance in animals which do not possess a language like ours. Also the expense of cinefilm and the absence of closed circuit television and videotape equipment was doubtless a factor since it is difficult to carry out fine-grain analysis without sophisticated recording tools.

The concepts of dominance and territory as used by ethologists were neglected, though a considerable amount was written on the forms and frequencies of aggressive behaviour. Jack (1934), Page (1936) and Cates (1939) discussed 'ascendance' (an equivalent term to dominance) in preschool children. They refer to the contemporary work of Maslow (1936) on monkeys and of Schjelderup-Ebbe (1935) on chickens and employ a similar situation paradigm to examine dominance relations in children, for example, two children would be placed in a room with a toy or sand-box. However, the applicability of the 'dominance hierarchy' concept was not examined (though see Hanfmann, 1935) nor were the characteristic facial expressions and postures associated with agonistic behaviour adequately described. Situational determinants such as group density (Hutt and Vaizey, 1966) were also seldom considered either in this or other contexts.

In the majority of studies the observations were made by passive observers present in the nursery school or playgroup. The reactions of children to strange adults is of some interest in its own right, but was never systematically examined; nor was behaviour when greeting or separating from the mother. Reactions to novel objects and to new group members (Washburn, 1932; Slater, 1939) were also topics inadequately investigated. A few studies were made of children's behaviour in a strange room or clinic (Arsenian, 1943; Shirley, 1942) and of teacher–child interactions in the nursery (Moore, 1938; Landreth, Gardner, Eckhardt and Prugh, 1943).

SAMPLING TECHNIQUES

Many of the findings made during the period under discussion are summarised in Arrington's (1943) review; fortunately this appeared towards the end of the productive period, though it is exclusively concerned with time sampling studies. These are therefore not discussed individually here. Half of Arrington's paper is devoted to considerations of observational methodology, on which considerable work was done, and this merits further discussion.

The inability of diary records, without the aid of film recordings, to capture *all* the relevant behaviour of a child was soon recognised (Barker, 1930; Arrington, 1931) and time sampling of selected behaviour categories became the dominant observational technique. Goodenough (1928) described this technique as 'the observation of the . . . behaviour of an individual or a group of individuals for definite short periods of time and the recording of the occurrence or non-occurrence of certain specified and objectively defined forms of behaviour during each of these periods. The number of periods in which the report is positive for a given individual is then treated as his score'.

Early studies (Goodenough, 1930; Arrington, 1931; Loomis, 1931; Beaver, 1932; Thomas, 1932; Olson and Cunningham, 1934) developed such techniques, and a spirit of substantial optimism concerning their future applicability can be felt in reading these papers. Some later evaluations of methodology were more critical and restrained (Jersild, 1933; Robinson and Conrad, 1933; Berne and Kelly, 1934; Charles, 1937; Landreth, 1940).

The great advantage of the time sampling technique is that it allows a comparison of measures of behaviour frequency, objectively defined, for different individuals and in different settings. Age and sex differences, and correlational analysis, follow naturally from this. Although the method does not lend itself so naturally to the detailed sequential studies of behaviour in specific situations now being made by some ethologists, it nevertheless represents a considerable advance in objectivity and comparability of results over diary records and rating methods.

Some of the later criticisms can be related to the use of such techniques by the experimenters rather than necessary defects in the method itself. Although comparability of records for individuals in the same study was satisfactorily obtained, comparability of results from one study to another was rarer. This was not only because the behaviour categories were different and more complex, but because the kind of time sampling used was different also.

In time sampling a large number of short observations are made on each subject. The length of each observation may vary from a few seconds to fifteen minutes or more, and the number of samples per subject similarly shows wide variation. The samples are distributed usually in a balanced design across subjects, and through the duration of the experiment; the latter has varied from a single day to a period of several months.

The standard procedure is the all-or-none recording described by Goodenough (1928). The samples may be discontinuous, or sequential, in which latter case a fairly long sample period is broken down into smaller (often five or ten second) units, and occurrence or non-occurrence scored for each unit. An alternative but related procedure is incident or frequency sampling, in which the number of occurrences within the time sampling period is noted. Which form of sampling to use, and the meaning of the data obtained, depends considerably on the frequency and duration of the behaviours to be observed.

If the time sample period is much less than the behaviour duration (bout length) then the distinction between frequency and all-or-none recording vanishes. Use of sequential samples gives information on both number of occurrences and durations. Swan (1938) attempted recording every second, and Arrington (1931) every five seconds, through five minute periods. However (especially when observing a large number of behaviours) such approximations to continuous recording by means of direct observation are in practice very difficult. One solution is to observe for one short time sample and record during the next (e.g. Updegraff and Herbst, 1933); or alternatively (as in the study on social behaviour reported in this chapter) to record ongoing behaviour at the end of each time unit. Sequential information begins to be lost here and the only reliable measurement usually obtained is the proportion of time spent in the particular behaviour. This is the only statistic obtainable when discontinuous, brief time samples are used (e.g. Parten, 1932).

If the time sample period is much greater than the duration of the behaviour then all-or-none recording is inefficient; frequency recording is preferable and gives information on the number of occurrences. The distinction between discontinuous and sequential sampling vanishes. Frequency sampling over a fairly long time period is useful for behaviours occurring rather rarely, such as fighting and crying (Ricketts, 1934; Landreth, 1940, 1941); often all the children in the sample can be observed simultaneously.

If the time sample period is of the same order of magnitude as the behaviour duration, then the meaning of the measure obtained is inexact, lying somewhere between number of occurrences and proportion of time spent in the behaviour. This may not be too important in terms of simply comparing individuals (provided behaviour duration does not show marked individual variation). Indeed for all-or-none recording this is the most efficient in terms of information extracted per time sample.

THE PROBLEM OF RELIABILITY

The number of time samples made is especially relevant to the reliability of the data obtained (this is referred to by Arrington as validity). The split-half reliability is obtained by correlating scores for two equal samples, usually obtained by odd–even splitting of the records. It will depend on (a) the consistency with which the behaviour is recorded by the observer, (b) the intrinsic stability of the behaviour concerned and (c) the adequacy of sampling. See Olson and Cunningham (1934) for further discussion of this. Assuming (a) and (b) are satisfactory the number of samples, together with sample length and distribution, should be such as to give sufficiently high split-half reliabilities for behaviour categories across individual subjects.

The term reliability was used in another sense, namely inter-observer agreement (perhaps better referred to as such). Much concern was evident for this, and periods of intensive training, often of weeks or even months, were undertaken in order to get agreement, usually of 0.9 or above, between two or three observers. Values such as these should refer to concordances rather than correlation coefficients (Arrington, 1943, p. 92). Such training procedures were obviously necessary if several observers were cooperating in collecting data. However, in the more usual case where a single observer (O_1) made all the main observations, it might be argued that such ' reliabilities ' were considerably over-valued. The ultimate figure obtained will depend on (a) the consistency of O_1, and of O_2 (the second observer) and

(b) the agreement between O_1 and O_2. The consistency of the observer is already reflected in the split-half reliability and satisfactory values of the latter will not be obtained if O_1's criteria are not consistent. The fact that O_1 and O_2 agree after considerable training is of little interest to others; the implication being that without training agreement would be lower, but by how much? It is only to be expected that after sufficient training two observers can come to share each other's interpretations and schemata. As far as communication with later readers is concerned, agreement with an untrained observer or observers might well be considered of greater interest. This would give an indication of how well the verbal category definitions can be understood by someone who does not have the benefit of the author's personal training in their interpretation. There are difficulties with this idea too; to be useful there should be several such observers. Moreover, should they be untrained in the most general sense of not having watched children previously? Undoubtedly this sort of experience is important (Connolly and Stratton, 1968).

The considerable emphasis on inter-observer agreements might well be thought of as a reflection of the complex and culture-bound nature of many of the behaviour categories. If the scheme mentioned above was used inter-observer agreements would be lower. In the case of more precisely defined or finer categories however, one might tentatively expect concordances in the range 0.6 to 0.9. Without individual training, it may well prove difficult to improve inter-observer agreements beyond this, even for the finer ethological categories of posture or facial expression. Although definition is more precise there are also many more alternative categories to choose from at this finer level of analysis. For example, the amount of observer variation in deciding whether a child's eyebrows are raised or not may be just as great as in saying whether a child is playing in a group or not; given that both categories are defined as precisely as possible relative to their own level of complexity. The answer may lie in attempting definitions which are as unambiguous as possible (often with the help of photographs and film records) and to generalise over a number of studies by different investigators.

THE ANALYSIS OF DATA

Treatment of the data obtained was usually in the form of a comparison of behaviour frequencies. In addition correlation coefficients were often computed. Factor analyses were rarely carried out, since the technique itself was new and high speed computing facilities were not available. Those which were undertaken (Williams, 1935; Alstyne, 1936; Richards, 1940; Maurer, 1941; Koch, 1934, 1942; and later Cattell and Peterson, 1958) are of limited value. The selection of categories was not very comprehensive and the data were often teachers' ratings rather than overt behaviour. Hence factors of ' pupil desirability ', ' self-sufficiency ', and ' conformity ' emerged.

Split-half reliabilities were not extended to the factor analysis, and in general it seems that more factors were extracted than can be considered reliable, though these seem to be common faults in the application of factor analysis in other fields as well (Armstrong and Soelberg, 1968).

SUMMARY

In summary, some characteristics of the early literature on social behaviour which limit its value in present-day terms are:

(1) a prevalent bias in the categories used and situations examined towards behaviours considered desirable or undesirable by teachers and parents,

(2) uncritical use of categories of a high level of complexity, often defined in motivational terms, with resultant emphasis on high inter-observer agreement after considerable training,

(3) reliance on methods of time sampling, or incident sampling, with a lack of sequential analysis of behaviour sequences, or temporal association of behaviour clusters in specific situations,

(4) little interest in looking for explanations of behaviour in terms of underlying motivations and immediate environmental influences,

(5) lack of any inter-species perspective.

The lack of inexpensive filming equipment, or of computing facilities, must inevitably have contributed to these limitations. In addition the general restriction of studies to white urban (usually American) children, without mental or physical handicaps, should be mentioned. This is however also a limitation of most present day research, though more attention is now being paid to handicapped children (Hutt and Ounsted, 1966; Hutt, Hutt and Ounsted, 1965). Gatewood and Weiss (1930) discussed race and sex differences in neonates whilst Stevenson and Stevenson (1960) have examined social interactions in an inter-racial nursery school.

While the above criticisms may indicate why further descriptive and ethological work on young children is needed, it is probably true to say that the literature of the 1930s has suffered an unjustified neglect. Many of the methodological findings are of relevance, especially for time sampling studies which will continue to have application. A great deal of basic knowledge on the type of behaviour to be expected in pre-school children, their behaviour problems and their social groupings, is also to be found. A few of the studies can be regarded as concerning themselves with quite specific situations, or using quite fine and precise behavioural categories. As interesting and perhaps relevant examples of work of this kind, anticipating the more ethologically oriented research of the 1960s might be mentioned the articles by Kenderdine (1931, experimental study of situations producing laughter), Ricketts (1934, study of anger; wide range of categories with definitions), Johnson (1935, how variation in the amount of play equipment affects behaviour), Parten (1933, size and composition of play groups, sex differences in toy preferences), Updegraff and Herbst (1933, differences in social behaviour stimulated by blocks and clay), Swan (1938, moderately detailed examination of facial expressions and vocalisations, including category ' clusters '), Ames (1949, situations in which smiling occurs, developmental sequences from eighteen months to four years), and Gilmer (1933, very detailed descriptions of behaviours in neonates using film records).

Some reservations concerning the Ethological Approach

Bateson (1968) has discussed ethological methods of observing behaviour and argued that the broad inclusive techniques of the ethologist complement those of the psychologist and may be regarded as preliminary to more precise experimental analyses. Whilst entirely accepting Bateson's point our reservations turn on how ethology is defined, a notoriously difficult problem, and how well the behaviour in question is understood. Probably the most powerful tool in the ethologist's armoury is the description of specific motor patterns. However, there are questions with respect to the feasibility, in the first instance at least, of using very fine behavioural categories without an immense amount of time and effort. Whilst a scientist must be prepared to give both of these there is nothing particularly edifying in watching him struggle with the impossible; as Medawar (1965) has said ' science is the art of the soluble '. To get down to the ' basic ' categories of human behaviour which are unitary in the sense discussed above would seem to imply more than fifty categories for facial expression alone and well over a hundred for behaviour generally (Grant, 1969; Blurton Jones, in press). Even so, whether bodily activities or postures such as *walk* or *bend forward*, are unitary in the motivational sense is questionable unless reference is made to the environment – is the child bending to pick up a toy for example? Admittedly situation analysis is used as an aid to motivational analysis by ethologists, but often to a limited extent; and there may be special difficulties in the case of man, who while not the only tool-using animal, is certainly unique in the degree to which he manipulates his environment. It is possible that in the case of the human species there may be much more motivational ambiguity in purely physically defined behavioural units. Thus problems present in animal ethology (Hinde, 1953; Blurton Jones, 1968) are magnified in human ethology.

In theory this could be overcome by sustained sequential analyses combined with observation of the situational factors. However it is here that the very large number of behavioural units, and the generally long time span over which human motivations are operative (especially in adults), may make this approach unrewarding. Either great simplifications would have to be made, thus losing some important features of the ethological approach, or an undigestible mass of detail would result.

This difficulty can be brought out vividly by considering the social nature of behaviour in a young child, which for practical purposes is often an important variable to measure. This would be prohibitively difficult if one is to measure a large number of micro-categories. Even use of all these micro-categories themselves may prove to be unsatisfactory unless the data is integrated over an appreciable time period, such as a minute or more. For example, a child in a group may run off to fetch a toy to add to a collection being made by the group. This is ostensibly solitary behaviour if the observer picks up and analyses the immediate motor pattern, over a slightly longer period of time it is clearly social behaviour.

A human observer brings his own information-processing system to bear on situations such as this and from a mass of complex perceptual data makes a judgement, on, for example, the social nature of the activity, using rules and criteria of which he is often only partly aware. Whilst he may apply the rules consistently himself the difficulty lies in comparisons with other observers and in the uncritical use of the concept concerned. Consequently ethologists strive to become aware of such rules and criteria and to describe them explicitly to other observers.

On an ideal ethological approach (in Bateson's terms (1968) a physical description) micro-categories are carefully defined and the occurrence of hundreds of such categories over a suitable time span is analysed by computer. This massive computer analysis now provides an opportunity for examining the rules and criteria involved and of re-evaluating the usefulness of the behaviour categories employed. The question remains, however, whether the complexity of human behaviour will render this approach prohibitive in time and resources. Pre-school children and neonates are more hopeful in this regard than adults since their behaviour is perhaps less complex, or at least their environment is more circumscribed. However, it must be clearly understood that these are the young of the species and general conclusions about human propensities and motivations cannot be drawn from them alone.

These criticisms are not to deny the undoubted use of the ethological method in many situations. There is ample evidence of its efficacy. Rather what we are questioning is whether the ' pure ' approach will provide a comprehensive account of human behaviour. These reservations will to some extent explain the compromises in the research described below where certain categories, such as the social nature of play, are complex and used rather uncritically. The gains made in the comprehensiveness of description are achieved without commensurate increases in the problems of data collection and analysis. Our strategy has been determined by the need to demonstrate unequivocally that there are problems which merit detailed study before a great deal of time, effort and skilled manpower is invested.

P. K. SMITH AND K. CONNOLLY

Social behaviour of children in day nurseries

The investigation which is outlined below bears some similarity to the kinds of research carried out in the 1930s on pre-school children. The study was designed to obtain an overall picture of the behaviour of these children and to examine their behaviour in relation to age, sex, and other variables. An important departure from the approach typically used in earlier investigations was the definition of behaviour categories. The behaviours examined were in most cases carefully defined in terms of facial expression, vocalisations, bodily postures and motor patterns rather than the more complex, and perhaps culture-bound, categories which characterise much of the early work. Altogether some sixty categories were used though far more will be necessary for a complete description of the children's behaviour.

Correlations of the behavioural categories (between subjects) were obtained, and a principal component analysis to obtain major dimensions of individual variation in behaviour carried out.

DESIGN

Observations were recorded on standard record sheets by one observer, who remained passive to any approaches by the children.

A time sampling technique, on free play activity, was employed. Twelve five-minute samples were taken on each child, ongoing behaviour being sampled every ten seconds (sequential information was not retained).

In the nurseries free play is usually allowed from 9.30 to 11.00 a.m.; 2.30 to 3.00 p.m. and 3.30 to 4.30 p.m. during which periods the children are free to play as they wish with a large number of toys. The types of apparatus and toys usually available are: climbing frame, steps and slide, rocking horse, trucks, doll's house, doll's pram, balls, toy cars, guns, dolls and so on. There were no easels, and games with clay, paper or sand were rare. During these periods of free play the interaction of the nursery staff with the children was limited.

Altogether forty children were studied in three nurseries of closely similar design, facilities and daily routine. Each nursery was approximately 850 sq. ft in area (indoors). The sample formed a balanced $2 \times 2 \times 2 \times 5$ design for age (2 years 9 months – 3 years 9 months and 3 years 9 months – 4 years 9 months, mean age 3 years 9 months), sex (males and females) and parental background (with or without father in the home *). This permitted the use of a three-way analysis of variance to examine any differences due to these variables in the frequency of the various behaviour categories. A smaller, 3×8 subgroup was balanced for these factors and in addition for the particular day nursery.

For thirty-seven of the forty children half the records were obtained in

* Approximately half the mothers of the day nursery children are unmarried, separated or divorced, though paternal substitutes may be present.

the mornings and half in the afternoons thus permitting a comparison between these two times of day. A number of records were made during play sessions out of doors in a yard attached to each nursery. Although small, the number of records obtained was sufficient to allow comparisons of pairs of 'indoor' and 'outdoor' records for individual children. Wilcoxon matched-pairs tests were used for these two variables.

Data were also obtained on: the social class of the children, the number of siblings, and the nursery experience of each child (the length of time over which child had been attending the nursery). These latter data are summarised in Table 3·1.

TABLE 3·1. *Background data (social class, number of siblings, length of nursery experience) on children in sample*

Social class	A	B	C	D	E	F
	5	3	15	13	17	0

Social class data for parents by occupation, using the Registrar-General's classification as in the Sample Census 1966 (General Register Office, 1968–9). Unemployed fathers and unmarried mothers are put in class E; unemployed married mothers are omitted.

A: managerial;   B: technical and professional;   C: clerical; D: industrial wage earners;   E: non-industrial wage earners; F: agricultural wage earners.

Number of siblings	0	1	2	3 or more
	19	8	10	3

Nursery experience	Range 1–37 months
	Mean 15.8 months; s.d. 11.1 months.

Split-half reliabilities were obtained from each behaviour category. Inter-observer agreement was also examined with an untrained observer (though one experienced in child watching), using only the written definitions given below. The overall level of concordance * was just over 0.7. The full details of all the results obtained are not given in this report, but the influence of the various variables examined is summarised; some of the more interesting results are discussed in detail. The results of principal component analyses are dealt with in a subsequent section.

---

* Concordance is defined here as the number of occurrences for which both observers agree, divided by the total number of occurrences (estimated by taking the mean for both observers). Thus agreement as to the absence of a behaviour does not enter into the concordance estimate.

DEFINITIONS OF BEHAVIOUR CATEGORIES

FACIAL EXPRESSION

Smile – Corners of mouth withdrawn and turned upwards. No distinction was made as to mouth open or closed, teeth visible or not. No audible vocalisation.

Red face – Reddening of cheeks or of face generally.

Puckered face – Tightening of the muscles or wrinkling of the skin around the eyes and the mouth. Brows puckered.

Stare – A look lasting for three seconds or more.

VOCALISATIONS

Talk – Any utterance containing one or more recognisable words, excluding *play noise, exclaim,* or *sing.* Scored *S* if talking alone, *C* if to another child, *N* if to nurse and *O* if to observer.

Play noise – Noises made in play (see p. 80) such as ' brr-brr ', ' bang ', and also repeated or stereotyped phrases such as ' I'm Batman '.

Laugh – Open-mouthed smile together with audible vocalisation (rapid or staccato expulsions of breath).

Scream – A single or repeated forceful high-pitched vocalisation. Excluding squeals occurring in a play context.

Cry – Repeated usually low-pitched vocalisations; ' waah ', ' aaah-hah '.

Sing – Any utterance of a continued (three or more seconds) rhythmical or musical nature.

Exclaim – Single interjections or exclamations (' oh ', ' ah ') or a sudden intake of breath.

SPECIFIC MOTOR ACTIVITIES

Climb, slide – Gross physical activity on steps, slide or climbing frame. Also scored if child is raising himself up on a chair, table or other apparatus.

Run – Any locomotor activity faster than a walk or a shuffle. Running up the steps is scored as *climb.* Exclude *chase, flee.*

Hop, jump – Jumping up or down, or just jumping down from apparatus; hopping on one leg; skipping.

Arm flap – Arms wave or flap around by the child's side.

Play beat – Beat made with extended arm in play context (see page 80), usually with open fists and without contact (see Blurton Jones, 1967).

Wrestle, fall over – Play such as mock fighting or rolling around, involving gross physical contact. Exclude *dance.*

Chase, flee – Non-contact play in which a child pursues or is pursued by another, accompanied by an open-mouthed smile or laugh.

Dance – Gross rhythmic movements of the arms, body and legs.

Read – Looking at books, magazines, comics.

Reach, search – Arm extended for object, or searching for an object.

Point – Arm extended outwards but not in contact with any other object, the child looks or stares in the same direction.

Suck – A digit or a toy in contact with one or both lips.

PLAY AND SOCIAL INTERACTION

AGONISTIC BEHAVIOURS

Threat – Threat of attack as indicated by verbal utterance ('get out of the way', 'I'll hit you') or by expression or posture (stare with a low frown).

Hit – Hit or beat with extended arm in an agonistic context. Contact is sometimes made, but not necessarily so.

Fight – Agonistic behaviour involving gross physical contact.

Submissive – Submissive behaviour as indicated by allowing another child to take possession of a toy or apparatus (e.g. going first on the steps or the slide), without any substantial attempt at resistance (excluding *flight*).

Flight – Locomotor behaviour away from a threat or immediately after surrendering a toy or an apparatus to another child (distinct from *flee* in a play context).

Try to take toy – Taking or attempting to take a toy (which has not been offered) from another child. This is separate from *fight* and is scored when a child's orientation and physical contact is with the toy rather than with the other child *per se*.

Try to keep toy – In response to another child trying to take a toy, holding on to the toy and/or following the child who has taken it, trying to get it back.

SPECIFIC SOCIAL INTERACTIONS

Holds out object – Arm extended to child (*C*), nurse (*N*), or observer (*O*), holding toy or other object.

Walk to, run up to – Direct approach from at least three feet away to nurse (*N*) or observer (*O*) when apparent from context this is not just accidental.

Physical contact – Any non-accidental physical contact to child (*C*), nurse (*N*) or observer (*O*), (e.g. holding hands, hand on the back of another child). Excluding contact which is involved in rough and tumble play or wrestling, contact in an agonistic context, and *cuddled by nurse*.

Rejection – Rejection of a physical contact or object held out, or a verbal play invitation by another child (*C*), or nurse (*N*).

Appeal to nurse – Appealing to nurse for help or assistance, either verbally or standing close and looking, staring or holding out an object to her, or crying.

Cuddled by nurse – The child is cuddled by nurse; includes gross physical contact, child lifted off the ground, but not minor physical contact as, for example, in drying eyes or leading a child somewhere else.

Helps child – Helps another child in some activity, e.g. tying a ribbon in hair, helping a younger child down the slide.

Cooperation with nurse – Cooperates with request or command by nurse.

Non-cooperation with nurse – Ignores or refuses to obey a request or command by nurse.

PLAY AND OTHER ACTIVITY

Whilst recording the behaviour, ticks could be placed in any of the categories defined above, or in none of them. In addition certain further discriminations were made and recorded at every (ten second) observation. They were (*a*) *play*; *activity*; *looking-on play*; *nothing* (*b*) *moving*; *stationary* (*c*) *self*; *parallel*; *group* and (*d*) *toys*; *no toys* (only in the case of *play*). Detailed definitions are given below. The advantage of this procedure was that it allowed a fairly unambiguous comparison for different children of comprehensive measures such as social participation and physical activity, made up on common sense grounds from these categories.

(a) PLAY; ACTIVITY; LOOKING-ON PLAY; NOTHING

The definition of play behaviour is notoriously difficult, and in practice the observer uses many criteria and makes a complex assessment on the basis of them. Problems of definition have been discussed by Loizos (1967). Bearing these difficulties in mind no rigid definition has been applied.

Play – The manipulation of toys, use of apparatus such as steps and slide (but excluding simply inactive behaviour, when the child is merely in contact with or leaning against them), general physical activity with or without contact with toys or apparatus, painting, looking at books or pictures, use of water, clay, or sand, imaginative or fantasy behaviour (e.g. pretending to be dead).

Activity – Standing in a group talking (only), watching other activity, wandering around, obeying the nurse, agonistic behaviour, pulling up socks and other routine activities.

Looking-on play – A particular intermediate category in which the child watches others play, follows them around, stands or sits within speaking distance so that he can see and hear what is taking place, but does not interact with the children or take part in the play behaviour himself.

Nothing – Minimal activity, either physically or socially. Possibly talking softly to self, sucking or doing some simple, repetitive non-essential action. Usually doing nothing at all.

(b) MOVING; STATIONARY

Moving – Child's feet and body moving relative to the ground

Stationary – Child's feet stationary relative to the ground.

(c) SELF; PARALLEL; GROUP

For *play* a distinction was made between *self*, *parallel* and *group* behaviour. The definitions of these categories correspond closely to those of Parten (1932). *Group play* here corresponds to her associative and cooperative play. *Looking-on play* here corresponds to her on-looker behaviour. A similar distinction was made for *activity* and *nothing*; but here *parallel* was subsumed under *group*, since it was difficult to distinguish the two.

Self – The child plays alone and independently, if he is playing with toys the toys are different from those used by nearby children. If he is playing without toys then no other children close by are engaged in similar behaviour. In either case there is no interaction with other children, a child makes no effort to keep close to or speak to other children, his interest is centred on his own behaviour which is pursued without reference to what others are doing.

Parallel – The child plays independently, but the behaviour he chooses naturally brings him among other children. If playing with toys then these are like those which nearby children are using, but he plays with the toys as he sees fit. If play is without toys then he uses the same apparatus or his behaviour is of a similar nature to that of nearby children. In either case he does not attempt to influence the behaviour of nearby children and there is little or no interaction with them. He plays beside, rather than with, the other children.

Group – The child plays with other children, interacting with them in the nature of the behaviour. Interactions here include conversation, borrowing or sharing toys, following or chasing one another, physical contact, and organised play involving different roles.

(*d*) TOYS; NO TOYS

Toys – Includes all the usual nursery toys, also sand and water, clay, painting, reading, dressing up, and play with any objects (e.g. flower, stick), or apparatus (swing, rocking horse) which can be manipulated or moved around by the child.

No toys – Includes not only play where there is no contact with material objects (running around, etc.) but also play with apparatus such as steps and slide, climbing frame, trampoline, chairs or tables, provided these are not moved around.

RESULTS

(1) *Effects of principal variables*

All the results quoted below are significant at or beyond the 5% level on two-tailed tests unless otherwise stated. The methods of analysis have been summarised on pp. 76–7.

(*a*) Differences related to the particular day nursery. The distribution of behaviour amongst the different kinds of play and activity (with or without toys, etc.) differed between the three nurseries without any significant differences in overall social participation or physical activity (definitions below).

(*b*) Differences related to age. *Talking* to other children and social *play* are more frequent amongst the older subgroup. *Staring, crying, sucking, pointing* and *submissive/flight* behaviours occur more frequently in the younger subgroup.

(*c*) Differences related to sex. *Talking* to another child and *sucking* are more frequent in girls. *Play noises*, rough and tumble play (see definition below) are more frequent in boys, and the overall physical activity level of the boys is higher.

(*d*) Differences related to presence or absence of father in the home. Significantly more aggressive behaviours were observed in boys without fathers when compared to boys with fathers, or compared to girls. The younger children without fathers cried more.

(*e*) Differences related to length of nursery experience. Sociability in play behaviour, rough and tumble play, *laughing* and *smiling* were all found to correlate with nursery experience rather more highly than with age.

(*f*) Differences related to activity indoors versus outdoors. Out of doors there are still many toys but because of the greater area for play the group density was reduced. There was more *running, moving play, laughing, smiling*, rough and tumble play and also wandering alone doing nothing. There was less *stationary play, staring, sucking* ($p < 0.06$), or aggressive behaviours (p >0.1, probably owing to the small size of the sample). No differences in the social nature of the play were observed.

(g) Differences relating to time of day. No significant differences were observed between the nature of the behaviour in the morning as compared with the afternoon session.

(2) Selected categories

Some of the more interesting findings are discussed below in greater detail. All the frequencies quoted refer to means per hour, sampling ongoing behaviour every ten seconds as described above.

(a) Vocalisations. The mean number of all vocalisations was 68.3 with a wide individual range, from 11 to 146. Split-half reliability was found to be 0.82. The two most important categories were *talk* (to another child) and *play noise*. The means for these two categories respectively were 38.9 and 15.8, reliabilities 0.83 and 0.86. Total vocalisations show a highly significant (p <0.005) age difference but no sex difference, see Table 3·2. For *talk* (to another child) the age difference is significant at p <0.002; in addition there is a sex difference, girls talk more p <0.02. For *play noise* the age difference is not significant but there is a significant sex difference (p <0.005), boys make more play noises. These sex and age differences in types of vocalisations are related to differences in kind of play. *Talk* to another child correlates highly with *group, stationary, play, toys* and social play. *Play noise* correlates highly with *moving, play, no toys*, irrespective of its social nature (see also Fig. 3·1). The sex difference in talkativeness has been noted several times before (see Arrington, 1943) though the distinction between talking and play noises was not usually made. However, Swan (1938) made a similar distinction and found more play noises were made by boys, though no sex differences in talking were reported.

TABLE 3·2. *Distributions of vocalisations as a function of age and sex. See text for significance levels of differences*

		Vocalisations boys	girls	Talk to C boys	girls	Play noise boys	girls
Age group	Older	82.9	82.4	47.0	65.6	27.7	7.6
	Younger	52.8	54.9	24.3	36.7	19.8	8.2
	Mean of both groups	67.9	68.7	31.8	46.0	23.8	7.9

(b) Social participation. A composite measure of social participation was obtained by weighting *group, parallel* and *self play* as 2, 1 and 0 respectively.

The split-half reliability was 0.88. Using this composite measure a higher correlation was obtained with nursery experience than with age.* The partial correlation with nursery experience, holding age constant, is 0.44 and with age, when nursery experience held constant, 0.29. This is a good indication that the nursery environment is conducive to an improvement in the ability to interact and play with other children. Mallay (1935) showed that the social techniques of 2-year-olds in nursery school improved in six months' nursery experience by an amount greater than the initial 2–3-year age difference. Hattwick (1936) and Jersild and Fite (1939) also examined the effects of nursery school attendance. These and later studies are discussed by Swift (1964) and Eyken (1967). Parten (1932) using a similar index of social participation obtained a higher correlation with age which probably reflects the wider age range of her sample.

(c) Physical activity. This composite measure was obtained by weighting *moving play* or *activity* as 1, and in addition *run*; *hop, jump*; *wrestle, fall over*; *chase, flee* and *dance* as 1, and *climb, slide* as $\frac{1}{2}$. Split-half reliability was 0.73. This was only a gross measure of physical activity, but it was found that boys had a higher score than girls ($p < 0.005$). There was no significant age difference. The sex difference has been noted previously (e.g. Goodenough, 1930), though obviously the actual measures used will be of importance.

TABLE 3·3. *Rough and tumble play in relation to age and sex.*
See text for significance levels of differences

		Total rough and tumble play		Non-contact play		Contact play (wrestle, fall over)	
		boys	girls	boys	girls	boys	girls
Age group	Older	21.4	8.5	15.8	7.7	5.6	0.8
	Younger	14.8	10.4	11.4	8.7	3.4	1.7
	mean	18.1	9.5	13.6	8.2	4.5	1.3

(d) Rough and tumble play. In this study rough and tumble play was taken as covering categories *wrestle, fall over*; *chase, flee*; *play beat* and *group, moving, play, no toys* involving *run* or *hop, jump*. The typical patterns have been described by Blurton Jones (1967) for humans and by Harlow and Harlow (1965) for rhesus monkeys. Harlow and Harlow distinguish

---

* In this sample the correlation between age and nursery experience was only 0.34.

between contact play (*wrestle, roll, sham beat*) and non-contact or approach–withdrawal play (*chase, flee*). They report a sex difference, with males exhibiting the former more often and females the latter more often. There is some evidence suggesting that these differences may be under hormonal control in monkeys (Young *et al.*, 1960). Blurton Jones (1967 and Ch. 4) has suggested that a similar sex difference is found in humans; both contact and non-contact play are more frequent in boys although the sex difference for non-contact play is less pronounced. Some support for this is to be found in the results reported here, Table 3·3. The sex difference is significant for contact play $p < 0.01$, for non-contact play $p < 0.05$. It must be remembered however that the category is relatively unreliable (split-half reliability 0.56) probably because it was observed infrequently, especially contact play. Both components were found to occur more frequently out of doors, but the majority of observations were made indoors.

(*e*) Sucking. Age and sex effects for *suck* are shown in Table 3·4; the age difference is significant at $p < 0.04$ and the sex difference at $p < 0.03$. The split-half reliability was found to be 0.76. The fact that young girls suck more than boys has been noted several times previously and the evidence on this point is summarised by Honzik and McKee (1962), who also discuss possible explanations. Honzik and McKee reject the activity level hypothesis, that boys being more active suck less, and also the suggestion that parents have a more permissive attitude to girls sucking. Instead they propose that the difference is due to a greater cutaneous sensitivity on the part of girls.

TABLE 3·4. *Mean frequency of sucking shown by boys and girls in the two age groups. See text for significance levels of difference*

		boys	girls
	Older	3.0	6.5
Age group	Younger	6.2	16.1
	Mean	4.6	11.3

In the results obtained from the present study the correlation of *suck* with overall activity is -0.06 which is non-significant. On the basis of the activity level hypothesis a high negative correlation would be predicted. J. Newson (personal communication, 1969) has found a sex difference in thumb sucking in 4-year-olds, but no differences in maternal attitudes to non-nutritive sucking in boys or girls at one year. The connection between enhanced sensitivity and greater oral pleasure from sucking proposed by Honzik and McKee (1962) is not self-evident. Sex differences in cutaneous sensitivity have been reported (Weinstein, 1968; Bell and Costello, 1964) but these are small; Weinstein quotes pressure sensitivities for the upper lip of 1.9 for adult males and 1.65 for adult females.

There is, however, another possible explanation. Sucking often appears to be a way of reducing arousal in anxiety producing situations. There is some evidence (Mendel, 1965; Goldberg and Lewis, 1969; Hutt, 1970) that girls are less exploratory and more passive in a stress situation. Zazzo (1958, p. 57) observed 7–12-year-olds watching a film and noted that in moments of excitement boys tended to make reaching out movements, whereas girls tended to withdraw the limbs back towards their bodies. These differences in response to stressful or arousing situations may have some relationship to the sex differences in sucking behaviour; boys perhaps have a higher optimal arousal level.

Component analyses of category interrelations

One of the problems associated with observational studies of the kind described above is that of data reduction and the maximisation of useful information extracted. An attempt to simplify the results and obtain some indication of the major dimensions of individual variability in behaviour was made by using a principal component analysis on the inter-correlation matrix obtained from the study on social behaviour. To this end thirty-five behaviour categories which occurred with a frequency of at least one per hour and had split-half reliabilities of 0·48 or above were selected. To obtain sufficient reliability three of the categories used were composite ones; *threat* plus *hit*, *submissive* plus *flight*, and *walk/run to nurse* plus *cuddled by nurse*. The categories were all mathematically independent.

The use of factor analysis techniques has at times been much abused and its indiscriminate or undisciplined use has resulted in justly deserved criticism (Armstrong and Soelberg, 1968). Factor analyses have often been published without any measures of reliability or validity; consequently the meaningfulness of the results, in the sense that (*a*) are they reliable simplifications of the original data, and (*b*) will they enable valid generalisations to similar samples, can be held in doubt. An attempt has been made to avoid these pitfalls. The number of subjects (forty) and of categories (thirty-five) is adequate for the application of factor analytic techniques. The data are certainly of a kind amenable to a simplification of this sort.

RELIABILITY

All of the categories used had split-half reliabilities above 0.48 and 28 are above 0.60. There are 144 correlations in the matrix of 0.308 or above (significant at $p < 0.05$, two-tailed), whereas only about 35 would be expected on a chance basis. Since some of the split-half reliabilities are rather low, the reliability of the principal component analysis was checked by performing identical analyses on the two split-half samples. This gives a clear indication of the component reliabilities and should perhaps be considered as standard procedure wherever possible in factor analytic work (Armstrong and Soelberg, 1968).

VALIDITY

This is of course a more difficult problem. In the present case, it was expected *a priori* that the first factor would be an age-linked, maturity factor, and

TABLE 3·5. *Results of principal component analysis of 35 behaviour categories. Main category loadings for the three largest components, split-half loadings in brackets*

Principal component 1: variance accounted for 19.8% (17.9%; 18.2%)

talk child	+0.29 (+0.27; +0.26)	*stare*	−0.31 (−0.29; −0.29)
group, moving, play, no toy	+0.27 (+0.20; +0.31)	*stationary, activity, self*	−0.27 (−0.29; −0.18)
group stationary, play, toys	+0.23 (+0.28; +0.12)	*self, moving, play, toys*	−0.25 (−0.18; −0.21)
age	+0.22 (+0.22; +0.22)	*try to keep toy*	−0.24 (−0.16; −0.21)
nursery experience	+0.22 (+0.26; +0.19)	*self, stationary, play, toys*	−0.22 (−0.20; −0.26)
group, stationary, play, no toys	+0.21 (+0.15; +0.25)	*moving, alone, nothing*	−0.21 (−0.22; −0.15)
run	+0.19 (+0.12; +0.25)	*looking-on play*	−0.17 (−0.13; −0.13)
group, moving, play, toys	+0.17 (+0.22; +0.05)	*stationary, nothing, group*	−0.16 (−0.13; −0.10)
smile	+0.16 (+0.15; +0.19)		
moving, activity, group	+0.16 (+0.23; +0.03)		

Principal component 2: variance accounted for 14.4% (13.6%; 13.8%)

parallel, moving, play, toys	+0.25 (+0.19; +0.17)	*parallel, moving, play, no toys*	−0.36 (−0.38; −0.31)
group, moving, play, toys	+0.22 (+0.12; +0.30)	*climb, slide*	−0.35 (−0.36; −0.35)
hold out object	+0.20 (+0.20; +0.07)	*self, moving, play, no toys*	−0.34 (−0.28; −0.31)
group, stationary, play, toys	+0.19 (+0.15; +0.25)	*parallel, stationary, play, no toys*	−0.32 (−0.28; −0.30)
		group, moving, play, no toys	−0.22 (−0.29; −0.13)
		hop, jump	−0.20 (−0.21; −0.18)

Principal component 3: variance accounted for 9.6% (9.0%; 9.8%)

age	+0.28 (+0.32; +0.15)	*cry*	−0.40 (−0.25; −0.39)
		suck	−0.37 (−0.17; −0.39)
		hold out object	−0.34 (−0.06; −0.06)
		puckered face	−0.31 (−0.08; −0.35)
		submissive/ flight	−0.25 (−0.14; −0.19)

that the second might well be sex-linked. Given the nature of the subject sample and the many differences due to age and sex already noted, these would seem to be two major sources of individual variability in behaviour. Furthermore two factors such as these could well be orthogonal, given the balanced sample population. Further factors might reflect personality syndromes, though the ability of an orthogonal analysis to extract many meaningful factors in this way may well be limited. All factors obtained could be expected to have considerable face validity.

The particular factors extracted may nevertheless reflect merely the limited number of categories used, or the particular sample population. As a check on this, further analyses were run. One was on the same subject sample using however fifty-three categories rather than thirty-five. Another was an analysis of correlational data published by Arrington (1931) on a sample population of twenty children of mean age 2 years $2\frac{1}{2}$ months, and using a smaller and different set of behaviour categories. The results of these analyses are discussed below. All are principal component analyses, which give a unique solution.

MAIN COMPONENT ANALYSIS

Three components from this analysis were found to be reliable, on the basis of the split-half comparison, and also to have face validity. Together

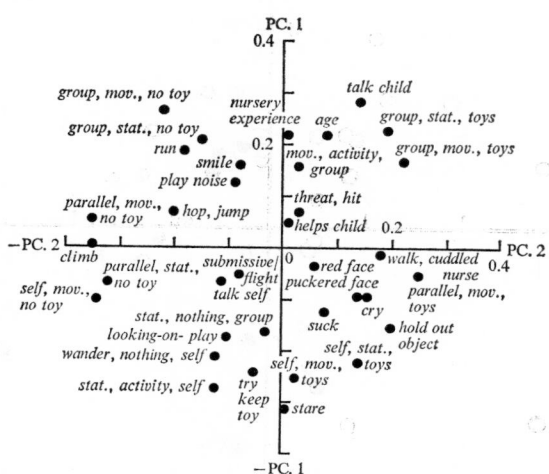

Fig. 3·1. Plot of category loadings on first two principal components from main analysis. Further details in text.

they account for 44% of the total variance. The highest ranked categories, and their loadings for these three components, are shown in Table 3·5. In brackets are the loadings for the split-half analyses. The components from the latter form a very similar rank ordering, the main discrepancy being that for one analysis *cry* and *suck* do not have the largest loadings on the third component, though they are still high. The analysis using fifty-three categories gives very similar results, the only exception being that *holds out object* is not high on component 3. The low split-half loadings also indicate that its position there is unstable. Two plots of component 1 against component 2 (for categories and for subjects) are shown in Figs. 3·1 and 3·2.

INTERPRETATION OF THE CATEGORIES

Component 1

This is clearly a factor which may be called ' social maturity '. *Talk* to child and all the *group play* behaviours are heavily loaded on one side, *stare* and *self* behaviours on the other. *Parallel play* categories have near zero loadings. This factor conforms to prior expectations. It is interesting that both age and nursery experience have equal loadings on this component.

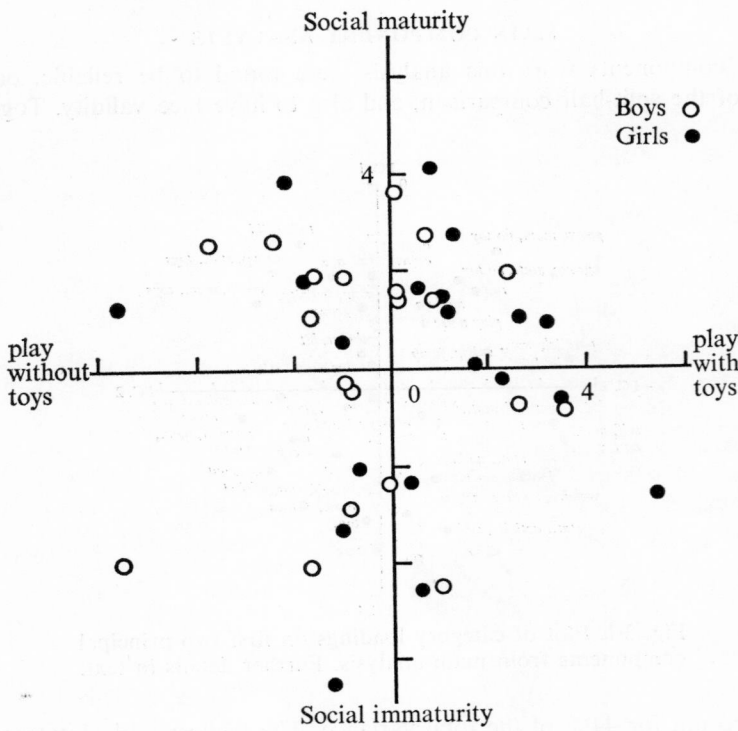

Fig. 3·2. Plot of subject scores on first two principal components of social maturity/immaturity and play with/without toys, from main analysis. Further details in text.

Component 2

This factor is also readily interpreted as reflecting whether the child is playing with toys or without toys, remembering that the latter includes play with immovable apparatus, as well as general physical activity. All the *play, toys* categories are loaded positively, and the *play, no toys* categories negatively including those with smaller loadings which are not shown. The loading of age is only 0.08 and of nursery experience, 0.01.

From Fig. 3·2 a suggestion of a sex difference on component 2 can be seen (there is no sex difference on component 1); the means are boys −0.47, girls 0.47, suggesting that girls play more with toys, while boys play more with apparatus, or run about and take part in rough and tumble play. This corresponds with the differences in vocalisations mentioned earlier. The difference is not significant overall, but using the smaller subgroup of twenty-four (see p. 76) balanced for particular day nursery, and allowing for this factor and for age in a three-way analysis of variance, the sex difference is significant at $p < 0.01$ (two-tailed).

Component 3

This is also strongly age-linked, with younger children showing more of the *cry, suck, puckered face* syndrome. It is interesting that this should be independent of the first component. Thus, both socially immature children, and children who cry and suck a lot, tend to be young, but there is no further connection between them.

One possible explanation for this might be that crying and sucking often, though not always, result from social interaction (e.g. *crying* when a toy is taken, *sucking* when anxious or afraid) by young children rather than immaturity, or activities in isolation.

TABLE 3·6. *Principal component analysis of Arrington's (1931) data. Main category loadings for the two largest components*

Principal component 1: variance accounted for 42.9%			
Material – self	+0.38	Non-material – active	−0.35
Material – active	+0.37	Non-material / self	−0.35
		Non-material – social	−0.34
		Non-material – inactive	−0.30
		Receives physical contact	−0.25

Principal component 2: variance accounted for 16.2%			
Talk person	+0.58	Receives physical contact	−0.20
Material – social	+0.51		
Age	+0.36		
Initiates physical contact	+0.27		
Talk self	+0.24		
Cry	+0.24		

RE-ANALYSIS OF ARRINGTON'S DATA

There is further evidence of the validity of these results from analysing the inter-correlations given by Arrington (1931) between categories of behaviour among twenty children age 1 year 4 months to 2 years 8 months (mean 2 years 2½ months). This is a sample about 1½ years younger than that described above. The behaviour categories are also different, though they do have some similarity. As many categories as possible were selected from her data, and principal component analyses performed. One of these was on twelve completely independent categories. This gave results very similar to those obtained from a second analysis on fifteen categories, some of which are not mathematically independent. Since the results were substantially the same the latter, more complete analysis, is quoted (see Table 3·6). No split-half analyses could be performed, but the quoted reliabilities are high. Two components appear to have face validity and to be very similar to components 1 and 2 above, bearing in mind that the children are younger, and that 'material' implies contact with any material object, so 'inactive-material' should not be considered play behaviour. A category plot of component 1 against component 2 is shown in Fig. 3·3.

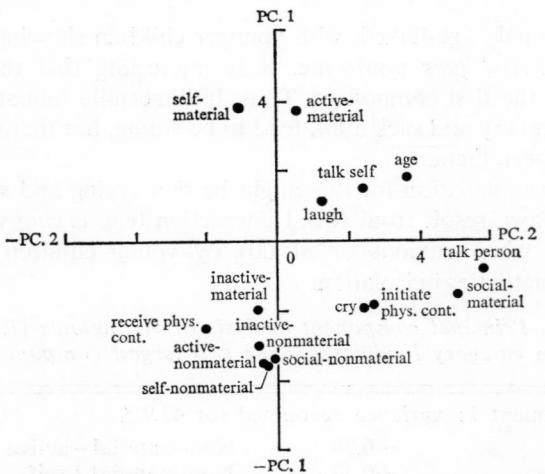

Fig. 3·3. Plot of category loadings on first two principal components from a re-analysis of Arrington's (1931) data. Further details in text.

It is apparent that components 1 and 2 here correspond to components 2 and 1 respectively of our analysis. Minor differences, such as the comparatively high loadings of 'age' on component 1 here, and 'talk self' on component 2, probably reflect the fact that the children are considerably younger.

The components obtained from these analyses are obviously limited by the categories used, nevertheless the results are certainly not trivial. For example, a general activity factor might well have emerged from the categories, but this was not the case. The fact that a major source of individual differences concerns whether play is with toys or not, and that this is related to sex differences in behaviour, has formed the starting point for a further study to analyse play behaviour beyond the provisional categories used here.

Conclusions

The methods of research described in this paper are concerned primarily with normal patterns of behaviour which are readily observed in pre-school children and rather less with motivational analyses based on very detailed categories. Whilst being perhaps less fundamental it nevertheless has the advantage of making data collection and analysis somewhat easier. The results are also readily interpreted.

These methods may be developed in a number of ways. Once the typical patterns of behaviour in the age group are defined the influence of particular environments can be estimated. Findings from such studies may have a bearing on how nurseries can best be planned and equipped. Information of this kind may be of particular relevance to the management and education of handicapped children; observational studies should enable us to discover what kinds of social techniques or forms of play behaviour are missing or inadequate. Once such information is available attempts may be made to alleviate these deficits, by special training or by environmental engineering.

Individual differences in personality may also be defined in terms of differences in overt behaviour. More detailed investigations of particular behaviours may be of special interest in this context (such as for example, the child's reaction to the observer). Longitudinal studies are also of value in studying the emergence of stable personality characteristics (Thomas *et al.*, 1964) though as yet they have been little exploited.

The authors are grateful to the Medical Officer of Health and the Director of Education of the city of Sheffield, and the staff at the various nurseries for their help and cooperation. One of us (P. K. S.) is in receipt of a research studentship from the Medical Research Council which is gratefully acknowledged.

REFERENCES

Alstyne, D. van (1936). A new scale for rating school behaviour and attitudes in the elementary school. *J. ed. Psychol.* **27**, 677–93.

Ames, L. B. (1949). Development of interpersonal smiling response in the pre-school years. *J. genet. Psychol.* **74**, 273–91.

Armstrong, J. S. and Soelberg, P. (1968). On the interpretations of factor analysis. *Psychol. Bull.* **70**, 361–4.

Arrington, R. E. (1931). *Interrelations in the behaviour of young children.* New York: Teachers College, Columbia University.

Arrington, R. E. (1943). Time sampling in studies of social behaviour: a critical review of techniques and results with research suggestions. *Psychol. Bull.* **40,** 81–124.

Arsenian, J. M. (1943) Young children in an insecure situation. *J. abnorm. soc. Psychol.* **38,** 235–49.

Barker, M. (1930). A technique for studying the social-material activities of young children. *Monog. Soc. Res. Child Develop.* **3.**

Bateson, P. P. G. (1968). Ethological methods of observing behaviour. In *Analysis of behavioural change.* Ed. L. Weiskrantz, London and New York: Harper and Row.

Beaver, A. P. (1932). The initiation of social contacts by preschool children. *Monog. Soc. Res. Child Develop.* **7.**

Bell, R. Q. and Costello, N. S. (1964). Three tests for sex differences in tactile sensitivity in the newborn. *Biol. neonat.* **7,** 335–47.

Berne, E. van C. and Kelly, H. G. (1934). The adequacy of samples of behaviour obtained during short observation periods. *Univ. Iowa Stud. Child Welf.* **9** (3).

Blurton Jones, N. G. (1967). An ethological study of some aspects of social behaviour of children in nursery school. In *Primate ethology.* Ed. D. Morris, London: Weidenfeld and Nicolson.

Blurton Jones, N. G. (1968). Observations and experiments on causation of threat displays of the Great Tit *(Parus major). Anim. Behav. Monog.* **1,** 75–158.

Blurton Jones, N. G. (in press). Criteria for use in describing facial expressions of children. *Hum. Biol.*

Brackbill, Y. (1967). (Ed.) *Infancy and early experience.* London: Collier-Macmillan.

Cates, T. (1939). A study of the dominative and submissive behaviour of eight preschool children. In K. S. Bernhardt, *et al.* (1951). *Twenty-five years of child study: University of Toronto Institute of Child Study.* Toronto: Univ. Toronto Press.

Cattell, R. B. and Peterson, D. R. (1958). Personality structure in 4–5-year olds, by factoring observed, time-sampled behaviour. *Ras. Psico. Gen. Clin.* **3,** 1–21.

Charles, M. (1937). Motion pictures versus direct observation – a study of method in social analysis. In K. S. Bernhardt, *et al.* (1951). *Twenty-five years of child study: University of Toronto Institute of Child study.* Toronto: Univ. Toronto Press.

Connolly, K. and Stratton, P. (1968). Developmental changes in associated movements. *Develop. Med. Child Neurol.* **10,** 49–56.

Esser, A. H. (1965). Social contact and use of space in psychiatric patients. *Amer. Zool.* **5,** 676.

Eyken, W. (1967). *The preschool years.* Harmondsworth: Penguin Books.

Gatewood, M. C. and Weiss, A. P. (1930). Race and sex differences in newborn infants. *J. genet. Psychol.* **38,** 31–49.

General Register Office (1968–9). Sample Census 1966. London: H.M.S.O.

Gilmer, B. H. (1933). An analysis of the spontaneous responses of the newborn infant. *J. genet. Psychol.* **42,** 392–405.

Goldberg, S. and Lewis, M. (1969). Play behaviour in the year-old infant: early sex differences. *Child Develop.* **40,** 21–31.

Goodenough, F. L. (1928). Measuring behaviour traits by means of repeated short samples. *J. Juv. Res.* **12,** 230–5.

Goodenough, F. L. (1930). Inter-relationships in the behaviour of young children. *Child Develop.* **1,** 29–47.

Grant, E. C. (1968). An ethological description of non-verbal behaviour during interviews. *Br. J. med. Psychol.* **4**, 177–84.

Grant, E. C. (1969). Human facial expression. *Man.* n.s. **4**, 525–36.

Hanfmann, E. (1935). Social structure of a group of kindergarten children. *Amer. J. Orthopsychiat.* **5**, 407–10.

Harlow, H. K. and Harlow, M. K. (1965). The affectional systems. In *Behaviour of nonhuman Primates,* II. Ed. A. M. Schrier, H. F. Harlow and F. Stollnitz, London: Academic Press.

Hattwick, B. W. (1936). The influence of nursery school attendance upon the behaviour and personality of the preschool child. *J. exp. Educ.* **5**, 180–90.

Hattwick, B. W. (1937). Sex differences in behaviour of nursery school children. *Child Develop.* **8**, 343–55.

Hinde, R. A. (1953). Appetitive behaviour, consummatory act, and the hierarchical organisation of behaviour, with special reference to the Great Tit *(Parus major). Behaviour* **5**, 191–224.

Honzik, M. P. and McKee, J. P. (1962). The sex difference in thumb-sucking. *J. Pediat.* **61**, 726–32.

Hutt, C., Hutt, J. S. and Ounsted, C. (1965). The behaviour of children with and without upper CNS lesions. *Behaviour,* **24**, 246–68.

Hutt, C. and Ounsted, C. (1966). The biological significance of gaze aversion with particular reference to the syndrome of infantile autism. *Beh. Sci.* **11**, 346–56.

Hutt, C. (1970). Specific and diversive exploration. In *Advances in child development and behaviour,* vol. 5. Ed. H. Reese and L. P. Lipsitt, London: Academic Press.

Hutt, C. and Vaizey, M. J. (1966). Differential aspects of group density on social behaviour. *Nature, Lond.* **209**, 1371–2.

Jack, L. M. (1934). An experimental study of ascendant behaviour in preschool children. *Univ. Iowa Stud. Child Welf.* **9** (3).

Jersild, A. T. (1933). The constancy of certain behaviour patterns in young children. *Amer. J. Psychol.* **45**, 125–9.

Jersild, A. T. and Fite, M. D. (1939). The influence of nursery school experience on children's social adjustments. *Monog. Soc. Res. Child Develop.* **25**.

Johnson, M. W. (1935). The effect on behaviour of variation in the amount of play equipment. *Child Develop.* **6**, 56–68.

Kenderdine, M. (1931). Laughter in the preschool child. *Child Develop.* **2**, 228–30.

Koch, H. L. (1934). A multiple-factor analysis of certain measures of activeness in nursery school children. *J. genet. Psychol.* **45**, 482–7.

Koch, H. L. (1942). A factor analysis of some measures of the behaviour of preschool children. *J. genet. Psychol.* **27**, 257–87.

Landis, C. and Hunt, W. A. (1936). Studies of the startle pattern: III. Facial pattern. *J. Psychol.* **2**, 215–9.

Landreth, C. (1940). Consistency of four methods of measuring one type of sporadic emotional behaviour (crying) in nursery school children. *J. genet. Psychol.* **57**, 101–17.

Landreth, C. (1941). Factors associated with crying in young children in the nursery school and home. *Child Develop.* **12**, 81–97.

Landreth, C., Gardner, C. M., Eckhardt, B. C. and Prugh, A. D. (1943). Teacher child contacts in nursery schools. *J. exp. Educ.* **12**, 65–91.

Loizos, C. (1967). Play behaviour in higher primates: a review. In *Primate ethology.* Ed. D. Morris, London: Weidenfeld and Nicolson.

Loomis, A. M. (1931). A technique for observing the social behaviour of nursery school children. *Monog. Soc. Res. Child Develop.* **5**.

Mallay, H. (1935). Growth in social behaviour and mental activity after six months in nursery school. *Child Develop.* **6**, 303–9.

Marston, L. R. (1925). The emotions of young children. *Univ. Iowa. Stud. Child Wel.* **3** (3).

Maslow, A. H. (1936). The role of dominance in the social and sexual behaviour of infra-human primates. IV. The determination of hierarchies in pairs and in a group. *J. genet. Psychol.* **49**, 161–98.

Maurer, K. H. (1941). Patterns of behaviour of young children as revealed by a factor analysis of trait ' clusters '. *J. genet. Psychol.* **59**, 177–88.

Medawar, P. B. (1965). *The art of the soluble.* London: Methuen.

Mendel, G. (1965). Children's preferences for differing degrees of novelty. *Child Develop.* **36**, 453–65.

Moore, S. B. (1938). The use of commands, suggestions and requests by nursery school and kindergarten teachers. *Child Develop.* **9**, 185–200.

Olson, W. C. and Cunningham, E. M. (1934). Time sampling techniques. *Child Develop.* **5**, 41–58.

Page, M. L. (1936). The modification of ascendant behaviour in preschool children. *Univ. Iowa. Stud. Child. Welf.* **12** (3).

Parten, M. B. (1932). Social participation among preschool children. *J. abnorm. soc. Psychol.* **27**, 243–69.

Parten, M. B. (1933). Social play among preschool children. *J. abnorm. soc. Psychol.* **28**, 136–47.

Richards, T. W. (1940). Factors in the personality of nursery school children. *J. exp. Educ.* **9**, 152–3.

Ricketts, A. F. (1934). A study of the behaviour of young children in anger. *Univ. Iowa. Stud. Child Welf.* **9** (3).

Robinson, E. W. and Conrad, H. S. (1933). The reliability of observations of talkativeness and social contact among nursery school children by the ' short time sample ' technique. *J. exp. Educ.* **2**, 161–5.

Schjelderup-Ebbe, T. (1935). Social behaviour in birds. In *Handbook of social psychology.* Ed. G. Murchison, Worcester, Mass.: Clark Univ. Press.

Shirley, M. M. (1942). Children's adjustments to a strange situation. *J. abnorm. soc. Psychol.* **37**, 201–17.

Slater, E. (1939). Types, levels and irregularities of response to a nursery school situation of 40 children observed with special reference to the home environment. *Monog. Soc. Res. Child. Develop.* **4**.

Stevenson, H. W. and Stevenson, N. G. (1960). Social interaction in an interracial nursery school. *Genet. Psychol. Monog.* **61**, 37–75.

Swan, C. (1938). Individual differences in the facial expressive behaviour of preschool children: a study by the time sampling method. *Genet. Psychol. Monog.* **20**, 557–650.

Swift, J. W. (1964). Effects of early group experience: the nursery school and day nursery. In *Review Child Development Research,* vol. 1. Ed. M. L. Hoffman and L. W. Hoffman, New York: Russell Sage Foundation.

Thomas, A., Birch, H. G., Chess, S., Hertzig, M. E. and Korn, S. (1964). *Behavioural individuality in early childhood.* London: Univ. London Press.

Thomas, D. S. (1932). An attempt to develop precise measurements in the social behaviour field. *Sociologus* **8**, 436–56.

Updegraff, R. and Herbst, E. K. (1933). An experimental study of the social behaviour stimulated in young children by certain play materials. *J. genet. Psychol.* **42**, 372–91.

Washburn, R. W. (1932). A scheme for grading the reactions of children in a new social situation. *J. genet. Psychol.* **40**, 84–99.

Weinstein, S. (1968). Intensive and extensive aspects of tactile sensitivity as a function of body part, sex and laterality. In *The skin senses.* Ed. D. R. Kenshale, Illinois: Charles C. Thomas.

Williams, H. M. (1935). A factor analysis of Berne's ' Social behaviour patterns in young children '. *J. exp. Educ.* **4**, 142–6.

Young, W. C., Goy, R. W. and Phoenix, C. H. (1960). Hormones and sexual behavior. *Science, N.Y.* **143**, 212–18.

Zazzo, R. (1958). In *Discussions on child development,* Vol. 3. Ed. J. M. Tanner and B. Inhelder, London: Tavistock Publications.

4

CATEGORIES OF CHILD—CHILD INTERACTION

N. BLURTON JONES*

SUMMARY

Twenty-five children selected as being the oldest (around 4 years old) or the youngest (around 2 years old) of their sex in the playgroup were observed during free play, each child for fifteen periods of five minutes. One child was observed at a time and the occurrence of twenty-two previously defined items of behaviour (such as *hit, smile, run, cry, point*) was continuously recorded during each five-minute recording. The number of occurrences of each behaviour item in a five-minute observation was correlated with the number of occurrences of each other item. Factor analysis of these correlations was done for each of four kinds of child: 2-year-old boys, 2-year-old girls, 4-year-old boys, 4-year-old girls. Three main factors, or axes, emerged in each of the four classes of child which were named ' rough and tumble play versus work ', ' aggression ', ' social behaviour '. A less reliable ' distress ' dimension also showed up. Another analysis was based on correlations between individuals. The frequency of occurrence of behaviour was totalled for all the observations on each individual and factor analysis between individuals was done using this data.

Comparisons of behaviour between the age and sex groups and across individuals tended to dissect the aggression dimension. Taking toys did not change in the same way as fighting over toys changed. Individuals who did more rough and tumble did less aggression, but the evidence suggests that this was because they were less often using toys and therefore less often in aggression-provoking situations. Boys did more *wrestling* and *hitting-at* during rough and tumble than girls did. The amount of behaviour to the teacher decreased with age in boys but not in girls.

The main dimensions of individual variation concerned all social behaviour, age and experience in the nursery. Working alone and watching children seemed to be younger forms of behaviour. Subsidiary dimensions of individual variation concern play with toys versus without toys, and active or passive interaction.

The implications of these and other findings for developmental studies are discussed.

Introduction

This paper concerns some of the most conspicuous aspects of social behaviour of children of nursery school age. It covers much the same ground as an earlier paper (Blurton Jones, 1967). The aim of the study was to show whether the same phenomena were still evident, even in the more restricted

* Department of Growth and Development, Institute of Child Health, University of London.

environment of our playgroup. As a subsidiary aim I hoped that, even with the small number of children involved, I would find some of the most obvious age and sex differences in behaviour. But the main aim was to test the groupings of behaviour which I described in my 1967 paper.

I have to redescribe some elementary aspects of ethology in order to introduce this subject. The business of grouping behaviour items derives from an interest which is almost unique to ethologists. Other students of social behaviour seem happy to pick on a *kind* of behaviour like attachment, aggression, fear, and to record it in one of two ways:

(1) they may rate children for the level to which they feel that this kind of behaviour is present: or

(2) one step better, they may seek a single criterion to measure it by, like crying on separation, hitting, or making others cry, or withdrawing.

Ethologists have acquired the important habit of asking themselves, as soon as a category like attachment or aggression comes to mind, what they mean by the term and whether it is indeed one kind of behaviour or more than one kind. This is not simply a difference between taxonomic ' splitters ' and ' lumpers '. There are ethologists who lump behaviour into large categories (e.g. the stimulus contrast scale proposed by Andrew, 1963; arousal theory as used by Hutt and Hutt, 1968), but they are concerned that these categories should have a reality justified by data and not by armchair theory. There are many pieces of observable behaviour that some or many people would call aggressive. But do they tend to occur at the same time as each other, or in the same situation? Do individuals who do a lot of one of them also do a lot of the others? These are just some of the likely empirical implications of such categorisations of behaviour. If any of them are not confirmed then the use of the original category is likely to obscure important relationships, as well as to lead to theoretical confusion.

These questions are initially questions of correlations between observed output of behaviour. One of the most sophisticated statistical techniques dealing with the large numbers of measures involved is factor analysis. The present chapter employs this to deal with categorisation of behaviour of one child to another. That is, to show which behaviour items tend to occur at much the same time as which others. To see how far these categories persist with age I also compare the frequency and proportion of the constituent behaviour items in a small sample of 2-year-olds with a small sample of 4-year-olds. Theories of causation of behaviour can be derived from the correlations (a process very similar to that of social survey studies, subject to the same misinterpretations of correlation, and benefiting to the same extent from statistical common sense). The theories can produce hypotheses about the effects of experimentally manipulated causal factors (e.g. Blurton Jones, 1968; Tugendhat, 1960). Perhaps even in man they can lead to ethical experiments on causation of behaviour.

Factor analysis gets over two important problems which simple correlations cannot deal with. Some psychological theory makes great play of behaviour patterns which are a substitute for other more obvious patterns. Thus scratching the body might be regarded as a substitute for overt aggression in certain situations. Animal behaviour studies have used a similar concept in the study of bird displays. Some displays are held to occur when a tendency to attack is balanced by a tendency to flee. There need be no correlation between such a display and actual attack or fleeing. An example occurred in my Great Tit study (Blurton Jones, 1968) and, though the correlation matrix appeared to give no evidence to link it with attack or fleeing, experimentally contrived conflict situations did so quite clearly. Recently I did a factor analysis of the observational data and this categorises the display in question along with attack and the other threat displays. This argument is put forward at greater length by Wiepkema (1961). Wiepkema argues that this happens because the factor analysis takes into account all the relationships of a measure to all the other measures. Sometimes two mutually uncorrelated behaviour items will have similar correlations with all the same other behaviour items. 158932

A similar problem arises when behaviour at different ages is compared. Behaviour at one age may be replaced at another age by different behaviour which has the same relationship to the rest of the behaviour. This, however, is only a first step towards deciding that the two items of behaviour are the same. The main point in deciding whether they are the same is to see whether individual differences in this behaviour have any consistency with age. If individuals who score high on category A at a young age are those who score high (or significantly low) on category B at an older age, this is interesting. If they do not, then there is no point in trying to relate these categories to each other. Space permits only this brief outline of the methodology behind this kind of descriptive ethology. Further details and discussion can be found in Tinbergen (1959) and Hinde (1966). It should be remembered that this represents only a very preliminary stage in investigating the causation of behaviour.

Subjects and methods

The children in the study were six boys and seven girls aged as near 4 years as possible (37–55 months) and six boys and six girls aged as near 2 years as possible (24–33 months). They were selected, on the basis of their age alone, from the children attending the research playgroup in the department. The playgroup consists of four different groups each of six to seven children of mixed age and sex who come for two visits of two hours each week. They are not selected with any particular end in mind, the original children being some of those on the waiting list of the local nursery school. Subsequently children have come from parents who heard about the playgroup from the original parents and from the local authority ' well baby ' clinic. Fathers' occupations are mostly in the Registrar-General's social class group 3 non-manual. The mothers do not work, their children are with us for too short a time. Most of them seem genuinely to bring their children for the child's sake. All the children were from intact homes but with varying accommodation and varying numbers of siblings. We have a few children from other sources (see Leach, Ch. 10); these were excluded from the present study.

The playroom is small, measuring just over 11ft × 14 ft, and is well equipped with toys and the usual play apparatus. Observations were made from an observation room through a one-way screen. The sound system involved monitoring a twin-track tape recorder which was modified to give a stereo sound image from three microphones in the room.

The observations were written on paper in a form of shorthand devised by Leach (Ch. 10), with the time marked at the end of each minute. Particular attention was paid to recording the behaviour items mainly used in this paper, which were taken from Blurton Jones (1967). But I also intended

TABLE 4·1a. *Result of factor analysis of correlations of each behaviour item with each other item between observation periods in 4-year-old children*

	Older boys				
Factor	1	2	3	4	5
% of variance	14.135	10.664	9.615	8.512	8.516
Age	−0.105	0.158	−0.197	0.663	−0.026
Expnce	−0.269	0.090	−0.030	0.539	0.093
Cry	−0.054	0.033	0.904	−0.010	−0.022
Pucker	−0.127	0.580	0.304	−0.192	−0.052
Red	−0.069	0.143	0.939	−0.104	−0.050
Fixate	−0.049	0.870	0.152	0.049	−0.148
Frown	−0.098	0.517	−0.114	−0.066	0.378
Hit	0.054	0.642	−0.142	0.338	0.068
Grabtg	0.007	0.324	0.006	−0.149	0.378
Push	0.211	0.334	0.175	0.336	−0.142
Wrestl	0.613	−0.070	0.005	−0.074	0.063
Hit at	0.611	0.245	−0.064	0.238	−0.203
Jumps	0.727	−0.003	−0.053	−0.230	0.123
Run	0.691	−0.083	0.004	−0.072	0.046
Laugh	0.827	−0.002	−0.081	−0.236	0.017
Work	−0.520	0.259	−0.377	−0.413	−0.079
Paint	−0.071	−0.239	0.052	0.543	0.006
Smile	0.147	−0.028	0.152	0.162	0.550
Talk	0.411	−0.060	−0.057	0.070	0.528
Receive	−0.193	0.290	−0.041	0.364	0.517
Give	−0.026	0.037	−0.100	−0.177	0.505
Point	0.010	−0.132	−0.034	0.048	0.594

the observations to cover most of what occurred, and some of the resulting extra items are used in part of the analyses. I made no attempt to record the behaviour of reactors in any detail.

Each child was observed for fifteen observation periods, each of which lasted five minutes. Three observations were made on a child on each of the five days that it was observed. These days were spread over a period of about two months. During an observation period only one child was observed and the occurrence of twenty-two previously defined items of behaviour was continuously recorded.

I processed the data by counting the number of times each of the items occurred in a five-minute observation. I entered the numbers in one row of an E.D.P. coding sheet. I then had these punched on to eighty-column cards, each card containing the data from one five-minute observation, as well as identifying codes. Factor analyses were done using the Fortran program 'FACTOR' by Clyde, Cramer and Sherin (1966), modified by B. Carter for the University of London CDC 6600. The rotation used in this program is Varimax, Kaiser (1958).

TABLE 4·1b. *Result of factor analysis of correlations of each behaviour item with each other item between observation periods in 4-year-old children*

	Older girls				
Factor	1	2	3	4	5
% of variance	15.047	10.860	10.495	9.959	8.130
Age	−0.108	−0.051	0.053	0.910	0.057
Expnce	−0.113	−0.156	0.020	0.884	0.122
Cry	0.106	0.921	0.021	−0.028	−0.124
Pucker	−0.042	0.040	0.053	0.023	0.703
Red	0.084	0.112	−0.171	0.074	0.713
Fixate	0.038	0.898	−0.112	0.026	0.092
Frown	−0.011	0.552	0.009	−0.106	0.141
Hit	−0.170	0.539	0.045	−0.052	0.051
Grabtg	0.128	0.175	−0.476	−0.057	0.299
Push	−0.349	0.034	0.071	−0.110	0.410
Wrestl	−0.817	0.059	0.054	−0.028	0.080
Hit at	−0.370	0.045	−0.319	0.141	−0.233
Jumps	−0.766	0.027	0.132	0.164	0.121
Run	−0.689	0.052	0.154	0.198	0.231
Laugh	−0.726	0.000	−0.329	0.025	−0.170
Work	0.512	0.045	−0.160	−0.349	0.286
Paint	0.015	−0.022	−0.068	0.437	−0.304
Smile	−0.534	−0.064	0.062	−0.347	−0.093
Talk	−0.354	0.172	−0.707	−0.031	0.084
Receive	0.135	−0.095	−0.590	0.120	−0.175
Give	0.087	−0.114	−0.692	−0.018	−0.142
Point	0.075	−0.002	−0.641	−0.092	0.255

The number of times an item occurred correlates very closely between the twenty-five individuals with the number of observation periods in which the item occurred, except that the latter reaches a maximum and the curve flattens off. Within individuals the number of times an item occurred in an observation also correlates closely with the number of minutes within an observation in which the item occurred. Since these measures are so similar, the number of occurrences of an item was judged to be the best measure to use except in the four cases indicated in the list of behaviour items. Behaviour measures rarely have normal distributions, zero scores being the most abundant.

TABLE 4·2a. *Result of factor analysis of correlations of each behaviour item with each other item between observation periods in 2-year-old children*

	Younger boys				
Factor	1	2	3	4	5
% of variance	16.141	9.611	8.670	7.972	7.757
Age	0.151	−0.081	−0.508	0.023	−0.055
Expnce	−0.009	−0.178	−0.136	0.635	0.024
Cry	0.000	0.000	0.000	0.000	0.000
Pucker	0.124	−0.083	0.167	0.041	0.671
Red	−0.109	0.029	−0.061	0.693	0.048
Fixate	0.055	0.847	0.186	−0.028	−0.043
Frown	−0.173	0.238	0.516	−0.171	−0.051
Hit	−0.048	0.809	−0.045	0.181	0.067
Grabtg	0.072	0.058	0.712	−0.120	0.367
Push	−0.008	0.526	0.038	−0.301	−0.032
Wrestl	−0.678	−0.042	0.212	−0.155	−0.168
Hit at	−0.512	0.442	0.018	0.535	−0.065
Jumps	−0.794	−0.053	0.198	0.040	−0.113
Run	−0.700	−0.030	0.044	0.276	0.272
Laugh	−0.828	−0.042	0.118	0.039	−0.146
Work	0.493	−0.068	0.043	−0.272	−0.296
Paint	−0.007	−0.122	0.490	−0.106	0.109
Smile	−0.684	0.174	−0.223	−0.107	0.172
Talk	−0.425	0.018	−0.265	−0.328	0.374
Receive	−0.146	0.041	0.152	0.066	0.763
Give	−0.052	0.317	−0.347	−0.089	0.325
Point	−0.132	−0.065	−0.429	−0.305	0.092

The main analysis consisted of four separate factor analyses, each done between all the observation periods on a particular category of children. The analyses correlated the number of times a behaviour item occurred in an observation period with the number of times each other item occurred. The observations on the children in each category were taken together so that the N for each correlation was 15 (observations on each child) multiplied by the number of children (six or seven in each group). The four analyses were therefore on:

(1) 90 observation periods on 4-year-old boys (Table 4.1a);
(2) 105 observation periods on 4-year-old girls (Table 4·1b);
(3) 90 observation periods on 2-year-old boys (Table 4·2a);
(4) 90 observation periods on 2-year-old girls (Table 4·2b).

The factor analysis model assumes that each measure is a linear function of a number of basic factors. Such a model may sometimes not be applicable to this type of data (e.g. in cases where the functions are not linear), it may even be a gross over-simplification. However, it is worthwhile to apply this technique, as others have done. Care must be exercised if tests of significance are carried out since the usual assumption of normality may not be even approximately true (Cattell, 1965; Kendall, 1957).

The specific composition of the factors in the version used here is not ' suggested ' to the analysis by the experimenter, although other kinds of limitation are enforced by the particular technique chosen. The only limitations or constraints are those implicit in the method adopted: the most important being that in this instance the factors are orthogonal (uncorrelated with each other).

TABLE 4·2b. *Results of factor analysis of correlations of each behaviour item with each other item between observation periods in 2-year-old children*

	Younger girls				
Factor	1	2	3	4	5
% of variance	14.280	11.231	8.304	8.080	7.318
Age	−0.044	−0.060	0.740	0.056	0.216
Expnce	0.048	−0.296	−0.070	0.190	−0.111
Cry	0.049	0.879	0.027	0.024	0.037
Pucker	0.114	0.804	−0.107	0.075	−0.215
Red	0.017	0.945	0.006	−0.018	0.022
Fixate	0.000	0.000	0.000	0.000	0.000
Frown	−0.009	0.063	0.080	−0.054	−0.603
Hit	−0.128	−0.061	−0.493	0.110	0.136
Grabtg	0.043	−0.054	−0.145	0.026	−0.652
Push	−0.568	−0.014	0.055	0.032	−0.522
Wrestl	−0.630	0.009	0.009	−0.021	−0.182
Hit at	−0.655	−0.041	−0.274	0.090	0.183
Jumps	−0.704	−0.028	0.092	0.094	0.020
Run	−0.608	−0.011	0.126	0.100	−0.031
Laugh	−0.824	−0.002	−0.139	−0.102	0.037
Work	0.217	−0.157	−0.629	−0.048	−0.242
Paint	0.086	−0.096	0.503	−0.072	−0.113
Smile	−0.579	−0.083	0.003	−0.285	0.302
Talk	0.018	−0.080	−0.229	−0.779	−0.211
Receive	0.143	−0.027	−0.366	−0.519	0.086
Give	0.031	−0.073	0.067	−0.575	−0.341
Point	0.047	−0.006	0.172	−0.618	0.150

The interpretation of the factor analysis is achieved by examining values of loadings on the factors produced. The computer print-out from the factor analysis includes a table of factors with the loading of each behavioural measure on each factor. The loadings are the correlations, either positive or negative, of the measure with the underlying factor. The factor can then be labelled for convenience and ease of memory, either by the name of the highest loading item, or more speculatively by a hypothetical causal factor. In this study the computer was asked to print out only the first five factors.

The treatment of the data could confound (1) the effects of individual differences, if some individuals consistently score high on behaviours *a* and *b* with (2) variation from one observation to the next when behaviours *a* and *b* tend to occur in the same observation period as each other, which was my main interest. In the results it becomes apparent by comparison with an inter-individual factor analysis that this did not happen. For this between-individual analysis the frequency of occurrence of each behaviour item was totalled for all the observations on each individual and the factor analysis between individuals was done using this data.

I compared frequencies of occurrence of behaviour across age and sex groups by using the total occurrences for each child, and comparing groups of children with the Mann–Whitney U-test (Siegel, 1956). For groups of six children, only the very largest differences can reach statistical significance but for groups of twelve (old *vs.* young, boys *vs.* girls) more sensitive comparisons can be made. Correlations between some derived variables e.g. *hit/take, hit/have object taken,* were tested with the Spearman rank correlation coefficient.

DEFINITIONS OF THE BEHAVIOUR SCORED

Most of these items are taken from Blurton Jones (1967) because the study was aimed at checking the groupings of behaviours proposed in that paper. A few were added to illuminate age differences in other items. But the list was kept as near as seemed sensible to the list in the 1967 paper, particularly the table therein.

1. Age – Age in months (to nearest month) from date of birth until half-way through the observations.

2. Experience – Time in months from entering the playgroup until half-way through the observations.

3. Red – Face goes red.

4. Cry – Weeping plus vocalisations. Lumped regardless of pitch i.e. both high and scream-like and low roaring crying.

5. Pucker – As Blurton Jones (1967). Frown and orbicularis oculi contraction, and *oblique* brows (Blurton Jones, in press). With or without mouth corner retract, or upper lip square.

6. Take – The child takes an object from another, grasping it and pulling before the other moves it towards him. Includes attempted takes, i.e. where owner pulls object back again.

CATEGORIES OF INTERACTION

7. Have object taken – Another child takes an object from the child under observation, who has not held it towards the thief. The 'owner' may hold on and pull at the object. Includes times when the 'owner' child successfully retains the object.

8. Fixate – Looking directly at eyes of the other child for more than about two seconds, with rapid onset of this position and with no smile. Much as Blurton Jones, 1967, but it is very hard to define what I really see that makes these look different from friendly looks.

9. Low frown – Brows lowered with no obvious vertical furrowing of forehead as Blurton Jones, 1967 and Grant, 1968. Plus any record of frown (*general frown*, Blurton Jones, in press) where not also called *pucker* or *oblique*.

10. Hit and beat – *Beat* as in Blurton Jones, 1967. A forceful downward movement of flexed arm from above shoulder height. Plus any other form of hard blow to the object child, i.e. includes *punch* and *side beat* as defined by McGrew (in press), and 'open beat' with contact. Excludes 'pat', 'poke', 'kick', 'pinch', 'twist', 'pull hair' and 'bite'.

11. Take–tug–grab – A combination (i.e. any one or more) of the following three:

(1) Taking an object from someone's hands (or an object which they are obviously using) when they have not held it out towards the subject (same as number 6).

(2) *Grab* is faster version of (1) and often with resistance from other.

(3) *Tug* is holding and pulling object which another is also holding and does not immediately release.

12. Push – Includes forearm push (backhand action) and two hands in front at waist to shoulder height forcing against other's body or arm. Does not include grasping other's hand and moving it.

13. Mins.' slide – Number of minutes during which the child goes down the slide at any time in the minute.

14. Wrestle – Clasp other with both hands, hands usually cupped (rather than clenched on clothes, hair or flesh), plus twisting, lifting or pulling, often by bending own trunk or walking forwards or backwards. Excludes pushing movement of arms.

15. Hit at – Sharp movement of hand towards another child, almost always with arm bent and hand held above shoulder before sharp downward movement. Sometimes hand out at side. But no actual contact with other child. Can include punch, beat with closed or open fist, with and without object in hand, so long as no contact with other child. Could have (though it didn't occur) included 'Pat' if no contact. Did not include 'shooting' gestures, or 'poke' where finger moved directly forward towards other child (again no cases of this movement without contact). Would include occurrences which looked like an attempt to hit. But these could be defined and treated separately as hitting movements where the movement does not stop short of the usual target (i.e. around shoulder height) but follows through often as far as waist level with temporary loss of balance (attempted side beat would involve hand going across midline and probably again loss of balance or brief stumble).

16. Jumps – Jumping up and down with two feet approximately together. Orientation as *laugh*.

17. Run – Any running (except run to teacher or adult). Includes run to slide even if, as often happens, the teacher is standing nearby.

18. Laugh, playface – Smiles with open jaws, with or without laughing noises. Records are counted when interaction with child is concerned (excludes teacher), but often not facing child so when performed in among other behaviour to children. Includes behaviour during slide time.

19. Minutes' work – Number of minutes in which any record of work. Work being using objects, excludes sliding, excludes watching child or teacher. Glueing paper (using brushes) is counted as work, not as painting.

20. Minutes' paint – Number of minutes in which there is any record of painting, which involves use of paints.

21. Behaviour to teacher – Any record (except look at *T*) where teacher is the object of the behaviour. Includes quick repetitions. Includes ' watch *T* ' and ' next to *T* '.

22. Smile – All kinds of smile except with teeth well separated (*laugh, playface*) or with lower lip square (*oblong smile* – Grant 1968), when facing towards another child.

23. Minutes' talk to child – Number of minutes in which any words were said while looking at another child. (I may sometimes also have used context and content to identify who, if anyone, was being addressed but I tried not to.)

24. Receive – Child extends arm and takes in its hand an object given by another, does not flex arm until other has released his grip (contrast *take – tug – grab*).

25. Give – Child holds object out to other below the line between the shoulder height of both children, and releases grip immediately the other grasps the object, or places it on substrate close in front of other. *Show* can be indistinguishable from this action when the reactor does not receive the object, or when the children are far apart.

26. Point – Hold out arm and often index finger towards some person or object. Usually at or little below shoulder level but depends on distance of object. Index finger often on line from actor's eye to the object which makes line of arm misleading to reactor.

27. Watch C – Looks for long time (more than five seconds) at another child's face or hands or both. A better measure than the number of bouts would have been the duration of watching, or scores from interval sampling.

28. Play with or next to child (Op in *C*) – Number of minutes recorded as near (about two feet or less) or next to a child, or in which recorded as playing with a child. *Play with* implies that they are using the same play materials and perhaps exchanging or discussing them. The exchanges and talking should go down under *give, receive, take* and *talk*.

29. General exchange – The sum of *give* plus *receive* plus *take – tug – grab*. The number of movements related to objects changing hands.

30. General hit movement – The sum of *hit* and *beat* plus *hit at*, i.e. the number of movements including sharply moving the hand towards another child.

31. General smile – The sum of *laugh – playface* plus *smile*, i.e. the number of smiles regardless of degree of mouth opening.

Results

From the five factors requested of the analysis (Tables 4·1a, *b* and 4·2a, *b*), three appeared with good or reasonably consistent ' contents ' in the different groups of children. A fourth (*cry, red, pucker* in one case) was less consistent. The fifth factor was an age factor, which had low and very variable loadings from group to group. Although temporal (between observation period) and individual variations are in theory confounded in these analyses, the emergence of age and experience as a separate factor indicates that at least the other factors were not results of regular age or experience differences between individuals. The different results obtained by the inter-individual analysis confirms that the present results were due mainly to temporal variation.

The consistency of the three behavioural factors across the four groups of children implies a basic similarity of the organisation of behaviour of both sexes at both ages. It also indicates that the analyses were fairly reliable. But having said this, the small differences between the groups cannot be allocated with any certainty between (*a*) unreliability due to an inadequate sample, as perhaps for *cry, red, pucker* which occurred very seldom, or (*b*) unreliability due to recording errors, or (*c*) real age or sex differences, unless the analyses were repeated on split data. Age and experience are investigated in another section with a cross-individual factor analysis.

In the sections that follow I describe and analyse further the behaviour items which load high on the factors hereby colloquially labelled: (1) rough and tumble versus work; (2) aggression; (3) social. In summary, ' rough and tumble versus work' has the highest loadings for *work* (positive) and *laugh, run, jumps, hit at, wrestle* (negative). 'Aggression' has the highest loadings for *fixate, frown, hit, push, take-tug-grab*. 'Social' has the highest loadings for *point, give, receive, talk, smile*.

ROUGH AND TUMBLE

The first factor for most of the analyses had high loadings for the movements which in 1967 I included in rough and tumble play. These were *laugh–playface, run, jumps, hit at, wrestle*. This factor had *work* at the other end with strong negative loading. This was unexpected but makes clear sense. These two sets of activities clearly exclude each other and they also give the impression of coinciding with very different moods, i.e. they last for much of an observation period. However, my original expectation was based on the occurrence of some rough and tumble items, *laugh* and *jumps*, during *work* (especially at water or dough) and on the readiness with which *work* occurs with and without social interaction.

The rough and tumble behaviour is clearly different from the other aggressive-seeming behaviour which was recorded. However, one must ask whether this separation would be reduced if more of the repertoire had been included. How would *pinch, bite, kick, shoot, slap, pat, fall, punch* or *throw* have affected the factors? Since each of these was rare they would have had little effect but my impression is that even if they were common the distinction would still have been clear, perhaps even more clear.

Following the argument that rough and tumble may represent a different kind of aggression, rather than, as I argue, having nothing to do with aggression, I have looked at the way these two groupings vary across individuals and across the age and sex groupings.

Among the older children there is a negative correlation ($r_s = -0.57$; $P = <0.05, >0.01$) between the number of aggressive items scored and the number of rough and tumble items scored. This means that if rough and tumble represents a different way of expressing 'aggressiveness' then individuals tend to specialise in their form of aggression and high levels of one kind do not predict high levels of the other. The negative correlation can however come about in at least three other ways.

(1) The most likely explanation is that children who spend more time in rough and tumble have less time to spend playing with objects. Playing with objects next to the other children is the commonest single situation for fights and quarrels (see also McGrew, 1969). This interpretation is supported by the fact that there is no significant correlation between rough and tumble and 'aggression: *have object taken*' (see section on aggression for description of this measure) ($r_s = 0.15$; $P >0.05$). It is also supported by the loading of work with aggressive items and opposite to rough and tumble in the cross-individual factor analysis.

(2) The more aggressive children may have few friendly relationships of any sort and thus less often get involved in rough and tumble play. This seems to be the opposite of my impressions. Children who score low on the social group of behaviour items also do very little rough and tumble or aggression. They appear generally hesitant about any kind of contact with other children (they are discussed further in the section on social behaviour). However, this is one factor, albeit a negative one, which is common to aggression and rough and tumble.

(3) It could be that rough and tumble play 'uses up' the child's aggressiveness. This implies popular but unsubstantiated theories about the nature of aggression and again at first glance contradicts my impressions. Aggression is usually, as others also found (Dawe, 1934; Green, 1933), very brief and entirely bound to the situation. (I do not wish to imply that this is therefore true of adults or adolescents as well: there is little direct evidence about this.) Rough and tumble play on the other hand may possibly start and finish according to the duration of confinement and non-performance or the duration of performance. However, we will see evidence below that the situation can elicit it. For instance, when the slide is put up in the playroom or when the door is opened and children are allowed into the corridor there is commonly a period of rough and tumble. I think, but do not know for sure, that the response to these situations depends on how long the children have been playing less actively. Clark, Wyon and Richards (1969) saw no

rough and tumble in a purely indoor nursery school but they report that mothers say this is the prevalent behaviour immediately the children get home. I have examined my data to see whether the amount of aggression is less or greater in observations before or after a period of rough and tumble play. There is no suggestion of a difference.

Arguments about these subtle kinds of relationship between rough and tumble and aggression are made more difficult by the possibility that some individuals can be found for whom each theory is true. One has to play the game fairly however and not put too much stress on the occasional individual. If evidence can be produced which shows that one individual uses rough and tumble to express aggression then the same evidence must be used on other individuals, where it will show that this is not so.

Rough and tumble items were much more common among the older children than the younger. Young girls did much more than young boys but they also did more of all other social behaviours (except ' aggression ') and these age and sex differences probably reflect the difference in social maturity or readiness to settle without the mother (four of the boys had cried at separation from the mother but none of the girls). Among the 4-year-olds no overall sex difference in rough and tumble was evident at first. This was surprising to me since there was a fairly clear suggestion of a sex difference in my data from nursery schools. Much rough and tumble occurred when the slide was put out. I therefore checked to see whether the slide had been available to the girls more than to the boys. This was not so, but I noticed that most of the rough and tumble items by girls occurred when the slide was available, but this was not so sharply true for boys ($\chi^2 = 31.35$; $p = <0.001$). For time when the slide was not available boys totalled almost twice as much rough and tumble as girls but the U-test is not quite significant ($U = 12$, $p = 0.117$). However, this implies that girls do more in response to the slide. It would be interesting to know if girls also spend more time on slides when they are constantly available.

The proportion of the different items in rough and tumble differed between the sexes. Boys did relatively more wrestling and hitting at ($U = 8$, $p = 0.037$). This was not merely an effect of the slide. The difference was only present during non-slide rough and tumble (29 occurrences of *wrestle* or *hit at* versus 97 other rough and tumble patterns for boys, 10 versus 82 for girls, $\chi^2 = 4.61$, $p <0.05$). In both sexes *wrestle* and *hit at* were relatively and equally rare (8 versus 44 other rough and tumble items for boys, 13 and 78 for girls) while the slide was available. A greater amount of body contact in play by males is also described by Harlow and Harlow (1965) and by Young, Goy and Phoenix (1964) and Phoenix, Goy and Resko (1968) for rhesus and pigtailed monkeys. I cannot account for my failure to repeat the sex difference in running and laughing which I reported in 1967, except by suggesting that the difference may apply when children are out of doors more than when they are indoors, as they were in the present study (see also Clark, Wyon, Richards, 1969).

WORK

I had expected that occupations involving manipulations of the various play materials would come out on a separate factor of their own. However, *work* and *painting* often loaded in opposite directions and *work* loaded highest on the rough and tumble play factor but in the opposite direction to rough and tumble. To this extent the popular categorisation of both these activities as *play* is justified but so is the separation of rough and tumble from the other sort of play. It appears that work and rough and tumble are mutually exclusive on the time scale of my observations (this does not mean that they necessarily will be correlated on a longer time scale, only long periods of almost pathological inactivity would change this relationship) and that social, aggressive, or distress behaviours can occur equally often during either of these major occupations.

During the observations I gained the impression that younger children spent more time doing nothing. However, they scored the same number of minutes which included work as the older children. The difference seems to be that they spent more of this alone or with the teacher and spent more time watching other children. It is evidently a mistake to suppose that because they are quieter and more solitary in their work that they are any less occupied.

AGGRESSION

Among older children a moderately consistent factor emerges with high loadings for most of *fixate, frown, hit, push, take–tug–grab*. This corresponds closely to the grouping which I described in 1967 as being concerned mostly with disputes over property and as being clearly separable from rough and tumble play. I have already discussed the inter-relationships between these two kinds of behaviour.

There was no indication of a sex difference in the overall frequency of behaviour items in the ' aggressive ' group. Because this conflicted with findings reported before, I went to some trouble to see if there were sex differences in any of the details of aggressive behaviour. I could find no difference in the amount of aggressive items when *tug* was excluded, no difference in the proportions of these to *take* or to *have object taken*, no difference in *take* or in *have object taken*, and no difference in the frequency of the individual items nor in the amount of aggression without *take, tug* or *have object taken*. There was no difference in the proportion of physical attack (*hit* and *push*) to *tug*. There was a slight but not significant difference in the proportion of pushing to hitting (more *pushing* by girls, among whom *pushing*, however, loaded quite high on the rough and tumble factor at both ages).

Dawe (1934) and Green (1933) both report a greater amount of aggression by boys but they do not describe the behaviour which they classified as aggressive nor do they give statistical tests or raw data on this topic. The lack of description makes it impossible to rule out the inclusion of substantial amounts of rough and tumble play in their scores, which would give such a difference. However, recent observers who are conscious of this distinction also find more aggression by boys (McGrew in Oxford and Edinburgh, pers. comm., and Burke, pers. comm. in our laboratory). An explanation could be that our small playgroup attracts the mothers of the more gentle and timid boys (we get fewer boys than girls). It may also be that girls are generally quieter or somehow less conspicuous to event-sampling observers when they quarrel though this seems to be excluded by the range of techniques used (direct observation, CCTV, silent film). It seems from Burke's study most likely that my sample is in fact unrepresentative of the larger sample (including mine) which he studied. His data suggests that there are a few highly aggressive (but all the more interesting) individuals. These are usually boys, but one who was a girl was included in the present sample.

A particularly interesting point is how far *taking* objects can be regarded as a part of aggressive behaviour. My impression is that *taking* is really the situation that evokes aggression, rather than being a behaviour controlled by the same things as aggression. This relates to my impression that most aggression is evoked by simple situations and ceases when these situations change. (But there are rare individual children who give a different impression.)

If taking and aggressive behaviour shared some causal factors one might expect that when a child often responds aggressively in *take–tug–grab* situations, it also often takes objects, thus initiating these situations. This relationship could be examined in day-to-day variation, or in individual variation. I chose the latter and correlated three measures: (1) the number of *takes* by the child; (2) the percentage of the times when the child did *take* in which it also did other aggressive movements (very likely to be affected by behaviour of other child, i.e. whether it resists or not) and (3) the percentage of the times when it *had objects taken* by another that it also did aggressive movements (much less readily affected by behaviour of other). The last two, readiness to behave aggressively in two provoking situations, correlated very closely (Spearman $r = 93$, $p < 0.01$). But neither of these correlated with the amount of taking.

One has to be cautious about these measures as they could be affected by both group composition and dominance hierarchy. However, it seems likely that a subordinate child would seldom dare *take* from a dominant and would seldom retaliate. This would tend to give a positive correlation of *take* with measures (2) and (3) which was not found. It could well account for the positive correlation between measures (2) and (3). However, whatever the factors are, those which make individuals *take* often are not the same as those which make them more likely to show aggressive behaviour in a provoking situation.

This independence is important when one considers the behaviour of 2-year-olds. This is a notoriously 'snatchy' age and quarrels seem more frequent and harder to stop than among older children. But it is arguable that even though snatching things evokes crying and screaming or attack and threat from the victim, its motivation is not always aggressive. It may indicate a lack of response to these reactions but it need not indicate an aggressive response in the sense of a tendency to hit or use other physical violence. That the independence of *taking* and aggression is even greater in 2-year-olds is indicated by the very loose relationship of *take–tug–grab* on the *fix, frown, hit, push* axis in the factor analyses for these children (Table 4·2a, b).

The age comparisons also separate *take* from aggressive behaviour. Aggressive behaviour other than *tug* was significantly more common in older children ($U = 33$, $p < 0.02$). But *take* gave no clear difference. The readiness to show aggression when taking an object was greater in older children ($U = 40$, $p < 0.05 > 0.02$). The ratio of *take* to *have taken* was significantly higher in the older children ($U = 42$, $p = < 0.05$). This suggests that older children were taking things from younger ones more than younger took them from older. I have no figures for the readiness to show aggression to younger or older children once a *take* situation has arisen.

The readiness to show aggression when taking an object was usually (but not significantly) less than if the child has something taken (Sign Test $p > 0.10$). This seemed to be the same for both ages but oddly enough was more true of boys ($p > 0.02 < 0.05$) than girls ($p > 0.20$). The results for girls were probably determined by two outstanding individuals commonly described as 'bossy'.

Some of the youngest children seem to *take* almost as a sign of interest in others, as if the combination of another child and a toy are very powerful stimuli for attracting attention as Bridges (1932) suggested long ago. In fact there is a positive correlation across individuals between the amount of *take* and the amount of social behaviour ($r_s = 0.915$, $p < 0.01$). But this may in fact arise only because these individuals interact more in all respects.

I have the impression that this is not due to the increased opportunity to *take* when playing more with other children because 2-year-olds often run up from far off to take things. There are older children who do this as well and they seem more unusual or even abnormal. I have no suggestion as to why this arises, except to point to their failure to do as many older children do, which is either to persuade a child verbally and non-verbally (with head tilted on one side, and turning the head slowly from side to side) to give them something, or to ask if they may use it together. There is also the question of why they resist the apparently strong adult pressure to share and not snatch.

CATEGORIES OF INTERACTION

Although the relationships described were all significant to $p < 0.05$ the very small and homogeneous population sampled indicates caution in generalising from these findings. What may be safely generalised is that any investigator of the development or causes of aggression should be very clear what he means by ' aggression '. He should also make it very clear in his reports. In the age range studied, rough and tumble, taking and ' aggressive ' behaviours perform separately. They may or may not also do so at later ages. One of them may be more relevant than others to later developments, and one cannot at this stage say which. Also if one is interested in the pathological extremes of aggression one may need to follow those individuals in whom the separation does not exist. Their development may follow a quite different path from that of even the quantitative extremes of the children with normally structured behaviour.

SOCIAL

This factor has high loadings for *point, give, receive, talk, smile*. This is a factor connected with social interaction between children other than rough and tumble, or aggression. It is a rather different measure from those used in studies of friendships and sociability, e.g. Parten (1933), Green (1933) and Clark, Wyon and Richards (1969). I have been concerned with what children do to each other, or what kinds of friendship or friendly behaviour there are, rather than with whom they do it. But presumably Parten's co-operative play involves more of these behaviour items than does parallel play. Had I included showing objects in the analysis this too would probably have loaded high on this factor, although the data in Blurton Jones and Leach (Ch. 9), and in Leach (Ch. 10) suggest that *show* and *point* play separate roles in behaviour to adults.

Subjectively this factor, more than any other factor, should be susceptible to subdivision. The sequential reorganisation of these items may be important and might differentiate categories like seeking help, giving help, showing-off achievements, conversing, giving presents, telling people what to do. But it may be that one's everyday subdivisions of this factor are misleading. The only certain test is to try both classifications in the same study of effects of background factors.

The social items are much commoner in the older children than in the younger (true for both sexes separately, boys $U = 2$, $p = <0.010 > 0.005$, girls $U = 1$, $p = <0.005 > 0.002$. Social behaviour is also more common in older children even if talking is omitted (see below). The *play with or next to child* score increases with age ($U = 17$, $p = <0.002$). The ratio social items: *play with or next to child* increases with age ($U = 30$, $p < 0.02 > 0.002$). So not only are older children close together more but they interact more while close together.

Two other items which were recorded make an interesting comparison with social items. These are *watching children* and *being next to children*.

Because *watching* involves long, non-overtly aggressive interest, and often an approach to about four to five feet of the child being watched, it appears moderately social and perhaps inhibitedly social. It is no commoner in younger children ($U = 51$, $p = >0.10$) but they show less of the other social behaviour (see last paragraph). The young girls *played with or next to children* nearly significantly more than the boys did ($U = 6$, $p = <0.10 >0.05$). But there was no difference in the amount of *watching other children* ($U = 12$, $p = <0.40 >0.30$) nor in number of social items. This implies that girls spend more time near other children but not interacting and that boys spend more time watching others from far off. The boys differed from the girls mostly in having resisted separation from their mothers at some time or other. This fits our impression from many other children that distress over separating goes with reduced interaction with other children. But it may not go with lack of interest in other children. I cannot produce satisfactory evidence, but my guess is that *watching* occurs when the tendency to interact is rising but when it is offset either by a tendency to keep away from other children (especially true for the younger ones) or by a tendency to work alone with play material. Longitudinal studies over quite short times could show whether the children, who on arrival at play-group watch other children most, are those who later show the most social behaviour. Persistence of *watching* might, on the other hand, predict later isolation and reduced interaction.

The possibility of simultaneous arousal of tendencies to approach and to stay away or avoid seems to have been ignored also in the studies of 'fear of strangers' in children of various ages. The occurrence of prolonged blank stares also seems to have been ignored (in so far as one can tell anything about what is observed from the published accounts). This may mean that one loses useful data as well as losing the possible clarification of the developmental relationship between avoiding strangers and approaching or interacting with them. It is sometimes not realised that, besides the two possibilities of shy versus sociable, there could also be highly sociable but very timid individuals, and unsociable and un-shy ones. Analyses along the lines of the numerous studies of conflicting motivation in animal communication should clarify the situation (e.g. Andrew, 1956, 1957; Tinbergen, 1959; Grant, 1963, 1968; Stokes, 1962 *a, b*; Blurton Jones, 1968), as Tinbergen and Tinbergen (in press) also argue.

The behaviour of the young girls is reminiscent of some child–child behaviour which Sears, Rau and Alpert (1966) used as measures of dependency. In Chapter 10 Leach describes how 'dependency' in the sense of staying near the mother tends not to involve interaction (see also Rosenthal, 1967), and in Chapter 9 we (Blurton Jones and Leach) show how staying near mother and protesting at separation are commoner in young boys. Perhaps the girls by this age have (as Sears implies) become able to transfer 'dependency' to other children whereas boys have not, although the occasional boy follows the teacher around like his mother. But children who follow adults around hold their hands, climb onto their laps or beg to be carried, and one sees none of this directed to children (except in rare cases to an older sibling). It may be that maintenance of proximity is a part of the social repertoire which occurs on its own if there is no tendency to withdraw. But whether any interaction will take place may depend on age, proficiency, ability to gain attention, or other factors. In other words 2-year-old girls may approach and watch, boys being more timid may watch from further off. Whether interactions also occur must depend on factors such as social skills in addition to the basic social interest in other children. The occurrence of protests at separation in some of these children makes comparison of these measures with McGrew's (Ch. 5) older, readily separating, children very difficult.

Behaviour towards the teacher predominantly consists of social behaviour items but with some rough and tumble and *watching*. Many of these behaviours are also performed to the mother (see Leach, Ch. 10) and one wonders whether there is any transfer of ' affection ', ' attachment ', ' sociability ', from the mother via the teacher and other adults to other children, with increasing age. This might imply that social behaviour to children is partly acquired in interaction with adults, and will appear earlier to adults than to children. The young children showed more behaviour to the teacher than social behaviour to children. The older ones did about equal amounts. The ratio:

behaviour to teacher : social behaviour to children

was significantly lower for the older boys compared to the younger boys. This was not so for girls. The older girls scored significantly more behaviour to teacher than did older boys. This means that boys interact less with the teacher as they come to interact more with children but that girls do not. The kinds of interaction with teacher probably change, with *showing, giving* and *talking* increasing and *watching* and *staying near* decreasing. This is also suggested by the finding by Stith and Connor (1962) that ' helpfulness ' increases and ' dependency ' decreases with age. These results could mean that social behaviour to teacher and to children develops in parallel. My impressions about the sex difference resemble the findings (see Garai and Scheinfeld, 1968) that girls have a greater need for approval of their achievements. They are continually showing the teacher what they have done whereas boys work on with less frequent reference to the teacher. It would clearly be important in pursuing this to differentiate *showing* and *giving* at least, if not to make more extensive divisions into ' approval seeking ' versus ' sharing '. However, I feel that the conclusions quoted by Garai and Scheinfeld may involve premature interpretations of the meaning of these social interactions. Although, as nursery school teachers are usually female, this difference may result from the teacher interaction being more rewarding with girls than with boys. The female teacher may more readily bestow praise (rewarding to girls) than share tasks or explain about objects (rewarding to boys). Alternatively, adult feminine interests may simply differ from masculine interests so that boys achieve fewer responses of any sort from the teacher and come to interact with her less.

Age change and inter-individual variation

In this section, I attempt to summarise the age changes mentioned above. I also used another approach to the age and individual differences, a factor analysis of individual total scores, partly in order to compare it with the similar analysis of individuals which Smith and Connolly present (Ch. 3).

TABLE 4·3. *Results of principal components analysis of correlations of each behaviour item with each other item between scores of individual children*

Factor	1	2	3	4	5
% of	7.910	4.032	3.257	2.819	2.319
variance	24.720	12.599	10.178	8.810	7.248
Sex	0.098	−0.014	−0.159	0.421	0.666
Age	0.773	0.032	0.022	−0.034	0.025
Expnce	0.771	0.130	−0.096	0.052	−0.050
Cry	−0.249	0.262	0.415	0.532	0.292
Pucker	−0.089	0.009	0.059	0.746	−0.040
Red	−0.349	0.251	0.221	0.698	0.265
Take	0.424	−0.493	−0.419	0.018	0.094
Havetak	−0.424	−0.342	−0.192	0.069	−0.289
Fixate	0.147	−0.470	0.366	−0.448	−0.146
Frown	0.135	−0.337	0.043	−0.427	0.347
Hit	0.289	−0.619	0.491	0.011	−0.314
Grabtg	0.231	−0.663	−0.572	0.104	0.074
Push	0.280	−0.475	0.161	−0.067	0.039
Minsld	0.212	0.420	−0.581	−0.255	−0.131
Wrestl	0.705	0.365	−0.192	0.004	−0.181
Hit at	0.407	0.263	0.134	0.396	−0.616
Jumps	0.469	0.655	−0.151	−0.123	0.196
Run	0.555	0.534	−0.348	−0.129	0.047
Laugh	0.721	0.241	−0.242	0.266	−0.144
Work	−0.499	−0.430	−0.210	0.272	−0.249
Paint	0.530	−0.179	0.248	−0.004	0.020
Teachr	−0.281	−0.079	−0.648	0.254	−0.049
Smile	0.575	0.111	0.279	−0.213	0.031
Talk	0.801	−0.138	0.172	0.070	0.052
Receive	0.341	−0.124	0.025	0.416	−0.033
Give	0.655	−0.406	−0.152	0.110	0.284
Point	0.554	−0.151	0.287	0.056	0.271
WatchC	−0.274	0.080	0.569	−0.148	0.448
OpinC	0.775	−0.062	0.264	0.181	0.210
Exchng	0.421	−0.666	−0.428	0.224	0.250
Hitmov	0.434	−0.183	0.371	0.317	−0.594
Gensml	0.819	0.208	0.086	−0.037	−0.046

I combined all four groups, giving twenty-five children in all. With this small number of individuals and the large number of variables the factor analysis could be rather unreliable. However, it agrees well with the age and sex differences examined above. It gives a markedly different appearance from the factor analyses between observation periods within the groups of children. Despite the expected unreliability there is a surprising amount of similarity in the first factor to the results of Smith and Connolly. Of the eight items present in both sets of results all eight load in the same direction in both analyses. Table 4·3 presents the results of the principal components analysis for comparison with their results.

The first factor is the only one with a high loading for age (0.773). It accounts for 24% of the variance. Experience also loads almost exclusively on this factor (0.771) and therefore cannot be separated from age in our sample. Along with the increasing age go *playing with or next to children*, *talk*, and other social items, rough and tumble, and *paint*. Negative loadings on this factor, items going with decreasing age, are *work*, *have object taken*, *behaviour to teacher*, *cry* and *watch children*. The second factor in the principal components analysis appears to concern mobility versus immobility. This seems comparable with Smith and Connolly's ' with versus without toys ' factor because play without toys is likely to involve rough and tumble items, and with toys will involve social and aggressive items which occur when children are less mobile. The third factor might with imagination be designated ' active versus inactive interaction '. The only positive loadings of any size are *watch* (0.569) and *cry* (0.415) and *hit* (0.419). Negative loadings cover both social- and aggression-provoking items. The Varimax rotation does not change the picture radically.

The difference between these factors and those from observation periods surprised me. But it does at least imply that the latter factors were not so much a result of individual variation as of genuine temporal variation within individuals. Thus my expectation that most individuals show the same sort of temporal clusterings of behaviour (even across the 2–4-year-old age range) is tentatively confirmed. But my expectation that age and individual differences would consist of changed frequencies of items in these clusterings is disproved.

Besides being unable to separate effects of age from effects of experience there is another problem in interpreting the overall age changes. I am unable to exclude effects of separation from the mother on the behaviour of the younger children. It could be that the age differences are entirely due to separation. The ultimate test of whether this is so is to observe children of both ages in the presence of their mothers. There were four of the young boys who at some time cried on separation, and this may well account for the differences between them and the young girls, none of whom cried. The two boys who never cried showed much more behaviour to other children than did the others. This fits with our impression that distress at separation goes with reduced activity during the play session. This relationship may be causal in either direction. Separation could suppress other behaviour, or lack of social behaviour could make the children cling more in this situation. Possibly both of these are separate age effects. The young girls did of course still show less social behaviour than the older girls, and I feel it is safe to expect to find these kinds of age differences in behaviour to children even if the mother is present. (Unfortunately Leach's sample is not comparable as it includes only three children as young as any of my ' 2-year-old ' group.)

One might expect the ' social ' behaviour items (*smile, talk, give, receive, point*) to be involved in ' co-operative play ' and not in ' parallel play '. It is thus a surprise to find them being done by 2-year-olds to other children, even though less often than by 4-year-olds and perhaps often in response to interaction initiated by 4-year-olds. I had expected to find that rough and tumble was the earlier appearing kind of sociable behaviour, being matched by ' co-operative play ' by 4 years of age. However, the proportion of rough and tumble to social items does not differ between the two groups. The amount of all these items increases with age.

There is, of course, little data in the literature on what 2-year-olds do. Apart from the rarity of children under 3 in pre-school groups, there is the appalling lack of description in the literature. It therefore came as something of a surprise to me to find all the behaviour items I was recording (and many more) already present and organised in much the same way (i.e. similar factor loadings emerge) as in 4-year-olds. Anderson (Ch. 8 and pers. comm.) describes considerable amounts of interaction of these types between children aged 14–24 months. Bridges (1932) describes chases, ' conversations ' and aggressive interactions over toys between children around 1 year old in an institution.

As I have shown, between 2 and 4 years old there was an increase in the frequency of each behaviour item towards children. The difficulty of ascribing this to a switch from behaving predominantly to the adults to behaving predominantly to peers was discussed in the section on the social factor. It may represent a transfer from responding to parents to responding to children which we cannot observe in the absence of parents. If it is, it is important that the change in opportunity provided by the absence of parents does not immediately increase response to children. I must provide an anecdotal caution. I have seen more than one baby of 6 months onward suddenly attend to and watch other children and babies, and if they can crawl or are made mobile in a baby-walker they follow, smile, laugh, finger their faces and run away and towards them. Clearly children are highly attractive objects in their own right from an early age. But it may still be that children have to learn that many of the things they do with adults can be done with children as well. In the context of the early origins of behaviour to peers I may also refer to my suggestion in the section on aggression that *take* is as much social as aggressive, perhaps resulting from the combined attention-getting power of a toy and a child.

EFFECT OF SIBLINGS

With this sample it was impossible to separate effects of experience in the playgroup from age differences. Very few children start at the playgroup at age 4, none have been coming for long at age 2. But effects of presence of siblings in the family can be examined quite conveniently, age and sex being well balanced among sibling status. Presence of siblings in the family does not obscure the age difference in social behaviour. The age difference in social behaviour (excluding *talking*) among children with no siblings is very significant ($U = 0$, $p = 0.008$), and so is that for children who have siblings ($U = 10$, $p = <0.05 >0.03$). If talking to children is included the differences are comparably clear. Within age groups the effect of presence of siblings on social behaviour is not significant, perhaps because of the small numbers involved. There is a suggestion of a difference in non-talking social behaviour (*talking* is excluded because it is widely held that the ability to talk is higher if there are no siblings and, although we found no difference in amount of talking, this could work in the opposite direction to the effects on sociability) among the younger children, those with siblings doing more ($U = 9$, $p = <0.15 >0.10$) but this is quite absent among the older ones ($U = 17$, $p >0.360$). So even if, when they come to the playgroup, children who have siblings are slightly more likely to show social behaviour to children, by the time they are 4-years-old this difference has completely disappeared. But still, because the 4-year-olds all had long nursery experience, we cannot say whether this is due to experience in the playgroup or whether it is an age change independent of playgroup experience, a sort of maturational catch up.

In both age groups there is a non-significant tendency for children without siblings to do less aggressive behaviour ($U = 11$, $p = 0.172$ for young children, $U = 11$, $p = 0.172$ for older children, comparable result with combined age groups). There were no significant differences for the general category 'responses to teacher'.

Among the 2-year-olds there is no sign that having siblings has any effect on rough and tumble play. But among the 4-year-olds there is a reversal of what one might expect. The children with no siblings did significantly more rough and tumble ($U = 6$, $p = 0.046$). This difference may in fact be a 'firstborn versus later child' difference. But whichever it is, the interpretation that springs to mind is that the children who play most, whether only children or older siblings, are the children who have least opportunity to do rough and tumble play at home. Clark, Wyon and Richards (1969) remark on mothers' reports of the frequent occurrence of rough and tumble on return from a nursery school at which none occurred. If at home there are no siblings or neighbours to play with or only much younger siblings, then the pressure to play while at playgroup is increased. These observations add to my impression of rough and tumble as being one of the rare kinds of behaviour which may show the kind of spontaneity which Lorenz (1950, 1966) ascribes to many kinds of behaviour, including aggression. While behaviour on my 'aggression' factor is predominantly set off by immediate situations which quickly pass, rough and tumble may differ from this. I have shown that rough and tumble can be elicited by the slide. I regard Bandura, Ross and Ross (1961, 1963) as producing some evidence that it is elicited by the sight of other people performing it (and my impression is that it is very infectious in the playgroup), but the readiness to respond to these stimuli, and the eventual cessation of rough and tumble, may depend on the time from last performance and duration of the present performance. This is at least a point which now seems to require investigation.

Discussion

The factor analysis of behaviour scores in observation periods was expected to give certain results. This determined my choice of the number of factors to request, and also implied that the Varimax rotation was quite suitable. The results agreed with my expectations to a considerable extent. However, the percentage of the variance accounted for by the five factors was low. That no outstanding first factor appeared even before the rotation, was expected, since I felt that the five factors should be of equal importance. Inserting extra variables into the analysis, such as behaviour to teacher and watching children, was expected to account for more of the variance, but this had no marked effect.

The factor analysis of the total scores of individuals was done with no specific expectation beyond the hope that the first factor in the principal components analysis might resemble that of Connolly and Smith, and that subsequent non-age factors might resemble the factors found from observation period scores. There was indeed a largish first factor, concerned with age and all forms of social behaviour. Comparisons with Connolly and Smith's first factor depends on sufficient overlap of behaviour items and must be left to the reader's judgement, although I regard the similarities as close.

The factor analysis of scores in observation periods could have confounded temporal variation with inter-individual variation. The difference between the results of the two analyses suggests that in practice the first was resulting much more from short-term temporal variation than from inter-individual variation.

In the factor analysis of observation-period scores most of the factors were 'one-ended', i.e. high loadings were found only with either all positive or else all negative sign. This was also true of Wiepkema's (1961) results and again is rather what one expects of most behaviour. However, one of the important points about behaviour is that some items may play two or more different roles, or result from two or more sets of causes. Factor analysis, with the possibility of one item loading strongly on two or more orthogonal factors allows for this much better than any technique which attempts to classify behaviour into non-overlapping groups. Two points arise from this.

Although very distinct factors, like rough and tumble as opposed to aggression, come out it may be difficult to use a particular behaviour item as diagnostic of one kind of behaviour or another. Just how difficult this can be is indicated by the similarity of the loadings on the two factors. Thus in girls *push* loads quite strongly on both, so one cannnot say all *pushes* are aggressive or all pushes are playful. On the other hand *laugh* loads very high on rough and tumble and low on aggression. This gives a position which ethologists would traditionally find quite anomalous, that *laughing* is the best criterion for rough and tumble. Traditionally one would not use a signalling movement as a criterion, one would aim to find other movement (e.g. *wrestling*) with which to link it (but see Loizos, 1969).

The other point is that since distinct factors can emerge with a behaviour item strongly loaded on both of them, the size of the original behaviour items may matter rather less than previously suggested (Blurton Jones, 1967, 1968). At least, if an item overlaps two factors this will show up. As a test of this I repeated the factor analyses with some of the items combined into general items (Table 4.4). *Exchange* was the sum of *take–grab–tug*, *give* and *receive*. *Hit movement* was the sum of *hit* and *hit at*. *General smile* was the sum of *laugh* and *smile*. Despite substituting these general items for their component items the social, aggression, rough and tumble factors seemed to me to be surprisingly identifiable (Table 4.4).

Of the possible errors in selection of behaviour items this appears to cover two. Hopelessly general categories like ' locomotion ' or ' arm movement ' may be split up meaningfully if there are enough specific items to allow identification of a factor. Failure to subdivide forms of *smile*, for example, may still allow their detection, or prediction from the factor analysis. The selection of very specific but erroneous items may not show up. If a certain combination of components of behaviour is recorded but the components on their own are not recorded, then a false result cannot be avoided by factor analysis.

The criteria by which I am judging behaviour items as correct or misleading are those of Altmann (1962, 1965). They will be those items that give the clearest relationship to reactions of other individuals, and which give the clearest indication of what has just happened or will happen next. In my non-sequential analysis in this paper this is perhaps equivalent to saying that they will give the sharpest differences in loadings between one factor and the next.

TABLE 4·4. *Results of factor analysis between observation periods with a more general classification of behaviour items. (On 4-year-old boys.)*

Older boys

Factor	1	2	3	4	5
% of variance	14.913	10.308	10.981	8.982	11.291
Age	−0.079	−0.040	−0.178	0.759	0.157
Expnce	−0.200	0.024	−0.077	0.584	0.133
Cry	−0.035	−0.049	0.898	−0.027	0.042
Pucker	−0.171	0.048	0.258	−0.133	0.648
Red	−0.069	−0.021	0.930	−0.118	0.156
Fixate	−0.106	0.012	0.167	0.066	0.854
Frown	−0.018	0.180	−0.187	0.032	0.513
Grabtg	−0.023	0.859	0.045	−0.127	0.196
Push	0.238	−0.180	0.185	0.253	0.359
Wrestl	0.643	−0.192	−0.016	−0.101	−0.012
Jumps	0.715	−0.012	−0.081	−0.249	0.035
Run	0.684	−0.017	−0.007	−0.111	−0.050
Work	−0.554	−0.030	−0.396	−0.344	0.245
Paint	−0.089	0.077	0.152	0.572	−0.311
Talk	0.501	0.360	−0.058	0.136	−0.129
Point	0.146	0.383	−0.119	0.031	−0.179
Exchan	−0.076	0.878	0.026	0.106	0.220
Hitmve	0.420	0.038	−0.085	0.317	0.488
Gensml	0.722	0.236	−0.031	−0.103	0.023

It was very gratifying to find that the identity of the factors did not vary greatly with changes in the behaviour items, or with addition of new items, and that they were similar in the different age and sex groups. How far they would still be the same if yet more behaviour items were added remains to be seen. The more new items one adds, the rarer they are, and they may fail to affect the results by virtue of their rarity. While extracting the data I was struck by the way that if I had included more items the categorisations usually would have been likely to become more distinct.

Although one can argue for the greater 'academic respectability' of the present technique over interview, rating and questionnaire techniques, it is perhaps appropriate to ask in this chapter whether it makes any difference in practice. Without repeating a longitudinal study such as that of Sears (1961), one cannot give an empirical answer on issues like the way parental behaviour affects various kinds of child behaviour. The ability to get relationships, as in Sears' study, is some evidence that they are measuring real variables, unless the results are already built into the ratings of child and parent behaviour. This would seem to be a danger in any study which uses measures of dimensions chosen beforehand from theory or everyday language. That the findings fit with the 'common sense' of anyone acquainted with learning theory or psychoanalytic theory, may simply reflect the fact that the measures were drawn from these theories in the first place. But it would be a useful function of ethological studies if they could confirm important studies of this type while avoiding the same possible loopholes.

The data presented in this chapter is relevant to the studies of imitation of aggression by Bandura, Ross and Ross (1961, 1963), and Nelson, Gelfand and Hartman (1969), and it partly modifies their conclusions. They do not define aggression, their use of the word in response measures is redundant, nor do they in any way derive their experiment from the real life occurrences but merely draw it from pre-existing theories. They do not make any distinction between play fighting and other fighting, but the illustrations in the 1963 paper (showing a clear *playface* among other things), and the inclusion of the category ' gun play', make it clear that there were many predominantly rough and tumble behaviour items in the responses. The relationship between rough and tumble and other aggression is no doubt more complex than I have claimed (for instance actual physical contact with the doll in their experiments is unlike rough and tumble in our playgroup (but see Konner, Ch. 11) where hitting movements normally do not connect with a child partner but do connect with objects that it holds, and often do connect with an adult playmate), and there are occasions when one cannot allocate an event to one or other category. But the clear distinction of these two factors makes it obvious (*a*) that one should investigate how far the newly acquired movements are subsequently used in natural fights and (*b*) that one cannot conclude from these experiments that seeing aggression makes children more likely to be aggressive.

It is very clear to anyone who watches pre-school children and keeps up to date with children's television programmes, that much rough and tumble play contains items of behaviour acquired from television (often use of fictional weapons or imitation of deadly automata!) which in their television context are aggressive, or defensive, or at any rate deadly. But the children use them in rough and tumble and not in aggression. In other words these items would load remarkably high on the rough and tumble factor and very low indeed on the aggression factor. Although the most valid conclusion of Bandura *et al.* appears to be that new *potentially* aggressive movements are acquired by imitation, one might also challenge the novelty of much of the example behaviour in the Bandura study. Throwing the doll in the air seems to be the only thing not commonly done to children either in rough and tumble or in real aggression.

One other important lesson comes out of the aggression data. The separation of *take* from readiness to *hit*, *push*, *frown* and *fixate*, warns against the confusion of functions or effects with causes. Because most of us would probably dislike having an object snatched from us just as much as we would dislike being hit, we tend to assume that both of these have the same hostile motivation. They may of course become more closely linked as a child learns from the effects these have on another (this makes typical and unwarranted assumptions about what is reinforcing about aggression) but their origins in development appear likely to be distinct. The reduction in individual variation in behaviour from 2 years old to 4 (which was apparent in the data) may in part result from this sort of learning process. This throws an interesting doubt on the assumption that learning is implied by an increase in individual differences with age. Conversely, data on height (Tanner, 1962) shows that genetically determined similarities and differences can show up more clearly as age increases. It is evidently impossible to infer things about control of development from the direction of change in variation.

It may be important to distinguish the development of a linkage between *take* and aggression from the development of peaceful (tactful) ways of acquiring objects. Deferring the use of an object, arranging to share it, tactfully acquiring it, snatching it, will clearly not fall on one dimension. The choice of these tactics will be influenced by many independent short- and long-term factors. The aggressiveness and the status in hierarchy or friendship of the potential victim and the proximity of the teacher might be short-term factors. Long-term factors might be the experience of effects on the other child (in turn affected by whatever determines whether and how these effects are responded to), and experience of interruption by adults in a variety of forms. This is really just an illustration of a point discussed by Hinde (1959, 1966): it is impossible to maintain a unitary drive theory when investigation is pushed beyond a certain level, and too great a dedication to a major theory phrased in drive terminology may prevent investigation beyond this level. It may be that this level has been reached in studies of aggression and dependency by social and developmental psychologists. But nor are ethologists immune to this error, as may be seen in the popular writings of Lorenz (1966) and Russell and Russell (1968).

The cross-individual analysis suggests that the main dimensions of individual variation cut across the temporal groupings of behaviour. All the children seem to show the same groupings but children do not differ mainly in the frequency with which they show behaviour in each group. Normal children vary in how much of any form of social behaviour they show and in whether their behaviour centres round toys or not. Obviously normal individuals vary in how much they show behaviour in each group, but this is a minor part of their variation, and the other major factors have to be held constant in order to examine differences in the temporal groupings (with a view to working out how they develop). Our limited experience with abnormal children suggests that subtler differences in the organisation of the behaviour are more important than differences in quantity of the usual groupings. The very general effects of age or experience on social behaviour are probably mimicked by other background factors. Existence of siblings and amount of distress (*crying* and *approach*) at separation from the mother appear to have a similar blanket effect on interaction, at least among younger children (see also McGrew, Ch. 5).

Speculation on the implications for development is too tempting to resist, and may eventually aid research. I would suggest that factors which bring about the development of the main groupings of behaviour are present in the life of almost all (i.e. normal) children and that these factors are different from the factors which cause the development of the normal range of individual differences. Furthermore I think this implies that the development of the temporal groupings is a very stable system not easily put off course, and self-regulatory to the extent that wild variation of one group or item in a group separately from others is not common.

This position is very different from the rapidly disappearing, over-simplified view that (to put it crudely) the child is taught to do behaviours *A*, *B* and *C* and that how much it does *A*, *B* or *C* depends on how much it was taught, or rewarded, for these particular behaviours. Ambrose (1968) has already shown how studies of development in animals have pushed the emphasis away from any such simplistic applications of information on learning. My remarks are another small step in this change of outlook, and are made because I feel that the change has not spread as widely as it might.

Acknowledgements

I wish to thank Professor J. M. Tanner for his encouragement and the excellent facilities of the Department of Growth and Development; the Nuffield Foundation for financial support; Professor Tanner, H. Goldstein and Dr M. F. Hall for criticisms on earlier drafts of the paper; Miss S. Drysdale for running the playgroup and providing a constant source of subjects; Miss J. Forrest for secretarial assistance and Mrs P. Cox and Mr B. Carter for data processing and computing assistance.

REFERENCES

Altmann, S. A. (1962). A field study of the sociobiology of rhesus monkeys, *Macaca mulatta. Ann. N.Y. Acad. Sci.* **102**, 338–435.

Altmann, S. A. (1965). Sociobiology of rhesus monkeys II. Stochastics of social communication. *J. theor. Biol.* **8**, 490–522.

Ambrose, J. A. (1968). The comparative approach to early child development: the data of ethology. In *Foundations of Child Psychiatry.* Ed. E. Miller. London: Pergamon.

Andrew, R. J. (1956). Some remarks on behaviour in conflict situations, with special references to *Emberiza* spp. *Br. J. Anim. Behav.* **4**, 41–5.

Andrew, R. J. (1957). The aggressive and courtship behaviour of certain Emberizinae. *Behaviour* **10**, 255–308.

Andrew, R. J. (1963). The origin and evolution of calls and facial expressions of the Primates. *Behaviour* **20**, 1–110.

Bandura, A., Ross, D. and Ross, S. A. (1961). Transmission of aggression through imitation of aggressive models. *J. abnorm. soc. Psychol.* **63**, 575–82.

Bandura, A., Ross, D. and Ross, S. A. (1963). Imitation of film-mediated aggressive models. *J. abnorm. soc. Psychol.* **66**, 3–11.

Blurton Jones, N. G. (1967). An ethological study of some aspects of social behaviour of children in nursery school. In *Primate Ethology*. Ed. D. Morris, London: Weidenfeld and Nicolson.

Blurton Jones, N. G. (1968). Observations and experiments on the causation of threat displays of the Great Tit (*Parus major*). *Anim. Behav. Monog.* **1**, 75–158.

Blurton Jones, N. G. (in press). Criteria for describing facial expressions in children. *Hum. Biol.*

Bridges, K. M. B. (1932). Emotional development in early infancy. *Child Develop.* **3**, 324–41.

Cattell, R. B. (1965). Factor analysis: An introduction to essentials. II. The role of factor analysis in research. *Biometrics* **21**, 405–35.

Clark, A. H., Wyon, S. M. and Richards, M. P. M. (1969). Free-play in nursery school children. *J. Child Psychol. Psychiat.* **10**, 205–16.

Clyde, D. J., Cramer, E. M. and Sherin, R. J. (1966). *Multivariate statistical programs.* Biometric Laboratory, University of Miami.

Dawe, H. C. (1934). An analysis of 200 quarrels of preschool children. *Child Develop.* **5**, 139–57.

Garai, J. E. and Scheinfeld, A. (1968). Sex differences in mental and behavioural traits. *Genet. Psychol. Monog.* **77**, 169–299.

Grant, E. C. (1963). An analysis of the social behaviour of the male laboratory rat. *Behaviour* **21**, 260–81.

Grant, E. C. (1968). An ethological description of non-verbal behaviour during interviews. *Br. J. Med. Psychol.* **41**, 177.

Green, E. H. (1933). Friendships and quarrels among pre-school children. *Child Develop.* **4**, 237–52.

Harlow, H. F. and Harlow, M. H. (1965). The affectional systems. In *Behaviour of non-human primates*. Eds. A. N. Schrier, F. Stollnitz, H. F. Harlow, London: Academic Press.

Hinde, R. A. (1959). Unitary drives. *Anim. Behav.* **7**, 130–41.

Hinde, R. A. (1966). *Animal Behaviour.* London and New York: McGraw-Hill.

Hutt, S. J. and Hutt, C. (1968). Stereotypy, arousal and autism. *Human Develop.* **11**, 277–86.

Kaiser, H. F. (1958). The Varimax criterion for analytic rotation in factor analysis. *Psychometrika* **23**, 187–200.

Kendall, M. G. (1957). *A course in multivariate analysis.* London: Griffin.

Loizos, C. (1969). An ethological study of chimpanzee play. *Proc. 2nd. Internat. Congr. Primatol. I*, 87–93.

Lorenz, K. (1950). The comparative method in studying innate behaviour patterns. *Symp. Soc. exp. Biol.* **4**, 221–68.

Lorenz, K. (1966). *On aggression.* London: Methuen.

McGrew, W. (1969). An ethological study of agonistic behaviour in preschool children. In *Proc. Second Internat. Congr. Primatol.* Ed. C. R. Carpenter, Basel: Karger.

McGrew, W. (in press). *An Ethological Study of Children's Behaviour.* New York: Academic Press.

Nelson, J. D., Gelfand, D. M. and Hartman, D. P. (1969). Children's aggression following competition and exposure to an aggressive model. *Child Develop.* **40**, 1085–99.

Parten, N. B. (1933). Social play among preschool children. *J. abnorm. soc. Psychol.* **28**, 136–47.

Phoenix, C. H., Goy, R. W. and Resko, J. A. (1968). Psychosexual differentiation as a function of androgenic stimulation. In *Perspectives in reproduction and sexual behaviour.* Ed. M. Diamond. Bloomington: Indiana Univ. Press.

Rosenthal, M. K. (1967). The generalization of dependency behaviour from mother to stranger. *J. Child Psychol. Psychiat.* **8**, 117–34.

Russell, C. and Russell, W. M. S. (1968). *Violence, Monkeys and Man.* London: Macmillan.

Sears, R. R. (1961). Relation of early socialization experiences to aggression in middle childhood. *J. abnorm. soc. Psychol.* **63**, 466–92.

Sears, R. L., Rau, L. and Alpert, R. (1966). *Identification and Child Rearing.* London: Tavistock Publications.

Siegel, S. (1956). *Non-parametric statistics for the behavioural sciences.* New York: McGraw-Hill.

Stith, M. and Connor, R. (1962). Dependency and helpfulness in young children. *Child Develop.* **33**, 15–20.

Stokes, A. W. (1962a). Agonistic behaviour among blue tits at a winter feeding station. *Behaviour* **19**, 118.

Stokes, A. W. (1962b). The comparative ethology of Great, Blue, Marsh, and Coal tits at a winter feeding station. *Behaviour* **19**, 208.

Tanner, J. M. (1962). *Growth at Adolescence.* Oxford: Blackwell.

Tinbergen, N. (1959). Comparative studies of the behaviour of gulls (*Laridae*): a progress report. *Behaviour* **15**, 1–70.

Tinbergen, N. and Tinbergen, E. A. (in press). Social interactions in normal and autistic children – an ethological study. *Z.f. Tierpsychol.*

Tugendhat, B. (1960). The disturbed feeding behaviour of the three-spined stickleback. I. Electric shock is administered in the food area. *Behaviour* **16**, 159–87.

Wiepkema, P. R. (1961). An ethological analysis of the reproductive behaviour of the bitterling (*Rhodeus amarus* Bloch). *Archs. néerl. Zool.* **14**, 103–99.

Young, W. C., Goy, R. W. and Phoenix, C. H. (1964). Hormones and sexual behaviour. *Science, N.Y.* **143**, 212–18.

5

ASPECTS OF SOCIAL DEVELOPMENT IN NURSERY SCHOOL CHILDREN WITH EMPHASIS ON INTRODUCTION TO THE GROUP

W. C. McGREW *

SUMMARY

Children of 3 and 4 years old in an Edinburgh nursery school were observed with two aims: to explore the possibility of short-term changes immediately after entry into the nursery and to compare these with long-term social changes. Earlier research on pre-school children's social development had neglected this or covered it only generally. Twelve children (six boys, six girls) were introduced singly into the nursery and observed during their first five days; a follow-up five-day period of observation was made approximately three months later.

Children's behaviour at entry varied greatly, but the group's reaction to the newcomer was a more consistent neutral curiosity. During his first nursery day, the incoming child was subdued and exhibited signs of ambivalence. He silently investigated the novel surroundings and inhabitants and avoided performing conspicuous behaviour patterns. Nursery members were indifferent or friendly, not hostile. Older siblings shepherded younger sibling newcomers.

Conspicuous changes in the new child's behaviour occurred within five days of entry. Nervous exploration decreased and social approaches, including agonistic ones, increased, but participation in quasi-agonistic 'rough and tumble' play remained rare. Differences between the two five-day periods followed trends existing over the first five days, and the newcomers were behaviourally indistinguishable from the others after approximately sixty-five days of nursery experience. Unexpected day-to-day consistencies were found in some behavioural pattern frequencies within morning observation periods. These periodicities generally resembled differences found between days.

The discussion emphasizes the usefulness of comparing social development in human and nonhuman primates but points out the many factors which could account for the differences found. The daily periodicities in behaviour may be attributable to each morning's arrival being a lesser repetition of the original introduction to the group.

The aims of this study were two-fold: first, to investigate the possible occurrence of short-term changes in children's behaviour immediately after introduction into an established group, and second, to examine the

* Department of Psychology, University of Edinburgh. Present address: Gombe Stream Research Centre, Kigoma, Tanzania.

behavioural details of long-term social changes in the introduced children. Observations of the introduced individuals will be emphasized, as changes during the group's formation will be presented elsewhere (McGrew, in press). The study is part of a continuing research programme in ethological studies of children's social behaviour being conducted in the Department of Psychology, University of Edinburgh.

Stimulation for the study came from three sources: (1) traditional developmental psychology; (2) nonhuman primate behaviour studies; and (3) recent advances in human ethology. The first was a 'negative' stimulus: the realization that behaviour patterns involved in 'socialization' had never been elucidated. The second type of studies has increasingly produced exciting findings about processes of social organization and development which appear to have important relevance for human primates. This relevance cannot be demonstrated by superficially transferring conclusions across primate species; instead, ideas resulting from studies of one species must be used (if possible) as a basis for similar investigation of other species. The third stimulus source, human ethology, has moved out of the stage of speculation and through much of the descriptive phase, so that research workers are now attacking more selected problems, as exemplified by this volume.

Earlier research

An important point which emerges from most nonhuman primate studies is that the first few hours, even minutes, after a new individual's introduction into a group may see important social behaviour changes. It is not unreasonable that similar processes may exist in *Homo sapiens*, especially when young children enter large peer groups for the first time. However, examination of the developmental psychology literature yields little information on this. Studies of long-term social development, in terms of months or years, abound. But even a lengthy monograph such as that of Jersild and Fite (1939) omits information about dates and times of observations as related to the child's date and time of entry into the nursery. Initial social contacts have been largely ignored.

An exception to this is Washburn's (1932) attempt at grading children's reactions in new social situations. She recorded a child's behaviour during its first fifteen minutes in a nursery group, using three categories (each for five minutes): number of attentional shifts and social contacts, amount of activity and amount of vocalization. The children observed ranged in age from 18 months to 4½ years old and were of varying social experience: eleven children had attended a nursery school for eight months. These children's behaviour on their first day in the nursery school and their first day in Washburn's nursery group were compared.

The older long-term studies of social development were reviewed by Jersild and Fite (1939), who observed eighteen children in the fall and following spring of a nursery year. Later studies have followed the same vein, usually examining selected aspects of long-term social experience. In a series of studies, nursery children were examined at four consecutive ten-day intervals; relationships were found between sociometric score, teacher judgement of friendship, and observations of free play (McCandless and Marshall, 1957). Stott and Ball (1957) used cross-sectional samples of children from under 3 to over 12 years old in studying the development of ascendance–submission in social interaction. Emmerich (1964) examined thirty-four social behaviour categories in thirty-eight children over four terms of nursery school. One of the few studies to separate age and length of time in nursery was that of Raph and her co-workers (1968) who observed social interaction in ninety-seven 3 to 5-year-olds.

All the above-mentioned studies seem to agree with the general conclusions reached by Jersild and Fite: ' It appears that nursery school experience aids in the development of " positive " personality traits, promotes social skills, prepares the child to adjust somewhat more effectively to future group situations which he may be called upon to meet ' (1939: 10).

But although thirty years have elapsed, the detailed study of the behaviour patterns involved in this development largely remains undone. What are the overt behavioural correlates of the ' positive personality traits '? What are the vocalizations, facial expressions, gestures, postures and locomotion which constitute the ' social skills '? How does the preparation for adjustment take place on a day-to-day interactional basis in the nursery?

The above studies used behavioural categories which cannot be used to answer these questions since most of the categories are general, inferential or undefined. For example, Washburn (1932) recorded ' activity ', which she defined as motion of the trunk or limbs; such a category is objectively defined but is too general to be socially useful. Emmerich (1964) used thirty-four behaviour categories, but his items, e.g. ' maintain and enhance own status ', seem too inferential to be replicable. Finally, Raph, Thomas, Chess and Korn (1968) used a seven-category system, e.g. ' negative behaviour ' defined as ' interactions in which the S's behaviour was predominantly negative, destructive, argumentative, and the like '. This behavioural classification may provide useful general knowledge about children's sociability, but it cannot be used in seeking to understand development and inter-relationships of detailed behaviour patterns.

Methods and procedures

SUBJECTS

Twenty-nine children (fifteen girls, fourteen boys) between 3 and 5 years old participated in the study. Group size varied between thirteen and nineteen as introductions of new individuals were made. Individual information

TABLE 5·1. *Individual information on 'new' children introduced into nursery group. (Names are pseudonyms)*

Child	Sex	Age at entry (months)	No. of siblings	Siblings in nursery	Previous peer groups
Isabel	F	39	2	—	—
Moira	F	36	1	older sister	—
Kathy	F	36	1	—	—
Hazel	F	36	1	—	—
Carrie	F	36	1	older brother	—
Teresa	F	39	1	—	—
Tommy	M	36	1	older sister	—
Ian	M	37	2	older brother	Sunday school
Norman	M	49	3	—	—
Sammy	M	36	1	older brother	—
Kenneth	M	36	0	—	—
Charles	M	36	1	—	—
6—F, 6—M		median=36	median=1	5 +, 7 —	1 +, 11 —

TABLE 5·2. *Individual information on children in nursery group. (Names are pseudonyms)*

Child	Sex	Age at entry (months)	No. of siblings	Siblings in nursery	Previous peer groups
Karen	F	49	1	—	—
Heidi	F	43	1	Moira	—
Marcia	F	47	1	Edward	Sunday school
Nora	F	40	3	—	—
Cora	F	40	1	Tommy	—
Ellen	F	36	1	—	—
Kristine	F	36	0	—	—
Gladys	F	56	1	—	—
Bertha	F	36	1	—	—
Evan	M	48	2	—	—
Ivan	M	45	2	Ian	Sunday school
Brian	M	39	1	—	—
Timmy	M	46	1	—	—
Oliver	M	42	2	—	—
Homer	M	40	1	Carrie	—
Gary	M	36	1	—	—
Edward	M	37	1	Marcia	Sunday school
9—F, 8—M		mean=42.1	median=1	6 +, 11 —	3 +, 14 —

is given in Tables 5·1 and 5·2. The children were from middle socio-economic backgrounds (primarily Classes 2 and 3 in the Registrar-General's classification, as determined from father's occupation), and only two children's parents were connected with the University. Children had a mean of 1.2 siblings, mostly younger. All were Caucasian, native English-speaking, in good physical health, and most were of Scottish national background. One child exhibited prolonged 'anxious' behaviour in connection with maternal separation.

Twelve children (six girls, six boys) were introduced into the nursery as vacancies occurred and were individually observed. Most had just turned 3 years old. Only one had previous experience with large peer groups. Five children entered the nursery while older siblings also attended.

Most of the remaining seventeen children (nine girls, eight boys) were nursery members before introductions began, but five children were introduced without systematic observation during the study, due to scheduling difficulties or observer illness. The non-observed group (Table 5·2) were older (mean age, 42 months), but of similar social experience: only three had participated in large peer groups before entry. Six had younger siblings present with them in the nursery.

PHYSICAL ENVIRONMENT

The study was conducted in the Epworth Halls Nursery School, administered by the Department of Psychology, University of Edinburgh. It included a play room (a converted church hall), an adjacent outside play area, a cloakroom and a bathroom.

Most observations were made in the rectangular, carpeted play room (36 ft × 22 ft). It contained standard nursery equipment: a slide, Wendy House, sand tray, building blocks, painting easels, book corner, assorted table toys, etc. During dry weather in the summer and early autumn, children also played in the small, irregularly-shaped outdoor play area. Besides a large sand pit, various toys were available: see-saw, balls, slide, skipping ropes, etc.

Nursery routine

A nursery nurse and assistant (both female) were present throughout the morning in the nursery. Male experimenters from an associated cognition study came in and out of the room for short periods. One full-time male observer and two part-time female observers (one who also acted as nursery assistant) were present in the room during free play sessions. Mothers left soon after bringing their children, most of them coming only to the door. Similarly when fetching children, mothers entered the nursery only after termination of the day's observations.

Children attended the nursery Monday–Friday mornings from late August to the first week of July. They arrived at the nursery between 9.15

and 9.30 a.m. Between 9.30 and 10.15 they engaged in free play, i.e. activities undirected by adults, in which all facilities (weather permitting) were accessible to all children. Between 10.15 and 11.00 there was a break for story, organized games or music-time, then milk and snacks. From 11.00 to 11.45 children engaged in a second free play session before their mothers arrived to pick them up.

During free play adults remained largely onlookers and rarely interfered in children's play unless asked to do so by them. Other grounds for interference were potentially dangerous or damaging situations, or prolonged agonistic encounters when a child seemed unfairly persecuted. In this atmosphere the children were largely self-sufficient, only occasionally consulting adults for solace or help with toys. No physical punishment was used, and most children performed routine toilet activities without adult aid. Many procedural rules were passed from child to child directly.

As a conspecific, the observer's potential interactional capacities posed special problems, particularly as some observations constituted continuous periods of up to 45 minutes. Two extremes of observer conduct were rejected: (a) intentional, initiated interactions with children, which would make objective, complete observation impossible, and (b) a totally detached 'wooden Indian' attitude which also might be 'unnaturally' disruptive. A compromise was achieved: the observer did not initiate interactions with children, but if they initiated an interaction with him, he did not refuse but terminated it as soon as was gracefully possible. Such interactions caused negligible interruption to the observer's recording, and no such interactions occurred between the observer and the child being observed. Generally, observers quietly stood or sat at the room's periphery or moved slowly about, marking on clip-boards. Maximum distance allowing accurate recording was maintained between observer and subject, and the observer used short glances and avoided facing the subject when looking at him. When the child moved, the observer moved with him, attempting to keep his face in view.

Throughout the study no child evidenced awareness of 'being followed'. Apparently children concluded early that observers were dull prospects and ignored them more than other adults. For example, more attention was paid to the experimenters who took single children for 'games' (ten-minute perceptual or cognitive tests in another room).

OBSERVATION PROCEDURES

Newcomers were introduced singly into the established group at a minimum of seven days apart, as soon after their third birthdays as possible. They were observed from the moment they entered the play room on their first day. These observations lasted an average of 82 minutes/day over the child's first five mornings in the nursery. Only one mother (Charles') stayed longer than ten minutes with her child: that was for half the morning on his second day, and recording was suspended while she remained.

The observer wrote a running account of the child's behaviour, emphasizing social interactions and using a previously prepared glossary of ninety-three behaviour patterns. Patterns referred to in the text but not yet analysed in detail are listed briefly in the Appendix and italicized in the text, and detailed descriptions are presented in a later publication (McGrew, in press). Every time a pattern started, it was scored once, regardless of its elapsed time, and scores given in the tables represent mean daily number of these bouts per child. Group members' behaviour toward the newcomer was noted when possible. The most commonly occurring patterns have been analysed first, and analysis of others is proceeding. Definitions of behaviour patterns so far analysed, and inter-observer reliability coefficients for them, are given in Table 5·3, and are also italicized in the text. These were obtained by having the observer and a co-worker simultaneously record ongoing behaviour in the nursery over ten-minute periods. Later comparison of their records produced a coefficient using the following formula: agreements/agreements plus disagreements. In general, inter-observer agreement improved steadily, and satisfactory coefficients were reached by the third day of testing.

TABLE 5·3. *Definitions of behaviour categories*

Immobile – Prolonged (longer than three seconds) cessation of gross movements of the trunk, limbs and head. Often accompanied by fixed gaze and occurring in any posture, but usually while sitting or standing (0.83).

Automanipulate – Use of the fingers, particularly thumb and forefinger, to manipulate a body-part. Usually consists of scratching, rubbing or otherwise fingering the mouth, nose, ears or hair. Similarly, fumbling movements of a small object or a limited aspect of a large object (see McGrew, 1969). Point manipulated is not visually fixated (0.85).

Run – Rapid forward locomotion on alternate legs, with both feet instantaneously off the ground during each stride. Trunk usually tilted forward (0.94).

Walk – Moderate forward locomotion on alternate legs, with one foot placed firmly on the ground before lifting the other during each stride. Trunk upright (0.86).

Glance – Rapid head movement orienting the face is followed within three seconds by another head movement re-orienting the face (0.93).

Verbalization – Vocalizations whose printed representations are found in dictionaries (0.95).

Look – Head movement re-orienting the face is maintained for at least three seconds (0.71).

Children who had been observed at introduction were re-observed for five mornings approximately sixty-five nursery days later. The follow-up observation series was done by the same observer under the same conditions.

Results

NURSERY ENTRY

A 'new' child usually walked into the nursery with his mother; the exceptions were Tommy, Carrie and Ian, who entered with their older siblings. The child usually walked with short, slow steps, held his mother's hand with one hand and either carried a snack with the other or sucked his thumb or fingers. After being greeted by the nursery nurse and handing his snack to her, the child often clung to his mother, leaned away from the nursery nurse and avoided her gaze.

The mother then usually stooped down beside her child, caressing and verbally encouraging him. Several mothers took their children in hand and walked about the play room pointing out toys and handing them to the children. Sometimes the nursery nurse did this while the mother looked on. As soon as the child was involved in some play activity or interacting with the nursery nurse, the mother usually said good-bye and left quietly. A mother's failure to take leave properly initiated the worst disruption seen on a child's first day: Teresa's mother sneaked away while her daughter's attention was diverted, but within seconds Teresa glanced toward her mother's former location. A few more seconds of agitated searching followed before Teresa ran from the play room screaming for her mother.

New children's reactions at entry varied greatly. Four of sixteen cried (*weeping* and *vocalizing, red* and *puckered face*) when their mothers said good-bye or soon after they left, and two had to be restrained by the nurse from running after their mothers. However, some children quickly entered into play activities, ignoring their mothers, who usually left within two or three minutes of arrival. One new boy, Edward, 'walked' on his knees into the nursery with a friend, both singing the 'Diddy men' song, on his first morning. His mother didn't have to enter the play room. Children with older siblings in the nursery seemed less upset with the mother's departure, as did some children who knew nursery members from outside the nursery. The numbers of such children were too small to warrant conclusions, however, and other children, e.g. Kathy, who knew none of the nursery children prior to entry, behaved similarly.

The reaction of nursery group members to a newcomer's entry ranged from neutrality to non-agonistic approach; no aggressive responses were seen. Children paid considerable attention to the morning's arrivals between 9.15 and 9.30, and on some days congregated by the play room door and greeted arriving children. This assured that a new face was obvious. Upon initially noticing a new child, a group member visually fixated him; the

136

visual inspection ranged from a brief glance (usually by a seated child engaged in manipulative activity) to staring while immobile (often by upright children unengaged in activity). The facial expression usually remained neutral, but some slight frowning (not *low frown*, see Blurton Jones, 1967) occurred.

Some group members then walked slowly toward a new child, maintaining visual inspection which seemed to focus on the face. The visual inspection did not seem 'hostile', and it was unaccompanied by aggressive patterns of behaviour. If the new child was interacting with the nursery nurse, they often glanced back and forth between the two. Although they approached within touching distance, group members did not usually touch a new child at this point although they sidled around him and leaned sideways keeping his face in view. A few group members exhibited patterns similar to those of the newcomers, e.g. *automanipulation, walk step*, silence. This sometimes involved a 'regression': Heidi had shown the peculiar pattern of sucking her two middle fingers at nursery entry, and this sometimes returned on days when new children were introduced. Similarly, Marcia, an older, 'well-adjusted' girl rarely thumb-sucked except when newcomers entered, and the pattern was identical to that exhibited at her entry eighteen months before.

A new child with an older sibling who was already a group member experienced different entry. Some older siblings took charge from the first moment in the play room: they verbally announced the stranger to be their brother or sister; they physically directed the new child's movements by holding his hand or walking with an arm on his shoulders. After instructing the new child to give his snack, toy, etc. to the nursery nurse, the older sibling sometimes steered him directly into a play activity. This often meant that he was not as readily available for inspection as the unaccompanied child, who often hung about or followed the nursery nurse for a few minutes before becoming involved in a play activity.

FIRST DAY IN THE NURSERY

The nursery nurse often spent the first few minutes with a child after his mother left. When crying occurred it lasted briefly, and the nursery nurse wiped the child's eyes before introducing him to a play activity, usually the zoo or a table toy, e.g. jigsaw puzzle, bead-stringing. Non-crying children generally went directly into activities or exploration of the room. In either case, the nursery nurse left the child on his own within five or ten minutes. Thereafter, she checked on him throughout the morning, especially if he appeared to be wandering aimlessly or remained immobile and inactive. The nursery nurse sometimes introduced a newcomer to table-mates if he were active at a table, but this was not stressed (as children were not given any special instructions about newcomers), and the stranger was left to meet group members on his own. In general, the nursery nurse's behaviour allowed the new child freedom to explore and encounter the others, only intervening if he seemed ' lost ' or excessively troubled.

In response to attention from the group members and the nursery nurse, the new child seemed inhibited and shy. All new children displayed much *automanipulation* and all but one showed periods of *immobility* during the first few minutes. Four of fifteen *sucked* or mouthed objects or digits and one child *rocked* briefly. Other conspicuous patterns were *chewing* or rolling the lips and repeatedly *shrugging* the shoulders. In response to eye contact, the new child *glanced* or *looked away* (usually down); sometimes this amounted to a permanent *chin in*, i.e. the face tilted down with the chin pulled in toward the neck. The *slope* posture described by Grant (1965) was common, as were *sidling locomotion* and *shuffling* (irregular foot-movements while standing still). The ratio of *backing* and *walking* to *back step* and *walk step* (each being one unit of the former) was less than normal, giving the effect of hesitant locomotion. *Running* was infrequent, and three of thirteen new children did no running on the first day.

New children spent much time in ' passive ' exploration, e.g. sitting or standing in one location and slowly surveying the room. They also intently observed children engaged in play activities but entered into few themselves. A few children remained most of the first morning at the toy first given them by the teacher. Engagement in new activities was usually superficial and brief, but older siblings aided new children considerably, e.g. giving instruction on a toy's workings. New children usually avoided gross, boisterous activities and often appeared to seek out quiet locations, e.g. book corner, empty Wendy House, which they vacated if group members approached or occupied. They usually declined requests, e.g. ' You pick up that big block! ' and invitations, e.g. ' Do you want to be the baby? ' by moving silently away.

Newcomers exhibited few agonistic (attack, threat, submission) and quasi-agonistic (see rough and tumble play, Blurton Jones, 1967) patterns. They appeared to avoid competitive (e.g. queueing up for the slide) and potentially quarrelsome situations (e.g. several children at one toy). If he had unwittingly blundered, e.g. picked up toy parts being used by another child, a new child usually gave way. There were exceptions to this, apparently because of the stranger's ignorance of ' status ' and ' protocol ', e.g. on her first day Ellen contested Timmy, an older experienced male, over the slide and won. Usually, however, the new child's actions were the antithesis of aggressive: arms kept down and close to the trunk, face and eyes averted, movements slow, silent.

The amount of *verbalization* exhibited by new children varied. Most were conspicuously silent, at least initially, or spoke softly; they answered many questions with head nods and shakes. None yelled or squealed as was common during quasi-agonistic bouts, nor did they make loud, non-vocal noises although children around them might be producing a din. Again children with older siblings present were more 'normal' in their behaviour and verbalized more; most of it was directed to the sibling and did not generalize immediately to unknown group members. Three new children, Hazel, Moira and Carrie, exhibited the opposite extreme: they verbalized excessively on the first day, and their verbalization decreased during the second through fifth days. Excessive verbalization was directed equally to adults and children and seemed 'normal' in content, i.e. not concentrated on mother's absence or complaints.

The group members' interactions with the new child continued largely non-agonistically during the first day. After initial inspection some children ceased to pay special attention to a newcomer, although they might *look* instead of *glance* if he walked by later. Others initiated friendly approach: asking him questions (e.g. 'What's *your* name?'), including him in play activities (e.g. 'You can sit *there*'), offering explanations of nursery procedure (e.g. 'The clay goes on the shelf') or even offering toys (e.g. holding out a sand tool to a newcomer watching sand play) as described by Blurton Jones (1967). Such approaches included *smiles, head tilting* to the side, soft touching of the newcomer's arms or trunk, and 'pleasant' vocal modulation. Not all group members approached new children, and some did so only tentatively; others questioned adults about newcomers instead.

Girls seemed to attend more to newcomers than boys, and several girls (especially Cora, Nora, Teresa and Marcia) displayed a remarkable degree of maternalistic attentiveness. This included *verbalization* apparently intended to comfort, often in response to a new child's specifically-expressed fears, e.g. 'All the Mummies come back after milk. When the bell rings' in response to Charles' question 'When's my mummy coming back?' The soothing tones (sometimes recognizably similar to their mother's inflections) were accompanied by tactile comforting: *holding hands, hugging, hand on child's back, shoulder hug, patting, kissing.* These 'Little Mothers', one as young as three, smiled frequently at the new child and 'joked' with him, e.g. pointing out incongruities in a painting while *laughing* and *glancing* back and forth between it and the child's face. They often diligently reported a new child's difficulties to the teacher.

Boys could be friendly to newcomers, but most seemed to exhibit indifference. Newcomers did not often participate in predominantly male activities on the first day, e.g. building with big blocks, marching with 'guns', etc., and this may account for the lack of interaction. The three male older siblings observed (Ivan, Norman, Homer) did not spend as much time with their younger newly-introduced siblings as did the female older siblings. Homer and Ivan virtually ignored them unless the younger sibling initiated interaction while Norman alternated between seeming 'protectiveness' and 'annoyance' at being followed about. One older sibling, Cora, completely dominated her younger brother Tommy's first day. They entered the nursery holding hands, and throughout the morning's first play period

she steered him from activity to activity, monopolizing his attention. This
included ' defending' him from the other children's advances; this she did
with verbal threatening, *low frowns* and *pushing*. The defence was especially
directed to Kenneth, the new child's best friend outside the nursery, who
was repeatedly repulsed. When Kenneth joined the sibling pair at a table,
they left, often with Cora pulling Tommy away. Later in the morning she
left him alone but returned if he were joined by others. Tommy usually
responded passively although he joined his older sister in some threatening.
This was a unique case, but another older group member, Moira, followed
her younger sibling more than vice versa on the latter's first day.

FIRST FIVE NURSERY DAYS

Conspicuous changes in new children's behaviour occurred during their first
five days in the nursery. Changes in the incidence of specific behaviour
patterns are given in Table 5·4; the first two columns are mean frequency

TABLE 5·4. *Mean frequencies/child of behaviour patterns. Comparison of a
new child's first day with the fifth and approximately sixty-fifth days*

Behaviour pattern	(N=12) First day	(N=10) Fifth day	p [1]	(N=9) Approx. 65th day	p [1]
Immobile	14.1	10.1	0.033	7.8	0.02
Automanipulate	13.3	6.6	<0.025	4.9	0.002
Run	12.6	16.8	n.s.	19.7	<0.05
Walk	60.7	71.3	n.s.	64.4	n.s.
Glance	59.0	45.9	0.033	54.9	n.s.
Verbalization (total)	37.2	42.6	n.s.	62.1	0.02
Child-oriented	20.3	27.4	n.s.	41.4	0.035
Adult-oriented	9.8	5.8	n.s.	7.4	n.s.
Other ♀♀	9.3	11.2	n.s.	7.8	n.s.
♂♂	5.0	7.8	n.s.	20.0	0.014
Look (total)	46.4	36.2	0.025	38.1	n.s.
Child-oriented	34.5	29.2	n.s.	32.1	n.s.
Adult-oriented	8.6	6.9	n.s.	5.9	n.s.
Other	2.2	1.7	n.s.	1.9	n.s.

[1] (Sign Test, checked with Mann–Whitney *U*-Test)

counts for the new children's first and fifth days. Four patterns showed
statistically significant decreases: *immobility*, *automanipulation*, *glancing*
and total *looking*. Sex differences (see Fig. 5·1, Table 5·5) were seen: boys
showed significantly less *immobility* and *automanipulation* and more *running*,
and girls significantly less *looking* on the fifth day than on the first, but in
each case the other sex's non-significant change showed similar directionality.
Frequency of *looking* oriented to other children remained the same for boys

but decreased significantly for girls. Finally, one directional sex difference was seen: incidence of boys' *walking* increased significantly over the first five days, while girls' *walking* decreased non-significantly during that period.

Non-agonistic social interaction involving new children occurred from the first day and increased steadily between first and fifth days for most of them.

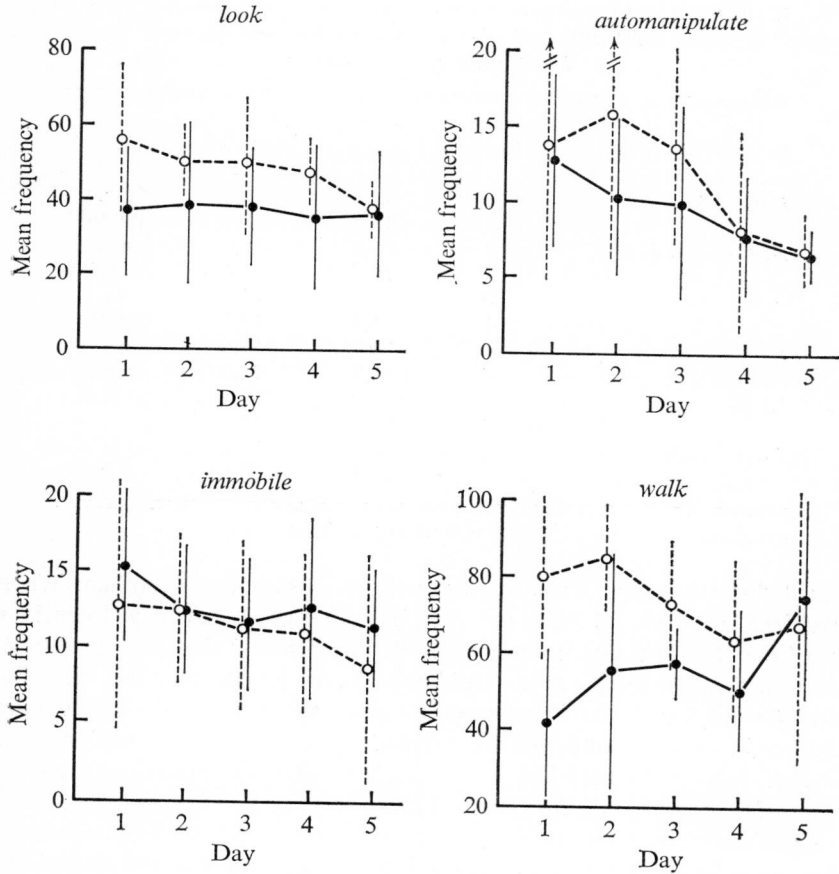

Fig. 5·1. Possible sex differences in behaviour over the first five days in nursery. Boys=solid line, Girls=broken line.

Both number of activities and number of children with whom they interacted increased while interaction with adults remained the same. New children expanded their play activities to include more ' gross ' pastimes, e.g. see-saw, slide and more social interchange, e.g. group play in Wendy House and block corner, which they had initially avoided. The increase in number of children successively interacted with appeared to occur fastest in children previously unacquainted with nursery group members, but children initially dominated by older siblings or friends also increased their contact ranges.

One new child, Charles, displayed the most 'anxious' behaviour of any newcomer, and on his fourth day still exhibited periodic bouts of *weeping, red* and *puckered face*, sobbing, *automanipulation*, digit *sucking*, etc. He

TABLE 5·5. *Mean frequencies of behaviour patterns comparing first and fifth day of nursery experience, illustrating sex differences*

Behaviour pattern	Sex	(N=6.6) First day	(N=5.5) Fifth day	p [1]
Immobile	♀♀	12.8	8.8	n.s.
	♂♂	15.3	11.4	0.026
Automanipulate	♀♀	13.8	6.8	n.s.
	♂♂	12.7	6.4	0.041
Run	♀♀	19.7	21.4	n.s.
	♂♂	5.5	12.2	0.026
Walk	♀♀	79.7	67.6	n.s.
	♂♂	41.7	75.0	0.041
Look	♀♀	56.2	36.6	0.012
	♂♂	36.7	35.8	n.s.
Look (child)	♀♀	40.5	29.8	0.026
	♂♂	28.5	28.6	n.s.

[1] Mann–Whitney *U*-Test.

repeated a seemingly constant stream of questions about his mother: Where was she? When would she come? etc. Yet Charles also displayed considerable 'social adjustment': on his first day he directed three times as many *verbalizations* to adults as to children; by the fourth day, the ratio was even. On his fourth day he entered into sustained, non-agonistic interaction with eight children although he seemed an unrewarding social partner. Several children directed him to the teacher with hand placed on the small of Charles' back (see Blurton Jones, 1967).

Agonistic interaction involving a new child was much less common but it also appeared to increase over the first five days. This was manifested in a new child's failure to defer to a group member's threats or attempts at claiming toy possession. Often a new child increasingly ignored developments which he earlier had fled from or avoided. 'Fearful' patterns (e.g. *fleeing, backing away*, giving up toy possession) seemed to give way to 'defensive' patterns (e.g. *raising the forearm, flinching* but not *turning away*, covering with the hands or hunching over the disputed toy). 'Passive resistance' predominated and active aggression by a new child was rare during his first five days. Several of the instances of active aggressive behaviour involved new children acting with protection from an older

142

sibling, e.g. Tommy *beat* and *kicked* group members early on while his older sister *beat, pushed, pinched* and *pulled the hair* of his attackers.

New children rarely participated in quasi-agonistic interactions. New children with older siblings present did so first, sometimes joining them in mobile, rowdy play groups. This seemed to occur mostly in the latter part of the five days, and new children seemed to prefer non-contact play, being the first to drop out if play became rough, e.g. if *running, jumping* and *laughing* turned into *pushing, wrestling* and falling. However, the majority of newcomers exhibited no quasi-agonistic interactions during the first week.

Behaviour of group members toward the new child also changed during his first five days. By the third or fourth day, newcomers received no special visual attention nor did they evoke digit *sucking, automanipulation*, etc. from group members. Group members knew the newcomer's name within a few days and recognized his mother. They often gave roles in imaginative play to new children, e.g. 'You be the baby and I'll be the mummy, all right?'.

However, even on a new child's final observation day he was still granted some social latitude by group members. E.g. a group member, Tommy, was unsuccessfully constructing a block stack; whenever he nearly completed it, another child would move the adjacent box or brush against it, causing it to fall. Tommy *pushed, verbalized* with loud, negative expletives ('Don't!' 'Get out!') and otherwise threatened these children, but when a newcomer, Charles, apparently unwittingly stumbled into the blocks, Tommy treated him differently. Tommy pushed against Charles' trunk with conspicuously less force and quietly told him to go away, following this soon afterwards with 'Now, you go to see Mrs Bruce' while patting Charles' back.

LONG-TERM BEHAVIOUR CHANGES

Many statistically significant changes in a child's behaviour occurred between his first five nursery days and the five-day follow-up period about sixty-five days later. Specific pattern frequencies are given in Table 5·4, which compares the first nursery day and approximate sixty-fifth day, and Table 5·6, which compares the two five-day totals. Significant long-term decreases were noted in: *immobility, automanipulation* and *looking* (total, child-oriented and adult-oriented). The only long-term sex difference seen was in other types of *verbalization* (i.e. those undirected to individuals or unidentifiable) which increased significantly in boys but not in girls.

By re-observation time, the new children were completely integrated into the group and indistinguishable behaviourally. No significant day-to-day changes were found in the second observations, an indication of behavioural stability. Excepting *look*-other, no significant sex differences were found between the second-period totals.

McGrew (1969) showed that winners and losers of struggles over objects could be ranked in a ' dominance ' hierarchy which correlated significantly with adults' ratings of aggression. Though no quantitative records were kept on this group's object struggles, observers felt that Tommy won most consistently over other males as of September 1969. If so, he achieved this

TABLE 5·6. *Mean frequencies/child of behaviour patterns. Comparison of totals from two five-day observation periods approximately sixty-five days apart*

Behaviour pattern	(N=10) First period	(N=9) Second period	p [1]
Immobile	61.3	39.9	<0.01
Automanipulate	48.0	21.8	0.008
Run	76.2	109.8	<0.05
Walk	331.6	325.2	n.s.
Glance	259.2	269.1	0.035
Verbalization (total)	206.5	351.4	<0.01
Child-oriented	128.2	234.0	0.001
Adult-oriented	35.1	48.3	n.s.
Other ♀♀	46.8	54.8	n.s.
♂♂	39.8	87.2	0.008
Look (total)	215.3	178.6	0.039
Child-oriented	171.5	146.9	0.05
Adult-oriented	42.7	29.8	0.027
Other	10.5	10.2	n.s.

[1] Sign Test, checked with Mann–Whitney U-Test.

' dominant male ' status in less than eight months of nursery experience, in spite of being only fourth oldest among the group's males. Two other factors may have aided his rise: his older sister's initial presence in the nursery, and the fact that he knew more group members outside the nursery than any other child.

WITHIN-DAY CHANGES

Daily periodicity in children's behaviour was recorded in the nursery group: i.e. if daily observations were sequentially quartered (into four sections of slightly over twenty minutes each), significant frequency differences in patterns were found between quarters, and some differences recurred persistently throughout both five-day periods (see Fig. 5·2).

To confirm that quarterly differences were statistically significant and not due to chance variation, group totals for each of the ten observation days were examined using the Kolmogorov–Smirnov One-Sample Test (Siegel, 1956). Group totals were used because individual quarterly totals were often too small for analysis, and inspection indicated that individual trends were similar. (N's for daily group totals: 14, 14, 12, 12, 11 for first five nursery days; 9, 9, 9, 9, 8 for five-day re-observation period.)

Looking decreased gradually throughout the morning during both sets of observations. The pattern was remarkably regular: the fourth quarter mean frequency/child was always less than the first and second quarter means ($p=0.001$, Sign Test), as was the third quarter mean with one exception ($p=0.011$, Sign Test). The distribution of *looking* by quarters was significantly different from chance on seven of ten days, and the other three days closely approximated the prevalent pattern. The children's first nursery day proved the most aberrant from the general pattern: the difference between first and fourth quarter means was smallest on the first day; it also included the only instance of a third or fourth quarter mean exceeding a first or second quarter mean.

Walking provided the opposite extreme: only one (second re-observation day) of ten days showed significant variance from chance between quarters, and this was at the 5% level. However, differences between the two five-day periods existed. Comparing the first and fourth quarter means: *walking* decreased over every morning in the first five days and increased over every morning during the second five-day period sixty-four days later ($p=0.031$, Sign Test).

Glance patterning resembled *looking*: the fourth quarter mean was less than the first quarter mean on nine of nine days with one tie ($p=0.002$, Sign Test), and the third quarter mean was less than the first on eight of nine days with one tie ($p=0.020$, Sign Test). Again the first nursery day deviated most: differences between its quarters were smallest, and it included the exception and one of the ties mentioned above.

Running increased throughout the morning. The third and fourth quarter means were greater than the first quarter means on nine of ten days ($p=0.011$, Sign Test). The first nursery day was also most extreme: it contained the only example of the combined third and fourth quarter means more than doubling the combined first and second quarter means. The first and second quarter means on the first day were the lowest of all ten days.

Other patterns so far analysed showed similarities: *automanipulation* and *immobility* decreased throughout each morning ($p=0.001$, Sign Test) with the first quarter of the first day producing the highest number in both cases; *verbalization* increased throughout most mornings during the first five days but was unchanged during the second observation series.

For most of the behaviour patterns so far analysed, the child's first day was the most aberrant from the usual periodicity seen throughout the ten observation days. The aberrancy took two forms: ' enhancement ' of inter-quartile differences (e.g. *run*) or ' flattening ' of inter-quartile differences

145

(e.g. *glance*). This finding is not surprising, as the first day's disruption was probably the most extreme.

Discussion

The importance of short-term behavioural changes immediately after nursery entry appears to have been underestimated in previous studies of children's behavioural development. Such changes are not accounted for by maturation alone, as the time scale is too small: as few as five days. Nor does rapid learning of the patterns explain the changes; children in practically all cases displayed ability to perform the behaviour patterns from the first day, and no changes were seen in the pattern form over the

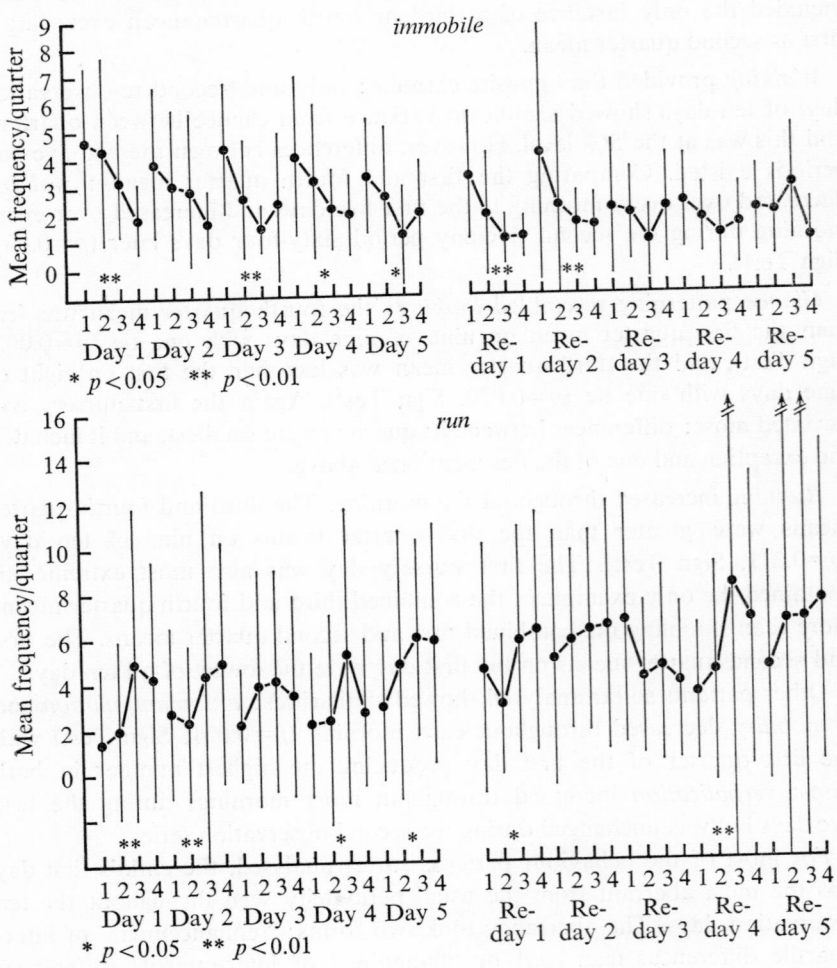

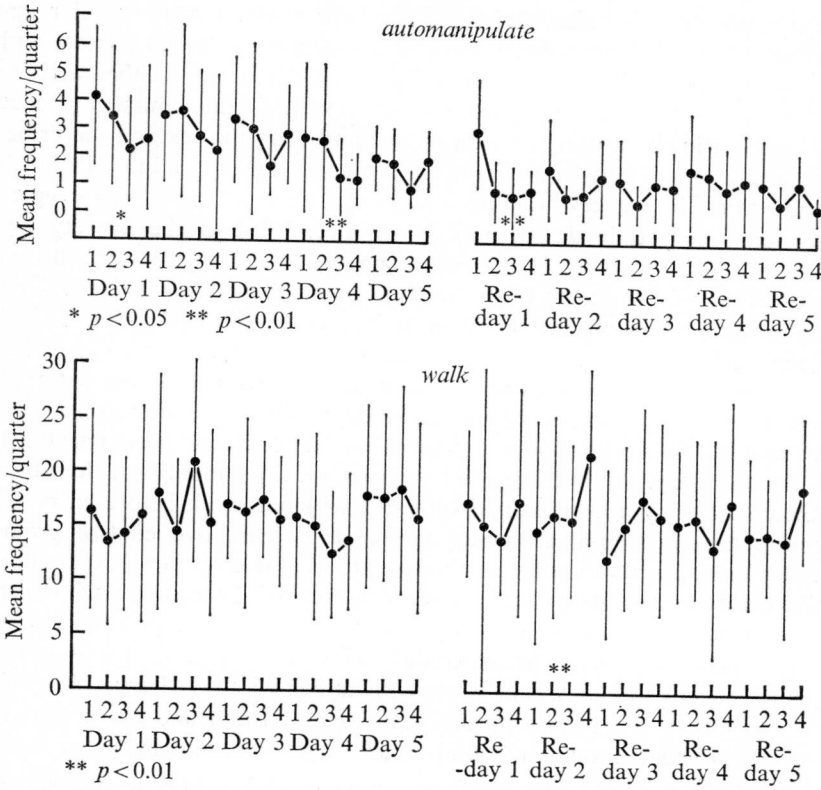

Fig. 5·2. Periodicity in children's behaviour during first five days in nursery and five-day period approximately 65 days later.

child's first five days. It is likely that the nursery situation, which for all but one of the introduced children was the first regular contact with a large age-peer group, presented a radically novel impact sufficient to force re-adjustment of a child's established social communicatory habits. I.e., although each new child's behavioural 'repertoire' already contained efficient *running, laughing, smiling*, etc., his existing systems of deployment (based on experience with siblings, neighbourhood friends, etc.) were inadequate for dealing with the nursery situation. This inadequacy may have been due to inability to respond with appropriate patterns to other's advances or failure to do so because of fear or both.

It is possible that the nursery's novel impact was unrelated to peer-social factors and instead due to other situational factors, e.g. strange building, strange toys, strange adults. This seems unlikely as at least nine of the twelve new children had been in the play room at least once before, and six of them had visited many times, usually accompanying their mothers bringing and picking up older siblings. Such brief visits, usually regular and twice-daily, enabled preliminary nursery exploration although contact with nursery group members was minimal since children were either arriving or leaving. The visits also included interaction with the same nursery teacher, who worked in the nursery before, during and after the research described here, and at least visual familiarity with other associated adults, including the observer. The nursery building, a converted church annexe, was a typical Victorian structure in design and appearance. Most of the nursery toys were of familiar commercial origin although some large objects were custom-made. From this, it seems likely that the nursery's social novelty and not other novel factors produced the most impact on the new child. This is augmented by another socially significant fact: several of the children had never been separated from their mothers and left with strangers before.

The relative contributions of maturation and social experience to the short-term and long-term behavioural differences found cannot be delineated in the present study. All but one child were within three months of their third birthdays at entry and most had turned 3 within a week before entry. To separate the two variables, observations of at least two control groups entering the nursery would be required: a group of peer-group-inexperienced older children, e.g. 4-year-olds, and a group of 3-year-olds who were socially experienced through previous peer contact in play groups or other nurseries but who were unacquainted with the Epworth Halls group. Whether such children would show similar behavioural changes is prob-lematical but it is hoped to pursue such studies. Raph and her colleagues (1968) found that amount of child–child 'negative interactions' at age 5 was highest in children with one-year nursery experience, lower in children with two-year nursery experience and lowest in children with three-year nursery experience. (However, age at nursery entry is confounded with amount of social experience.) Alexander (Harlow and Harlow, 1969) found similar differences between rhesus monkeys which were peer-deprived or peer-experienced. It is likely that the later peer-group contact is withheld, the more difficulty the socially inexperienced primate will have in redeploy-ing appropriate behaviour patterns to fit the new situation.

Many similarities exist between the nursery school social situation in Western society and the infant play group in nonhuman primate troops. Both constitute groups of very young primates experiencing initial age-peer contact. Although of mixed sex, both groups included same-sex subgroupings displaying differing behaviour types, e.g. rough and tumble play. Like non-human primate play groups, the Epworth Hall nursery group spent the majority of time in free social play. In both cases this was monitored by and sometimes interfered with by adult females of the species, either the nonhuman primate mothers or the nursery nurse and assistant. Some young nonhuman primates use the same area for daily social play, e.g. the 'arena' of young free-living patas monkeys, *Erythrocebus patas* (Hall, 1965). In both cases, play group members spent part of the day together and the rest with parents, siblings and other individuals engaged with them in eating, sleeping, travelling, etc. This is not to say that the nursery school and the nonhuman primate play group are completely equivalent nor that findings from one are transferable to the other, but from an evolutionary viewpoint the nursery school is not so culturally unique and 'artificial' as might first be supposed.

Ethologically, the most important comparisons between primates involve specific, recurring motor patterns. If we are to appreciate the evolutionary significance of human facial expressions, gestures and postures, particularly when faced with the variety of culturally imposed modifications, we must compare notes among those living animals with whom we most recently shared common ancestry, i.e. the nonhuman primates. (The other important comparisons, between the communicational patterns of different human cultures, are obviously also important, but their discussion is not possible here.) The grounds for inter-primate comparisons are on several levels: many patterns show *morphological* similarities, e.g. use of similar body-parts (eyelids, fingers, shoulders) involving similar musculature and inner-vation (particularly the face, see Blurton Jones, in prep.). Many patterns show *operational* similarities, i.e. structures acting similarly, *e.g.* hair erection, flushing, combinations of muscle groups contracting together. *Functional* similarities exist: inter-individual sequences of patterns may result in similar social consequences, e.g. one individual's staring at another may lead to the latter's averting his gaze, one individual's directed, hori-zontally-outstretched arms may lead to the other's approach and physical contact. Finally, *situational* similarities abound: e.g. patting of one individual by another may occur when the former is disturbed or agitated, abbreviated versions of hitting behaviour may produce flight by another individual in conflicts over object possession. A listing of such patterns can only be tentative but includes: *bite, gaze fixate, play face, play crouch, beat, kiss, slap, stamp, kick, hug*, etc.

The absence of aggression by nursery group members toward a new child introduced into the group was most surprising, particularly since this ran counter to the rule among nonhuman primates (Kawai, 1960; Bernstein, 1964, 1969; Southwick, 1967; Gartlan and Brain, 1968). In most of the nonhuman primate studies, incidence of aggression was greatest during the first few minutes or hours, and this persisted until the animal was killed, left the group, or was withdrawn by experimenters. If the animal succeeded in remaining in the group agonistic interaction gradually subsided.

Several possible explanations exist for the difference: one relates to temporary/permanent introduction. All children introduced became 'per-manent' nursery members, usually until moving on to primary school at age 5. Several nonhuman primate experiments included repeated temporary introductions and removals (e.g. Southwick, 1967); such alterations of group membership may have disrupted social stability, producing chronic frustration and attendant increased aggression. Frustration–aggression may also have been involved in those studies using exposure to strangers instead of their introduction (e.g. Ploog and MacLean, 1963). Efforts by zoo primates to interact and make physical contact with adjacently-housed animals are well known, and it seems probable that degree of frustration is related to intelligence level, so that exposure of strange individuals to caged nonhuman primate groups might produce extreme frustration and attendant aggression. Also the strangers may have been prevented by the exposure techniques from displaying appropriate submission and appease-ment patterns, which may have prolonged or exacerbated aggression. In the nursery, new children went immediately into group free play and were accessible to all group members.

Age of group members may influence the group's reaction to newcomers, and could account for the difference between the children's behaviour and that usually reported for other primates. Only Harlow and Harlow (1969) have used infant groups for nonhuman primate introduction studies – most workers used adult groups or groups assembled to approximate the natural troop's age-sex structure. In the nursery, only two adults interacted to any extent with children during free play, and almost all child–child interactions proceeded without adult interference. Group ' permeability ' may decrease with age in primate groups as dominance and sexual activities assume increasing importance. This certainly appears to be true at a gross level, e.g. an adult male vervet's differential treatment of juvenile and adult male intruders (Gartlan and Brain, 1968), a male gibbon's altered response to the maturing juvenile male (Bernstein and Schusterman, 1964). In Bernstein and Draper's (1964) study of a juvenile rhesus group, the first animals to approach and make contact with the introduced adult male were the smallest (youngest?) while the largest juveniles reacted aggressively toward him.

Also, some form of ' territoriality ' may have been operating in most of the nonhuman primate studies, as they were observed in home cages which they occupied all the time. The children spent only a fraction of the day in the nursery and most of the rest at home.

Any or all of these factors may have contributed to the differences seen between human and nonhuman primate group's reactions to introduced strangers, but it is tempting to consider possible phylogenetic differences. Whether the fact that the gibbon group's response to strangers (studied by Bernstein and Schusterman) more closely approximated the human one than any of the lower forms is significant or not awaits further examination. But the ' open ' group structures described in free-living gorillas and chim-panzees contrast strongly with the ' closed ' groups usually found in monkey populations. (However, Lindburg's recent (1969) study of wild rhesus macaque groups in India has shown them to be more ' open ' than previously supposed, i.e. during the breeding season incidence of males changing groups increases markedly.) In human evolutionary terms, protohominid 'open' groups, i.e. those which allowed easy entry and exit to members of neighbouring groups, presumably facilitated gene dispersal and therefore accelerated evolutionary rate. The probable importance of 'open groups' has been discussed by Reynolds (1966).

Other observational studies of human response to strangers also found a lack of aggression but signs of fearfulness. Blurton Jones (1967) found that if shortly after entering a nursery school he returned the gazes of nursery children, they looked away and avoided him. Adult chronic mental patients responded to the presence of strange adults in their ward room by increasing 'way station' behaviour, i.e. making non-functional stops at certain objects in the room (e.g. water fountain), before walking away from the nearest stranger. This behaviour decreased significantly after six days' exposure to the strangers (Hershkowitz, 1962).

The equivalent to Southwick's (1967) finding that rhesus group members interacting most with intruders matched their age–sex class has not yet been analysed for children. But consistent sex and individual differences in reaction to strangers have been shown, e.g. the 'Little Mothers'. Washburn (1932) also noted this: one boy in the nursery she studied always approached a newcomer, observed him a few seconds, then hugged him. It would be interesting to seek correlations between a child's behaviour toward strangers and other behavioural characteristics.

It is difficult to compare the introduced individual's behaviour in the human and nonhuman studies because of the radically different group responses. Castell (1969) has stressed the 'collective aggression' of a group directed toward an introduced stranger in both squirrel monkeys and rhesus macaques. Bernstein (1969) observed three newcomer response types: strong defence against attack, attempts to initiate play/grooming with residents, and avoidance/escape attempts. The last somewhat approximates the new child's behaviour but there was no attack by residents as in the pigtail macaques. Again the closest nonhuman approximate was supplied by the gibbon: newcomers avoided most animals for the first few minutes but were engaging in usual types of social interaction within fifteen or so minutes (Bernstein and Schusterman, 1964).

If the new child is characterized as 'fearful' and 'uncertain' at nursery entry, many changes in frequency of specific patterns are explainable. For example, *looking* and *glancing* represent examples of visually exploring and monitoring the new environment and its inhabitants. An 'uncertain' child might be expected to do more visual shifting than usual because he can take nothing for granted: the potentially unpleasant unexpected is everywhere. In fact, *looking* and *glancing* significantly decreased in frequency over the first week, presumably as familiarity with the nursery increased. 74% of looking was child-oriented, and this could represent another indication of social as opposed to non-social novelty's importance. Washburn

(1932) recorded attention shifts (both social and non-social) during 3–3½-year-olds' first five minutes in nursery: all fourteen subjects exhibited observing behaviour. Intra-daily observations support the idea that amount of visual exploration decreases as ' uncertainty ' decreases. On the first day, mean frequencies for *looking* and *glancing* were high throughout all four quarters; from the second day on they decreased as the morning progressed.

Both *immobility* and *automanipulation* are indicators of ' fearfulness ', e.g. Washburn (1932) described as an extreme of newcomer behaviour a ' period of " frozen " observation ' which some children exhibited for the first five minutes. Both patterns seemed to occur in ' social stress ' situations: after losing a conflict, when crowded into a small space, while another child was being scolded. Grant (1965) described children's *automanipulation* as a displacement activity occurring in ambivalent situations. In another study (McGrew, 1969) subordinate pre-schoolers displayed significantly more *automanipulation* than dominant individuals, these labels being based on win–loss record in object struggles. *Immobility* and *automanipulation* decreased significantly in frequency as the first five-day period progressed, presumably reflecting decreasing fearfulness as familiarity with the nursery developed. The same trend existed within mornings: incidence decreased throughout the morning, especially during the first five-day period. The highest single mean frequency/quarter of both *automanipulation* and *immobility* occurred in the child's first twenty minutes of nursery school.

The demonstration of regular periodicity in children's behaviour could be an important variable neglected in most previous observational studies of children. In several cases it revealed differences masked by daily totals, e.g. daily means of *running* did not show significant short-term change, and *running* only increased significantly in the long-term comparison (see Table 5·4). However, increases in *running* over the morning were present from the child's first day in nursery (see Fig. 5·2). In addition to remaining unchanged in the short and long-term comparisons, *walking* was also unaltered over the morning.

It is unlikely that the periodicity was an artefact of the nursery or observational procedures. All observations were made during free play when children were undirected by adults, and the two daily play sessions were identical in routine and conditions. No difference in the observer's behaviour over quarters has been found, e.g. it is unlikely that ' observer fatigue ' was responsible, as some frequencies increased as well as decreased over the mornings. Some circadian activity rhythm may have been the source of quarterly differences, but 82 minutes/day is an insufficient sample for determining this. It is most likely that periodicity was related to the situation's social structure: each morning's arrival probably constituted a lesser repetition of the original introduction. Patterns which had tailed off the previous morning probably rose again the next morning in response to ending the overnight separation from the group and to renewal of group contacts. A consistent rate of recovery after waning of a pattern's frequency is a common behavioural phenomenon (e.g. Hinde, 1966: 211).

The significance of the possible sex differences is difficult to judge (e.g. apparent sex differences may result from differential maturation rates), but none was spectacular. Most short-term changes occurred in the same direction for both sexes, with one showing statistical significance, and all but one disappeared by the follow-up observation period. If any pattern emerged it was that boys seemed more fearful than girls at nursery introduction. They showed more significant drops in *immobility* and *auto-manipulation* over the first five days and lower initial frequency of locomotion (*walk, run*). However, girls exhibited more *looking* than boys, which may be another fearfulness measure. The one long-term sex difference (in *verbalization* not oriented to adults or children) was probably the result of frequent quasi-agonistic play shown by experienced boys but not girls. This involved considerable yelling back and forth across the room, much of which seemed undirected at any individual or was considered unassignable by the observer.

Long-term behavioural changes continued in the same direction as short-term and intra-daily ones, with one exception (*glance*) which is at present inexplicable. Most specific changes seem to fit well into the general picture of increased 'socialization'. But it is anticipated that after more pattern analysis, the picture will become more complicated. It will be interesting to see if within-day changes retain their apparent predictive utility for later short and long-term behavioural changes.

In summary, the socially 'naive' child entering the nursery was shown to exhibit significant behavioural changes within the first day, over the first five days, and over a long period of nursery experience. The direction of change was shown to be consistent, and this consistency was sometimes augmented by regular daily periodicity. These preliminary findings underline the importance of examining the 'socialization' process in detail; they emphasize that while 'socialization' is a time-consuming process it also appears to have important short-term facets. The use of knowledge derived from nonhuman primate research has re-emphasized the value of comparative studies, both as sources of stimulating ideas for expanding research and as help in interpreting and classifying results in an evolutionary framework.

Acknowledgements

The research was generously supported by grants from the Population Council (1968–9); the National Institute of Mental Health, U.S. Public Health Service (1969–70); and the Social Science Research Council (1968–70). The author is also grateful for aid and encouragement to: Prof. D. M. Vowles, Dr Margaret Manning, Mrs L. Bruce and Mrs P. L. McGrew.

APPENDIX

BRIEF DESCRIPTIONS OF BEHAVIOUR PATTERNS

1. *Back* – Walk backwards.
2. *Back step* – One unit of *back*.
3. *Beat* – Overarm blow with lightly clenched fist.
4. *Bite* – Hold object forcefully between teeth.
5. *Chew lips* – Press teeth against lips.
6. *Chin in* – Face forward and down, chin pressed to neck.
7. *Flee* – Run with arms flailing, frequent veering and direction changing, quick glances over shoulder.
8. *Flinch* – Shoulders flexed, face down and to side, arms flexed to shoulders.
9. *Forearm raise* – Forearm raised to horizontal position in front of head.
10. *Gaze fixate* – Eyes oriented to another's eyes, usually prolonged.
11. *Hand on back* – Palm placed on another's back.
12. *Head nod* – Head moved forward and down, then back and up.
13. *Head shake* – Head moved from side to side.
14. *Head tilt* – Head leaned sideways to diagonal position.
15. *Hold hands* – Grasp another's hand, palm-to-palm.
16. *Hug* – Arms flexed horizontally and toward trunk, encircling an object.
17. *Jump* – Extension of legs launches body into air, landing on flexed legs, two feet.
18. *Kick* – Leg rapidly extended toe-first.
19. *Kiss* – Protruded lips contact another.
20. *Laugh* – Series of short, rapid, open-mouthed vocalizations.
21. *Lean away* – Trunk extended at hips.
22. *Low frown* – Brows lowered and brought together.
23. *Pat* – Palm repeatedly touched to object.
24. *Pinch* – Thumb and forefinger pressed together.
25. *Play crouch* – Arms and legs partially flexed, feet wide apart, shoulders slightly hunched.
26. *Play face* – Mouth opened wide with corners up, teeth only partially visible.
27. *Pucker face* – Forehead and nose wrinkled, brows together with inner ends up, eyes screwed up.
28. *Pull* – Arms flexed to body, hands hold object.
29. *Push* – Arms extended from body, palms pressed to object.
30. *Red face* – Facial skin flushed.
31. *Rock* – Trunk moved back and forth or sideways, rhythmically repeated.
32. *Shoulder hug* – Arm is flexed around and on another's shoulders.
33. *Shrug* – Shoulders flexed and extended in rapid succession.
34. *Shuffle* – Feet moved repetitively while standing.
35. *Sidle* – Walk sideways.
36. *Slap* – Palm-first, sidearm blow with hand open.
37. *Slope* – Shoulders hunched, chin in, hands clasped together at waist.
38. *Smile* – Mouth partially open and corners up, eyes partially closed, teeth partially visible.
39. *Stamp* – Sole of foot moved forcefully down onto object.
40. *Suck* – Lips closed around object inserted into mouth.
41. *Turn* – Trunk rotated.
42. *Vocalize* – Laryngeal sound production.

43. Walk step – One unit of *walk*.
44. Weep – Tear secretion.
45. Wrestle – Gross body movement while grappled in physical contact with another.

REFERENCES

Bernstein, I. S. (1964). The integration of rhesus monkeys introduced to a group. *Folia primat.* **2**, 50–63.

Bernstein, I. S. (1969). Introductory techniques in the formation of pigtail monkey troops. *Folia primat.* **10**, 1–19.

Bernstein, I. S. and Draper, W. A. (1964). The behaviour of juvenile rhesus monkeys in groups. *Anim. behav.* **12**, 84–91.

Bernstein, I. S. and Schusterman, R. J. (1964). The activity of gibbons in a social group. *Folia primat.* **2**, 161–70.

Blurton Jones, N. G. (1967). An ethological study of some aspects of social behaviour of children in nursery school. In *Primate Ethology*. Ed. D. Morris, London: Weidenfeld and Nicolson.

Castell, R. (1969). Communication during initial contact: a comparison of squirrel and rhesus monkeys. *Folia primat.* **11**, 206–14.

Emmerich, W. (1964). Continuity and stability in early social development. *Child develop.* **35**, 311–32.

Gartlan, S. and Brain, C. K. (1968). Ecology and social variability in *Cercopithecus aethiops* and *C. mitis*. In *Primates: Studies in Adaptation and Variability*. Ed. P. C. Jay, New York: Holt Rinehart and Winston.

Grant, E. C. (1965). An ethological description of some schizophrenic patterns of behaviour. In *Proc. Leeds Symposium on Behavioural Disorders*, Dagenham: May & Baker.

Hall, K. R. L. (1965). Behaviour and ecology of the wild patas monkey, *Erythrocebus patas,* in Uganda. *J. Zool.* **148**, 15–87.

Harlow, H. F. and Harlow, M. K. (1969). Effects of various mother–infant relationships on rhesus monkey behaviours. In *Determinants of Infant Behaviour*, vol. 4. Ed. B. M. Foss, London: Methuen.

Hershkowitz, A. (1962). Naturalistic observations on chronically hospitalized patients: I. The effects of ' strangers '. *J. Nerv. ment. dis.* **135**, 258–64.

Hinde, R. A. (1966). *Animal behaviour. A synthesis of ethology and comparative psychology*. New York: McGraw-Hill.

Jersild, A. T. and Fite, M. D. (1939). The influence of nursery school social experience on children's social adjustments. *Child Develop. Monog.* **25**, 1–112.

Kawai, M. (1960). A field experiment on the process of group formation in the Japanese monkey (*Macaca fuscata*) and the releasing of the group at Ohirayama. *Primates* **2**, 181–253.

Lindburg, D. G. (1969). Rhesus monkeys: mating season mobility of adult males. *Science, N.Y.* **166**, 1176–8.

McCandless, B. R. and Marshall, H. R. (1957). Sex differences in social acceptance and participation of preschool children. *Child develop.* **28**, 421–5.

McGrew, W. C. (1969). An ethological study of agonistic behaviour in preschool children. In *Behaviour*. Ed. C. R. Carpenter, *Proc. Sec. Inter. Congress of Primatology*. Zurich: Karger.

McGrew, W. C. (in press). *An Ethological Study of Children's Behavior*. New York: Academic Press.

Ploog, D. W. and MacLean, P. D. (1963). Display of penile erection in squirrel monkey (*Saimiri sciureus*). *Anim. behav.* **11**, 32–9.

Raph, J. B., Thomas, A., Chess, S. and Korn, S. J. (1968). The influence of nursery school on social interactions. *Amer. J. orthopsychiat.* **38**, 144–52.

Reynolds, V. (1966). Open groups in hominid evolution. *Man.* (n.s.) **1**, 441–52.

Siegel, S. (1956). *Nonparametric statistics for the behavioral sciences.* New York: McGraw-Hill.

Southwick, C. H. (1967). An experimental study of intra-group agonistic behaviour in rhesus monkeys. *Behaviour* **28**, 182–209.

Stott, L. H. and Ball, R. S. (1957). Consistency and change in ascendance–submission in the social interaction of children. *Child develop.* **28**, 259–72.

Washburn, R. W. (1932). A scheme for grading the reactions of children in a new social situation. *J. genet. psychol.* **40**, 84–99.

6

REACTIONS OF PRE-SCHOOL CHILDREN
TO A STRANGE OBSERVER

KEVIN CONNOLLY AND PETER K. SMITH *

SUMMARY

Many studies of pre-school children have involved the presence of an observer in the nursery. The effect of his presence on the behaviour of the children is a problem of methodological importance and is also of interest in itself. An initial comparison of approaches to a male observer at a nursery school, a day nursery and a residential children's home revealed certain differences. There were fewest approaches to the observer on the part of the children in the nursery school and most from the children in the residential home. In the day nursery and nursery school the incidence of approach responses declined rapidly over a series of eight visits. These differences in behaviour might be due to the different environments or, to some extent, to a lack of parental care in the case of some of the children. A further study was made in three day nurseries using a carefully defined set of behavioural categories. The nurseries used in the experiment were closely similar in routine and physical environment. The same observer visited each nursery for five days in successive weeks, behaving completely passively at one nursery, smiling when approached at a second nursery, and both smiling and talking at a third. The conditions under which these responses were made by the observer were carefully defined. From time sampling observations over a one-hour period each day the kinds of approach made to the observer were classified into some seven main types. Almost all kinds of approach occurred with increased frequency at those nurseries where the observer responded to the children. In all three nurseries there was a tendency for younger children in the group to show more responses than the older ones. No consistent sex difference was found, nor was any difference found between children with or without their father in the home. This finding suggests that the nursery environment rather than the home background may be more important in accounting for the differences found between the children from the three institutions in the first study. A few children in the day nurseries, however, showed especially high levels of approach to the observer and for some of these the absence of a father-figure may be an important factor. Evidence was obtained of a decline in approach frequencies both through individual one-hour sessions and through successive weekday visits. It is concluded that, for the majority of children at least, responses to a passive observer in the nursery fall to a very low level within a few sessions.

Introduction

A great deal of the descriptive work carried out on pre-school children both recently and in the 1930s (see Smith and Connolly, Ch. 3) has entailed

* Department of Psychology, University of Sheffield.

the presence of an observer or observers in the nursery. The observer sits or moves around discretely, reacting little or not at all to the approaches made to him by the children. Alternative methods of observation have usually involved watching or filming children through a one-way screen; these facilities are not generally available in nursery institutions, however, and such methods often imply a rather artificial environment.

An implicit assumption in those studies where the observer has been present in the nursery is that any disruption of the usual environment caused by the presence of the observer will be short-lived, and that any reactions by the children will be few and will rapidly decline. His presence is thus regarded as not interfering with their 'natural' behaviour.

Even casual observations show, however, that there are often marked reactions to an observer on his first visit, and that there are considerable differences in this respect between different nursery institutions. Apart from the methodological importance of this problem, these observed differences in behaviour also require an explanation. The research reported in this chapter describes the kind of approaches which are made to an observer, and considers the importance of factors such as age, sex and family background of the children, as well as the particular kind of nursery. The effect of the observer's own behaviour is also considered.

The literature does not contain any previous systematic work in this area. Blurton Jones (1967) reported some casual observations on the kinds of approaches made by children in a nursery school and Kellmer Pringle (1965) includes some observations made whilst comparing children in nursery schools and residential nurseries. The only other related work with pre-school children has been where the child has been brought to a strange room or clinic (Shirley, 1942; Arsenian, 1943) or introduced to a nursery group (Heathers, 1954; McGrew, Ch. 5) but these situations are not really comparable. Morgan and Ricciutti (1969) described the reactions of infants between 4 and 13 months, with and without their mothers, to strangers, and Hershkowitz (1962) described 'way-station' behaviour on the part of chronic psychiatric patients entering a ward containing a stranger; this behaviour declined markedly over six sessions.

First study: comparisons between types of nursery

A preliminary study of four kinds of approach in three different types of nursery institutions was undertaken. The behaviours recorded and their operational definition were as follows:

Fixate – A sustained look of not less than four seconds directed at the observer.

Talk to – Any verbal behaviour consisting of two or more recognisable words directed to the observer. Squeals, shouts and play noises such as ' bang, bang ' were excluded, and also *requests*.

Physical contact – Any non-accidental physical contact between the child and the observer which was initiated by the child.

Requests – Requests made by the child to the observer. These were usually verbal such as 'pick me up' though some were by gesture, for example extending the arms up to the observer by way of request to be picked up.

The three institutions in which the investigation was carried out were as follows:

(1) A nursery school containing twenty-five children, administered by the Education Office. Ten children, five boys and five girls, were observed. Their mean age was 4 years 0 months.

(2) A day nursery with twenty-six children, under the direction of the Medical Officer of Health. Ten children, five boys and five girls were observed. Their mean age was 4 years 2 months.

(3) A residential children's home with eleven children, administered by the Children's Department. Seven children, four boys and three girls were observed. Their mean age was 4 years 0 months.

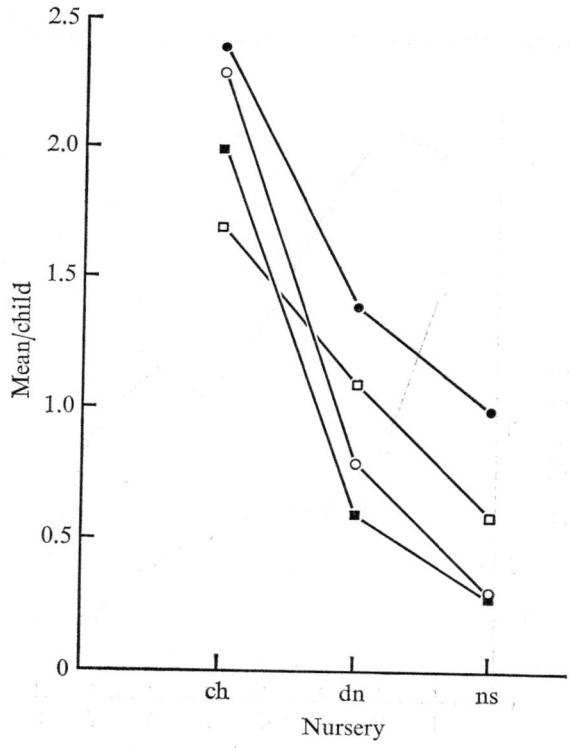

Fig. 6·1. Mean number of responses per child at children's home (ch), day nursery (dn) and nursery school (ns), for *fixate* (●), *talk to* (□), *physical contact* (○) and *requests* (■). Further details in text.

159

One visit was made to each nursery, each child being observed for a two-minute period. A time sample technique was employed and sampling of ongoing behaviour was carried out every ten seconds. The observer was positioned in the corner of a room and remained totally passive to all approaches.

TABLE 6·1. *Means per child at a children's home CH, a day nursery DN, and a nursery school SN, for four categories of approach to the observer. Significance levels for differences between nurseries (2-tailed Mann–Whitney U-test)*

	Mean			Significance level		
	CH	DN	SN	CH–DN	CH–SN	DN–SN
Fixate	2.4	1.4	1.0	0.02	0.02	(>0.1)
Talk	1.7	1.1	0.6	(>0.1)	0.02	(>0.1)
Request	2.0	0.6	0.3	0.02	0.02	(>0.1)
Physical contact	2.3	0.8	0.3	0.02	0.02	(>0.1)

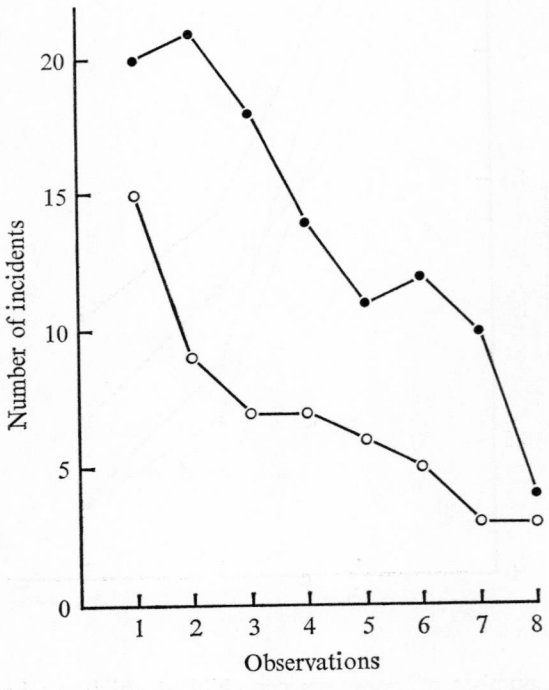

Fig. 6.2. Number of occurrences of *fixate* at day nursery (●), and nursery school (○), over eight successive observation periods. Further details in text.

Considerable and significant differences were found in the reactions to the observer for the three institutions (Fig. 6·1 and Table 6·1). All four approach behaviours were most frequent in the children's home and least frequent in the nursery school. Physical contacts and requests were especially common in the children's home, where approaches were sometimes very persistent and, besides stroking or leaning against the observer, included climbing on him and making forceful play requests or invitations.

Although these differences are reported for only one nursery of each type, they are not infrequently mentioned by people who have occasion to visit different nurseries, and have indeed been experienced by the authors at a variety of nurseries and institutions. The behaviour of the residential children is especially striking as regards physical contact, and suggests an abnormal disregard for the 'personal space' of the observer (Little, 1965). Several possible explanations present themselves. One is concerned simply with the immediate environment; the nursery school has most toys (especially paint, easels, jigsaw puzzles, etc.) which occupy a child's attention, whereas the day nursery and the children's home were less well

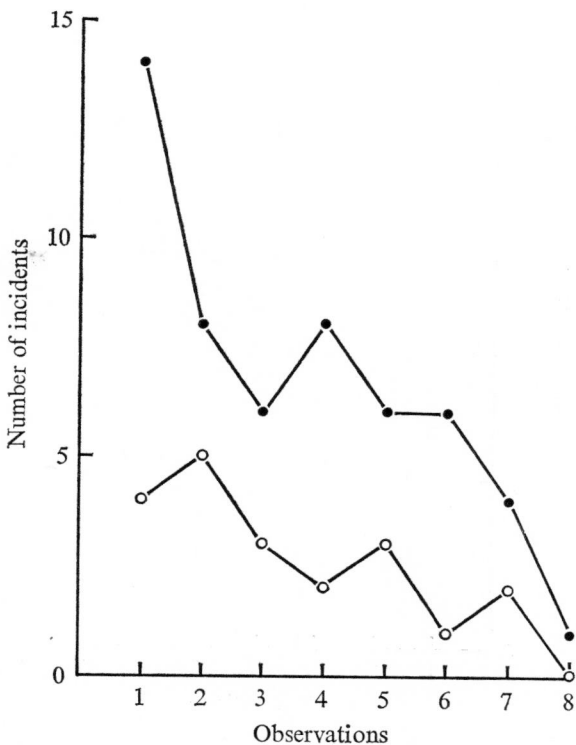

Fig. 6.3. Number of occurrences of *talk to* at day nursery (●) and nursery school (○), over eight successive observation periods. Further details in text.

equipped. In the case of the children's home it must be noted also that the playroom area was smaller (26ft×24ft compared with approximately 30ft×28ft for the other two) and the observer would be more conspicuous amongst a smaller number of children. Another factor which may be relevant is the frequency of visitors; in the children's home visitors are infrequent. In the case of all three institutions the staff were female whereas the observer was always a male. The effects of the number and sex of the observers were not investigated.

An alternative and perhaps more interesting explanation may lie in the home background of the children. The nursery school children came from an ostensibly stable family background with both parents present in the home. Many of the day nursery children came from broken homes, their mothers being divorced or unmarried; the absence of a father figure was common. The children in the children's home are in long-term residential care and they seldom see their parents (if, indeed, they have any known

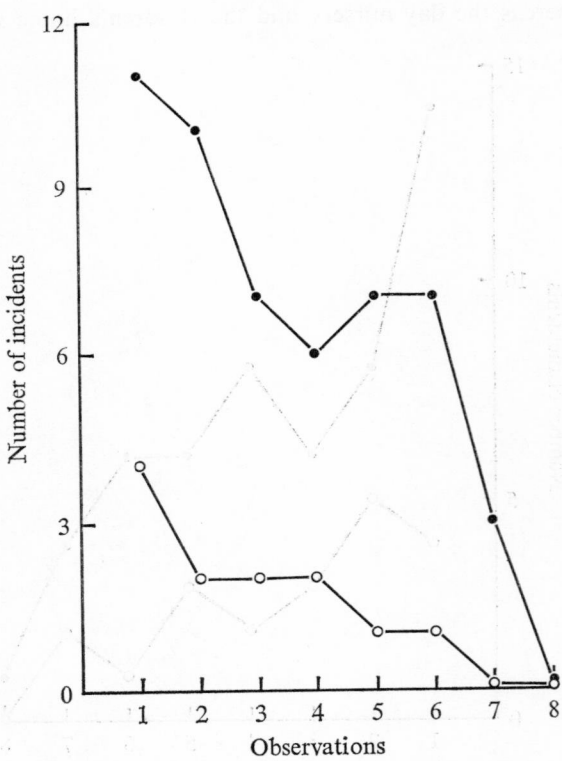

Fig. 6.4. Number of occurrences of *physical contact* at day nursery (●) and nursery school (○), over eight successive observation periods. Further details in text.

TABLE 6·2. *Means per child (over eight sessions) at a day nursery DN and a nursery school SN, for four categories of approach to the observer. Significance levels for differences between the two nurseries (2-tailed Mann–Whitney U-test)*

| | Mean | | Significance level |
	DN	SN	DN–SN
Fixate	10.9	5.5	0.001
Talk	5.3	2.0	just>0.1
Request	3.9	1.0	0.05
Physical contact	5.1	1.2	0.025

living parents). This suggests that 'parental deprivation' may be a contributory cause of the observed differences. This is discussed further below.

Data were also obtained on variations in the frequency of approach responses at the day nursery and nursery school in a series of eight sessions extending over a two-month period (Figs. 6·2, 6·3, 6·4 and 6·5 and Table 6·2). At each session each child was observed for five minutes, with ten-second ongoing sampling as before. It is apparent that there is a considerable

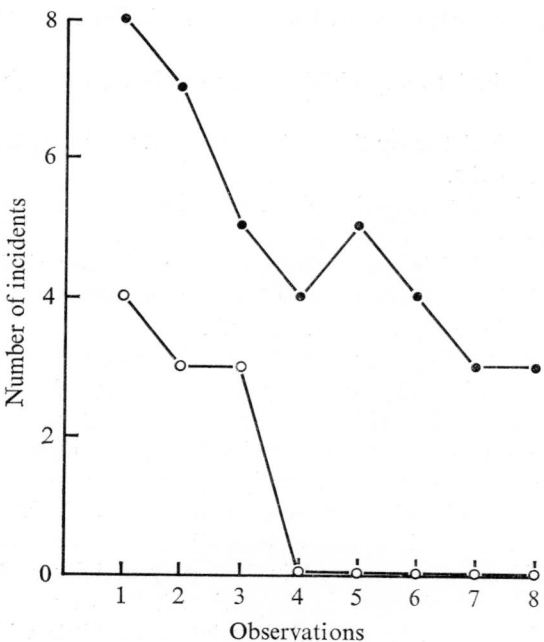

Fig. 6.5 Number of occurrences of *requests* at day nursery (●), and nursery school (○), over eight successive observation periods. Further details in text.

decline in all the responses over this period in both institutions, and the difference between the two nurseries is confirmed.

Second study: observer's behaviour and patterns of approach

A further study was subsequently made solely on day nursery children. Three nurseries (*A, B* and *C*) were visited. No observer had visited these nurseries for a period of at least four months previously. A considerably wider range of approach responses was recorded with the aim of looking for behavioural clusters of different kinds which might constitute patterns of approach. The investigation was also designed to examine possible differences among the day nursery children, between those with both parents as compared to those with only one parent. This was an attempt to explore further the ' parental deprivation ' hypothesis while controlling the factor of nursery environment as far as possible.

An additional aim of the study was to examine the effects of the observer's reactions to the approaches made by the children. This could not be accomplished at one nursery, because of the inevitable confounding of the results due to a temporal decline in responses. Instead the observer behaved differently, but consistently, at each of the nurseries. The three nurseries used were chosen because of their similarity in design and available equipment, and also because each had a similar number and kind of children:

(1) Nursery *A* had twenty children (eleven boys, nine girls), mean age 3 years 9 months.

(2) Nursery *B* had twenty-three children (thirteen boys, ten girls), mean age 3 years 5 months.

(3) Nursery *C* had twenty-six children (twelve boys, fourteen girls), mean age 3 years 6 months.

Although not identical in composition the nurseries are similar enough to make it improbable that differences of any magnitude can be attributed to small differences in group size and so forth.

The observer visited each nursery for one hour (between 9.45 and 10.45) each morning from Monday to Friday, the three nurseries being visited on consecutive weeks. A few children who were present on fewer than three mornings at any nursery have been omitted from the nursery compositions above and from all subsequent analyses. On entering the nursery the observer positioned himself near the centre of one wall, clear from toys or any obstruction. Recording began immediately. During the observation period the children were engaged in free play activity and could almost always approach the observer as they wished. Two or three nurses were present in each nursery. In general they interacted little with the children apart from stopping fights and comforting any child who was distressed.

At nursery *A* the observer assumed a totally passive attitude to the child;

he adopted a neutral expression at all times and did not look at the children (apart from the glances necessary for observation), smile, talk or make any other overt responses. At nursery *B* he met a child's glances and smiled at any child making an approach (see operational definition below) and repeated this once a minute if the approach was maintained, no other responses being made. At nursery *C* in addition to looking and smiling the observer replied to vocal initiations by a child, typically with one or two word replies such as 'hello', or 'yes', but so as to make a sensible reply in the context. If offered a toy he took it, looked at it briefly and then returned it, or if the child had moved away he put it on the floor. Brief vocal acknowledgements ('uh-huh', 'that's nice') were made when shown a painting or a toy. Play invitations were declined with 'sorry' or 'I'm busy'. No other responses were made.

A sample time of one minute was used; each minute a record was taken of every child making an approach. An approach was defined as the child being within six to seven feet of the observer and: either *fixating* him or *glancing* at him several times, or *talking* to him, or making physical contact with him, or *holding out an object* to him. Details of each approach were recorded in coded form using the behaviour categories defined below. This could normally be achieved satisfactorily though 'information overload' was experienced at nurseries *B* and *C* at the commencement of observations on the first two days.

DEFINITION OF BEHAVIOUR CATEGORIES

The categories listed below were selected, and their use practised, on the basis of extensive unstructured observations at a fourth nursery. For brevity the observer is referred to as *O*.

Glances – Several looks of less than two to three seconds duration at *O*.

Fixate – A look lasting for three seconds or more at *O*.

Smile – Corners of mouth withdrawn and turned upwards. No distinction was made as to mouth open or closed, teeth visible or not. No audible vocalisation.

Laugh – Open-mouthed smile together with audible vocalisation (rapid or staccato expulsion of breath).

Talk – Any utterance containing one or more recognisable words, excluding exclamations ('oh', 'ah') or *play noise*, directed at *O*.

Play noise – Vocalisations other than *talk* or *laugh*, including noises made in play such as 'brr-brr', 'bang' and also repeated or stereotyped phrases such as 'I am Batman'.

Walk up to – Walk up to within 3–4 feet of *O*.

Walk up and past – Walk towards and then past *O* but coming within 3–4 feet.

Walk past – Walk past *O* tangentially, passing within 3–4 feet.

Run up to – Run up to within 3–4 feet of *O*.

Run up and past – Run towards and then past *O* but coming within 3–4 feet.

Run past – Run past *O* tangentially, passing within 3–4 feet.

Situated at distance – Remaining more than 3–4 feet away from *O* (although making an approach, as previously defined).

Sit close facing – Sit or crouch within 3–4 feet, body oriented to *O*, stationary.

Stand close facing – Stand within 3–4 feet, body oriented to *O*, stationary.

Sit next to – Sit or crouch within 1½ feet, body not oriented to *O*, stationary.

Hold out object – Object held in hand, arm extended to *O*.

Show object – Object held in hand, child and object oriented to *O*, arm not extended.

With toy – Holds object in hand.

Suck – Digit or object in contact with one or both lips.

Point – Arm extended outwards but not in contact with object, looks or stares in same direction.

Touch – Gentle physical contact with *O*, by hand or similarly limited part of body. If contact made by toy then this is noted.

Hit – Hard physical contact with *O*, such as to cause pain, swift ballistic movement.

Lean against – Both feet on the ground, gross bodily contact with *O*.

Climb on – One or both feet off the ground, gross bodily contact with *O*.

In group – Child currently engaged in activity with other children.

RESULTS

The commonly occurring approach patterns listed below are derived from impressions gained in the course of making the observations and from inspection of the records at the end of the study, in the course of which each approach was assigned to one of these patterns. In some cases the records in themselves are not sufficiently detailed to allow the fuller descriptions given below, for example, the variants of pattern (vii).

(i) Child *fixates O* from a distance, usually while alone. He may be stationary, perhaps *sucking* finger or thumb, or moving past *O*. Sometimes returns a smile, occasionally *smiles* or *laughs* spontaneously. Relatively inactive if on apparatus.

(ii) *Fixates* or *glances* several times whilst passing in chasing or moving games. *Smiling* common though may be occurring anyway before *O* fixated.

(iii) *Fixates* and *talks* to *O* from a distance, often in a group or near other children, sometimes *smiles* or *points*. May be relatively inactive on apparatus.

(iv) *Walks up to* and *stands facing O, fixates*. Often, though not always, alone. May *smile* if smiled at. Occasionally *sits* or *stands next to*. May say 'hello'. Alternatively the child *walks past O* and 'hovers around'. In a somewhat different pattern, the child is crying, *fixates* or *walks up to O* and stays close to him.

(v) *Walks* or *runs up to O*, usually alone, may *fixate*. *Stands facing O* and *holds out* object as if it is to be taken. (If object taken by *O* child usually walks or runs away.) May say 'look' or something similar or 'ah'. Sometimes *smiles*.

(vi) *Walks*, or usually *runs up* and *past*. Child usually *in a group* and playing with toys. *Fixates*, usually *smiles* or *laughs*, makes *play noises* or *talks*. This pattern is quite different from (ii) in that child is much more oriented to O. In addition to vocalisations may wave a toy or *point*. Subsequently the child may make a pattern (vii) approach.

(vii) *Walks or runs up to O*, often with a toy or on a toy, stands facing O, *talks* or makes *play noises*. Often holds out or shows an object to O. More rarely physical contact is made, usually touching with the hand.

Variant (*a*). Usually *in a group*; usually *smiles* or *laughs*. Typical vocalisations are ' bang' (waving a gun) or 'Look, I've got an ice cream' (showing imaginary ice cream). These may be play invitations.

Variant (*b*). Often *smiles* before *walking* or *running up*; vocalisations are of an informational nature rather than a play invitation, e.g. 'there's a plane' (*pointing*), 'I'm going to a party tomorrow', 'We're playing over there'. The distinction from variant (*a*) may be one of degree only. Another common vocalisation was, 'What you doin' mister?', frequently accompanied by touching O's clipboard or stopwatch.

Variant (*c*). Usually alone and does not smile, vocalises in request context; 'Look' (holds out shoe which he cannot put on) or 'I've got a pain

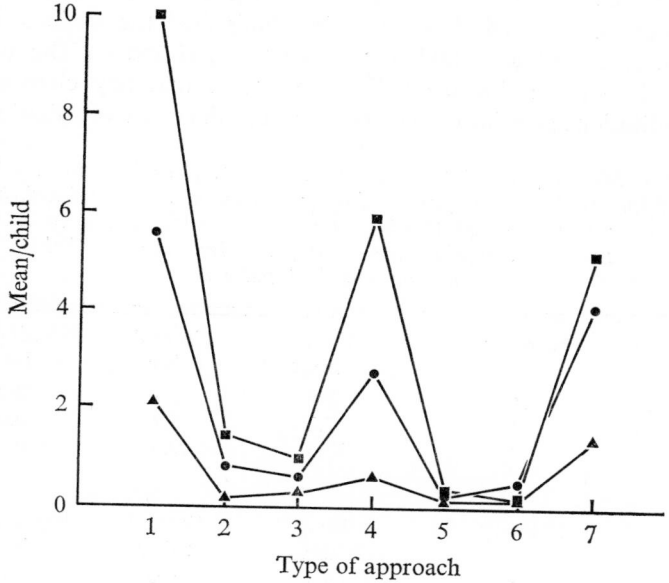

Fig. 6.6. Means per child for different types of approach at nursery *A* (▲), nursery *B* (●), and nursery *C* (■). Further details in text.

167

here' (shows arm). The crying variant of (iv) might be more appropriately placed here.

All the approaches could be placed in one of these patterns, though it must be made clear that pattern (vii) covers a number of approaches which may well have different motivations. Unfortunately further analysis of pattern (vii) is precluded by the limitations of the data obtained. Patterns (i), (v) and (vii, *a*) seem to correspond to those mentioned by Blurton Jones (1967) for nursery school children.

TABLE 6·3. *Means per child (over five sessions) at day nurseries A, B and C, for total number of approaches to the observer and for three categories of approach. Significance levels for differences between nurseries (2-tailed Mann–Whitney U-test)*

	Mean			Significance level		
Total	*A*	*B*	*C*	*A−B*	*B−C*	*A−C*
approaches	4.6	12.9	23.1	0.002	0.05	0.001
Smile	0.9	7.3	9.0	0.001	(>0.1)	0.002
Talk	1.0	3.6	6.0	0.1	(>0.1)	0.05
Physical contact	0.5	0.7	0.4	(>0.1)	(>0.1)	(>0.1)

For these day nursery children, patterns (i), (iv) and (vii) are much the most common. Fig. 6·6 shows the distribution of the various kinds of approach, as means per child, for nurseries *A*, *B* and *C*. The categories correspond to those documented above except that any close approach with vocalisations goes into (vi) or (vii) because the exact vocalisations could

TABLE 6·4. *Means per child at day nurseries A, B and C, for total number of approaches (a) for first half-hour compared to second half-hour (over five sessions) (b) for first two days compared to last two days. Significance levels for differences (2-tailed Wilcoxen matched pairs test)*

(a)	Nursery	First ½ hour	Second ½ hour	Significance level
	A	2.5	2.1	0.02
	B	7.2	5.7	0.05
	C	13.5	9.6	0.01

(b)	Nursery	First 2 days	Second 2 days	Significance level
	A	2.4	1.3	0.05
	B	5.6	4.0	0.1
	C	11.6	7.8	0.01

often not be recorded. This probably leads to an underestimate of pattern (v). A similar distribution of types of response is present in each nursery though approaches are most frequent at nursery *C* and least at nursery *A*.

This difference between the nurseries is also apparent in Fig. 6·7, where the mean per child for total approaches, total *smiles*, total *talks* and total *physical contacts* * are shown. Means and significance levels are given in Table 6·3.

The temporal variation of approach responses showed some irregularity, but evidence for their decline is given in Table 6·4*a* and *b*. Table 6·4*a* compares approaches made in the first half-hour to those in the second half-hour (mean for five days). Table 6·4*b* compares approaches made on Monday plus Tuesday with those made on Thursday plus Friday.

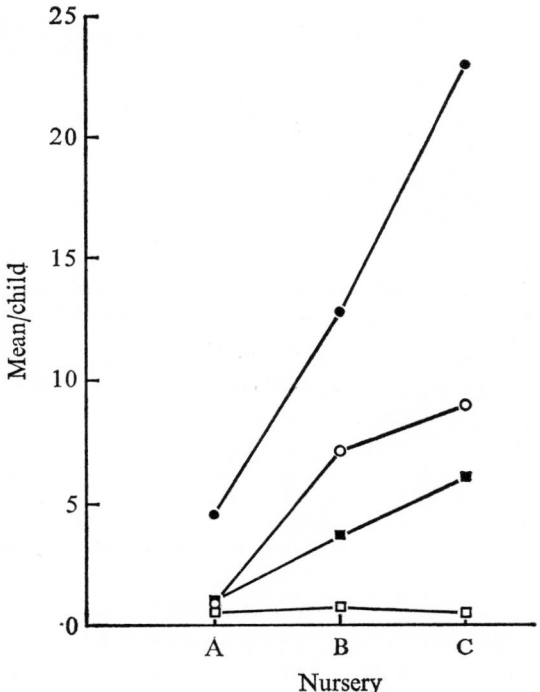

Fig. 6.7. Means per child for total number of approaches (●), number of *smiles* (○), number of *talks* (■), and number of *physical contacts* (□), at nurseries *A*, *B*, and *C*. Further details in text.

While more detailed evidence of decline in approaches could no doubt be obtained with a longer run of sessions, these results do agree with the general impression of the authors that after a week or two's visits to a nursery

---

* *Touch, hit* and *lean against.*

the observer is largely ignored and the children's behaviour is not disturbed (cf. Hershkowitz, 1962). Sometimes indeed it is evident that children will fight or 'misbehave' in the proximity of the observer but will look guilty or stop as soon as a nurse or teacher appears.

Inasmuch as overt approaches to the observer provide a satisfactory measure it would appear that the completely passive attitude most quickly

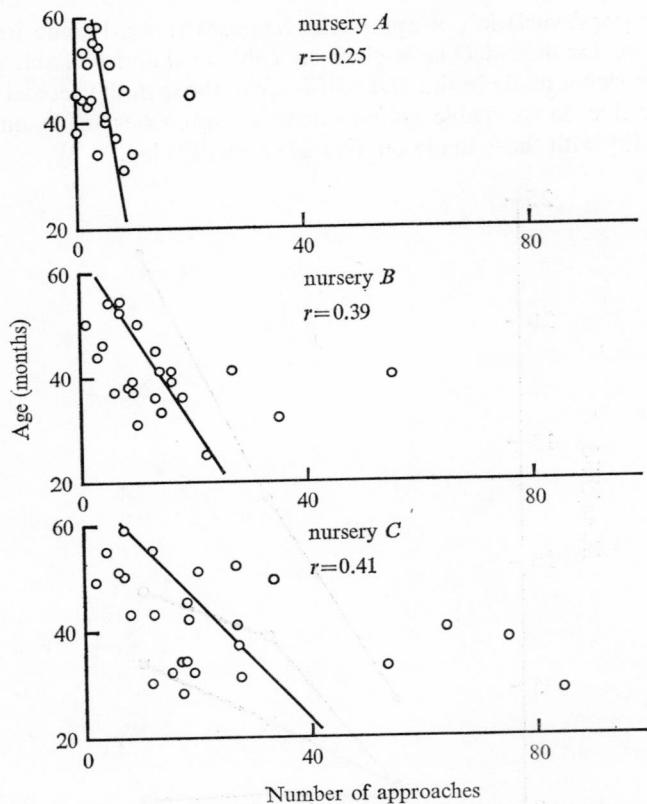

Fig. 6·8. Scatter diagrams of number of approaches made by each child, against age in months, for nurseries A, B, and C, with regression lines of number of *approaches* on age. Further details in text.

results in the children ignoring the observer.† At the end of the week at nursery A each child was making on average well under one approach per hour, and about half of these were only staring from a distance.

The difference between nurseries A and B, which is due entirely to the observer's facial expression, is striking and supports the notion that a smile

† This does not preclude the possibility that the presence of the observer affected behaviours which were not directed to him.

has a definite communicatory function to children of this age. The possibility remains however that the greater number of approaches is due simply to the fact that facial expression changes (irrespective of how it changes). A frowning or 'threat face' observer would provide a suitable control for this.

The total number of approaches made by the children in the three nurseries is shown in Fig. 6·8. No stable sex differences emerged but there is clearly a prevalent tendency for younger children to make rather more approaches. The correlation of total approaches with age are; nursery A, -0.25 ($p > 0.1$), nursery B, -0.39 ($p < 0.1$), nursery C, -0.41 ($p < 0.05$). This may be simply because the older children tend to play in groups, often in semi-organised activity, and hence would not notice the observer so often. Dependence on adults (i.e. teachers) has been found to correlate negatively with popularity and age (McCandless, Bilous and Bennet, 1961).

A further point of interest from the graphs is that at each nursery there are one or a few children who make an unusually high number of approaches. These children appear to be of two kinds; sociable children who often make play invitations, trying to incorporate the observer into a group game which they are already playing, or alternatively rather isolated children who appear to like being close to the observer, and are either relatively inactive, or make tentative invitations for the observer to play or interact. Although no definite data are available experience suggests that these kinds of children may continue making approaches now and then to a passive observer, even after several weeks. For such children the assumption that the observer's presence does not change the child's behaviour is not entirely justified.

The parental circumstances of the children are sometimes difficult to determine accurately, the children 'without fathers' may frequently see their grandparents or the mother may be living with another man. Nevertheless from the available information there were no reliable indications that children without fathers made more total approaches than those having both parents. This throws doubt on the 'parental deprivation' hypothesis advanced to explain the findings from the pilot study and suggests rather that the nursery environment may be the principal variable. This is in agreement with certain conclusions drawn by Kellmer Pringle (1965) who compared children in residential nurseries with those in nursery schools, but from similarly impoverished homes. In addition to being less advanced in language development and less active or assertive in play, the residential children sought adult attention much more actively.

It is possible that those children in residential nurseries who pay a great deal of attention to adults are similar to the isolated kind of 'high approachers' in the day nurseries (in fact all three of the latter in our sample were without fathers). This may indicate that parentally-deprived children are more inclined to seek the attention of adults but that the moderately stimulating environment, with toys and other children, of a day nursery or nursery school, is sufficient to markedly reduce this attention-seeking for all but a few children. What remains to be discovered is what is missing in the residential nursery environment where this type of approach seems to be so much more common.

A more detailed comparative study of the kinds of approaches made in different institutions, perhaps in terms of the patterns described above, would be of value here. It would also be interesting to look at approaches made to a female observer, as compared to a male. A female observer would have less 'curiosity' value in the nursery, and perhaps also with respect to the home environment; thus the sex of the observer may be an important variable.

Acknowledgements

The authors are grateful to the Medical Officer of Health and the Director of Education of the City of Sheffield and the staff at the various nurseries for their help and cooperation. One of us (P. K. S.) is in receipt of a research studentship from the Medical Research Council which is gratefully acknowledged. The authors are grateful to K. Davis for his valuable assistance in this investigation.

REFERENCES

Arsenian, J. M. (1943). Young children in an insecure situation. *J. abnorm. Soc. Psychol.* **38**, 235–49.

Blurton Jones, N. G. (1967). An ethological study of some aspects of social behaviour of children in nursery school. In *Primate ethology*. Ed. D. Morris, London: Weidenfeld and Nicolson.

Heathers, G. (1954). The adjustment of two-year-olds in a novel social situation. *Child Develop.* **25**, 147–58.

Hershkowitz, A. (1962). Naturalistic observations on chronically hospitalised patients: 1: The effects of 'strangers'. *J. nerv. ment. Dis.* **135**, 258–64.

Kellmer Pringle, M. C. (1965). Language difficulties among emotionally deprived children. In *Children with Communication Problems*. Ed. A. W. Franklin, London: Pitman.

Little, K. B., (1965). Personal space. *J. exp. soc. Psychol.* **1**, 237–47.

McCandless, B. R., Bilous, C. B. and Bennet, H. L. (1961). Peer popularity and dependence on adults in preschool-age socialisation. *Child Develop.* **32**, 511–18.

Morgan, G. A. and Ricciuti, H. N. (1969). Infants' responses to strangers during the first year. In *Determinants of Infants' Behaviour*. vol. 4. Ed. B. M. Foss, London: Methuen.

Shirley, M. M. (1942). Children's adjustments to a strange situation. *J. abnorm. Soc. Psychol.* **37**, 201–17.

MOTHER–CHILD INTERACTIONS

7

AN OBSERVATIONAL STUDY OF MOTHER–INFANT INTERACTION

M. P. M. RICHARDS AND JUDITH F. BERNAL *

SUMMARY

This paper describes the methods used in an observational study of mother–infant interaction and some of the theoretical assumptions which dictated their choice. It is argued that the analysis of the interaction requires very detailed behavioural data and that this may only be obtained by direct observation. The importance of using data from several levels of analysis is stressed and this is illustrated by some preliminary results which compare breast- and bottle-feeding mothers and their infants and analyse some of the effects of obstetric medication on the infant and his behaviour with his mother.

Introduction

This paper describes the aims, methods and some preliminary results of an observational study of mother–infant interaction. Though interest in observational studies of human behaviour has increased in this country in recent years, the movement has not been without its critics. Much of this criticism seems to be based on a misunderstanding of the purposes of these investigations. As few accounts of observational work have been published – since much of it is still in the early exploratory stages – such misunderstanding is not surprising. Confusion has been increased by the recent spate of popular books on human ethology which contain theoretical assumptions very different from those which underlie our research. We hope to dispel some of the criticism by describing our aims and methods. We will also discuss some of the theoretical and practical considerations behind our decisions to use particular methods. We believe it is particularly important to do this in a relatively new field lest methods become traditional and generally accepted for no better reason than some one person's initial decision to do things in that way.

Though there are many similarities between our methods and those used in other observational studies, there are also differences which reflect the varying theoretical positions held by the investigators and the different problems they study. This paper can in no sense be a credo for the entire field.

* Unit for Research on the Medical Applications of Psychology, University of Cambridge.

The aim of our research is threefold. We want to describe some of the behaviour of an infant in his first year of life and some aspects of the environment in which he grows up, and to attempt an assessment of the influences of this environment, particularly the mother's behaviour, on the course of his development. We assume a two-way behavioural interaction between the mother and her child: the behaviour of each will be influenced by, and will in turn partially determine, the behaviour of the other.

Our task is not only to study the actual interaction, but also to provide relatively independent measures of the elements each participant brings to the situation. Though we cannot rear children in motherless environments, nor observe maternal behaviour in the absence of a child, by examining a series of mother–infant interacting pairs we may hope to discover the direction and effects of some of the influences which constitute this inter-action. This has been done in other primate species (e.g. Hinde and Spencer-Booth, 1968).

There is much evidence to show that individual infants do not respond to the same stimuli or experiences in the same way (e.g. Schaffer, 1966), and therefore the same style of maternal care may have very varied develop-mental consequences for different children. This makes it important to assess individual differences between infants, as far as possible independently of the mother, in the hope that characteristics related to differential respon-siveness to maternal behaviour may be isolated and also so that the infant characteristics influencing maternal behaviour may be detected. To make this assessment independently of the mother turns out to be more difficult than was anticipated, because there is reason to believe that, by the eighth day, an infant's behaviour has been moulded by his previous interactions with his mother (see below).

We also want to make an independent assessment of the mother's maternal behaviour. This presents problems. Even if the mother is absent, almost all of the infant's waking behaviour is of a sort that might, at some time or other, elicit a response from the mother, and is therefore potentially part of the interaction process and relevant to the infant's role in interaction. This is not true of the mother. A large range of her behaviour is not directly related to the infant and is unlikely ever to enter into the inter-action between them. For this reason the only behaviour on the part of the mother which enables us to estimate her responsiveness and her role in the interaction is her behaviour during the interaction itself. Further information may be obtained by examining characteristics and behaviour of the mother, which, while not immediately infant-directed, are likely to be related to maternal behaviour; for example, attitudes towards various aspects of infant care. We also are looking at mothers with two successive infants, whenever the opportunity arises, as a further way of disentangling the respective roles of the mother and infant in the interaction.

Our basic design is thus to assess the development over the first sixty weeks of a particular kind of infant interacting with a particular kind of mother. We describe the infant in terms of his behaviour seen soon after birth and during later observation periods, and his status in relation to other more general variables such as birth order and sex. The mother is described by our observations of her interaction with her infant and her parity, social and educational position, and the more nebulous categories of her attitudes to feeding, permissiveness and so on.

Work of the kind we are going to describe is often referred to as ethological. Ethologists study the behaviour of animal species in their own right rather than using them as experimental systems for the investigation of such processes as learning or perception, according to the more traditional psychological approach. They have stressed that the behaviour of a species is adapted to its environment, as is its morphology, and this belief leads them to watch animals in their natural settings with a minimum of interference or disturbance. We are trying to do the same for our own species. Unlike the animal ethologists we are able to ask questions of our subjects and investigate their attitudes and intentions. So alongside the observations we use a variety of interview techniques; not to do so would be to throw away a vital part of the available evidence. Our methods must at least approach the complexity of the phenomena we set out to investigate.

As well as collecting various kinds of information (such as the observations and interviews), we try to obtain data at several levels of analysis, from the sociological to the neurological and physiological. Our procedures are not reductionist, but arise from our conviction that analysis at a single level may be seriously misleading and must restrict explanation to the single level chosen. Spreading our analysis widely means that we cannot be as thorough and detailed at any one level as we could be by concentrating our efforts more narrowly. We regard this as the lesser of the two evils. The ways in which we use our multilevel analysis are illustrated in the final section of this paper.

Reasons for using observational methods

Before going on to the description of our methods, we must explain why we set such store by the use of direct observation. It might be argued that interview techniques would produce all the information we require, and would be far more economical in time and trouble. We have two general objections to interview techniques. Information required by the interviewer may be forgotten or distorted to fit into the interviewee's conception of what the interviewer expects (e.g. Colombotos, Elinson and Loewenstein, 1968). Behaviour which the interviewee regards as culturally unacceptable may not be reported. These kinds of effects can be reduced by training interviewers not to make any value judgements and not to show surprise however bizarre or strange reported behaviour may seem to them, but they cannot be eliminated entirely. For example, Newson and Newson (1963) found that replies from mothers about child rearing depended on whether the interviewers were health visitors or trained university personnel and, though one may speculate about the differences, there is no way of knowing which set of replies is a closer approximation to the truth. Little can be done about forgotten information. Several studies have shown this to be an important source of bias, even for things as neutral as the infant's birth weight (e.g. Minde, Webb and Sykes, 1958).

These are minor difficulties compared with our second objection. Experience with other primate species (e.g. Hansen, 1966; Rosenblum and Kaufman, 1967; Jensen, Bobbitt and Gordon, 1968; Hinde and Spencer-Booth, 1968) has indicated that very detailed records of behaviour are required to sort out interactions as complex as those between a mother and her infant. No mother can possibly remember events at the required level of detail; could she be expected to know how many times she smiled at her infant during a feed, and what were the stimuli evoking her smiles? Given that we believe behavioural interchange and sequences of this kind are important and significant, and that analysis must be made at this level of fine detail, observation is the only possible technique of investigation.

A common objection to this kind of analysis is that it is only concerned with very fine (and perhaps trivial) details and that it will miss the broad patterns and higher level characteristics of behaviour. But how are we to assess these more molar behavioural characteristics? Traditionally this has been done by deriving them from a pre-existing theoretical framework and then evolving rating scales or observational systems for their measurement. Dichotomies of maternal behaviour like permissiveness–restrictiveness have grown up in this way. When one sets out to characterise mothers on such dimensions there are great difficulties in fitting the observed behaviour into the dimensions. For example, a mother may be very permissive in determining the times of feeds, but highly restrictive and controlling during each feed. Our approach, like that of the ethologists, is to produce the more global categories from the fine level analysis, rather than the other way round. By the analysis of temporal and functional sequences we aim to produce constellations of associated behaviour which constitute the higher level categories. So, for example, we do not begin with a category called maternal stimulation. Instead we record the mother talking to, smiling at, holding and touching the infant, and we examine the associations between each of these low-level categories to see whether they give rise to more global patterns.

The other general objection to observational techniques is that we will never see 'real' behaviour as our presence will disturb the mother too much. It is our impression, as that of others who have observed mother–infant interaction (e.g. Levy, 1958; Moss, 1965) that mothers show few signs of nervousness or distraction. When asked in retrospect, most mothers report that they feel undisturbed during observation, perhaps because we emphasise to them that we are primarily interested in their infants. Breast-feeding mothers might be expected to be more disturbed by a male rather than a female observer. Our results do not support such a conclusion. Furthermore, behaviour which the mothers expect the observer to dis-approve of (e.g. reading during breast feeding, hitting small infants) is sometimes seen. The frequency of certain behaviour patterns (e.g. talking to infant) may be reduced by our presence but we assume that, even with these minor distortions, our records will have some fairly lawful relation to what would occur in our absence.

It might be thought that the removal of the observer from the situations, perhaps behind a one-way screen, would solve this problem. But it is our experience that mothers find it much more disturbing and 'unnatural' to be watched by an unseen observer than by someone they can see. Our technique is to sit unobtrusively in the room and to talk as little as possible to the mother while recording. Most mothers soon come to respect this convention and talk very little to the observer during the actual observation.

We have found that very good rapport is usually established with the mother after the first visit, perhaps partly through our being with them at moments of great intimacy and importance, and that although the mother may not be behaving as she would alone, the situation is no more disturbed than it would be by the presence of a friend of the mother.

Description of methods

To simplify the following discussion we will consider only the part of the project covering the perinatal period; the follow-up visits made at 8, 12, 20, 30 and 60 weeks will be described in a future publication. We hope that this

TABLE 7·1. *Outline of procedures used in the perinatal period*

2–6 weeks before delivery	Description of the project to mother, collection of medical, social and attitude information.
Delivery	Pre-coded medical information recorded by midwife. Observation of first mother–infant interaction and infant behaviour (when an observer is present).
Days 2, 3, 8, 9, 10	Observation of a feeding session and collection of attitude and interview information.
Days 0–10	24-hour mother's diary.
Day 8 or 9	Neurological examination of infant, sucking test and test of visual responsiveness.
Day 10	Rating of mother on attitude measures.

description of the methods used in the perinatal period will illustrate the general principles behind the methodology of the whole. An outline of the perinatal procedures is given in Table 7·1.

THE SAMPLE

In the selection of the sample, we have been guided by both theoretical and practical considerations. Because we initially chose to work with home-delivered infants * (homes provide a more informal atmosphere for observation, less bound by a rigid routine) and to contact the mothers through the district midwives, we are limited to the geographical area of their operation, the City of Cambridge. From this area we wanted a group of 'normal' married mothers and their first and second-born children. In an attempt to reduce the variability of the sample further, we exclude non-British parents and the two extremes of the distribution of socio-economic class. Our criteria of 'normality' are mostly derived from the Perinatal Mortality Survey (Butler and Bonham, 1963) and cover about thirty-five maternal, foetal and delivery factors. Our criteria are stricter than those used locally for hospital booking though not quite as severe as Prechtl's (1968) definition of optimal obstetric conditions. In the future we plan to compare our 'normal' sample with various 'abnormal' samples.

Our first idea was to build our sample so that it represented the distribution of socio-economic class found in the whole Cambridge population. On the assumption that many aspects of maternal behaviour are related to social class, this would allow findings to be generalised to the whole of Britain using the appropriate correction for the local idiosyncrasies of social class distribution. For several reasons we have abandoned this aim.

In particular, we are impressed by the wide differences between geographical subcultures which may make generalisation on a social class basis meaningless. So now we aim to provide a description and analysis of behaviour for the sample we have selected in Cambridge. We hope that some of our findings will be applicable to other populations in Britain and elsewhere but we do not assume this *a priori*, and regard it as an empirical question. Furthermore, a rigid use of traditional social class classifications may lead to the setting up of the typology of 'the middle class' and 'the working class mother and child' rather than focusing on a more ecological analysis (see Richards, 1971).

The district midwives in Cambridge give us names of mothers who fulfil our criteria, and talk to the mothers about the project before we see them – this is probably a reason for our low refusal rate (less than 10% of the mothers we approach) – and they exercise an unknown amount of selection

* Early in 1969 the policy for selection for hospital delivery in Cambridge was changed. Now all primipares are given the opportunity of hospital delivery. Therefore we are attempting to collect equal numbers of hospital-delivered, 48-hour discharge mothers in each of our subsamples.

against mothers they do not think are likely to co-operate with us. The extent of some of these biases will be checked as we are planning an analysis of data from the whole population we sample using the midwives' records.

At the initial visit the project is described to the mother and the procedures and visits are discussed with the emphasis that we are interested in the behaviour of the infant rather than the mother. This interview is made up of 120 pre-coded and open-ended questions. It includes fairly standard sociological questions concerning the education and occupation of the mother, husband and grandparents, and about the amount of contact between members of the family. Medical data on this and previous pregnancies is obtained, and the midwives' records are also consulted. Some rather detailed questions are asked about intended family size and contraceptive methods; we are interested to see whether attitudes on this subject are related to behaviour with children, and whether the experience of having children alters the attitudes; similar questions are asked later in the project as the children grow up. Attitudes and intentions about infant feeding are explored so that we may see how far they are related to observed behaviour. Other questions cover preferences about the sex of the child; this seems important when differences in behaviour towards children of each sex are to be looked at later on.

DELIVERY

In cases where the general practitioner and midwife have given their permission, we ask the mother if we may attend her delivery. All three agree in about half our cases. We want to be present to record the first mother–infant interaction, and to examine the early (particularly visual) behaviour of the infant. Pre-coded categories of behaviour are not recorded at this visit; instead a shorthand account is written of what occurs from the beginning of the second stage of labour until after the infant is bathed. If there is a period when the infant is left alone in his cot, as often happens during the third stage of labour, we concentrate on describing his behaviour and may attempt to elicit visual tracking.

When an observer is not present at delivery, the midwife records some basic medical data on a pre-coded form. This covers the duration of various stages of labour, drugs given to the mother and the state of the infant at birth.

FIRST TEN DAYS' OBSERVATIONS

During the first ten days post partum the midwives make regular visits to home-delivered mothers, and the mother usually has other assistance in the house from friends and relatives. We set out to record mother–infant behaviour during this initial phase; to minimise the inconvenience to the mother and to economise on our own time we decided to restrict our visits to days 2, 3, 8, 9, 10. This distribution was chosen to provide an adequate sample of the post partum period, and to allow assessment of changes in behaviour over the period. On each day the observation covers the time from when the infant is picked up for a feed until he is returned to his cot, and so samples one period of interaction including feeding and changing the baby. If possible we take such a period between 9 a.m. and 2 p.m. to minimise the effects of diurnal variation in behaviour.

There are two general techniques used in direct observation. Behaviour may be recorded by film or videotape for later analysis or analysed on the spot into a series of pre-coded categories. Filming has the advantage that a minimum of data is thrown away at the initial recording, and films may be re-run many times so that items of behaviour may be scored from them in fine detail and the reliability of analysing them can be assessed accurately. This method has two disadvantages: it is expensive, and it is much more disturbing to the mother than an observer making a written record; these led us to choose direct recording.

In the tradition of the ethologists, we have attempted to record mother–infant interactions with a minimum of theoretical pre-suppositions, apart from those set out above (see Marler and Hamilton, 1966; Bateson 1968, for general accounts of ethological recording techniques).

We sought categories of behaviour that are species typical, i.e. common to most mothers and infants, and that seemed to be functional (in the biological sense). Our recording categories grew out of our observations rather than being imposed on them by some pre-determined theoretical position. At first we watched without making any attempt to record. Later we began to note features of behaviour that recurred regularly and these were gradually refined into our behavioural categories. This preliminary phase involved watching about sixty mother–infant pairs for about 200 hours.

The construction of behavioural categories is the most difficult part of an observational study to describe to someone who has not had experience of this type of research. To an outsider, a category may often appear to be arbitrary, while to the observer it feels right, but he is often unable to give an explicit reason for that feeling. Perhaps categories are selected by setting up internal statistical models of recurring patterns of behaviour. There are two possible tests of what constitutes a ' good ' category. The first is that it is reliable and valid. Other observers will, or have, evolved the same or closely similar categories and a description of the behaviour pattern will enable another observer to record it with a high degree of agreement (the two will agree that the behaviour pattern has or has not occurred at least 75% of the time).

The second test is much less discrete: that the category will be useful in analysis – its occurrence will correlate with other factors or distinguish preselected groups of subjects. This is where pre-suppositions about which are the important variables can have a direct effect on structuring the outcome of the research.

In choosing categories, one is usually limiting the analysis to a particular behavioural level, somewhere between muscle twitches and the most molar level (e.g. the restrictiveness of the mother). The level is obviously related to the recording method; for example, it would not be possible to record changes in direction of gaze by pencil and paper methods, because it occurs too rapidly. During the preliminary phase of the work, we decided to use a thirty-second time grid for the observations, that is, to note the occurrence or absences of each behavioural category within each thirty-second period.

TABLE 7·2. *Some behavioural categories used in observing mother–infant interaction*

Mother
  Rubs or pats infant
  Kisses infant
  Rocks infant
  Changes nappies
  Stimulates infant to suck (e.g. by rubbing cheek or feet)
  Touches infant on bare skin
  Walks, carrying infant
  Talks to infant
  Talks to another person
  Looks at anything other than infant
  Leaves room
  Smiles at infant (and within 3 feet of infant's face)
Infant
  Nipple in mouth
  Arms free (not swaddled, can touch own face)
  Cries
  Fusses
  Burps
  Chokes
  Sneezes
  Vomits
  Hiccups

Infant position	Infant state
Cradled	1. Eyes closed, regular respiration, no movement
shoulder	2. Eyes closed, irregular respiration, no gross movements
sitting	
lying	3. Eyes open, no gross movements
	4. Eyes open, gross movements, no crying
	5. Eyes open, gross movements, crying
	6. Not observable
	7. Sucking

A description of these categories is given in the Appendix.

At this level, one cannot follow the second-by-second interaction of mother and child, but we decided that at the present state of knowledge it might be more productive to begin at a coarser level; beginning at a finer level would involve a greater pre-selection of the important factors, which could give a

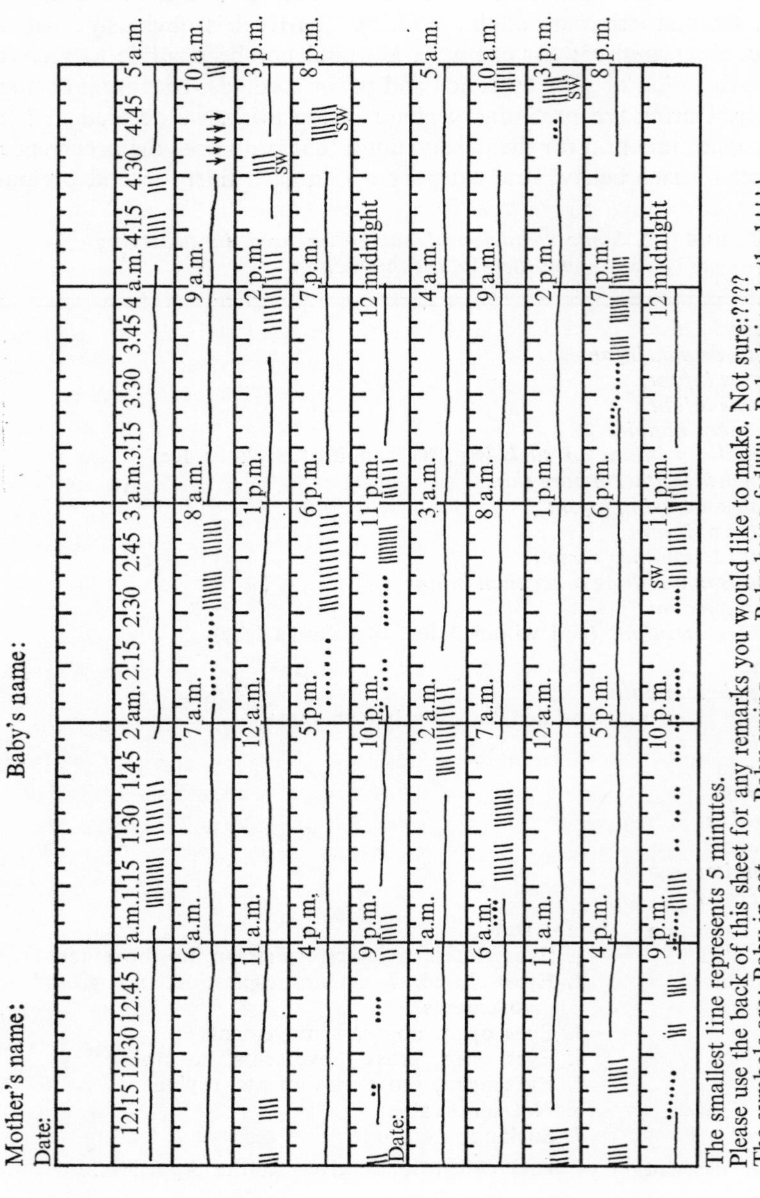

Fig. 7·1. An example of a mother's diary. This is a copy of a diary of a breast feeding mother for days five and six. 'SW' indicates feeds that were sugar water given in a bottle.

The smallest line represents 5 minutes.
Please use the back of this sheet for any remarks you would like to make. Not sure:????
The symbols are: Baby in cot——, Baby crying••••, Baby being fed‖‖‖, Baby being bathed ↓↓↓↓

184

stronger theoretical bias. In part this choice followed from the decision not to use film or videotape, as this ruled out the analysis of fine interaction.

Our categories are of three types, descriptive (e.g. mother talks to infant, infant sneezes), locational (e.g. position of infant relative to mother), and by outcome (mother stimulates infant to suck), or more accurately, by inferred intended outcome. Table 7·2 gives a partial list of the forty or so categories that are currently in use. These are more fully described in the appendix.

Reliability checks show that observer agreement is probably better than 75% for most of the categories. Recording is done on duplicated sheets: symbols for each category are written in columns which are divided by cross lines corresponding to each thirty-second interval. During recording an electronic interval timer is used which gives a sound pulse in the observer's ear every thirty seconds.

Our procedure samples five of the fifty or so feeding interactions that take place in the first ten days. This is a small proportion, and as the observations always sample the morning feed, it is biased in that it may miss any diurnal variations. To get a fuller picture of each day, mothers are asked to keep a diary for the post partum period on a standard form (Fig. 7·1). This records when the infant is in his cot, is fed, cries and is bathed. Somewhat to our surprise, mothers seem to enjoy keeping these diaries and it is our impression that they are filled in with reasonable accuracy. This can be partially checked during the periods we are in the house.

At each visit a number of questions are asked about the infant and the mother's attitudes to him. On the tenth day a more extensive questionnaire is used; this covers topics like the mother's attitude to the observers and the midwives, her intentions about method and scheduling of feeds, and the behaviour of the sibling (if there is one) towards the baby. The various attitude measures are brought together in a summary account which is written after the tenth-day visit. This describes the observer's impressions of the mother's behaviour under a series of pre-selected headings and a rating is given on the Brody general scale (Brody, 1956).

ASSESSMENT OF THE INFANT

As mentioned earlier, we attempt to assess the infant's behaviour when it is not interacting with the mother as well as during the observations. Three techniques are used: a neurological examination, an assessment of sucking behaviour and of visual responsiveness. The choice of these particular measures can probably be best described as an informed guess. We wish to assess individual characteristics that are likely to influence the style of interaction with the mother and the course of development of the infant, but until there has been much more analysis of mother–infant interaction, it is impossible to specify these characteristics.

On day 8, about an hour before the expected feeding time, a neurological examination is carried out by the Goningen method (Prechtl and Beintema, 1964; Beintema, 1968). The examination gives measures, among others, of general reactivity to stimulation and ease of quietening which are likely to be key determinants of the mother's behaviour towards her infant. The mother of a wakeful infant who often cries is likely to behave very differently from a mother with a drowsy (' good ') infant. The examination has the further advantage of providing a screen for neurological abnormalities.

As feeding is such a central issue in the post partum period for the mother, the sucking behaviour of her infant is likely to affect their interaction. The pattern of sucking behaviour is known to have wide individual variation but to show relative consistency for one infant (Halverson, 1938; Balint, 1948; Kron et al., 1967; Wolff, 1968). It is assessed by the method of Waldrop and Bell (1966) during the neurological examination. A sterile teat is placed in the infant's mouth for four minutes and the number of sucks per group is recorded for each minute. After removal, the latency to the first flexion of the knee and the first cry and the amount of crying in the following ninety seconds are noted.

The reasons for recording visual responsiveness are more of a guess than an informed guess. It is assessed at birth (when an observer is present) and on day 8. A red ring (two inches in diameter with a $\frac{3}{4}$-inch hole in the centre) is shown to the infant when he is in a quiet alert state. As the target is moved, horizontal and vertical tracking with the eyes or head and eye are recorded. The method is modified from that of Graham (1956).

Results

To illustrate some of the points made earlier, we will present some preliminary results for the first thirty-eight mothers recruited to our sample. As the number of mothers is very small, we are forced to use the simplest kinds of analysis. We have divided the group by a number of major variables, parity, sex of infant, method of feeding, and compared measures of mother and infant behaviour in each subsample. We have found differences for all these variables and evidence of interaction between them. A more subtle behavioural analysis and a more sophisticated statistical treatment to parcel our variance between the relevant factors must await a larger sample. Meanwhile, we will present a preliminary analysis of the behaviour of breast- and bottle-feeding mothers and their infants and of the influence of obstetric medication. We hope that, in particular, this will illustrate the importance of multilevel analysis.

BREAST- AND BOTTLE-FEEDING

The results of the non-nutritive sucking test indicate that breast-fed infants suck at higher rates and are more responsive to the removal of the teat than bottle-fed infants (Table 7·3). This is consistent with a previous finding that an anthropometric examination on day 3 or 4 produced higher levels of arousal in breast-fed than bottle-fed infants (Bell, 1966).

TABLE 7·3. *Non-nutritive sucking in breast and bottle fed infants on day 8 or 9*

	Mean no. of sucks in 4 min.	Median latency in sec. to cry after removal of teat	Mean crying totals for 90 sec. after removal of teat
Breast fed $N=20$	213.0	15	24.0
Bottle fed $N=11$	171.4	38	16.8
2-tailed Mann–Whitney U-test	$u=63.5$ $p<0.10$	$u=44$ $p<0.02$	$u=78$ N.S.

How may we explain these results? * There seem to be three main possibilities. Some aspects of the post-natal environment may differ in the two groups. Nutrition is the most obvious factor but there may be other differences in the treatment received by the infants. There may be aspects of maternal behaviour, apart from the actual feeding which co-vary with feeding method. The third possibility is that the infants were never similar. Perhaps the factors that lead a mother to choose a particular feeding method are associated with others that influence the post-natal behaviour of the

TABLE 7·4. *Observational data on days 2, 3, 9 and 10 for breast and bottle feeding mothers*

	Mean no. of 30 sec. periods			
	Breast $(N=17)$	Bottle $(N=10)$	2-tailed U-test U	
Length of feed	195.6	174.1	62	N.S.
Time *nipple in mouth*	107.6	79.7	41.5	$p<0.05$
On nipple with interruption	20.0	17.6	64	N.S.
On nipple with interruption as % of time nipple in mouth	22.4%	21.6%	69.5	N.S.
Touch infant	23.6	8.7	40.5	$p<0.05$
Stimulate to suck	18.8	15.0	80	N.S.
Smile at infant	11.0($N=13$)	8.6($N=8$)	34.5	N.S.
Talk to infant	68.9	45.5	50	$p<0.10$

* For further discussion of some of these problems, see Bernal and Richards (1970).

infant. We cannot test this directly as we do not have enough data on the independent behaviour of the infant before the eighth day but we can compare the two groups of mothers to see how similar they are.

Some of the observational data for the two groups are given in Table 7·4. One striking difference is that the breast infants are fed for longer periods as measured by the time the nipple was in the infant's mouth. The mothers' diaries show that the breast infants spend less time in the cot and this seems to be true from the first day. The diaries also indicate that breast infants cry more than the bottle infants. As this trend is apparent right from the start, it might suggest that the two groups differed from birth. We can find nothing in the birth histories (length of labour, maternal medication, etc.) that might be associated with such a difference.

Why do particular mothers choose to breast or bottle feed? Sociological work (Newson and Newson, 1963) has found a correlation with the Registrar General's classification of the husband's occupation. The Newsoms suggest that this correlation is explained by increased modesty and a lack of privacy for working-class mothers who are the least likely to breast feed. We find the same social class relationship (Table 7·5) and that bottle-feeding mothers had received less education. We cannot test the modesty hypothesis directly though we do find that other people are more likely to be present during bottle feeds than breast feeds (mean time others present during feeds, breast feeders 44%, bottle feeders 75%, $p=0.02$). Privacy does not seem to be important for our Cambridge sample, as we find no difference in the number of rooms per house for the two groups (mean number of rooms, breast feeders 3.9, bottle feeders 4.2, not significant).

TABLE 7·5. *Registrar-General's classification of the husbands of breast- and bottle-feeding mothers*

	Class I and II	III and IV	
Breast	16	9	$\chi^2=5.5$
Bottle	2	10	$p=<0.02$

Some other variables do seem to distinguish the two groups. The breast-feeding mothers were older at the birth of their second child (26.6 years against 24.3 years, $p=0.05$) and had a shorter gap between the births of their first two children (24 months against 31.4 months, $p=0.10$). These two differences are also found for the social class 3 and 4 mother alone. Paradoxically our data on contraceptive practice suggests that the bottle feeders are using less efficient methods. This, coupled with the absence of a lactational suppression of ovulation, might be expected to lead to a shorter interval between successive births. From our results we may tentatively conclude that there is a fertility difference between the two groups, perhaps related to differences in the frequency of intercourse. The mothers in the two groups also intended to have a different family size before the birth of their second child (Table 7·6). However, this difference disappears if the social class 1 and 2 mothers are removed from the sample.

TABLE 7·6. *Intended family size for breast- and bottle-feeding mothers*

	Two children	More than two children
Breast	10	14
Bottle	12	0

$\chi^2 = 9.13$
$p = <0.01$

We may conclude that bottle- and breast-feeding mothers differ on a number of factors apart from their social class and therefore we feel it is unwise to assume that the two groups will produce infants that will behave in similar ways. This possibility indicates a defect in the design of our study. We had initially assumed that we could assess infants relatively independently of their post-natal experience on the eighth day. This may well be too late. We are now reconsidering our decision and intend to make some kind of assessment nearer birth.

MATERNAL MEDICATION IN LABOUR

We have examined the preliminary data for possible correlations between the infants' and mothers' behaviour and the drugs given to the mothers during labour. Of the thirty-three mothers in the group for this analysis, 23 received one or two intramuscular injections of 50 or 100mg Pethilorfan (Roche Products, Pethidine: Levallorphan Tartrate: 100: 1.25) between 9 hours and 30 minutes before delivery. In addition, in the Pethilorfan group, four mothers were given Trichloryl (monosodium triclofos), seven Sparine (promazine hydrochlor), one Welldorm (dichloralphenazone), and one Trichloryl and Welldorm. Two mothers who did not receive Pethilorfan were given Trichloryl. Except for three mothers who had no Pethilorfan, all mothers had a variable quantity of some form of inhalant anaesthesia (Trilene, nitrous oxide and air, or nitrous oxide and oxygen).

We would have liked to have computed a drug score for each infant based on the dose and time of administration of Pethilorfan to the mother. However, the kinetics of placental transfer of Pethidine has not been adequately studied (Moya and Thorndyke, 1963; Moya and Smith, 1965; Beckett and Taylor, 1967) and no accurate data appears to be available for Pethilorfan. Thus we are forced to make the crudest comparison, that between the infants of mothers who were given Pethilorfan at any time during labour and those who did not receive the drug.

189

At birth, all infants were rated on three point scales for colour, reflex irritability and muscle tone by the midwife in charge of the delivery. An infant in an optimal condition would receive a score of 3, while a maximally depressed infant would receive a score of 9. The time from birth to the first

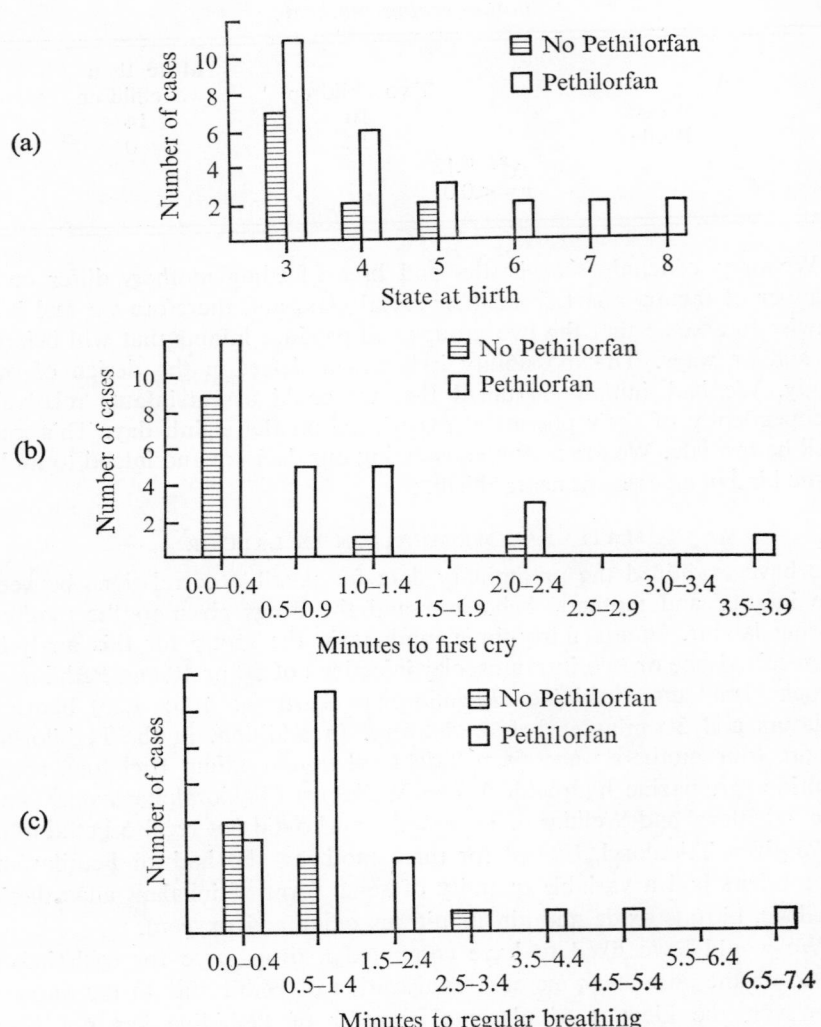

Fig. 7·2. Assessments of the infants at birth in the Pethilorfan and no Pethilorfan groups:
(a) Rating of colour, muscle tone and reflex irritability. Three is the optimum score.
(b) Minutes from birth to first cry.
(c) Minutes from birth to the establishment of regular breathing.

cry and to phythmical breathing were also recorded. Fig. 7·2 shows the results for the two groups. Infants in the Pethilorfan group tended to be given a higher rating at birth and to have longer latencies to the first cry and to rhythmical breathing.

TABLE 7·7. *Presence of eye signs (nystagmus, strabismus and sunset signs) in the Pethilorfan and no Pethilorfan groups*

		No eye signs	Eye signs
Pethilorfan	$N=22$	9	13
No Pethilorfan	$N=10$	10	0
$\chi^2=7.65$, $p=<0.01$			

Two infants, not included in this table, both in the Pethilorfan group, did not open their eyes during the course of the examination.

As part of the neurological examination on day 8 or 9, the presence or absence of three eye conditions, strabismus, nystagmus and sunset signs, was noted. One or more of these signs were found in more than half the infants in the Pethilorfan group but they were not seen in any infant in the other group (Table 7·7). The sucking test (p. 186) did not give statistically significant differences between the two groups but the results suggest that

TABLE 7·8. *Non-nutritive sucking test results for the Pethilorfan and non-Pethilorfan groups*

	Mean no. of sucks in 4 min.	Median latency in sec. to cry after removal of the teat	Mean no. of cries in 90 sec. after removal
Breast-fed Pethilorfan $N=13$	208.2	15	26.5
No Pethilorfan $N=6$	233.2	11	21.3
Bottle-fed Pethilorfan $N=6$	169.5	44	11.0
No Pethilorfan $N=4$	192.3	31	23.3

the Pethilorfan infants have a reduced non-nutritive sucking rate and are less responsive to the removal of the teat (Table 7·8). If the Pethilorfan infants do show altered sucking behaviour it is likely that this will influence the interaction with the mother. As we mentioned earlier, this was why the sucking test was included in the procedures used in the study. The observational data indicates that the Pethilorfan infants tended to be fed for shorter periods, to have fewer thirty-second periods with the nipple in their mouths, more periods in which feeding was interrupted and received more stimulation to suck from their mothers (Table 7·9).

We have tried to determine why particular mothers are given Pethilorfan. Using an argument analogous to that given for the bottle-breast infants, there may be other maternal factors associated with receiving Pethilorfan which might give rise to the differences in the infants, so that we could not conclude that Pethilorfan had any direct effect on the infant. The criteria used by the midwives are that the mother should be 'distressed' and that,

TABLE 7·9. *Some measures of mother–infant interaction in the Pethilorfan and no-Pethilorfan groups*

	Mean no. of 30 sec. periods during feeding sessions on days 2, 3, 9 and 10			
	Feed duration	Nipple in mouth	Nipple in mouth with interruption	Maternal stimulation
Breast-fed Pethilorfan $N=13$	184.0	99.3	24.0 [2]	21.6
No Pethilorfan $N= 6$	226.7	123.3	16.3	12.0
Bottle-fed Pethilorfan $N= 5$	146.2 [2]	65.4	20.0[2]	17.0
No Pethilorfan $N= 4$	186.3	96.5	12.5	12.5
Total Pethilorfan $N=18$	175.8	91.8	22.8 [2]	21.2 [2]
[1] No Pethilorfan $N=11$	207.0	108.6	15.5	12.0

[1] One additional mother who both bottle and breast fed is added here.
[2] Indicates comparisons between the Pethilorfan and no-Pethilorfan groups significant at <0.05 (2-tailed) on a Mann–Whitney U-Test.

where possible, the drug should not be given within one and a half hours of delivery. Though we found that Pethilorfan was not given to mothers who had brief labours, there was no significant association between the presence of eye signs and the length of labour (Fig. 7·3). We also compared the two groups on a number of other factors and did not find differences with respect of parity, maternal age, maternal education, minor complications of pregnancy, the sex of the infant, birth weight or the method of infant feeding. So we tentatively conclude that the Pethilorfan effect is a direct

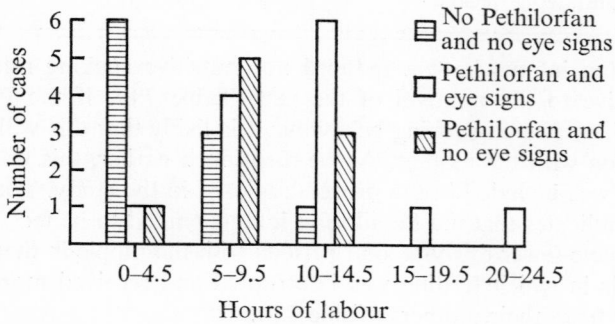

Fig. 7·3. The association between the length of labour, the administration of Pethilorfan and the presence of eye signs in the infant.

one and the differences in the mother–infant interaction are the result of the infant bringing altered behavioural characteristics to that interaction.

The number of subjects is very small for a definitive drug study and clearly the importance of these changes in the new born period cannot be evaluated until the results of the follow-up visits are analysed. But the results are very suggestive and complement those found with barbiturates and other kinds of maternal medications (Brazelton, 1961; Stechler, 1964; Kron, Stein and Goddard, 1966).

Conclusions

Our very preliminary results indicate that breast- and bottle-fed infants may differ at birth (as their mothers do) and have a different interaction with their mothers during the first ten days of their lives. Either or both of these influences and, of course, the quantity or quality of the nutriment they receive, may contribute to the differences in their behaviour we find on the eighth day. Looking at any one factor or any one level might have led to the suggestion that the one factor investigated was the cause of the behavioural difference found. The situation is clearly much more complicated than that. An analysis of the mode of interaction in both the groups must await the collection of more data.

Using a similar kind of analysis we can show, at least tentatively, that Pethilorfan given to the mother during labour will alter the infant's behaviour and so in turn influence the mother–infant interaction. The consequences of this may be profound because it is possible that the 'style' of interaction is determined in this early phase. So, even if the direct effects of the drug on the infant's mother may continue, this could have developmental consequences for the infant. This is one of the possibilities that only longitudinal studies can investigate.

The Pethilorfan findings also illustrate the necessity for analysis at many levels. In a population where mothers are commonly medicated during labour it is necessary to consider the possible influences of the drugs on the mother and infant and their interaction.

To do this successfully, the analysis must include biochemical and physiological data about placental transfer and metabolism of the drug, and data about its effects on the mother's and infant's behaviour as well as the social reasons that lead to particular mothers receiving the drug. So far we can only sketch in a few of the relevant factors and merely acknowledge the existence of some of the others.

In this paper we have attempted to describe the methods used in an observational study of mother–infant interaction and some of the theoretical assumptions which dictated their choice. Our method involves the collection of a large amount of detailed information. This we believe to be essential. We are convinced that the understanding of human behaviour will not be advanced by an approach which, having acknowledged its complexity, goes on to attempt to analyse behaviour by recording a very small number of factors at any one time. Such an approach may be appropriate for physical systems but it has proved remarkably unsuccessful for human behaviour.

Acknowledgements

In a project of this nature one accumulates even more debts than are usual in scientific research. The greatest of these is to the mothers who have accepted our intrusions into their lives with good humour and have given us every possible assistance. The midwives first approach the mothers, inform us of births and record valuable data for us. We much appreciate their patience, skill and co-operation. The Nuffield Foundation supports the project with a generous grant; without them we would not have been able to begin. We also have numerous debts to friends and colleagues for many kinds of help and encouragement. In particular, we would like to thank Tony Ambrose, John Bowlby, Mavis Gunther, Robert Hinde, David Ingleby, Heinz Prechtl, Joanna Ryan and Oliver Zangwill. Jackie Deitch, Sheila Jackson and Caroline New have provided very efficient technical assistance.

APPENDIX

DESCRIPTIONS OF BEHAVIOURAL CATEGORIES USED IN THE MOTHER–INFANT INTERACTION OBSERVATIONS DURING THE FIRST TEN DAYS

GENERAL INFORMATION
Position of the infant in the cot, before and after the feed, is noted; the side on which he is lying or whether prone or supine.
Swaddled. Swaddled is recorded when the infant is not able to touch his face with his own hand.
Position of the mother during the feed, e.g. sitting up in bed.
Bottle, breast or cup feed.

MOTHER–INFANT CATEGORIES
Rubs or pats infant. Gross rubbing or patting movements which are usually seen during winding or if the infant chokes.

Kisses infant.

Rocks infant. Repetitive side to side movements of the infant.

Changes nappies/diapers. While this is carried out only a limited number of the other categories are recorded.

Stimulates infant to suck. Gentle rubbing of cheeks or feet or movements of the nipple or teat relative to the infant's lips.

Touch. Touching infant on bare skin for any other purpose than to stimulate; usually a light stroking of forehead or hands. The movements are lighter and at a lower frequency than rubs and pats.

Walk. The mother moving around room carrying her infant.

MOTHER-INFANT INTERACTION

Talks to infant. The content of speech is used to determine whether or not the speech is directed at the infant. Where possible the actual remarks are noted.

Talks to others. Talking to anyone other than the infant, including the observer.

Looks away. Looking at anybody or anything other than the infant.

Leaves room. The mother leaves the room containing the infant or is out of that room.

Smile. The mother smiles at the infant. This is scored whenever the mother smiles while facing and within three feet of the infant even if the infant's eyes are closed.

INFANT CATEGORIES

Nipple in mouth. The nipple or teat must be between the infant's lips. Stroking of the lips with a teat is scored as stimulate to suck and not nipple in mouth.

Nipple out. The nipple or teat comes out of the infant's mouth. This is recorded every time it occurs, rather than once each thirty-second interval. Where possible each occasion is qualified by the member of the diad who causes the nipple to come out, i.e. it may be pushed out by the infant's tongue or pulled out by the mother.

Free/swaddled. Whether or not the infant is able to touch his own face with bare or mittened hands.

THE INFANT'S POSITION

Cradled. Held more or less horizontally across the mother's body, supported by her arms.

Shoulder. Held more or less vertically against the mother's body, supported by her arms.

Sitting. Supported on the mother's lap or any horizontal surface with the infant's back at about 90° to his legs.

Lying. More or less horizontal across the mother's lap or any other horizontal surface.

For each of the categories where the infant is supported by the mother's body, it is noted whether the infant's head is towards the mother's left or right side. In all cases, if the infant is held by someone other than the mother, the same categories are used but a note is made of who is holding the infant.

Change. A change of position but not of category. This is recorded each time it occurs.

Not held. The infant is not in physical contact with the mother or any other person.

INFANT VOCALISATIONS, STATE, ETC.

Cries, fusses. A hard and fast definition cannot be given which distinguishes these two categories. In general, crying is louder and involves more reddening and contorting of the face than fussing.

Burps.

Chokes.

Sneezes.

Sick – vomits or spits up.

Hiccups.
Our definition of these categories follows common usage. A description in terms of mechanics or muscle contractions would only add to the reification of our recording system.

The predominant state is recorded for each thirty-second period.
1. Eyes closed, regular respiration, no movements.
2. Eyes closed, irregular respiration, no gross movements.
3. Eyes open, no gross movements, no crying.
4. Eyes open, gross movements, no crying.
5. Eyes open or closed, crying.
6. State not observable.
7. Sucking.
Eyes open or closed.

Vis-à-vis possible. This is recorded when the observer judges that it is possible for the mother to look into the infant's eyes, even if these are closed.

OTHERS PRESENT
All persons present in the room are recorded. Role designations are used, e.g. midwife, husband, sibling, etc.

OTHER/INFANT INTERACTIONS
These are recorded in exactly the same way as the mother/infant interactions.

REFERENCES

Balint, M. (1948). Individual differences of behaviour in early infancy and an objective method for recording them. *J. genet. Psychol.* **73**, 57–117.

Bateson, P. P. G. (1968). Ethological methods of observing behaviour. In *Analysis of Behavioural Change.* Ed. L. Weiskrantz, London and New York: Harper and Row.

Beckett, A. H. and Taylor, J. F. (1967). Blood concentrations of pethidine and pentazocine in mother and infant at time of birth. *J. Pharm. Pharmac.* **19**, Suppl., 508–25.

Beintema, D. J. (1968). *A Neurological Study of Newborn Infants.* London: S.I.M.P./Heinemann Medical Books.

Bell, R. Q. (1966). Level of arousal in breast-fed and bottle-fed human newborns. *Psychosom. Med.* **28**, 177–80.

Bernal, J. F. and Richards, M. P. M. (1970). The effects of bottle and breast feeding on infant development. *J. Psychosom. Res.* **14**, 247–52.

Brazelton, T. B. (1961). Psychophysiologic reactions in the neonate: II. Effects of maternal medication. *J. Pediat.* **58**, 513–18.

Brody, S. (1956). *Patterns of Mothering: Maternal Influences during Infancy.* New York: Internat. Univ. Press.

Butler, N. R. and Bonham, D. G. (1963). *Perinatal Mortality.* Edinburgh: Livingstone.

Colombotos, J., Elinson, J. and Loewenstein, R. (1968). Effect of interviewer's sex on interview responses. *Pub. Health Rep.* **83**, 685–90.

Graham, F. K. (1956). Behavioral differences between normal and traumatized newborns: I. The test procedure. *Psychol. Monog.* **70**, No. 427.

Halverson, H. M. (1938). Infant sucking and tensional behavior. *J. genet. Psychol.* **53**, 365–430.

Hansen, E. W. (1966). The development of maternal and infant behavior in the rhesus monkey. *Behaviour* **27**, 107–49.

Hinde, R. A. and Spencer-Booth, Y. (1968). The study of mother–infant interaction in captive group-living rhesus monkeys. *Proc. Roy. Soc. B.* **169**, 177–201.

Jensen, G. D., Bobbitt, R. A. and Gordon, B. N. (1968). Effects of environment on the relationship between mother and infant pigtailed monkeys (*Macaca nemstrina*) *J. comp. physiol. Psychol.* **66**, 259–63.

Kron, R. E., Stein, M. and Goddard, K. E. (1966). Newborn sucking behavior affected by obstetric sedation. *Pediat.* **37**, 1012–16.

Kron, R. E., Stein, M., Goddard, K. E. and Phoenix, M. D. (1967). Effect of nutrient upon the sucking behavior of newborn infants. *Psychosom. Med.* **29**, 24–32.

Levy, D. M. (1958). *Behavioral Analysis.* Springfield: Thomas.

Marler, P. and Hamilton, W. J. (1966). *Mechanisms of Animal Behavior.* New York: Wiley.

Minde, K., Webb, G. and Sykes, D. (1958). Studies on the hyperactive child. VI. Prenatal and perinatal factors associated with hyperactivity. *Develop. Med. Child. Neurol.* **10**, 355–63.

Moss, H. A. (1965). Methodological issues in studying mother–infant interaction. *Amer. J. Orthopsychiat.* **35**, 482–6.

Moya, F. and Smith, B. E. (1965). Uptake distribution and placental transport of drugs and anesthetics. *Anesthesiol.* **26**, 465–76.

Moya, F. and Thorndike, V. (1963). The effects of drugs used in labor on the fetus and newborn. *Clin. Pharmacol. Ther.* **4**, 628.

Newson, J. and Newson, E. (1963). *Infant Care in an Urban Community.* London: Allen and Unwin.

Prechtl, H. F. R. (1968). Neurological findings in newborn infants after pre- and paranatal complications. In *Aspects of Praematurity and Dysmaturity.* Ed. J. H. P. Jonxis, H. K. A. Visser and J. A. Troelstra. Leiden: Stenfert Kroese N.V.

Prechtl, H. and Beintema, D. (1964). *The Neurological Examination of the Full Term Newborn Infant.* London: S.I.M.P./Heinemann Medical Books.

Richards, M. P. M. (1971). Mother–infant interaction and its social context – some comments. Proceedings of a study group on 'The Origins of Human Social Relations' C.A.S.D.S./Ciba Foundation, July 1969. Ed. H. R. Schaffer. London and New York: Academic Press.

Rosenblum, L. A. and Kaufman, I. C. (1967). Laboratory observations of early mother–infant relations in pigtail and bonnet macaques. In *Social Communication among Primates.* Ed. S. A. Altman, Chicago: Univ. Chicago Press.

Schaffer, H. R. (1966). Activity level as a constitutional determinant of infantile reaction to deprivation. *Child Develop.* **37**, 595–602.

Stechler, G. (1964). Newborn attention as affected by medication during labour. *Science, N.Y.* **144**, 315–17.

Waldrop, M. F. and Bell, R. Q. (1966). Effects of family size and density on newborn characteristics. *Amer. J. Orthopsychiat.* **36**, 544–50.

Wolff, P. H. (1968). The serial organisation of sucking in the young infant. *Pediat.* **42**, 943–56.

8

ATTACHMENT BEHAVIOUR OUT OF DOORS

J. W. ANDERSON *

SUMMARY

This paper consists of deductions from observations made out of doors on the interactions between mother and infant with a view to ascertaining the distances he maintained when he was at liberty in a familiar environment. Thus, attachment behaviour, the infant's tendency to maintain proximity to its mother, hypothesized in Bowlby's (1958) account of the child's tie to its mother to be at its strongest during the period 18 to 30 months, came under observation in testing circumstances.

It was found that infants whose ages were estimated to range from just walking to 2½ years kept within sight or sound of the mother without their having to be recalled. Since cases in which prolonged feeding and other caretaking behaviour which cause a mother and infant to remain together had been excluded from the sample, the social basis of the bond which kept the child within a safe distance could be affirmed.

Subjects did not know that they were under scrutiny; observation periods therefore yielded samples of spontaneous behaviour. For instance, conspicuous gestures of communication occur every now and then, and from them mild states of arousal can be inferred. Since Darwin's time, it has been known that the expression of emotion provides a means of communication both for animals and for men; modern ethologists describe in detail the signals and gestures that unite a pair in lasting bonds. This paper isolates some of the communications that occur in a natural setting, thus preparing for the study of attachment in terms of factors that identify a mother–infant pair.

Introduction

This paper gives some results of a study of attachment in human infants out of doors. The study arose from a consideration of the effects on the character of long early separation from the mother (Bowlby, 1951); from studies of imprinting; from work on mother–infant interactions in higher animals, which records the stages by which the infant enlarges his environment while maintaining contact with the mother; and from a reformulation of the psycho-analytical theory of the child's tie to his mother (Bowlby, 1958). A further influence was a description of the altered relationships between animals when the spatial distances between them changed (Hediger, 1955). In contrast to the theories of observers who record the social interaction of the young with its parents, there are views of writers who empha-

* Institute of Education, University of London.

size the permissive and restrictive aspects of parents' behaviour to account for the proximity of their infant; Smart and Smart (1967: 146), for instance, state that if parents did not set limits on their infants' behaviour, 'there would be no more babies, since babies creep and toddle right into danger'.

Mothers' statements when presenting a history of their child at child guidance clinics were highly material to the general thesis. Some mothers had noticed a peculiarity in their child's attachment beginning at the time he had learned to walk: how, instead of enjoying the freedom which his first outings to the park afforded, he would cling close, not mixing with other people, scarcely ever taking his eyes off his mother. Or, in contrast, so far from being anxious when away from her, a child had persistently sought opportunities to depart; unless she was vigilant, he would get lost and remain missing until he was returned to her by neighbours, apparently untroubled by the loss of his mother.

Hence, one aspect of attachment, the tendency to remain in proximity to the mother, presented itself for testing. By making observations on mother–infant pairs when the infant had just begun to leave the mother's side, in surroundings where opportunities for exploring remote places might take him out of her control, it would be possible to isolate the social influence of the mother on his behaviour.

Method

The results below were derived from tape-recorded commentaries of infants' 'random' movements around a stationary mother in London parks, over observation periods which averaged fifteen minutes, without the subjects' awareness. The infants' ages were estimated to range from 15 to 30 months. The criterion of selection was that a mother should have positioned herself so far away from other people with children that interruption by them would be unlikely. The mother was not to be amusing the child with toys or otherwise deliberately influencing his behaviour. If she recalled him with an offer of food, recording was abandoned. It was hoped to exclude every feeding situation, but this requirement would have sacrificed most of the cases; however, it is not thought that what feeding that occurred biased the locomotion scores, for when a child went to his mother to fetch a feeding cup he simply resumed his peregrinations with it in his hand.

Results

RETRIEVAL BY THE MOTHER

The infants seemed to establish their own boundaries and with the exceptions noted below kept within a distance of approximately 200 feet from the mother without being recalled. Out of thirty-five infants, twenty-four were never far enough away to warrant retrieval. A further eight were followed by the mother; after he had been playing in her vicinity for a few minutes the infant would be attracted elsewhere (to a swing enclosure, for example) and the mother would leave her position to catch up and escort him to it. The remaining three infants were brought back when they wandered too far or remained out of their mother's sight.

Thus, in spite of the opportunities for wandering and the temptation to explore, the sample remain mother-oriented while establishing a distance which takes them out of her immediate control. This is not to say that the mothers relax vigilance when the children are at a distance, and it is broadly true that the infant's boundary coincides with that which she tolerates.

GENERAL LOCOMOTION

Infants move around in bouts which are typically short and (provided that they are not close to their mother) stop between each bout for similar brief periods. The distributions of walking and stationary bouts are, for all infants, positively skewed, that is, scores accumulate at the short end of the distribution, while long bouts tend to be very long and rare in comparison.

The median for the child with the shortest bouts of locomotion is 3 seconds, the median for the longest 8.5 seconds. The scores for stationary periods vary independently of the latter range, but the range of medians is similar; the lowest median is 2 seconds, the highest 9 seconds.

In order to determine whether the differences in infants' bouts of locomotion signified genuine population differences or whether they represented chance variations, the data for fourteen infants were tested by the Kruskal–Wallis One-Way Analysis of Variance (Siegel, 1956). The resulting H of 67 has a probability under the null hypothesis of <0.001 from which it is concluded that infants differ from each other significantly in the duration of their bouts of locomotion.

Two factors probably account for this result: the various ages of the infants sampled and the habitual performance of the different children. It is expected, when a sample's scores are compared over a period of years, that cutting across the changes that take place with age, characteristic similarities within individuals will remain.

SORTIE, RETURN AND STOP

When making the running commentary it was quickest to describe bouts which reduced the distance between the infant and his mother as *return* and those which increased it as *sortie*. These bouts turned out to account for most of the infant's locomotion. Occasionally he described a small circle or semi-circle or walked in a line circumferential to the mother; or he would revolve on his axis; or he might fall, crawl or jump, but most of his walking time is spent drawing nearer to or farther from the mother.

Another characteristic of the activity around the mother is the tendency to stop after a few seconds of locomotion rather than to run hither and thither. This period in which the child is not walking manifests such a variety of behaviours from immobility to energetic playing that an inventory was begun for subsequent analysis; for the present purpose, the terms stationary and stopped are used simply to mean not walking.

Since the stationary periods broke up those of locomotion, it was expected that the child's stationary bouts would occupy the largest proportion of the whole observation period. It was further hypothesized that since most of the children did not stray from their mothers, the time spent in *sortie* would be approximately the same as that spent in *return*. The data were ranked according to the proportion of total observation time which the infant spent under the three conditions of *sortie*, *return* and *stop* and these ranks put to the Friedman Two-Way Analysis of Variance test (Siegel, 1956). The result of $\chi^2 r = 17.7$ for fifteen children leads to a rejection of the null hypothesis at the $p < 0.001$ level; *return* occupies the least proportion of time, *stop* the greatest, and *sortie* comes intermediate. When the numbers of bouts in each condition constitute the ranks of the same test, the null hypothesis is rejected even more decisively; there are considerably more bouts of *stop* than of *sortie*, and of *sortie* than *return*.

Although the expectation in regard to stationary periods was confirmed, it was a surprise to learn that infants who do not need recalling to their mothers spend more time retreating from than returning to her. It is suspected that there is a difference in velocity, the infants tending to run to the mother but to walk away from her. The point could not be investigated because an infant's pace changes within one bout of locomotion.

STATIONARY PERIODS

The outline of graphs in which the infant's distance from the mother was plotted against time suggested that when a child was close to his mother he was stationary for longer periods than when he was away from her, but that these periods were fewer in number than those spent further away. (By ' close to ' a distance of some 3 feet is meant: a spot at which he could be reached by the mother without her leaving her position.) The median periods which the sample spent close to the mother range from 4 to 37 seconds. In contrast, the bouts spent away from her are shorter, the medians ranging from 2 to 9 seconds. When each infant is compared for his median period spent close to/away from the mother, the result is clear-cut; the longer median bout is spent beside the mother by sixteen out of seventeen infants. Then, each child's number of stationary bouts was divided into the proportions spent close to/away from the mother and the rank differences put to the Wilcoxon Matched-Pairs Signed-Rank test (Siegel, 1956): the result is that fewer bouts are spent close to mother ($p = 0.01$).

The hypotheses that infants differed from each other in the length of their stationary bouts when (i) close to the mother, and (ii) away from the mother, were tested. Under each of these two conditions, the scores made by eight infants (for this analysis I had to exclude cases where another infant intervened, and to separate those able to walk well from those just-walking toddlers, hence the reduced number of cases) over a ten-minute observation period were put to a Kruskal–Wallis One-Way Analysis of Variance and proved to represent only chance variations. Infants did not differ from each other in length of their average stationary periods whether they were close to or away from the mother. The generalization that remains from the stationary data is therefore the following: an infant stops close to his mother for long periods but infrequently; away from her, he stops for short periods frequently.

SORTIE AND RETURN IN FURTHER DETAIL

It was thought that the stationary mother might be the stimulus to a pattern of activities operating relatively independently of anything happening else-where. Thus, when an infant left her side, it need not have been that he wanted to pursue a remote object or because she urged him away but simply that he wished to put a distance between himself and her at that moment. Similarly, if an infant approached his mother, it would not necessarily be because he were called back to her, or be recoiling from strange objects. In short, locomotions to and from the mother are not specifically released in his external environment.

TABLE 8·1. *Evidence of stimuli to 49 bouts of return made by 7 infants*

Any event to stimulate the return	Full Return	Incomplete Return	Totals
Yes	2	0	2
No	26	21	47
Totals	28	21	49

Taking the *returns* first, the records were perused for evidence that the infant had been instigated to approach his mother by being called or signalled, by being frightened, hurt or surprised in any way. Forty-nine *return* bouts made by seven infants were divided into *full return* (a bout that took him to his mother's side) and *incomplete return* (where he had moved towards her but stopped short or walked away again) and tested for independence of events which might have produced the approach (Table 8·1). The resulting fourfold contingency table yielded a χ^2 which was no larger than would arise by chance. In only two instances out of forty-nine – the mother's being joined by a female companion – could the observer infer a reason for the infant's being impelled back to her.

To test the hypothesis that the child had been stimulated to return to the mother by his seeing her do something that might have interested him, forty-six bouts of return made by seven infants were divided into *full* and *incomplete return* and classed according to whether or not the child was looking at his mother just before he made the approach. Another non-significant combination of frequencies demonstrates that the infant is as likely as not to be facing away from the mother just before his approach is made and therefore no specific stimuli emanating from her can be held to account for his return.

There is a similar paucity of evidence of external events to account for his walking away from his mother when the *sortie* data was scrutinized. After leaving the mother's side he usually stops to look around; he may approach a passer-by or seek a patch of ground which had interested him previously, but he so often ignores both novel and familiar stimuli that it would be pointless to try to count instances of objects that might have attracted him but did not. The mother's wishes are not effective in stimulating or discouraging a *sortie*. When an infant intends to leave his mother's lap he sometimes struggles vigorously to get away; the mother may be holding, trying to feed or to amuse him, but with no evident motive other than the wish to be on his feet at a distance from her he wriggles free and moves some paces off, there to stand until the next bout of activity begins. Equally, her trying to send him off by pointing and exhortation or by throwing objects for him to play with is futile when he intends to remain at the base.

Finally, a feature of the *return* bouts – their tendency to end in some form of contact with the mother, was recorded. The end result of *full return* made by eight infants were grouped according to whether they terminated in *contact*, e.g. climbing on the mother's lap, leaning against her, pulling her hand; *near-contact*, e.g. handing an object to her, leaning against the bench where she is sitting; and *no contact*, e.g. squatting at the mother's feet, standing in front of her. The result of this grouping is that in 39 *returns*, the infants initiate 18 *contacts*, 6 *near-contacts* and 15 *no contacts*. With younger infants, the contact can be a part of the *return* itself. as when he runs into the mother, throws himself against her, his two arms striking her knees, or flops down upon her when she is recumbent. The vigour of the contact, which can evoke the mother's annoyance, suggests an aggressive element in the return.

EFFECT OF MOTHER'S CALLING CHILD

The effect of the mother's calling the child was put to test and it was ascertained that the majority of mothers do not recall their infant once he has begun his sortie. Out of 26 cases, the mothers of only 16 attempted to summon the child to their side and as often as not it was reasons other than excessive distance which prompted it: when he played with refuse, remained out of sight in bushes or was about to mingle with a passing group she would try to bring him back by calling. Of these 16 called cases, 12 infants either remained where they were or increased the distance from the mother, 2 decreased the distance slightly then went elsewhere and 2 returned to the mother. The mothers justifiably place little reliance on the efficacy of a call. The infant, on his side, never called his mother. Indeed, vocalization was rare: he would sing or talk to himself, or squeal with excitement. Whatever inaudible speech may have been taking place, no child addressed, from a distance, a verbal message to his mother at the base; talking to her was kept for around contact distance.

At a distance, he remained in contact visually. The extent to which the infants looked at their mothers varied greatly amongst them; they were recorded more often looking away from than towards her, and for briefer periods (around two seconds) when looking at mother than when staring at novelties (around eight seconds).

ARM GESTURES DURING NATURAL PLAY

The infant's play which results from the absence of customary park equipment, toys and food, is best described as experimentation. He runs a short distance from the mother, stops to look around, fixates the sources of sounds and visual stimuli and, in some cases, attracts the mother's attention to them. Intermingled with this scanning of the remote is an examination of the ground: he handles leaves, grass, stones and refuse; crawls or jumps backwards and forwards over verges, and attempts the shaking or climbing of obstacles; this section is a summary of activities emerging from a classification of the arm gestures.

Dealing with the infant's immediate surroundings first, the most common gesture in the area of manipulation is *picking up objects* from the ground (and, since most infants drop, at least once, what they are holding, the proportion for this category could be considerably augmented). The retrieved object may be dismembered, put into the mouth, discarded or carried back to the mother. One-half of the whole sample take an object back to the mother. Some infants do not wait for the mother to accept it; when she extends a hand, they carry it off again. Throwing away, in the manner of older children, rarely occurs in this sample; the object is more likely to be cast down and trampled on.

When studying a patch of ground, the infant usually scrapes his hand and/or foot in it. *Scraping the hand* on the ground would be among the commonest gestures, but its frequency cannot be compared with others' since some infants are reproved by the mother if they are about to dirty their hands.

Holding on to a fixture which offers support or a possibility for climbing or shaking is the second most common movement which could be called manipulatory. A bench, railings, tree-cage or push-carriage, besides the mother herself, provide a stimulus which infants react to by grasping. Whether the purpose is manipulation or balancing is not always clear. It is not long since these infants will have been making assisted walks around a room with furniture as support; their continuing dependence on support is demonstrated by the extent to which they fall when out of doors: two falls in ten minutes is the median frequency for the sample.

Other manipulatory movements are concerned with the particular object which the infant is handling, such as *pushing* his push-carriage to and fro or *playing* with its working parts, *holding up* a leaf to be blown away by the wind, *dusting his hands* with hand open, wiping palm against palm, after touching (or in resisting the temptation to touch) the ground, etc.

The second class of gestures occurs when the hands are not grasping an object; the infant is most likely to be seen scanning the environment between bouts of locomotion, fixating the direction of new sounds and nearby sights. Consequently, most gestures in this context indicate the direction of the stimulus which elicits them. Occurring particularly in the newly-walking is the gesture of *one arm straight forward* at or a little above shoulder level. The simplest context is when infants who have just attained the erect posture walk with one arm forward (an observation made in an early analysis of walking by Burnside (1927)). Even when the infant has abandoned this balancing aid for ordinary locomotion, it will recur when he is pursuing or hurrying for any other reason. Preceding an approach, it marks an intention to proceed. It is also a component of reaching – grasping; the fingers may open and close whether or not the infant can ever reach the object to be seized. The gesture also occurs *in vacuo* at least once in ten minutes, whether the child is moving, standing still or sitting down, with no identifiable stimulus to elicit it. That it is a signal whose meaning is distinct from pointing is apparent from the following three criteria: (1) Reaching – grasping can be directed to the mother; pointing is always directed away from her. (2) It can be made when the infant is walking; pointing is done when he is still. (3) The body-orienting response is to the stimulus and not, as in pointing, to the midline between the stimulus and the mother.

Flapping the extended arm and *waving the hand* are, when newly walking, at around 12 months of age, almost identical movements. The infant hurrying to his mother, flapping the extended arm excitedly as he nears her, makes a similar gesture as he stands in front waving 'goodbye', apparently about to depart on a sojourn. The end result, in both cases, is the same – the child will be beside his mother in a few seconds. His parting salute announces but the briefest sojourn. There is no goodbye sign – or any other – to precede a long sortie. It predicts rejoining rather than parting.

Among infants of the present age-range, the wrist is unstiffening and the older person's gesture of flapping the hand, rather than the arm, from a stationary position, has become established.

A feature is that, of the gestures recorded in this section, this is the one most readily imitated. If the mother waves to him from a distance, the infant stops to return the wave and may approach a few steps to fixate the mother, hand aloft, as if expecting a game of imitation.

When he is standing against the mother, the same wave-flap may be used to strike her knee, attracting her attention.

However, in the majority of instances, the observer cannot tell what elicits the gesture and the child is most often facing away from the mother when he makes it.

Two arms straight up. This is one of the commonest gestures which, in everyday life, a mother leading her child is seen responding to. The child moves to face the mother's front, looks up and stretches two hands above his head, whereupon the mother lifts him into the carrying position.

In the present situation (the mother is seated) the occurrence of the gesture was recorded for two-thirds of all infants at least once in ten minutes, whether the child was close to the mother or not, facing her or facing away, himself being stationary, walking or running. In the majority of instances, the infant can have had no expectation of being lifted. Nor was there any identifiable stimulus to elicit the gesture when the child was distant from the mother except when it was observed as an aid to balancing; if an infant of this age group loses balance, he falls back into the sitting position: the two arms may erect momentarily as he goes over or rectifies himself.

To evoke a response from the mother, the child must be close to her, preferably touching, and nearly always *en face*. If the seated mother does not take him on to her lap, the infant tries to climb up beside her; failing to do this he returns to her front, his hands aloft, which he may bring down hard upon her thighs. Her attention secured, she leans forward to talk to him. Then the child may persist by reaching for the mother's face.

Besides proximity, the difference between the posture when it is addressed to the mother and when it occurs *in vacuo* is the length of time the arms stay up. When the mother is not involved, the arms can be raised and lowered within two seconds. If the infant expects to be lifted, he will maintain the posture, often thrusting himself against her at the same time, until the mother acknowledges it.

Putting a part of the hand into the mouth. Two-thirds of the infants put a finger or thumb into their mouth at least once in ten minutes. To find some unity amongst the contexts in which the infant does this, positive and negative criteria must be introduced. He is not making a long sortie away from the mother, nor running about energetically. He is not engaged in an easily definable activity, like scraping a patch of ground or arranging small material. If other people are close by, he may stop to watch, but will not engage them. He is likely to be facing or be about to face the mother. He is likely to be stationary, and his next walk will take him to or towards the mother. To generalize: the gesture accompanies vacillation rather than involvement in a course of action and it presages increasing proximity to the mother.

POINTING: AN ORIENTATION RESPONSE

Pointing is the most common gesture made in the field. The sight or sound of any remote object that catches his attention is sufficient to elicit it. Its most conspicuous feature is that it is done only when the infant is stationary. The frequency of the occurrence of pointing varies greatly amongst infants, ranging from 0 to 14 times over ten minutes. The amount of pointing is not related to interesting events as an adult sees them, but to the individual child's tendency. An observer can seldom identify the source of the stimulus; mothers sometimes can, especially when the child is old enough to talk, but it can be imaginary things that engage his attention; a child will point to a part of the horizon where nothing is moving and tell the mother that a man is coming.

Pointing does not often occur in the newly walking, but by 15 months of age it is part of every infant's repertoire. Amongst the features of this gesture which distinguish it from other arm signals are the following. First, the mother herself is never pointed at. The hand points outwards; and the mother is fixated. Then the object is given scrutiny. Second, it is the most reliable criterion for the identification of a mother–infant pair. When other criteria fail to apply, the child will always relate the event which surprises him to the mother: when he is distant, by looking at her; when he is beside her, by tapping her with the other hand if she does not pay attention. In this respect, it differs from waving, smiling and other expressive gestures which are directed to strangers as well as to the mother. Third, it is the terminating point of a course of activity. Once an infant has run outwards, stopped to look at the mother and point into the distance, he does not usually proceed in the same direction but looks around and goes off elsewhere. Fourth, it is not mimicked from the mother. She and the child are never seen to imitate each other's pointing, as they do some other signals. Indeed, the mother seldom pays attention; she is unlikely even to be looking when he points, yet the frequency of the gesture does not decrease with age. Nor does its purpose appear to have been learned imitatively. In everyday life at home, mothers use it as an intention movement usually to indicate the involvement that will follow: she will either reach for the object he wants, or use it to select amongst alternatives. Infants, on the other hand, do not use it as an intention movement until they are around 3 years of age, by which time its conventional, adult applications have come into operation alongside the earlier.

When a mother rises, looks at the infant and points, the effect is to make herself conspicuous to him. For example, if she wants the child to come away from one area to go to another, her indication of the desired direction by pointing to it only results in the infant's gazing at her face or hand. It is generally believed (though no data are available) that the first year of life will pass before an infant can detach his gaze from the mother's hand, even in his own home, to look in the direction indicated. When he is out of doors, his inability to detach the gaze lasts longer. He will be around 2 years old before she can expect an adequate response to her signalled command to move away to another place. Until then, her pointing only draws attention to herself. Though the mother may emphasize the gesture and shout, the infant continues to stare blankly at her face, and this seems to be the only response that it evokes.

The child, in his turn, makes himself highly conspicuous to her by his orientation response. He comes to an abrupt stop, angles himself to the midline between the stimulus and the mother and raises one arm towards it while his head turns simultaneously towards her. The rigidity of this posture suggests that it should convey information. No obvious emotional state other than heightened alertness is transmitted. In the field, states of high arousal are accompanied by sounds. When distressed, the infant cries; when angry, he screams; when frightened, he whimpers; when excited, he squeals. Otherwise, his utterances during natural play consist of talking to himself. Hence, lack of vocalization during the orientation response has a communicative significance, i.e. the information is conveyed in the posture; no reinforcement by sound is necessary.

Something else is communicated by this gesture. Although mothers whom I have questioned do not give enlightening answers, their own reactions show an understanding of the difference between a sign to proceed and one of the unlikelihood of proceeding. When a toddler is going to move outwards from the mother, he faces the intended direction and erects one arm: this gesture seems to be a prolongation of the habit of putting an arm up for balance. It is common to see a child being given a smack when, after being reproved for going to a forbidden place, he puts an arm up in that direction. But when the child points, the mother is unconcerned. She seems to know that his pointing will disengage his attention from a source of interest.

The pointing has a definite referent. It can be elicited by any disturbance evoking surprise, by stimuli evoking mild fear, or those which if close by would arouse strong fear. An observer who cannot locate the referent will bear in mind the lack of veridicality in infant's distance vision: large objects which are far off appear to be small objects nearby. One mother stated that her infant was pointing at birds; another infant was pointing at aeroplanes; another at the absence of aeroplanes, because he expected to see them; another at the sound of wind in the trees; another at the noise of traffic in the distance. Although mothers' replies are not helpful in explaining the high frequency of infants pointing, they do indicate a feature that accords with the general interpretation of this gesture: the separateness or inaccessibility of the stimulus. Added to this might be the condition of inaccessibility without the mother's company: some infants point to where they want the

209

mother to take them: if she refuses to go the child does not proceed in that direction.

The fact that the gesture of pointing has a sender, receiver and external referent brings it into the category of a purposive communication, the function of which is to relate two persons by way of an independent object in the environment. It is the first – and only – purposive communication at a distance which the child is able to make until he can vocalize intelligibly. What is symbolized by other gestures in the field is appropriate to a simpler context, communicable by action, such as presence-seeking (by looking), proximity-seeking (by locomotion), contact-making (by touch), play-seeking (by waving) and other dyadic transactions which bring the pair together to prepare for other forms of interaction. When the referent is a remote object, however, a new relationship between the parties is set up. It has become a learning situation, appropriate to other kinds of experience. For instance, were the family's sojourn taking place in primitive territory, it would be important for the mother not only to be kept aware of possible dangers in the vicinity, but to be alerted before the situation developed into an emergency. Hamburg (1969) writes, on the basis of observations on non-human primates: ' The early learning of what to fear, what is dangerous in a particular environment, seems to be quite flexible; such fear may attach to different objects, in different circumstances, in different environments . . .' The orientation response of pointing, which signals minor disturbances in the environment, would serve just this function. The infant, in turn, learns by the mother's indifference to his communication what events are not dangerous.

FOLLOWING

If the mother moved off unexpectedly, following did not occur among field cases whose ages at the time of observation went up to about 22 months. Out of seventeen instances chosen for observation, the infant's response to the mother's departure was as under:

Continue playing	1
Make brief approach, then stop	2
Retreat briefly, then stop	2
Refuse to move, ' freeze '	12
	17 cases

When the infant is older, there is usually verbal exchange with the mother before she moves away, so following behaviour, the primitive animal's response to a parent's departure, is not applicable. When the mother persuades the child to accompany her, especially by making a game of the move off, he follows, though her leading has to be punctuated by stopping to wait.

FATIGUE AND CONFLICT

When an infant is tired (as confirmed by some mothers in an arranged sample), he wanders in different directions, not walking for long in a straight line nor stopping for long, alert, to scan. He looks to and from moving people, but his thumb is often in his mouth, or his hand flicks an ear or rubs the head or eyes, and the general direction of his locomotion takes him towards his mother, where he leans against her or ' asks ' to be lifted.

One form of conflict, decision at a choice point, came to light as a result of recording the arm movements of infants following the mother as she walked. The child's attention captured by an attraction which would take him along a different route to that taken by the mother, he would pause to look in each direction, touch the back of his head with the flat of his hand, then set off to rejoin the mother. Instead of an alternative path, a familiar person who brings the child to a stop by talking to or offering him something could elicit the same gesture just before he ran to pursue the mother. If the infant tended to suck his fingers, part of the hand was put into the mouth when the mother was about to be followed after the interruption.

When hesitancy is accompanied by either of these two gestures, it is resolved by the infant's seeking the mother; if he is going to separate himself from her, there is no prior indication of it. When the mother is stationary, the disturbing stimulus is not so easy to identify and the gestures are accompanied by vacillation: the child is obviously unsettled.

The appearance of apparently irrelevant gestures at this point occurs in the kind of situation which is usually contrived for experimental purposes to produce conflicting alternatives. In the full form of the expression movements, the arms are in a position infants commonly adopt in sleep; one hand cradles the head, the other is up to the mouth for thumb-sucking. Mothers recognize varieties of it as signs of tiredness: the infant tugs at an ear lobe, rubs his scalp or eyes, holds a cloth toy to his cheek and probably puts a thumb into his mouth as well. The adopting, at a choice point, of a posture indicative of sleep, brings to mind the phenomena called ' displacement activities ' in lower animals whereby a behaviour pattern determined by either of two incompatible tendencies can be superseded by one more often induced in other circumstances.

Behaviour comparable to that of these infants was noted in adults by Tinbergen (1951) who suggested that scratching behind the ear and sleep (at low intensity, in the form of yawning) occurred as displacement activities in situations of conflict. In Grant's (1968) study of adults and children, scratching and head grooming were ' observed in situations where ambivalence was clearly demonstrated, these situations consisting essentially of the (behaviour sequence) triad approach–X–retreat '. From his own and others' experiments on gulls, cats and rats, Delius (1967) presents evidence that grooming or preening, which are commonly involved in displacement behaviour, are 'largely controlled by neurophysiological mechanisms which are also responsible for de-arousal and sleep'; the occurrence of some displacement activities would cancel, through the activation of an arousal inhibiting system, the arousal increment generated by conflict or thwarting. Delius concludes that the occurrence of sleep as displacement in several species might be regarded as a regulatory overshoot, and grooming and other patterns as activities which conduce to de-arousal through stimulus reduction, switch of attention onto stimuli of little novelty, or generation of repetitive stimulation.

Amongst human infants, the evidence for displacement activity would be stronger if ear-flicking and thumb-sucking could be shown to be occurring out of their normal functional context. 'Brief skin-care activities' such as chewing, scratching and shaking have been located in monkeys subjected to mildly stressful situations by Rowell and Hinde (1963); it is likely that these activities partake, with the head-stroking and thumb-sucking of human infants, of a common base in the reaction to increased awareness of discomfort.

IDENTIFICATION OF THE MOTHER

Although the mothers' activity was marginal to the topic, one feature was noted which distinguished them from other women with whom the infant might mix; that is, the ventral orientation to the infant, which is maintained even in those cases where mother and child are not seen to be in contact during the observation period. When she is sitting or lying on the ground, she positions herself and changes position to face whatever direction he is playing in.

If she is sitting on a bench and therefore unable to orient her body towards the infant, she looks round frequently whenever he moves about behind her. It can be deduced that a mother is ill at ease unless her child is playing in front of her. This is not through fear of the distance he might go undetected, for there is usually a fence behind the bench she sits on; he may be allowed to go as far as he wishes in the forward direction, getting lost to sight through mingling with people, or pushed over by other children without her showing much concern, but he does not play in the rear for long without her looking round impatiently. Thus a mother can be singled out amongst a group of women when no other criteria of mother–infant identification apply, such as when the child comes under the influence of age-mates and no longer makes periodic returns to the base.

Discussion

There is ample evidence for the view that attachment, assessed in terms of proximity which the infant maintains to the mother, is strong at a 'period of life after the child is capable of free and independent locomotion but before he is able to fend for himself in an emergency' (Bowlby, 1958).

ATTACHMENT BEHAVIOUR OUT OF DOORS

The criteria of attachment in a study of this nature are the factors which assist the identification of a mother–infant pair under field conditions.

In a few minutes of liberty a child will give evidence of his affiliation by:

(i) frequently running to and from the mother;

(ii) keeping within sight or sound of the mother;

(iii) stopping for longer by the mother's side than he does when he is away from her;

(iv) glancing at the mother from a distance; on the move he orients himself to two objects simultaneously, looking back to the mother while moving away from her or at something afar when he is returning to her;

(v) physical contact of a quick make-and-break nature, not prolonged, as in the case of other higher primates at a comparable age.

These standards can only be disrupted by the presence of other children who come to play in the vicinity. Once the infant has joined two or three age-mates, he will go farther from the mother than usual and may stay away until she fetches him.

The ability to maintain contact also breaks down if the mother moves away unexpectedly. Once mother and infant are on the move, an illusion of successful following can be given when a mother waits frequently on her route, for whenever she stops the child's ability to regain contact with a stationary mother takes effect.

Other criteria belong to the areas of expression and communication. Returning to greet the mother, especially by touching and putting two arms up to be lifted are behaviours rarely directed to anyone but the mother, though the newly-walking have been seen to approach and cling to companions of the mother, and even to strangers. Picking up small objects from the ground to take back to the mother is a good indicator of affiliation, but if another woman offers to accept what the infant has retrieved, he may playfully bring back things to her. The infant's waving to a person is no guide at all to the degree of familiarity with him. The best way to identify a mother–infant pair is to see whom a child looks at when he is astonished or startled by external events like a noise in the distance or passing animal; only the mother's attention is sought in such circumstances and the orientation response, in addition to the purposes already mentioned, re-locates, for the infant, the mother's whereabouts when he turns to look at her.

There is probably survival value in the infant's tendency to use gestures out of context and with no expectation of a response from people. For there is no evidence that fear of a specific class of object (strangers, animals) operates in its absence to keep the child close to his mother. Persistence in the use of gestures such as raising the arms to be lifted, reaching for unattainable objects and pointing to imaginary novelties suggests a prolongation of that medium of communication (overlapping with speech development) the

213

functional significance of which would be to increase the probability of a response from the mother and other adults in the vicinity. By rendering conspicuous the sight of an unescorted infant, gesturing would protect him against some dangers which his new locomotor ability, coupled with inadequate distance vision, could lead him to. The identification of a particular infant amongst his age-mates is, of course, assisted by the sight of his arm movements, owing to the individual differences between children in this medium of expression.

Finally there are some internal conditions of the infant, such as being cold, hungry or ready for sleep, exerting an influence on proximity-seeking. The most obvious one seen in the open is that of fatigue, the signs of which are those given by infants at bed-time and which are observed to occur in some situations of conflict. Behaviours in fatigue and conflict may be connected through a common state which would subserve the function of attachment out of doors. For, although in fatigue, as in sleep, the child's interest is withdrawn from external stimulation, the mother's taking him on to her knee, cradling and talking to him, substitutes another kind of stimulation – one which is not incompatible with his going to sleep. The occurrence of such a common state, recognizable by the signs of tiredness as the child turned to face the mother when a remote stimulus competed for his orientation during a bout of following, would have an adaptive value in that stimuli from afar, likely to produce in the child decreased proximity to the mother, would become blocked in favour of stimulation provided by her.

In work in progress, sequences of behaviour are related to finer groupings within the 1 to 3-year-old age range. Besides randomly drawn cases, a sample of infants provided by volunteer mothers who attend Infant Welfare Clinics is under observation in field conditions.

Acknowledgements

The pilot study reported above forms an introduction to a three-year project on attachment behaviour in human infants from walking age to 3-plus, which is made possible by the award of a Leverhulme Trust Fellowship through the Mental Health Research Fund. The work is registered for the degree of Ph.D. under the supervision of Professor Brian Foss, Institute of Education and Dr J. Bowlby, The Tavistock Clinic. For introduction of the concept of the orientation response into this study, I am indebted to a suggestion by Professor R. A. Hinde.

REFERENCES

Bowlby, J. (1951). *Maternal Care and Mental Health.* Geneva: W.H.O. Monogr. No. 2.
Bowlby, J. (1958). The nature of the child's tie to the mother. *Internat. J. Psychoanal.* **29**, 1–24.

Burnside, L. H. (1927). Coordination in the locomotion of infants. *Genet. Psychol. Monog.* **2**.

Delius, J. D. (1967). Displacement activities and arousal. *Nature, Lond.* **214**, 1259–60.

Grant, E. C. (1968). An ethological description of non-verbal behaviour during interviews. *Br. J. Med. Psychol.* **41**, 177–83.

Hamburg, D. A. (1969). Observation of mother-infant interaction in primate field studies. In *Determinants of Infant Behaviour*. Ed. B. M. Foss, London: Methuen.

Hediger, H. (1955). *Studies of the Psychology and Behaviour of Captive Animals in Zoos and Circuses.* London: Butterworth.

Rowell, T. E. and Hinde, R. A. (1963). Responses of rhesus monkeys to mildly stressful situations. *Anim. Behav.* **11**, 235–43.

Siegel, S. (1956). *Non-parametric Statistics for the Behavioral Sciences.* New York: McGraw-Hill.

Smart, M. S. and Smart, R. C. (1967). *Children: Development and Relationships.* New York: Macmillan.

Tinbergen, N. (1951). *The Study of Instinct.* Oxford: Clarendon Press.

9

BEHAVIOUR OF CHILDREN AND THEIR MOTHERS AT SEPARATION AND GREETING

N. BLURTON JONES AND GILL M. LEACH *

SUMMARY

The behaviour of thirty-five mothers and their 2–4-year-old children was observed during separation at the beginning of a playgroup and during greeting at the end. The frequencies of the various items of behaviour (*smile, approach, touch, wave, show–give, point, leave, play,* etc.) were counted up for each individual and factor analysis showed the following main dimensions of behaviour: crying at separation leading to greeting with either rapid approach with arms raised and touching the mother, or no response except looking at the mother and pointing at an object. Ready departure from the mother went with greetings in which play continued or objects were shown or given to the mother. Smiling by mother and child was separate from these but went with smiling to the teacher.

The child's approach and arm raising were both shown to increase the chance of the mother's touching the child. When this effect was taken into account the mothers of children who cried at separation were found to behave no differently from mothers of children who did not cry. When we analysed separately children under and over 2½ years old (after which age crying is very rare) the mothers of young criers were found to be more responsive than mothers of young non-criers, and mothers of old criers were less responsive than mothers of old non-criers. Mothers of children who were less likely to move away from the mother were found in this and a second sample to be more responsive in terms of likelihood of touching a child who approached.

These results are compared with Ainsworth's and Schaffer and Emerson's findings on rather younger children. Comparison is made difficult by their not having explicitly taken the child's behaviour into account when assessing maternal responsiveness.

Introduction

This paper concerns the occurrence of a number of small items of behaviour shown by the child and its mother in two brief and restricted situations: when the mother leaves the child behind at playgroup, and when she returns to take it home later on. Two main points arise from this study. One is the relevance of our observations and analysis to the concept of attachment discussed in the recent book by Bowlby (1969). The other is the relationship

* Department of Growth and Development, Institute of Child Health, University of London.

between the behaviour of the child and the behaviour of the mother, with especial emphasis on the problem of separating influences of one on the other. This mainly centres around a search for the reasons why some of the children cried on separation and others did not. Our approach is very similar to that proposed by Bowlby (1969: 331–5) but covers a much narrower field.

The present study began in a deliberately undirected way. The only questions in mind were (1) will we see what Blurton Jones (1967) saw before and (2) how are the items of behaviour organised in separation and greeting? This traditionally unfashionable (non-hypothesis-testing) approach is quite usual in ethological studies and has proved valuable in research on animal behaviour. We feel that its use in human behaviour studies should be fully explored.

The interactions between children and their mothers are composed of a number of simple items of behaviour which can be observed repeatedly. While watching children with their mothers at nursery school Blurton Jones (1967) found it quite unnecessary to describe the behaviour even in this most 'psychological' situation by using predetermined categories like affectionate, reticent, dependent, joyful. Starting from the observable behaviour it should be possible then to build up the real pattern of occurrence of different kinds of behaviour without confusion resulting from ill-defined everyday or theoretical categories. Nonetheless, some preliminary discussion of the general theme of the child's attachment to its mother is necessary.

There are several interesting recent studies of 'attachment' and some signs of a convergence of the approach and ways of thought of child psychologists and ethologists. Psychologists have sought clear observable criteria for attachment (like crying on separation, as in Schaffer and Emerson, 1964), and have reached the stage of arguing about which are the best measures. But here there still seems to be a crucial difference between workers coming from psychology and those coming from ethology. The former are still writing as if there is a real entity which is 'attachment', existing over and above the observable measures (but see Walters and Parke, 1964; and Walters, 1968). Ethologists, asking themselves what they mean by words like 'attachment', find that the only use for such a term is as shorthand for a number of behaviour items which vary together, or are found to be related together in a more complex way in a causal system. It then becomes evident that the existence of a 'thing' like attachment can be justified in no other way than by the observable 'measures'.

One may then find it useful to decide as a first simplification whether 'attachment' is one thing or many. If the disputed 'measures' of attachment really are alternative measures of the same thing they must be correlated. They must to some extent be measures of each other. Otherwise, as Ainsworth says (1969b) attachment must be multi-dimentional, in other words not one ' thing ' at all but several unrelated groupings of behaviour. To study development of these unrelated groups as if they were one would tend to obscure any relationship to causal factors.

This argument may appear to be contradicted by the suggestion that some kinds of behaviour of children to the mother are mature forms of attachment, in contrast to others which are immature forms. For this use of the term attachment to mean anything more than ' behaviour to mother ', it must imply a relationship between the early forms and the later forms. The obvious meaning for this particular statement would be that individuals who scored high for the behaviour designated immature-attachment when young, would later score high for behaviour designated mature-attachment. No one seems yet to have examined their data for such a relationship. This relies on having longitudinal data, but even in a cross-sectional study such as ours, with a range of ages, one would expect immature forms to occur at a younger average age than mature forms of attachment.

Procedure

We recorded, as occurring or as not occurring, four items of mother behaviour and twenty items of child behaviour for the brief but flexible periods (*a*) separation: when the mother began to leave the room to when she went out of the child's view, and then (*b*) greeting: the first burst of activity when she reappeared at the end of the play session. The behaviour items recorded are named and defined in Appendix 1. Records were made on prepared sheets. The sheets had behaviour items listed down the side, the top half for arrival, the second half for departure from the playgroup. Each column represented one day's observation on a child. If a behaviour occurred a figure (1) was entered in the appropriate square. The sheets were designed to simulate coding sheets for punching cards and the results were subsequently punched onto cards. Total scores for the first ten complete (both separation and greeting) records for each individual were counted and punched on another series of cards used for inter-individual comparisons and correlations. Data from thirty-five children were used.

It was very difficult to collect these data. The main problems were: events occurring in the corridor instead of in the playroom, two children arriving simultaneously, mothers sharing the job of bringing each other's children, other adults or siblings occasionally bringing them, mothers coming much earlier than usual, children getting ill or going on holiday. We therefore have very few uninterrupted series of observations and have not tried to show serial changes in behaviour. We tried to collect as much data on as many children as we could. Where a choice had to be made we chose the younger child in order to increase the amount of data on ' difficult ' separations.

We each collected data on different sets of children but with some overlap; we have seventy-one simultaneous recordings for inter-observer reliability tests. N.B.J. always observed from the observation room, through a one-way screen with a sound system. G.M.L. observed from inside the playroom. The children and mothers were used to her being there because they were also subjects of her long-term observations of mother and child for which she wished to be in the room with them. This difference in procedure would appear to be the cause of the one difference in frequency of behaviour in our records: G.M.L. recorded more talking both by child and mother. Some of the analyses were repeated separately on the data from each observer. The results were almost identical.

The factor analysis procedures were the same as those used by Blurton Jones (Ch. 4).

The mothers knew that their children came to the playgroup for studies of normal behaviour of children but were not told that we also collected data on mothers. The children were recruited as is described in the chapter by Blurton Jones on child–child interactions and were basically normal healthy children from the immediate neighbourhood.

Analysis: 1 – Patterns of attachment

We have argued that the behaviour items which measure 'attachment' (if there is such a thing) should vary together. We have looked at the way behaviour items vary in four kinds of variation. These are (1) how the items of behaviour vary from one individual to another (the between-individual factor analysis), using the total scores for each individual's first ten complete records; (2) how the items of behaviour vary from one day to another, using the daily records from the first ten complete records (the between day analysis); (3) which items are performed mainly to the mother rather than to other women and (4) how they vary with age. The first analysis tells us about variation from one individual to another, the second tells us something about how this variation arises. We are primarily interested in the cross-individual variation but refer to the cross-day analysis where appropriate.

BETWEEN-INDIVIDUAL ANALYSIS: HOW THE ITEMS OF BEHAVIOUR VARY FROM ONE INDIVIDUAL TO ANOTHER

We have correlated each item with each other item and used factor analysis to summarise the resulting correlation matrix. This shows us the most economic way of looking at the data and gives a mathematical indication of the patterns of occurrence of the behaviour. It should allow us to make a decision as to which possible measures of attachment (*crying, smiling, approaching,* etc.) do in fact measure the same thing as each other, judged from the size of their loadings on the factor. We used the Varimax rotation giving orthogonal factors, employing the same computer program as in Blurton Jones (Ch. 4).

The reliability of factor analysis is hard to assess. In our inter-individual analysis there are too few individuals compared to the number of variables to allow us to split the data and compare the results. However, a preliminary analysis with twenty-seven individuals when we had completed that number gave what seemed to us to be the same picture as the final analysis of thirty-five individuals. The results of each observer for our simultaneous observations were analysed and the resulting factors compared. The patterns of loadings look very similar, suggesting that we were tending to record in a similar manner and that factor analysis of seventy records gave quite reliable results. The significant correlations also showed great similarity.

The various analyses seem to agree well on the patterns of greeting and of separation and to corroborate our impressions about the children's behaviour, but we find them less convincing on the relationship between these patterns. We have consequently examined the original correlations between the highest loading items in each pattern at separation with those at greeting. These patterns are now summarised before more detailed consideration of the factors.

Two patterns of greeting were characteristic of children who *cried* or did *pucker* at separation: (1) consists of *approach, arms up, touch*. The other (2) consists of no clear reaction other than continuing *play, pucker* and sometimes *point*.

On the actual days when *cry* or (less so) *pucker* occur, the most likely greeting is *pucker* and *point*. On days when the child did not *cry, approach, arm up, touch* are more common. The other patterns of greeting seem to be more characteristic of children who rarely or never did *cry* or *pucker* at separation. These are (3) *smiling* by child and mother; (4) *run, jump, laugh*; (5) *approach, touch, smile*; (6) *play, talk*.

Patterns of separation were (1) *cry, pucker, approach, touch*; (2) *away, play*; (3) *away, approach, kiss, smile*; (4) mutual *smile*, and *smile at teacher*.

In describing the factors or their loadings we try not to leap directly to putative causal factors. This involves some inaccuracy of language. The term ' pattern ' above for instance does not, as may have appeared, necessarily imply that each pattern occurs on its own exclusive of the other patterns. The factor analysis is only able to make this statement for certain pairs of patterns, others are orthogonal to each other.

Five factors (Table 9·1) were derived from inter-individual correlations. The first four, after Varimax rotation, each accounted for 10–12% of the variance. This is sometimes regarded as very little but we feel that (*a*) a large main factor was not really expected despite the unitary ' attachment ' theories and (*b*) it is realistic to expect behaviour to require many factors to account for the total variance. Age, sex, history of the mother–child dyad, mother's behaviour, the child's occupation when mother returns, and the amount of attention given by the teacher are a few of the possible influences that come to mind. (c) Even with the vastly superior techniques of measurement of physique, studies of physique in this department have found similar division of the first 50% of the variance between several factors (J. M. Tanner, pers. comm.).

We summarise the factors and our interpretation of them below.

TABLE 9·1. *Results of between individual factor analysis of behaviour of child and mother (M) at separation (A) and greeting (D) (ASMILET = smile at teacher on arrival)*

Factor	1	2	3	4	5
% of variance	11.824	10.962	10.273	11.243	7.753
SEX	0.084	−0.284	0.434	0.325	0.010
AGE	0.023	−0.340	−0.042	0.487	−0.032
DMTOUCH	−0.515	−0.147	0.058	−0.551	−0.107
DMAPPROACH	0.097	−0.165	−0.025	−0.613	0.042
DMSMILE	−0.042	−0.569	−0.136	−0.493	0.035
DPUCKER	−0.616	0.170	−0.105	−0.464	0.122
DJUMP	−0.133	0.190	0.570	0.427	−0.212
DPOINT	−0.152	0.521	0.090	−0.042	0.047
DSHOW	0.526	−0.014	0.035	−0.259	−0.061
DARM UP	−0.785	0.155	0.212	−0.218	−0.192
DTOUCH	−0.750	0.008	0.063	−0.303	−0.320
DTALK	0.185	−0.118	−0.374	0.314	0.103
DAWAY	0.582	−0.088	0.298	−0.252	−0.231
DPLAY	0.793	0.314	0.069	−0.092	−0.221
DRUN	−0.416	0.007	0.564	−0.006	−0.467
DWALK	−0.595	−0.134	−0.396	0.119	0.083
DSMILE	−0.135	−0.613	0.053	0.011	−0.432
AMTALK	0.027	0.146	0.490	0.106	0.550
AMTOUCH	0.110	−0.112	0.792	0.031	0.135
AMAPPROACH	0.058	0.047	0.741	−0.036	0.046
AMSMILE	−0.219	−0.583	0.350	0.099	0.275
APUCKER	−0.520	0.312	−0.110	−0.603	0.099
ACRY	−0.332	0.315	−0.263	−0.621	0.101
AKISS	0.158	0.426	0.580	0.263	0.096
AWAVE	−0.004	−0.045	−0.030	0.435	0.161
ATOUCH	−0.069	−0.137	−0.098	−0.098	0.449
ATALK	0.206	0.004	0.242	0.087	0.697
AAWAY	0.105	−0.493	0.000	0.563	0.225
APLAY	0.228	0.558	0.167	0.310	−0.111
ARUN	0.345	0.101	−0.135	−0.401	−0.410
AWALK	−0.042	0.562	0.083	−0.084	−0.024
ASMILET	−0.165	−0.521	0.321	0.272	−0.135
ASMILE	0.085	−0.678	0.126	0.229	0.295
ALOOK	−0.280	−0.052	0.099	−0.016	0.766

Factor 1

11.8% of variance (separation: *run* +0.345, *play* +0.228, *cry* −0.332, *pucker* −0.520; greeting: *play* +0.793, *away* +0.582, *show* +0.526, *arm up* −0.785, *touch* −0.750, *pucker* −0.616, *walk* −0.595, *mother touch* −0.515, *run* −0.416).

Here we have a clear approach and clinging greeting related to crying at separation. This contrasts with continuing or resuming *play* and showing things to the mother in children unlikely to cry at separation.

Factor 2

10.9% of variance (separation: *play* +0.558, *walk* +0.562, *kiss* +0.426, *cry* +0.315, *smile* −0.678, *mother smile* −0.583, *smile at teacher* −0.521, *away* −0.493; greeting: *point* +0.521, *play* +0.314, *smile* −0.613, *mother smile* −0.569, *avert* −0.516).

Here there is a contrast between mutual smiling both at greeting and separation by children who do not cry, and *approaching* and *kissing* during separation by children who cry, leading to no clear greeting behaviour except *pointing* and continuing to play. *Talking* (−0.118) also helps to differentiate this from the inactive greeting of non-criers in factor 1 (*talk* +0.185 with *show*, *away*, *play* which have much higher positive loadings). The existence of these two forms of inactive greeting is very interesting. It presumably represents, and provides with slightly more objective support than hitherto available, the distinction between minimal ' rejection ' of the mother by the child after separation and a simple healthy preoccupation with play rather than mother. It is surprising that ' smiley ' diads should emerge because one would expect smiling to relate to some other behaviour between child and mother. In factor 5 and in the between-day correlations this does seem to be the case. Comparison of frequencies of smiling and other behaviour in criers and non-criers showed the same for the data of both observers, so that this factor is not an ' observer ' factor. ' Smiley ' children also smile at the teacher a lot and this raises the related question of (*a*) whether all these responses differ in how specific they are to the mother and (*b*) how far some of the social behaviour which develops between mother and child is a precursor to social behaviour to other people. The contrasting loadings of *mother smile* and *cry* cannot really be taken as evidence for a reassuring effect of *smiling* although this would be well worth investigating.

Factor 3

10.2% of variance (separation: *mother touch* +0.792, *mother approach* +0.741, *kiss* +0.580, *mother talk* +0.490, *smile at teacher* +0.321, *cry* −0.263, *run* −0.135; greeting: *jump* +0.570, *run* +0.564, *walk* −0.396, *talk* −0.374, *sex* +0.434).

The conspicuous loadings on this factor are all forms of maternal behaviour at separation and *run* and *jump* at greeting. This factor has the highest loading for *sex* of any of the factors and it is hard to decide how this enters into the association of maternal behaviour at separation with *run* and *jump* greetings. *Kiss* also achieves its highest loading here and loads opposite to *cry* (in factor 2 they go the same way). This may mean that while *kissing* at separation is more typical of girls, there is also a sex difference in the meaning of kissing separations (maleness loads in the same direction as *kiss* and *cry* in factor 2, -0.248). The clustering of maternal behaviour may also depend on whether the child approaches the mother or calls to her to kiss the child goodbye. *Talk* ($+0.242$) loads with *kiss* on this factor. We think that it would be easy to over-exaggerate this suggestion of a sex difference in maternal behaviour at separation; it is more likely to reflect differences in the demands of the child than in the responsiveness of the mother.

Factor 4

11.2% of variance (separation: *away* $+0.563$, *wave* $+0.435$, *play* $+0.310$, *cry* -0.621, *pucker* -0.603, *run* -0.401; greeting: *jump* $+0.427$, *talk* $+0.341$, *mother approach* -0.613, *mother touch* -0.551, *mother smile* -0.493, *mother talk* -0.483, *pucker* -0.464, *touch* -0.303, *age* $+0.487$).

This factor corresponds closely to age differences found in another part of the study. We find there that the relationship of maternal greeting behaviour to age is exaggerated here. This comes about because (*a*) young children initiate more interactions with their mother and (*b*) the mother initiates more with the younger child. The responsiveness of the mothers does not change. It is important to remember that this 'age factor' is independent of the others, where age had considerably lower loadings.

Factor 5

7.7% of variance (separation: *look* $+0.766$, *talk* $+0.697$, *mother talk* $+0.550$, *touch* $+0.449$, *run* -0.410; greeting: *run* -0.467, *smile* -0.432, *touch* -0.320).

This factor accounts for rather less of the variance than the others, and the high loadings for *talk* might be regarded as an indication of inter-observer differences except that *talk* loads high only at separation and the observers disagreed on *talk* at both times. The greeting is of some interest in that it links *smile* to *approach* and *touch*, but leaves it unrelated to *crying*. The *talking* at separation must simply reflect the likelihood of saying goodbye along with any kind of separation. We also did not distinguish 'mummy' which goes with *approach* and *crying* from 'see you later' which often does not.

To try to summarise what is already a summary is difficult. It is clear that the child's reaction to separation and to its mother's return is multidimensional, there are many directions in which it varies. Perhaps only one of these should be ' attachment ', and it seems to us rather arbitrary as to which it should be. That *smile* with *run* and *jump*, and *smile* with *run* and *touch* as well as *show* are important aspects of the child's relationship to the mother would be denied by few. But they are different aspects from *pucker, walk, run, arms up, touch*, or *play* or *point*. To translate into everyday terms and oversimplify even further: some children need their mothers, some children like them. Some need and like their mothers, some need her but don't specially like her, some like her but don't need her. No doubt some could be found who don't like her and don't need her (they may, or may not, dislike her or in any sense be aggressive to her).

This result surprised us as much as it might disturb attachment theorists. For instance we had been interested in being able to show whether *smiling* reflected some ' sociable ' or proximity-seeking tendency in the child as suggested by Blurton Jones (1967). At the simplest level this would lead one to expect children who *cry* to *smile* more than those who do not cry. This is not so. Factor 5 and between-day analysis gives some grounds for linking *smile* to an *approach* tendency, but it is a different kind of *approach* from that associated with *crying*. The findings are more reminiscent of Ambrose's (1963) emphasis on the different kinds of interaction evoked by *crying* and by *smiling* in babies (leading perhaps to relatively independent developmental processes) than it is of Bowlby's (1969) emphasis on *smiling* as an important part of attachment behaviour. Our data, being cross-sectional (and as yet ignoring the selectivity of response to mother as opposed to others, which we see below is different for different behaviour patterns) does not allow us finally to solve this problem.

BETWEEN-DAY ANALYSIS: HOW THE ITEMS OF BEHAVIOUR VARY FROM ONE DAY TO ANOTHER

Between-day correlations and factor analysis gave basically very similar results to the inter-individual analysis, showing the same kinds of separation and greeting behaviour. There was one striking difference. *Crying* at separation was on the same factor with *point* at greeting and not with the *approach* and cling greeting. The original correlations confirm the impression that on the days when a child cried at separation, its response to the mother at greeting would be minimal. The clinging greetings occur in the same children but on other days. This analysis was also done separately on each of four sections of the data, that from: (1) N.B.J. observations on criers (children who at some time cried at separation); (2) N.B.J. observations on non-criers (who never cried); (3) G.M.L. observations on criers; (4) G.M.L. observations on non-criers. These showed that *smile* occurred with *approaching* and *touching the mother* in each group. *Crying* went with increased *approach, touch, arms up* but not increased *smiling*. Criers more often *approach* and *touch* without *smiling* than do non-criers.

SPECIFICITY TO MOTHER

Several children were sometimes brought by other familiar adult females instead of their mother (some were also brought by fathers and siblings but these are excluded from the present analysis). This allows us to look to a limited extent to see how far certain behaviour is shown predominantly to the mother. This seems to be one of the major criteria of attachment implied in Ainsworth's and Bowlby's discussions. The children who were brought by other women must differ from those who were only ever brought by their mothers but nevertheless some interesting results emerge.

For each of several of the characteristic separation or greeting behaviours (*touch, arm up, smile, jump, show–give, point, talk, kiss, away*) we calculated two percentages (Table 9·2). One was the proportion of observations of the child with another woman when it showed the behaviour to her. The actual number of observations with another woman was much lower than with the mother and this may distort some of the comparisons (e.g. comparing *arms up* and *touch* which are not abundant in response to the mother because these are the children who separate fairly readily, and which never occurred in response to another woman, and *smiling*, which was very common to both).

The behaviour items listed above divided rather sharply into those almost entirely confined to mother, and those relatively often seen in response to other women as well. *Touch, arms up, kiss, point, jump* were almost completely exclusive to mother. *Smile, talk, show–give* were common to other women as well as to mother. *Away* at separation was slightly commoner to other women than to mothers. In this connection we may point out that *smile to teacher* was recorded, and in the factor analysis loaded along with *smiling to mother*.

There is altogether a complete fit between these findings and the factor analysis. (It should be noted that data on response to other women was not included in the factor analysis and that the children in this specificity study were partly different from those in the factor analysis, including some additional children.) Nowhere does the separation into specific or general response cut into any grouping produced in the factor analysis. *Touch* and *arm up* on the first factor are mother-specific whereas the oppositely loading *away* and *show* are generalised. *Smile*, on factor 2, is generalised but the oppositely loading (with *cry* at separation) *point* is mother-specific. It is interesting that behaviour characteristic of two other clusters, *kiss* at separation and *jump* at greeting, were both mother-specific. The abundance of *show* to other women makes an interesting unexpected comparison with the finding of Blurton Jones (1967) and Connolly and Smith (Ch. 6) that

TABLE 9.2. *Specificity of behaviour to mother. The occurrence of each behaviour to the mother (as % of greetings or departures with mother) is compared with its occurrence to other adult females (as % of greetings or departures with them). Behaviour to mother is on left of each column*

Subject	touch	arms up	smile	(D) jump	show	point	(D) talk	(A) kiss	(A) away	(D) approach	Greeting	Separation	Number of Records Greeting	Number of Records Separation
A	25	0	100	0	17	0	50	0	83	75	12	2	6	4
B	12	12.5	62	0	0	12	37	0	22	25	8	0	9	2
C	20	7	80	20	0	7	40	0	57	60	15	4	7	5
D	71	23	36	18	0	0	50	27	0	86	14	1	11	3
E	9	0	82	0	9	0	27	0	57	63	11	1	7	6
F	42	0	92	0	0	0	17	0	14	58	12	5	21	0
G	–	–	–	–	–	–	–	0	23	–	0	0	22	3
H	20	0	50	0	0	0	50	20	20	20	10	3	5	2
I	8	19	38	30	12	12	50	10	21	50	16	7	29	1
J	8	15	100	8	23	0	62	22	30	46	13	8	27	2
K	0	27	72	25	0	18	45	5	33	18	11	8	18	2
L	50	21	86	21	0	14	21	46	–	57	14	6	24	0
M	28	11	78	17	5	0	33	19	44	44	18	9	16	14
N	23	8	46	8	0	0	46	21	50	69	13	2	14	2

these were common responses to a strange adult paying his first visits to a nursery school. The association of *point* with mother-specificity and with *crying* makes an interesting, if less easily understood, comparison with Anderson's (Ch. 8) observations on *pointing* in younger children.

These measures strengthen our finding of a number of different patterns of behaviour to mother and allow us to specify that four of them are to do with attachment in the sense of mother-specificity but that another two are to do with either low attachment (e.g. *away*, *show*) or with quite different dimensions or kinds of relationship (e.g. *smile*).

THE RELATIONSHIP OF GREETING AND SEPARATION PATTERNS TO AGE

Patterns of greeting and separation which are mature or immature reflections of the same basic attachment should differ in the average age at which they occur. Longitudinal studies should show closer relationships between them but in the present study we can only look at the relationship of age to the patterns.

In the factor analysis the highest loading for age is +0.487 on factor 4. This factor was described above as an age factor and concerns a contrast between *crying* and clinging, *arms up* and *touch* (young) as in factor 1, and *away*, *play*, *wave*, *talk*, and *jump* (old). Low age also goes with all forms of maternal behaviour at greeting. The second highest loading of age (−0.340) is on factor 2, the *smile* factor, and this is the only other substantial age loading. This may be taken to imply that *waving, jumping* and possibly *smiling* are mature behaviour and that we have not shown them to be completely different from the immature forms. However, there still appear to be several immature and several mature forms of child-to-mother behaviour. The distinctions between factors 1 and 3 must be of a different kind from maturity distinctions, and the high loading of *sex* on factor 3 suggests that *kiss, run, jump* are specialities of girls regardless of their age. The distinction within factor 1 of *crying* and clinging versus *moving away* and *playing* also suggests different kinds of relationship to mother, and we have no evidence to say which of these is the antecedent of which later forms. However, we have no evidence which conflicts with the supposition that early *clinging* may be an antecedent of later *smiling, jumping* and *waving*.

Analysis: 2—Why do some children cry at separation?

BACKGROUND FACTORS

To examine the effect of background features on whether children cry at separation, we have been surveying the seventy-four children who have attended the playgroup at the time of writing. This survey is continuing and we give only a brief outline here before going on to analyse differences in maternal behaviour to criers and non-criers.

Data on whether a child cried or not come from a variety of sources which agree closely (arrival and departure records, teacher's logbook, memory of teacher and of the two authors). Clear effects of age can be seen from Table 9·3 and of presence of siblings at the playgroup from

TABLE 9·3. *Numbers of children crying on separation at different ages*

Age in months when start at playgroup	Number of children who cried	who did not	% who cry
21–24	7	4	63
25–27	7	8	47
28–30	4	6	40
31–33	1	8	12
34–36	1	4	20
37–39	1	5	17
40–42	0	1	0
43–45	1	5	17
46–48	0	1	0
49–51	0	2	0
52–54	0	1	0
55–57	0	2	0
58–60	0	1	0

Table 9·4. *Crying* is common under $2\frac{1}{2}$ years old and rare after that age. Presence of siblings makes crying much less likely. Table 9·5 suggests a sex difference but this is not significant on an Exact Test. Boys appear more likely to cry than girls. Effects of siblings in the family (but not at playgroup) and of birth order are not clear. To see whether mothers differ in their ' expectations ' of boys and girls we are also recording the proportion of criers whose mothers take them home again with those who persist in trying to leave their child at the playgroup. So far no significant overall sex difference has shown up. As well as assuming that ' attitudes '

TABLE 9·4. *Effect of presence of siblings at the playgroup on crying by children aged 30 months or less who have siblings (some scored in each situation because still under 30 months when older sibling left the playgroup)*

	Cry	Not
Alone	10	4
Together	1	10
Fisher's exact test $p=0.025$		

and 'expectations' communicate to the child via overt behaviour we are assuming that nearly as often they will reveal themselves to us in the mother's overt behaviour.

TABLE 9·5. *Sex differences in crying on separation*

| | Children of all ages | |
	Cry	Not
Boys	11	16
Girls	11	35

DIFFERENCES IN MATERNAL BEHAVIOUR RELATING TO CRYING AT SEPARATION

From the arrival and departure data we have attempted to find differences in maternal behaviour which relate to crying. There are two contrasting expectations from other work. The view put forward by Bowlby (1969) and others (mainly based on extreme cases) seems to be that over-dependence results from too little mothering. Applied to the variation among normal children this might predict that clinging and *crying* were inversely related to amounts of mother behaviour. The view suggested by most work on mother–infant interaction in animals, e.g. Rosenblatt (1965) and Hinde and Spencer-Booth (1967, 1968), is that the development of independence results from an increase in rejection by the mother. It is important that these workers have not concerned themselves with the relationship between variation in very early mothering behaviour and later development of independence. It may be that both Bowlby's and the opposing view are right but that the factors they are stressing are applied at different ages. Too little mothering very early in life may make the infant unable to respond by increased independence to later rejection. This also implies that if we cannot find a correlation with maternal behaviour at age 24–48 months it does not prove that maternal behaviour has no effect on separation.

Yet another view is suggested by the monkey studies of Rosenblum and Kaufmann (1968). Comparing their Bonnet macaques (*Macaca radiata*) with their Pig-tailed macaques (*M. nemestrina*) they conclude that the more a baby was allowed to roam around and interact with other monkeys the less it was affected by the removal of its mother. Perhaps increasing familiarity with the physical and social environment is responsible for the eventual reduction of the effects of separation from the mother. It may be that the 'safe-base' function of the mother stressed by Harlow and Harlow (1965) and Ainsworth (1969b) controls the amount of experience the infant is able to acquire. Some caution has to be attached to the findings of the laboratory monkey studies because DeVore (1963) has shown how in wild baboons the normal pattern of rejection by the mother is a sharp increase at 9–10 months when lactation apparently ceases. The elegant effects of environment on maternal rejection which Jensen *et al.* (1967, 1968) have demonstrated may mean that in the rich and unconfined wild situation there is very little rejection by the wild mother until the new baby arrives. The findings of Goodall (1968) on chimpanzee mothers also suggest that the relationship in the apes may differ from that in several monkey species. (This is perhaps the place to point out that the range of practices concerning separation of the child from the mother is as wide in man as in the whole of the rest of the mammals.)

Our attempt to find correlations between maternal behaviour and crying on separation has been voluntarily curtailed for two reasons. First, it is necessary to isolate variations in mother behaviour which are independent of variations in child behaviour. Some of the calculations involved in doing this are very tedious to do by hand, and we do not have a suitable computer program for them. Second, we have concluded that during the brief period covered by these observations the mothers are in a 'responding mode', simply dealing with the task of leaving the child and then greeting it again. It is therefore unlikely that we would find many differences in these observations.

In the present study we start with the simple quantitative differences between mothers of children who cry and the others. Mothers of children who had at some time cried on separation (1) more often *approached* the child during the separation; (2) more often *slipped out* and (3) less often *smiled* at the child during the separation. At greeting they more often *touched* the child. These (like the factor analysis) cut across any simple classification of warm or cold (i.e. more or less *touching, approaching, smiling*, and *talking*) receptive–unreceptive mothers, and stressed the necessity of examining the child's behaviour to see how far this or other features were determining the scores of the mothers. Because the mother's behaviour at separation can be assumed to be organised around the task of leaving her child we have removed the analysis of separation to Appendix 2 and here concentrate on the difference in greeting. This illustrates our techniques and raises other interesting general questions.

The mothers of criers are more likely to *touch* their child in the greeting than are mothers of non-criers (Mann-Whitney U-test, Siegel 1956, $p < 0.002$). We are able to show that *touching* is associated closely with *approaches* and other behaviour by the child (see below). This raises the possibility that when the effects of these are removed there is no difference between the maternal behaviour. And, in fact, mothers of criers and non-criers under 3 years old (an age chosen to balance ages of criers and non-criers) are equally responsive to the child's behaviour.

Mother touch does not occur only on those days when the child cries on separation ($\chi^2 = 0.001$, n.s.), but it does tend to occur on days when, at greeting, the child runs towards the mother ($\chi^2 = 4.49$, $p = <0.05 > 0.025$)

and when it has its *arms up*. Partial association tests allow us to conclude the following:

(1) The association between child *approaching* and *mother touching* is unaffected by whether the child is a crier or not. (Partial association chi-squared=4.47, $p<0.05>0.025$. Second order interaction chi-squared= 0.29 with 1 d.f.)

(2) The strong association between *arms up* by the child and *mother touching* is unaffected by whether the child is a crier or not. (Partial chi-squared 24.49, $p<0.001$, interaction n.s.) Thus there is no significant effect of the child's status as a crier or non-crier on association of the mother's response with the child's behaviour. In other words, the mothers of criers are no more or less responsive than mothers of non-criers of this same age.

(3) *Arms up* is strongly associated with *mother touching*, independently of *approach*, both in criers (partial chi-squared 7.97, $p<0.005>0.001$, interaction n.s.) and non-criers (partial chi-squared 10.50, $p<0.005>0.001$, interaction chi-squared 2.70 with 1 d.f., $p>0.10$). Since the sequence in which these behaviour items can occur is very fixed, this is as near as one can get (without experimental control) to demonstrating that *arms up* has a signal function. The effectiveness of *arms up* is demonstrated both in criers and in non-criers and it seems to be equally effective in each.

So during the greetings the *mother touching* seems to be very strongly determined by the child's behaviour. Mothers of criers and non-criers appear equally ready to respond. This is better evidence for the feeling we had about the separations, that the mother is predominantly in a ' responding mode ' at these times, mainly waiting to receive and act on signals from her child. However, because of the marked decrease in incidence of crying after $2\frac{1}{2}$ years old, we felt it advisable to investigate separately the interactions of children above and below this age.

AGE DIFFERENCES IN INTERACTIONS

Non-criers

We have now to see how far the above finding applies to the age differences. That is, whether differences in mother behaviour to older or younger children can be accounted for by differences in the behaviour of the children. The analysis above was for children of under 3 years, the age of the oldest crier. Comparison of non-criers over and under $2\frac{1}{2}$ years (the age after which *crying* is rare) shows whether there were changes in maternal responsiveness with age, independently of child behaviour, and age differences in the relationship of maternal behaviour to child behaviour.

Among non-criers the amount of *arms up* (U-test, $p<0.02>0.002$) was less in older children although *approach* did not differ (U-test, $p>0.10$). However, six measures of the responsiveness of the mothers showed no difference in responsiveness in the two age groups. These were (1) comparison of the proportion of days on which the child approached the mother when the mother responded by touching the child. These showed no suggestion of a difference between age groups ($\chi^2 = 0.00$). (2) A similar comparison for proportion of times *arms up* led to *mother touching* gave the same figure (7 touches out of 10 *arms up*) for each age. (3) The scores from the first ten observations on each child show no difference in the proportion of *mother touch* to *child approach* (*U*-test, $p > 0.10$). (4) A similar comparison showed no difference in proportion of *mother touch* to *child approach* when the score for *arms up* was subtracted from each figure to give an approximation of the responsiveness to simple *approach* (*U*-test, $p > 0.10$). (5) Similar comparison of proportion of *mother touch* to *arms up* showed no difference (*U*-test, $p > 0.10$). (6) Correlation with age of child of individual mother's scores of the percentage of *approaches* by the child that led to *mother touch* gave a Spearman's correlation coefficient of -0.15 ($p > 0.5$).

The non-criers showed no difference in *smile* (*U*-test, $p > 0.10$) with age, but young ones were more often *approached* by the mother (*U*-test, $p < 0.02 > 0.002$). The figures for *mother touch* when the child did not *approach*, also showed more maternal behaviour to the young children ($\chi^2 = 4.10$, 1 d.f., $p < 0.05 > 0.025$). These suggest a greater frequency of initiations of behaviour by the mother to young children, although her responsiveness does not change over this age range.

Criers

The age differences in criers show some interesting differences from the situation in non-criers. Even though there were only four criers over 31 months their scores are similar enough to give some significant results. Older criers resemble older non-criers in showing less *arms up* (*U*-test, $p = 0.014$) and being less often *approached* by their mother (*U*-test, $p = 0.024$), and in no less often *approaching* their mothers (*U*-test, $p = 0.285$) than their young counterparts. But older criers differ from older non-criers in that they less often *smile* at their mother in greeting than do young criers or non-criers (*U*-test, $p = 0.055$) or all other children ($p < 0.05$). They are also peculiar in getting significantly less response from their mothers than do non-criers on each of three measures: (1) measure 3 for non-criers above, shows fewer responses of mother to *approach* (*U*-test, $p = 0.004$). (2) measure 4 above likewise (*U*-test, $p = 0.024$) and (3) measure 5 above shows less *mother touch* to *arms up* (*U*-test, $p = 0.024$). These measures (and measure 1 above) also give significant differences from the scores of old non-criers.

In summary, older criers are remarkable in getting a lower rate of response from their mothers. They are also unusual in less often smiling to their mothers than any other children. This makes an interesting comparison with Leach's results on her older pathologically bad separators. The low response rate cannot be taken as the definite cause of the bad separation of these older criers. It may be that the mothers have all given up responding to demands which they have come to find excessive, although *arms up* has shown the normal decline with age. But if this argument is used, it must then be admitted that this treatment produced no great improvement. In fact, the low responsiveness may not have been a result of such a kind of long experience by the mother, at least not at our playgroup, because each of the older criers started coming to us when already over $2\frac{1}{2}$ years old. But whichever is cause or effect there is a conspicuously abnormal relationship. The reduced amount of *smiling* is further evidence of a disordered mother–child relationship but again cannot certainly be attributed to the ill effects of unusually low responsiveness; it may equally well be a cause of reduced responsiveness (see for example Robson, 1967). The reduction in *arms up* but not in *crying* is also a difference from young criers.

Having found this peculiarity of older ($2\frac{1}{2}$–4 year old) criers it is necessary to return to the comparison of maternal responsiveness in under $2\frac{1}{2}$-year-old criers and non-criers. In this age group there is a difference in maternal responsiveness (Mann–Whitney U-test, $p = 0.051$) between criers and non-criers and it is the reverse of that found in the older children. Mothers of young criers were more responsive than mothers of young non-criers (using measure 1, above). We have not completely excluded short-term influences of all child behaviour, such as facial expression or speed of approach but our finding is in accord with the relationship claimed by Ainsworth (1969b) for 1-year-olds and Schaffer and Emerson (1964) for children aged 6 to 18 months. However, an added problem is the sex difference in incidence of crying. Most of these criers were boys, and most of the non-criers were girls. We could find no sex difference in maternal responsiveness in non-criers, which excludes a short-term indirect source of the correlation of responsiveness and crying. However, we cannot exclude, and even regard as a likely pointer to an explanation, the early sex differences in newborn responses to maternal calming attempts suggested by Moss (1967).

With the above exceptions the responsiveness of the mothers shows a surprising constancy. Neither age in non-criers, nor the frequency of *approach* (see below) in young criers affects the maternal response rate. Age (but not crier versus non-crier status) does affect the frequency of the mothers' initiations of behaviour to the child. These effects are interesting in relation to separation and attachment, so long as they are not purely restricted to the greeting situation. They also suggest something about the role of the mother in development. It may well be that as Bowlby (1969) implies, maternal behaviour at all ages is very largely a matter of responding to the child. This would probably be more expected by the layman (or rather lay-mother, see Newson and Newson, 1968) than by the psychologist or educationist, or by a Victorian parent. *Tabula rasa* thinking and the prevalence of operant conditioning theory lead one to expect the mother to be playing a very much more active role, constructing child behaviour as she goes along. (This argument is discussed more completely by Ambrose (1968) and Ainsworth (1969*a*) as well as Bowlby.) The child has been regarded as adapted to acquiring adult behaviour by being unprogrammed but good at learning. It is beginning to look more likely that its behaviour is very clearly programmed (as Bowlby (1969) implies) to direct the mother into providing stimuli within the range that the developmental system requires. The learning ability may also be constrained primarily towards certain directions, for instance, see Laughlin (1961, 1968). It is important to remember here that we have studied a very homogeneous and healthy set of mothers. A study covering pathological mothers might make one think very differently. That maternal responsiveness does vary between individuals and that this affects child behaviour is not denied and another possible example is described in the next section.

MATERNAL RESPONSIVENESS AND 'EXPLORATION'

Ainsworth (1969*b*) has emphasised a relationship between maternal responsiveness and exploratory behaviour. She claims that responsive mothers have ' secure-attached ' children who readily move away from them to explore the surroundings but who nonetheless (among her 1-year-olds) cry when the mother leaves them. Therefore having found possible differing relationships of maternal responsiveness to likelihood of crying in children over and under $2\frac{1}{2}$ years old we should see whether responsiveness also relates to readiness to explore.

We have plotted for all the children a measure of maternal responsiveness in greetings (% of times child approaches on which mother touches the child) against the number of times the child moved away from the mother during separations. The relationship, as shown by Spearman's ranked correlation coefficient, was a negative correlation ($rs = -0.50$ $p<0.01$). This was confirmed by analysis using a partial regression technique which showed that the relationship was independent of the number of child approaches during greeting, and which also showed that the relationship was linear. A second group of children on whom we had only incomplete records, where *away* was converted to a percentage of the records of separation, gave a similar result. The correlation suggests that more responsive mothers have children who move away less often. This relationship is not due to changes with age (there is no correlation between age of child and mother's responsiveness in our age range), nor does it appear to change with age nor to be affected by removal of criers from the sample. By plotting separately individuals who did and did not do *arms up* we feel that we have also removed possible effects of this aspect of the kind of approach on the responsiveness measures.

It is not certain that we can equate this moving away in a separation situation with exploring in Ainsworth's sense, indeed this seems rather unlikely. *Away* at separation had high loadings on the same factors as *crying* but opposite to *crying*. It is therefore nearest to a measure of the inverse of resistance to separation, and perhaps a more sensitive one than *crying* (for this sort of analysis one should probably use factor scores of individuals rather than single behaviour items). Ainsworth's discussion seems to imply that exploration and resistance to separation are either independent of each other, or in conflict, having a balance point determined by the quality of mothering. If our finding really represented a hump-shaped curve this could compare closely with Ainsworth's formulation. But, as it apparently represents a simple straight line, it becomes hard to argue, as many have done, that extremes of clingingness result from too little mothering, except as regards to the very small number of criers aged over $2\frac{1}{2}$ years. The possibility of changing relationships between clinging and responsiveness at different ages also has to be borne in mind.

Our result would fit better with the comparison of children in the U.K. and U.S.A. with the Zhun/twa mothers and infants in Konner's study (Ch. 11), and with the implications of Bowlby's stress on the survival value of the child's signals to the mother and of the resulting close attachment between them.

Discussion

In describing the results of the factor analysis we carefully refrained from ascribing causal factors to the statistical factors and have tried to describe them as kinds of behaviour patterns. It is hard to propose real causal factors that might be responsible for these dimensions of variation. Causal factors behind the individual variations are likely to be entangled in the history of each family. The factors with high age and sex loading, even if we regard sex or age as causes, may result from gradual effects of sex and age on the inter-actions of the mother and child. We need to know what determines the difference between clinging and ' rejecting ' greetings after crying at separa-tion, just as much as we need to know what causes some children to cry at separation more than do others. We also need to know what controls the amount of the other kinds of greeting and whether there is any develop-mental relationship between the various patterns. This topic is often con-fused by views about what is ' healthy ' in attachment behaviour. Some argue that a deep attachment is important and healthy. Others treat crying at separation as an unhealthy, problem behaviour, where the first would regard this as just an unfortunate by-product (brought about by the mis-match of the European–North-American way of life and the adaptations of child behaviour) of a healthy attachment. No doubt this is more complicated than either side has bargained for. How does the amount of early contact relate to later reactions to separation, to later amounts of other mother–child contact, to readiness to explore? We are unlikely to get the answers until longitudinal studies are done in which all these aspects are measured.

The simplest theory of a global attachment–independence dimension, a unitary theory of attachment, would predict a first major factor with high loadings for behaviour to mother and low loadings for behaviour which does not concern the mother (e.g. *away, play, smile T*). This seems to be a very bad summary of our observations. The loadings on the first factor do not closely correspond to the expected loadings. The rotation in factor analysis increases the discrepancy from the predictions of a unitary theory but since this is part of its intended function we must also cite the principal components analysis which precedes rotation. Even in the principal components analysis the first factor is little larger than the next. On the first component there are high negative loadings for *arms up, touch, walk, pucker, cry* and *point*, but the high positive loadings, although they include *play* at greeting and *away* at both occasions, also include *show* and *jump*, and at separation *smile, talk, wave* and *kiss*.

The choice of *crying* on separation as the main criterion of attachment was described by Schaffer and Emerson (1964). This has the all too rare advantage of being stated in terms of clear observables but, as Schaffer and Emerson say, perhaps it is too simple. This is clearly another single factor theory and therefore inadequate on the grounds of percentage of variance accounted for by the factors. But it is also inappropriate on the grounds that much behaviour towards the mother is unrelated to crying on separation. If *crying* measures 'attachment' then attachment is little more than *crying* because it does not include *smile, jump, kiss, wave, show, talk* nor does it measure *approach* or *touch*, or distinguish between clinging and ignoring 'attachment'. No single measure substituted for *crying* will get over these disadvantages. *Touch* will not distinguish criers from non-criers, nor distinguish non-crying 'ignorers' from crying 'ignorers'. It might be possible to manage with fewer measures than we used but even after our exploratory analysis a minimum of one chosen measure per factor is likely to be too few. In studies of possible background variables one should probably use the factor scores of individuals as the dependent variable rather than the single measures that we used in part 2 of our analysis.

Ainsworth's categorisation of 'secure–attached' versus 'insecure–attached' could form the basis of a two-factor theory and since she suggests (1969b) that attachment is likely to prove multi-dimensional this would be the fairest version of her theory to match to the data. The match is in our view a fairly good one. Supposing that security–insecurity and attachment–independence are the main dimensions, the high loading behaviour on the first principal component could be taken to correspond to secure versus insecure attachments. After rotation the first two factors are nearly equal in the amount of variance they account for (but so is the third). But the specific high loadings to be expected from Ainsworth's categories are hard to choose. The theory gives little indication of how to tell that a secure child is attached rather than simply independent. It is supposed readily to explore away from the mother. But presumably some other feature of its behaviour indicates that it has an attachment (e.g. returning to mother rather than strangers?). (It is likely that the children in Ainsworth's healthy families, at the ages she describes, are all attached to the mother and only older children or institution-raised children might be expected to show no attachment. Nonetheless this implies a difference in their behaviour which should be observable.) We might expect any of the behaviour to mother which is not closely associated with staying near, or crying on separation, to show the secure child's attachment.

The first two factors both have reasonable loadings for crying. This goes in the opposite direction to *away* at separation and goes along with approaches to the mother and therefore could correspond to the insecure aspects of Ainsworth's classification. The greeting behaviour associated on these two factors is (1) *approach, arms up, touch, pucker*, and (2) *pointing* and *playing*. Greeting behaviour with high opposite loadings to crying and staying by mother is (1) *play, away, show* and (2) *smile*. In so far as *smile* is regarded as any stronger indication of attachment than *show* then these results fit Ainsworth's classification. However, three points must be made (*a*) it may be somewhat inappropriate to try to apply Ainsworth's concepts, which may concern exploration versus non-exploration during the presence of the mother (in 1-year-olds), to the separation and greeting situation in 2–4-year-olds. (*b*) The first four factors account for almost equal variance and there is little justification for treating the first two as more important than the next two ('sex' and 'age' factors). (*c*) The 'specificity to mother' of the responses does not support separation of a secure–insecure dimension from an attached–unattached dimension on the above lines but possibly does with the use of *jump* and *laugh* as indicators of secure attachment.

We feel that Bowlby's recent book has put the study of attachment onto a new plane both conceptually and methodologically. He stresses the distance-reducing effects of behaviour between mother and child, which has survival value predominantly as an anti-predator device. While the predators of pre-agricultural man are not clearly known, still less their prey-catching behaviour, a comparative study of anti-predator devices and child-care practices in the mammals at large would probably show him to be largely right. However, other possibilities, for instance the more traditional but less likely assumption that attachment is an adaptation ensuring development of a social adult (necessary for hunting or exploiting large prey, but also possibly for protection), should be examined at the same time. If Bowlby's survival value is the correct one there is still the implication that attachment is the context in which the systems for acquiring other behaviour are designed to function.

Bowlby's theory also regards the behaviour which brings about attachment as becoming organised into one causal system having proximity as a goal situation. But even if proximity of mother and child has survival value, and several behaviour patterns have this effect, it does not necessarily mean that they are controlled in the same way. The history of the study of causation in ethology has largely been to do with the realisation (implicit in Tinbergen's 'four why's', 1951 and 1963) that a common function need not imply common causation, and with the discovery of cases where this was indeed not so (e.g. Hinde, 1959; Beer, 1961–3).

In the case of the child and its mother (or caretaker) *crying, smiling, arms up, approach* and sometimes *pointing*, and as Bowlby suggests, *sucking*, all bring mother and child together. They may even have this as their survival value, in a series of immediate plus long-term back-up systems, or of systems which replace each other through development. But (as Bowlby himself implies on p. 331 of his book) it is an open question as to how far, at each age, they have any short-term causation in common, or a common developmental course.

We feel we have evidence that the causation, and probably the development, of these behaviours of the child is not a unitary phenomenon. (We think that the survival value of each of the kinds of behaviour which we describe needs individual investigation but also point to the findings of Tinbergen and his colleagues (Tinbergen, 1965) on the compromise between opposing selection pressures.)

Cry, approach, arms up, touch and a tendency not to move away, is a clear 'clinging' pattern producing persisting contact. That *suck* was commoner in criers ($U=15$, $p>0.02<0.002$) can be taken to support Bowlby's view that thumb-sucking is causally a part of the attachment system. But sucking is often described as a response to high arousal, having a calming effect. This is a more vague explanation, if an explanation at all, but could be an alternative to Bowlby's. On the other hand, contact with the mother is likewise calming, and could be regarded as a response to high arousal in much the same situations as sucking. Both precede sleep and give the impression of inducing sleep in babies.

Smiling, and *jumping* and *laughing*, with or without contact, occur separately from the above (both across individuals and from day to day). Ambrose (1966) and Robson (1967) have found that smiling produces important and long-lasting effects on the mother, though different effects from crying. This may be a response that, like contact, acts as a reinforcer for the mother and therefore has some developmental connection with the mother's responsiveness to clinging behaviour (which Ainsworth (1969b), and Schaffer and Emerson (1964) suggest increases 'attachment' in the first year). Alternatively, the smiling, and other non-clinging social interactions may replace clinging at a later stage of development but this hardly seems compatible with their known history in the first year of life. While

Leach (Ch. 10 and pers.comm.) has evidence that this may be true for *giving*, *talking* and *showing*, our data for *smiling* suggests that it is not true for this. The smiling relationship runs nearly parallel in age with the clinging relationship but varies independently of it. Ainsworth's (1969*b*) description of a highly sociable 1-year-old (nonetheless and not surprisingly found to cry at his mother's departure) suggests to us that one should consider whether smiling between mother and child may have more to do with developing interactions with people in general than with the basic clinging form of attachment (even though smiling has sometimes been found to pass through an exclusive-to-mother phase (Gewirtz, 1965), and in contradiction to the comparative discussion of Ambrose (1966)). Effects on the mother of contact with the baby seem to have been too little investigated. Primate studies suggest that physical contact with the young is very important for initiating maternal behaviour (Meier, 1965; Harlow and Harlow, 1965). Human admirers (mostly female) of a new baby are seldom content until they have held it.

If smiling increases proximity by increasing the mother's readiness to respond to the child this may on occasion have surprising effects. The argument depends on our observations about older criers and may therefore not apply to normal mother–child couples. If a child smiles less (as do the older criers whose mothers are less responsive than others) and his mother becomes less responsive, the child may then cry more. Crying tends to exclude, or at any rate does not increase, smiling. The mother will then receive fewer smiles and become less responsive. The child will cry more and try to cling more. In the opposite cases, if the child smiles more the mother will respond more, the child cry and cling less and smile more. Thus smiling would have the opposite effect to that expected, it reduces proximity. But this assumes that the older criers are typical, and that the low responsiveness of the mother causes crying and clinging rather than crying causing low responsiveness. If we suppose that low responsiveness by the mother reduces clinging (as in the animal studies) then smiling will tend to increase attachments. It is of course possible, and the available data makes it look likely, that both these processes occur but at different times in development.

Schaffer and Emerson (1964) and Ainsworth (1969*b*) both describe high responsiveness of mothers as characteristic of strong attachments during the second half of the first year and first half of the second year. Assuming that they are really rating responsiveness and not simply amounts of behaviour resulting from the child's initiatives, this is the same as our results on responsiveness and *away* and on responsiveness and *crying* in the under $2\frac{1}{2}$-year-olds. But it is the opposite to our findings about crying after $2\frac{1}{2}$ years old. During the early phase smiling and crying could work together to build up the attachment. Once a clinging response has been built up, then the consequences of lowered responsiveness have to be assumed to be different. But at this later stage, persisting smiling by the child (via its effects on responsiveness of the mother), reduces the clinging response.

We feel that it would be wise to regard Ainsworth and Schaffer and Emerson's ratings of ' responsiveness ' with caution for the reason stated above. We also feel that our results on relationship of maternal scores to child scores could be affected by our sample being self-selected. Presumably mothers who do not expect their child to leave them easily, and who do not wish it to, do not come to a playgroup.

Those who wish to be tenacious about a unitary theory of attachment can legitimately find loopholes in our argument: (1) Just how appropriate are these fleeting, artificial situations to attachment as a whole? (2) Surely smiling must on a larger scale increase proximity? (3) Our separation situation may show differing effects of the strangeness of the environment to each child, rather than any general clingingness. Nonetheless it is important that resistance to staying in this environment went with *approach, arms up, touch, suck, point* and not with other behaviour. (4) Perhaps our different kinds of behaviour are alternative specialist ways of keeping mother close, or (5) perhaps they substitute for each other as the child ages.

So long as one does not indulge the unfortunately prevalent propensity to seek ' one grand theory of behaviour ', and remembers that it is very possible for relatively independent developmental systems to exist side by side (perhaps also subserving different functions) these counter arguments to our approach are well worth pursuing and may lead to yet more sophisticated theories about attachment.

One or two other authors have discussed the question of independent development of different kinds of interaction of the child and its mother. Rosenthal (1967) discriminated ' attention-seeking ' and ' proximity-seeking ' which sound as if they correspond to ' giving–showing–talking ' and ' approach–touch–next to ' in the observations reported here and in Leach (Ch. 10). She found that these behaviour patterns differ in how much they ' generalise ' to strange adult females (though in the opposite direction to our finding, probably because her strangers were instructed to make very few responses to the child) and that proximity-seeking is increased much more in an anxiety-provoking situation. Walters and Parke (1965) suggest that ' attention and approval seeking are not entirely derivates of early physical dependency gratifications but are habits that are developed from the beginning of life in the course of the infant's perceptual transactions with its environment, most of which involve visual and auditory stimulation '. We would extend this to say that even if ' attachment ' is distinguished from ' dependency ' it should also be still distinguished from ' attention and approval seeking ' and comparable ' give–show–talk–receive ' interactions and from ' smile–approach–touch ' interactions. Sears (1963) likewise suggested that physical-contact behaviour develops independently of ' attention and approval seeking '.

We appear to disagree with Bowlby and Ainsworth on some of the details of development of the child's interactions with its mother and other people. But we must emphasise that we find their approach and framework the most valuable contributions which can be found in the literature on human mother–infant interaction. In view of the related work in progress in this field by Anderson, Leach, Konner, and Richards and Bernal, and our own plans for further analysis of this data and investigation of this situation, and in view of the work which one hopes will spring from Bowlby's book, it is premature to attempt a general description of attachment behaviour in this paper. We would stress that the fastest progress will be made if many variables are recorded, and every child is observed in a variety of appropriate situations, and if wider aspects such as the child's relationships to siblings, peers, father and extended family are also taken into account. In short, we feel that the multivariate approach, even if arduous, is as important at this stage as is the more generally accepted need for longitudinal data.

Acknowledgements

We wish to thank Professor J. M. Tanner for his encouragement and for the excellent facilities of his department; the Nuffield Foundation for financial support; Professor Tanner and Dr M. F. Hall for criticism of earlier drafts of the paper; H. Goldstein for advice on much of the statistics; Miss S. Drysdale for running the playgroup and providing a constant source of subjects; Miss J. Forrest for secretarial assistance and Mrs. P. Cox and Mr B. Carter for data processing and computing assistance.

APPENDIX 1

DEFINITIONS OF BEHAVIOUR FOR ARRIVAL AND DEPARTURE RECORD SHEET

CHILD BEHAVIOUR

Look – Turns face and eyes towards mother, for whatever duration.

Smile – Smiles and faces towards mother. Remarkably high agreement is reached using 'smile' in its everyday sense. However, criteria usually present were mouth corners raised, mouth widened, lips separated exposing mostly upper teeth, sharpened shadow below eyes and line lateral to outer corner of eye and bulging cheeks.

Avert – Very difficult to record, intended to mean turning the face away from the mother other than when looking at teacher, child or at destination when moving away, also persistently not looking at mother despite her approaches to the child and her presence being quite obvious. Gaze is probably usually averted downwards.

Smile T – Smiling at the teacher.

T intervene – Child carried away from mother or door by teacher. Teacher then usually holds and carries child, talks to it, shows it things out of the window then tries to settle it into some occupation.

Walk – The child walks towards its mother.

Run – The child runs towards its mother.

Play – The child begins to manipulate play materials or talk to other children. (The possibility that we recorded the absent-minded fingering of objects while anxiously watching the mother could be worrying. But (*a*) this scarcely happened at all and (*b*) it anyway involves initially attending to the play material.) In the brief period covered no distinction beyond *play* ± *look at mother* can be made. *Look* is of course recorded in another column.

Away – The child moves away from the mother or has gone far away from her. We may have been inconsistent in using the second part of the definition. In greetings may include (*a*) moving away as soon as mother comes and (*b*) first moving towards the mother then moving away.

Suck – Recorded by N.B.J. only. The child puts fingers into his mouth. Sucking movements of jaw need not be seen. No serious attempt was made at discriminating between, e.g. sucking thumb, or fingers, biting nails, putting index finger to teeth, putting hand over mouth, arm to mouth, chewing digits, etc. My impression is that most of what occurs in these situations is anyway only the first of these possible subdivisions.

Talk – The child talks to its mother, i.e. produces words (including its own individual baby words, i.e. noises that we and the mother have learned to accept as words) while looking even briefly to the mother, or whose meaning indicates that they are addressed to the mother.

Touch – The child reaches out and actively touches the mother (important subdivisions could be made, e.g. taking hold of her hand, embracing her legs, or if lifted embracing her shoulder, leaning against her, taking hold of her clothes). No attempt was made to say whether child or mother touched first. *Touch* was not used for passive contact where the mother had reached out to touch the child first.

Arms up – The child holds its arms up rather straight, slightly in front of the head–body plane, and usually simultaneously looks at mother.

Show – Includes *showing* and *giving*. In both, the child holds an object in front of itself away from the body towards the mother at a level between pelvis and shoulder height. The mother may then take hold of the object and the child release it (*giving*) or she may look at it without taking it or ignore it.

Point – The child holds out one arm towards an object, often with index finger extended, and may alternately look at the object and the mother. Usually accompanied by saying 'look mum', or occurring just before or after other behaviour to mother.

Wave – The child waves its hand towards the mother (often to children when leaving but we did not record this). The forearm is raised near the vertical and the hand opened, palm towards the mother. The amount or number of waving movements, and whether wrist or upper arm joints or fingers provide the movement, seem to differ from one individual to another.

Laugh – Used for the laughing vocalisation here, not only for the facial expression. Orientated to mother. We can't improve on the description by Ambrose (1963). But there is a range of variation and we have not attempted to break this up, e.g. into high or low pitch, long or short sounds.

Jump – The child, facing the mother, jumps up and down, with both feet push-ing more or less together. We separate this from skipping and from stamping with one foot at a time.

Kiss – The child reaches up to mother's face with own face, with lips pursed and touches her cheek. Sometimes the kissing sound is heard, from opening the closed lips, which is a result of a slight suction. The mothers also kiss the children usually both more or less simultaneously, sometimes unreciprocated. We did not record mothers kissing children on the record sheet. One or two mothers regularly kissed their children on the mouth, most on the cheek. Many never kissed or were kissed by their child.

Cry – The well-known vocalisations, but again we made no distinction between variations, e.g. growling, roaring, or shrill or quiet, or very segmented sobs. It would be interesting to use such distinctions (if their description could be tidied up) because most people (including the mothers) have the impression that they have to do with different circumstances and are associated with different behaviour.

Tantrum – The child arches the back, twists the trunk, extends arms and legs or stamps with one foot at a time, and/or flaps (usually) both hands in fast, small amplitude, vertical movements with the hands well in front of the body at about shoulder height, with elbows well below the level of the hands (i.e. not far out at side).

Pucker – Oblique eyebrows or bulging inner end of brows without clear lower-ing of brows, with or without red face, orbicularis oculi contraction, lip re-traction or squaring of upper lip.

Extra items – We entered 1 if the child was given food by mother, 2 if its father came instead of mother, 3 if sibling came instead, 4 if another adult, e.g. mother of another child in the group was bringing the child, 5 for mother *slips out* of room when child is not looking (equivalent to no mother behaviour scored other than *look*).

MOTHER BEHAVIOUR

Mother look – Mother looks towards child.

Mother smile – Mother smiles when looking at child (regardless of whether the child is looking at her). Often mothers would smile at the teacher but not at the child and care was needed not to record these as *mother smile*.

Mother approach – The mother moves towards the child, regardless of whether the child is still or moving.

Mother touch – The mother touches the child. This lumps many kinds of touch. It could include hits but these were actually rare. It could be very useful to differentiate kinds of touch like picking up the child, taking its hand, dressing it (which was excluded from the category), stroking its head, putting an arm round its neck or onto its back, gripping its arm with pulling or shaking. These dis-tinctions were ignored in order to keep the list of behaviour as short as possible. It did not include passive contact initiated by the child such as when the child approaches and leans against the mother, unless as is common the mother then rests a hand on the child.

Mother talk – The mother talks while looking at the child or seems to address her remarks to it (i.e. we do not count times when the mother is talking to the teacher and briefly looks away at the child).

Time – The time of day (hour and minute) when the mother leaves, or (in columns 21 and 22) when she reappears.

COMBINED ITEM USED IN ANALYSES
Approach – Either walk or run.

APPENDIX 2

DIFFERENCES IN BEHAVIOUR OF MOTHERS OF CRIERS AND NON-CRIERS AT SEPARATION

1. MOTHER APPROACH

During separation the mothers of criers more often *approached* the child than did mothers of non-criers ($U=56$, $p=0.062$). However, if the older children (almost none of whom cry) are excluded there is no significant difference. Mothers of criers under 31 months approach no more often than mothers of non-criers under 31 months. However, the children who *cry* are more likely to *approach* their mother ($\chi^2=20.4$; $p<0.001$), leaving fewer opportunities (since mutual approach is rare) for the mother to approach. Taking only the occasions when the child did not approach there is still no significant difference in the proportion of times when the mother approaches criers and non-criers ($\chi^2=0.19$; $p>0.10$). So, mothers presumably initiate approaches to younger children more than to older ones but this has nothing to do with their readiness to cry (as was also shown for greetings). This might be taken to mean that, although the mother's attachment to the child wanes or changes form with age, it has no relationship to the child's changing attachment to the mother. It could mean that neither the child's attachment determined the mother's attachment, nor the mother's attachment determined the strength of the child's attachment. However, we would reserve judgement on such a statement on two counts. First, *crying* is only one measure on the child's attachment. Second, *approach* is only one measure of the mother's behaviour and one would like to see many more measures examined to decide on the differences implied by ideas like ' protectiveness ' or ' infantilising ' besides the idea of a more general maternal attachment.

2. MOTHER TOUCH DURING SEPARATION

Mothers of criers did not *touch* their child any more often than did mothers of young non-criers during separation. This is despite the fact that the criers more often *approach* the mother. This means that the mothers of criers are unusually unresponsive in terms of touching when the child approaches. It seems sensible to interpret this as a result of the necessity of getting away from the child, if she waits and touches it then it can cling on to her. The view that it reflects a reaction to the situation rather than the mother's customary behaviour is supported by the different findings in greetings where mothers of criers are no less likely to touch an approaching child.

3. MOTHER SMILE DURING SEPARATION

Mothers of criers were less likely to *smile* during the separation than were mothers of non-criers ($U=49.5$, $p=0.034$). We felt that this was likely to reflect the mother's anxiety over the child crying. Absence of *smiling* could just as well go with maternal *approach*, in a maternal version of the child's unsmiling *pucker* and clinging pattern of behaviour. But against this is the fact that *mother smiling* showed no age difference among non-criers ($U=59$, $p=0.810$). This is unlike *mother approach*. In support of our impression that mothers fail to smile because of the child's unsmiling upset state, is the observation that mothers of

245

criers appeared markedly (but not significantly) unlikely to smile on days when the child actually cried (table 9·6, $\chi^2 = 2.60$, $p = 0.10$). But they were also less likely to smile than other mothers on days when their child did not cry ($\chi^2 = 6.57$, $p = 0.01$). We cannot say much more about this. The mother might be worried that the child will be unhappy because it often is, or she might be unhappy herself at separating even though she decided to bring the child to playgroup. We are not confident that absence of smiling by the mother makes the child less likely to separate. All we can say is that smiling by both parties (as the factor analysis also shows) is more typical of separations of non-criers.

TABLE 9·6. *Association between crying and maternal smiling at separation from criers*

	Child cries	Does not cry
Mother smiles	1	21
Does not smile	20	64

REFERENCES

Ainsworth, M. D. S. (1969a). Object relations, dependency, and attachment: a theoretical review of the infant–mother relationship. *Child Develop.* **40**, 969–1026.

Ainsworth, M. D. S. (1969b). Attachment and exploratory behaviour of one-year-olds in a strange situation. In *Determinants of Infant Behaviour*, vol. 4. Ed. B. M. Foss, London: Methuen.

Ambrose, J. A. (1963). The age of onset of ambivalence in early infancy: indications from the study of laughing. *J. Child Psychol. Psychiat.* **4**, 167–84.

Ambrose, J. A. (1966). Ritualization in the human infant–mother bond. *Phil. Trans. Roy. Soc. B* **251**, 359–62.

Ambrose, J. A. (1968). The comparative approach to early child development: the data of ethology. In *Foundations of Child Psychiatry*. Ed. E. Miller, London: Pergamon.

Beer, C. G. (1961–3). Incubation and nest-building behaviour of black-headed gulls. *Behaviour* **18**, 62–106; **19**, 283–304; **21**, 13–77; **21**, 155–76.

Blurton Jones, N. G. (1967). An ethological study of some aspects of social behaviour of children in nursery school. In *Primate Ethology*. Ed. D. Morris, London: Weidenfeld and Nicolson.

Bowlby, J. (1969). *Attachment and Loss*, vol. 1. *Attachment*. London: Hogarth Press.

DeVore, I. (1963). Mother–infant relations in free ranging baboons. In *Maternal Behaviour in Mammals*. Ed. H. Rheingold, New York: Wiley.

Gewirtz, J. L. (1965). The course of infant smiling in four child rearing environments in Israel. In *Determinants of Infant Behaviour*. Ed. B. M. Foss, London: Methuen.

Goodall, Jane van Lawick (1968). The behaviour of free-living chimpanzees in the Gombe Stream Reserve. *Anim. Behav. Monog.* **1**, 165–311.

Harlow, H. F. and Harlow, M. K. (1965). The affectional systems. In *Behaviour of Non-Human Primates*, vol. 2. Eds. A. M. Schrier, H. F. Harlow and F. Stollnitz, London: Academic Press.

Hinde, R. A. (1959). Unitary drives. *Anim. Behav.* **7**, 130–41.

Hinde, R. A. and Spencer-Booth, Y. (1967). The behaviour of socially living rhesus monkeys in their first two and a half years. *Anim. Behav.* **15**, 169–96.

Hinde, R. A. and Spencer-Booth, Y. (1968). Review lecture. The study of mother–infant interactions in captive group-living rhesus monkeys. *Proc. Roy. Soc., B.* **169**, 177–201.

Jensen, G. D., Bobbitt, R. A. and Gordon, B. N. (1967). Sex differences in social interaction between infant monkeys and their mothers. In *Recent Adv. biol. Psychiat.* **9**, 283–93. Ed. J. Wortis, New York: Plenum.

Jensen, G. D., Bobbitt, R. A. and Gordon, B. N. (1968). Effects of environment on the relationship between mother and infant pigtailed monkeys (*M. nemestrina*). *J. comp. physiol. Psychol.* **66**, 259–63.

Laughlin, W. S. (1961). Acquisition of anatomical knowledge by ancient man. In *Social Life of Early Man*. Ed. S. L. Washburn, Chicago: Aldine.

Laughlin, W. S. (1968). Hunting: an integrating biobehaviour system and its evolutionary importance. *Man, the Hunter*. Eds. R. B. Lee and I. DeVore, Chicago: Aldine.

Meier, G. (1965). Maternal behaviour of feral and laboratory reared monkeys following the surgical delivery of their infants. *Nature, Lond.* **206**, 492–3.

Moss, H. A. (1967). Sex, age and state as determinants of mother–infant interaction. *Merrill-Palmer Quart.* **13**, 19–36.

Newson, J. and Newson E. (1968). *Four years old in an Urban Community*. London: Allen and Unwin.

Robson, K. S. (1967). The role of eye to eye contact in maternal–infant attachment. *J. Child Psychol. Psychiat.* **8**, 13–25.

Rosenblatt, J. S. (1965). The basis of synchrony in the behavioural interaction between the mother and her offspring in the laboratory rat. In *Determinants of Infant Behaviour*, vol. 3, pp. 3–41. Ed. B. M. Foss, London: Methuen.

Rosenblum, L. A. and Kaufman, L. C. (1968). Variation in infant development and response to maternal loss in monkeys. *Amer. J. Orthopsychiatry* **38**, 418.

Rosenthal, M. K. (1967). The generalization of dependency behaviour from mother to stranger. *J. Child Psychol. Psychiat.* **8**, 117–34.

Schaffer, H. R. and Emerson, P. E. (1964). The development of social attachments in infancy. *Monog. Soc. Res. Child Develop.* **29**, 3 (serial no. 94).

Sears, R. R. (1963). Dependency motivation. In *Nebraska Symposium on Motivation*, pp. 25–64. Ed. M. R. Jones, Lincoln, Neb.: Univ. of Nebraska Press.

Siegel, S. (1956). *Non-Parametric Statistics for the Behavioural Sciences*. New York: McGraw-Hill.

Tinbergen, N. (1951). *The Study of Instinct*. London: Oxford University Press.

Tinbergen, N. (1963). On aims and methods of ethology. *Z. Tierpsychol.* **20**, 410–33.

Tinbergen, N. (1965). Behaviour and natural selection. In *Ideas in Modern Biology*, vol. 6 of *Proc. XVI Internat. Zool. Congr.*, Washington 1963, pp. 521–42. Ed. J. A. Moore, New York.

Walters, R. H. (1968). The effects of social isolation and social interaction on learning and performance in social situations. In *Biology and Behaviour*. Ed. D. C. Glass, New York: Rockefeller University Press.

Walters, R. H. and Parke, R. D. (1964). Social motivation, dependency and susceptibility to social influence. In *Advances in Experimental Social Psychology*, vol. 1, pp. 231–76. Ed. L. Berkowitz, New York: Academic Press.

Walters, R. H. and Parke, R. D. (1965). The role of distance receptors in the development of social responsiveness. In *Advances in Child Development and Behaviour*. Eds. L. P. Lipsitt and C. C. Spiker, New York and London: Academic Press.

10

A COMPARISON OF THE SOCIAL BEHAVIOUR OF SOME NORMAL AND PROBLEM CHILDREN

GILL M. LEACH*

SUMMARY

A method of recording the social interactions of pre-school children and their mothers is described, and the problems of making an accurate record by direct observation are discussed. A shorthand code, specially devised for use with event-recorder, or by hand, is described; and a list of defined behaviour items is given.

One way of analysing the data is presented, and the results are discussed in summarised form. This analysis was designed to compare the way in which the children 'initiated' and 'responded to' interactions with other people. Differences were sought between the Problem and the Normal children, and between Normal Girls and Boys, and Normal Young and Old children.

The results showed that the Problem children had reduced, unsatisfactory interactions with both peers and mothers. They initiated less behaviour and were less responsive to other children than the Normals and they were less successful at eliciting responses from other children than the Normals. They were less responsive to their mothers than the Normals (which was surprising, in view of their 'clinging' behaviour towards their mothers). Also, the mothers of Problem children seemed to be trying to avoid interactions with their children. Several similarities between the Problem children and the Young Normals were found in the child–children interactions, but only two for the mother-child interactions. The results showed that, given enough data, this kind of analysis could examine the 'mechanism' of interactions in considerable detail.

Introduction

The observations for this study were made on twenty-four pre-school children, attending playgroups in the research nursery, at the Institute of Child Health. The nursery was a small room (about 11ft × 14ft), well-equipped with the usual nursery toys: puzzles, paints, dough, water, sand, etc., and a climbing frame. The children were supervised by one female teacher. There were four playgroups, each comprising seven children. Each child attended a playgroup twice weekly, for two-hour play sessions. Most children were recruited from the local neighbourhood (see Blurton Jones,

* Department of Growth and Development, Institute of Child Health, University of London.

Ch. 4 for details of recruitment). Eighteen of these children were used as a Normal group for the study.

The six Problem children were specially recruited from the Department of Psychological Medicine, the Hospital for Sick Children, Great Ormond Street. These children were said to have difficulty in separating from their mothers.

'Separation anxiety' is regarded as a normal response to separation from the mother in a young child, up until about $2\frac{1}{2}$ years of age (see e.g. Bowlby, 1960). But when it is manifest to an acute degree in an older child, it is generally regarded as abnormal. Five of the Problem children were more than 3 years old.

The purpose of the study was to discover in what way this separation anxiety affected the social interactions of the Problem children. To do this, data on the children's interactions was collected both by direct observation and on film, for various kinds of analysis. In this paper only one method of analysing the hand-written data will be described, in some detail; and the problems which arose will also be discussed.

Methods

COLLECTING DATA

Observations were made whilst the children were playing freely in the nursery. When the mothers were present during a play session they usually sat to one side of the room; but they were quite free to move around the room, and play with their children, if they wished. The mothers of the Problem children stayed for several sessions, until their children were settled enough to let them go. The mothers of the Normal children stayed too, so that comparable data could be collected on their children.

Data were collected on the children's social behaviour under two conditions: with mothers present, and with mothers absent; and for three kinds of social interaction which were available to them: child–children, child–mother, and child–teacher. Observations were made on each child in turn, for bouts of six minutes per child. As much data were collected on each child as possible. Usually two or three six-minute observations were made on each child in one day. The following sections describe the way in which the data were recorded, with discussion of the problems involved in making this kind of record.

Type of record

Observations were made using a running commentary, which consisted mainly of a list of coded behaviour items (see Appendix 1). The commentary method was chosen in preference to checklists, after both methods had been tried out. A checklist has certain advantages: (1) it should provide a more consistent record, for the items being recorded are constantly before one's eyes; and (2) the data are recorded in a form which is easy to analyse. However, a checklist has three serious limitations: (1) it is inflexible – one has to have in advance a complete list of items to be recorded, and then ignore any new items which may appear; (2) it has to be short, for it becomes too unwieldy to use if the number of items exceeds about ten; and (3) it does not readily allow the *sequence* of items to be recorded, although some kind of numbering system can be devised. In contrast, a running commentary allows considerable flexibility, one can use a large number of items and one can record sequences.

The commentary was hand-written, in a special shorthand code described below. Two alternative methods of recording that were also tried out were a tape-recorder and an event-recorder. The main reason they were not used was because at the beginning of the study it was not definite that all the data could be collected in the research nursery where these methods were available. The tape-recorder would, perhaps, have enabled me to record more information, for one can speak faster than one can write, and observation is not interrupted by glancing down to record. The main disadvantage is the laboriousness of making the transcription. The event-recorder likewise has the advantage that one need not look down, if one can touch-type. From our event-recorder, moreover, the data go straight onto punched tape ready for analysis; but owing to its internal mechanics, this event-recorder proved slower to use than writing a code by hand. (It should be useful for film analysis, however, or for recording fewer behaviour items.)

The use of a running commentary is widely accepted among ethologists, and with the help of the shorthand code the children's social interactions could be recorded in some detail. Yet there are at least two imperfections in the technique, which must affect the quality of the record. (1) Speed of interactions: even with the help of a code or tape-recorder there are many occasions when the record lags behind the action (especially when the children are playing vigorously, or quarrelling). It is necessary to disentangle and remember the sequence as well as possible. (2) Consistency of record: extensive preliminary training cannot ensure that all items are recorded with equal reliability, since one's awareness of items varies from day to day. Or one may have 'blind-spots' – items which are persistently under-recorded. Psychologists have attempted to combat this problem with extensive, repeated inter-observer reliability tests and training. Ethologists do not seem to have worried about it at all. They rely instead on the replicability of their observations by other workers. This is feasible when the observables recorded are carefully defined. Two ways are available to test the reliability of my observations: N. Blurton Jones did a series of observations with me, and we also have a film record covering some of the sessions which were recorded by hand.

Size of units

For the commentary it must be decided what size of unit to use, i.e. how much detail to record. The units for this study were chosen with two principles in mind: (1) the units should be readily definable, and so recognisable to other workers, and usable by them and (2) the units should have biological meaning, in terms of the recognition of social signals between the interactants.

The decision was, essentially, what items to split and what to lump. (For a good discussion of this, see Altmann's 1965 paper on rhesus monkeys.) To give an example: the verb ' to touch '. This verb can be defined as ' to bring part of the body, usually a hand, in contact with something or somebody '. The definition could be detailed further, to say whether the contact was sustained or abrupt, and whether its impact was hard or gentle. Each of these ' sub-units ' of *touch* could be recorded as a separate item, but how does one make the choice? Or to phrase the question differently, how can we justify lumping all these sub-units of *touch* under a common name, until we have studied their biological functions, and discovered their relationships with one another?

Biological considerations apart, there is the practical fact that there is a definite limit to how much detail can be seen and recorded during direct observations. (With film analysis this limit is raised.) The choice must also depend on the type of analysis planned. As a general rule, however, until one is very familiar with the behaviour being studied, it would seem sensible to try and record these sub-units wherever possible; they can always be lumped together in the analysis.

Communicative function of units

This study was concerned with social interactions between two or more people (or ' attempted ' interactions – which means simply that one person orientated his behaviour to another person, but did not get any immediate overt response). The manipulative or exploratory actions performed by the children were *not* recorded, unless they seemed to be being used as part of a social interaction (for example, squirting another child with water); but the name of the play material being used was always recorded.

Every action that is done, however, in the company of other people is communicative, in that it conveys information about oneself. For this study the record was deliberately restricted to the more obvious interactions (as defined below), because my interest was to discover how the Problem children compared with the Normals in the way they initiated, or responded to, specific behaviour items.

Duration of units

The units which were recorded varied considerably in their respective durations. Compare, for example, *hit*, *smile* and *lean on*. Ideally one should have units of about equal time-span, but this is not feasible with real behaviour. So some kind of policy must be worked out to deal with the differing durations. Some researchers separate out the lengthier items (usually ' positional' items, like *stand by*), and record them in a special column, with an arrow running down through several time-intervals, to indicate where the behaviour terminates. With some event-recorders it is possible to hold down certain keys, whilst tapping away on other keys representing shorter items. Altmann (1965) used the special code 99 to indicate termination of a long item. Bobbitt, Jensen and Kuehn (1964) marked the termination of behaviours which were not terminated by the start of another behaviour by the code 10. In my record long items were re-recorded at the beginning of each minute subsequent to the one in which they first appeared, until they had ceased. In retrospect I think this was not a satisfactory method, for two reasons: it does not discriminate between items which are momentary and those which last as much as a minute (like *touching* mother); and it complicates the analysis of sequences.

Number of subjects observed

During each observation bout my attention was centred on one child at a time. But, in order to record his interactions fully, behaviour directed to him by others had also to be recorded. Fortunately, from my point of view, the children tended to interact with only one person at a time, and these interactions were fairly easy to follow and document. But during the more vigorous games, like ' Batman ', which might involve three or four children, the interactions were complex and rapid. Not only was it difficult to record all that was happening, but often I could not tell to whom some particular behaviour was being directed. In this case it would be recorded as directed to ' all '. But this was not a satisfactory solution, because it made the sequence ambiguous for analysis.

Shorthand code

Some kind of shorthand was essential to cope with the recording. My code was specially devised for use both with hand-written notes and the event-recorder. The code consisted of 2-letter units for verbs, and 3-letter units for nouns. (This gave a large number of possible combinations.) Behaviour was arbitrarily divided, for convenience, into five categories. Each category had a vowel prefix, which identified it, and then a consonant to represent the name of the verb. (I found subsequently in the analysis that the vowel prefix aided visual recognition of the units for counting purposes; they were also intended to simplify analysis by machine.)

The five categories were:

(1) Facial expressions (*e*)   e.g. *smile es, frown ef*
(2) Speech or noises (*u*)   e.g. *talk ut, laugh ul*
(3) Locomotion (*i*)   e.g. *walk iw, run ir*
(4) Actions (*a*)   e.g. *give ag, touch at*
(5) Occupations (*o*)   e.g. *paints opn, sand osn*

The items of behaviour that were recorded are defined in Appendix 1. (They are listed there under three headings described below in the analysis, which combine locomotion and actions under the heading Actions.)

METHODS: ANALYSIS OF DATA

For the analysis described below data from fourteen children was used. Table 10·1 lists these children (with pseudonyms), with their ages and sex, and gives the amount of data available for each child, with and without their mothers. Four of the fourteen were Problem children, viz. Samuel, Kevin, Karl and Lorna. Although all six Problem children did show behavioural disturbances of various kinds, only three (Samuel, Kevin and

TABLE 10·1. *List of children used for AFS analysis*

N.B. No data for Samuel without his mother, because she was never able to leave him

Pseudonyms of children	Age in months (halfway through observations)	Number of 6-minute observation bouts	
		(1) with mother present	(2) with mother absent
Boys			
Kenneth	33	17	19
Peter	33	40	19
James	41	15	28
Samuel	45	34	–
Kevin	53	16	18
Karl	56	15	28
Stewart	58	17	14
Girls			
Katherine	31	21	19
Theresa	34	21	20
Lesley	36	19	26
Susanna	36	15	17
Annabel	48	21	20
Lorna	48	14	28
Doris	54	21	20

Lorna) actually *behaved* as ' bad separators ' in the nursery. Moreover, their differences from the Normal children proved to be varied and rather subtle in nature. This made comparison with the Normal group much harder than it would have been with a more profoundly disturbed group, such as autistics (who exhibit marked mannerisms or stereotypes, like repetitive *rocking* and *gaze-aversion*).

The three Bad Separators showed two clear differences from the Normal pattern: they spent more time in close proximity to their mothers (although not necessarily interacting with them), and they showed great hesitation in exploring the nursery and interacting with other children. These differences were not in themselves surprising. But observation of the Problem children's social interactions made me aware that these interactions were somehow unsatisfactory, and so this analysis was aimed at trying to pin down what was ' unsatisfactory ', in terms of observable behaviour items.

The analysis was done by hand. Although it was quite simple in principle it involved a very considerable number of computations, as will become apparent. The labour will be much reduced when a computer program, called Primate, which is specially designed to deal with this kind of data, is completed. It is being written by P. Humphreys (of University College, London). Appendix 2 gives a summary of this program.

AFS INTERACTION ANALYSIS

This analysis was devised to manipulate the data in *very* simplified form. The following paragraphs will describe how the data were tabulated and the calculations were done, so that the children could be ranked and compared for various behavioural measures.

PREPARATION OF DATA

There were three stages in the preparation of the data, before the calculations could be done. Firstly, the commentary was re-written in columns, to separate out the interactants. Table 10·2 shows how a two-minute sample of Samuel's data was written in columns. The first column contained the time-marker (minutes), a record of what the child was playing with, if anything, and any behaviour items by the child which were not specifically orientated to someone (the children often talked to themselves, for example). The remaining six columns subdivided the child's record for the three kinds of pair-interactions: mother–child, children–child, and teacher–child. Interactions with *all* other children were placed together in the children–child columns, but the children's names were always given (e.g. Ke) so that they could be treated separately or together in the analysis. They were lumped together for the analysis reported in this paper.

Each behaviour item was written on a separate line, in the sequence in which they occurred. But if two or more items happened simultaneously either from one person or two, then they were placed on the same line.

Table 10·2 gives some examples of this: *look + smile, look + stand by, look + ask*.

Next, a list was made of all the behaviour items, and they were arbitrarily regrouped into just three major categories: Faces, Actions, and Speech (and noises). These categories correspond to the major headings in Appendix 1.

TABLE 10·2. *A two-minute sample of commentary data, re-written in columns, from Samuel's record*

Key: Sa=Samuel, M=Mother, Ke=one of the children

N.B. This is a modified version: the data were in fact re-written in code

Time marker	Samuel to mother	Mother to Samuel	Samuel to children	Children to Samuel	Samuel to teacher	Teacher to Samuel
1	Sa approach M					
		M look+ smile Sa				
	Sa ask M question					
		M shake head +talk Sa				
	Sa leave M					
2				Sa approach Ke		
				Sa standby +look Ke		
	Sa look M					

INTERACTION TABLES

Thirdly, a number of interaction tables were constructed. Certain quite arbitrary rules had to be devised in order to tabulate the interactions consistently. To explain these rules the sample of data for Samuel and his mother given in Table 10·2 will be used.

Firstly, Samuel was taken as Initiator and his mother as Reactor. Each interaction between them was broken up into 'initiation and response dyads'. In the sequence given in Table 10·2 there are three such 'dyads' with Samuel as Initiator:

(1) Samuel *approaches* his mother – she *looks* and *smiles* at him.
(2) Samuel *asks* his mother a question – she *shakes her head* and *talks* to him.
(3) Samuel *leaves* his mother – no response.

Simplified down into the three major categories (Actions *A*, Faces *F*, and Speech *S*) these dyads become:

(1) Samuel *A* – Mother *F*
(2) Samuel *S* – Mother *F* + *S*
(3) Samuel *A* – Mother *0*

There are seven possible combinations of *A*, *F* and *S* which the Initiator and Reactor can use to each other (plus a 'no response' 0 for the Reactor); therefore the dyads can be tabulated as shown in Table 10·3 – in which the three dyads for Samuel and his mother have been marked with asterisks, one, two and three asterisks respectively. Table 10·3 gives the complete table of interactional dyads which occurred between Samuel (as Initiator) and his mother. This table shows, for example, that on 123 occasions Samuel directed an Action to his mother which received no response; on 15 occasions she responded with Speech; and so on.

TABLE 10·3. *The AFS interaction table for Samuel as Initiator and his mother as Reactor*

N.B. Asterisks explained in text

Reactor: mother's responses to Samuel

		No response, O	Responses 1 A	2 F	3 S	4 A+F	5 A+S	6 F+S	7 A+F+S	Totals
Initiator:	1. A	123***	6	2*	15	1	3	6	2	158
Samuel's	2. F	33		6	2			4	1	46
behaviour	3. S	51	3	2	24		4	**16	1	101
to mother	4. A+F	2			1			1		4
	5. A+S	14		1	9		3	2		29
	6. F+S	13		3	5			24	5	50
	7. A+F+S	6						9	1	16
totals		242	9	14	56	1	10	62	10	404

The eighty-four tables which were calculated in this manner were for the following pairs of interactants:

(1) Child as Initiator and mother as Reactor
(2) Mother as Initiator and child as Reactor
(3) Child as Initiator and other children as Reactors, mother present
(4) Other children as Initiators and child as Reactor, mother present
(5) Child as Initiator and other children as Reactors, mother absent
(6) Other children as Initiators and child as Reactor, mother absent

For this analysis the interactions with all other children were lumped together on the tables. The data were split for the two situations: mother present or absent, because it was thought likely that there would be differences in the children's behaviour in these two situations.

The interactions were broken up into these 'initiation and response' dyads and the behaviour items were lumped into the *AFS* categories, because this was the simplest technique that I could devise for dealing with the data. Whether it was in fact a valid way to treat the data can be assessed to some extent from the results.

One problem which arose concerned the lumping of the verbs. Most verbs fell clearly into one or other of the three *AFS* categories. But there were a few difficult ones, e.g.: *headshake* — an Action or a Face? *Laugh* — a Speech or a Face? Such verbs could quite reasonably be placed in either of the two categories. The only solution was to try putting them in the category which seemed to be the better choice, and see how the analysis worked.

Another problem concerned the intervention of a third person in an interaction. Most interactions were straightforward: *A* to *B*, *B* to *A*; but sometimes *C* intervened thus: *A* to *B*, *C* to *B*, *B* to *A*. In this instance *B* may have ' responded ' to *A*, but not directly. For this analysis an interaction was only scored between *A* and *B* if the sequence was uninterrupted by a third person. This rule meant that the number of interactions was slightly underscored.

The lumping of the verbs into the *AFS* categories was necessary for numerical as well as manipulative reasons; whereas a few verbs occurred very frequently, the majority occurred rather seldom. The two most frequent verbs were *look* and *talk*. Actions were much rarer. For the first part of the analysis, in which the verbs were in the *AFS* categories, there was a statistically adequate number of verbs. But in the more detailed second part of the analysis, where these three categories were being broken down, lack of adequate numbers became a problem.

CALCULATIONS AND RESULTS

Various questions could be asked of the data, using these interaction tables. For example: do the Problem children direct less behaviour to other children, and more to their mothers, than the Normals? How do the proportions of their Actions, Faces and Speech compare with the Normal? Are the Problem children more responsive to their mothers than the Normals? Are the Problem mothers more responsive to some kinds of behaviour than to others? Do the Problem children resemble the *younger* Normals, or are they quite different? And so on.

The four series of tests described below were designed to answer some of these questions. In each case the aim of the procedure was the same: to set out the data in such a way that the children could be ranked. Then three significance tests were done on these rankings: the Mann–Whitney *U*-test was used (i) for comparing the Problem children with the Normals; (ii) for comparing the Normal boys with the Normal girls; and (iii) a correlation between age and behaviour was sought in the Normals, using Spearman's Rank Correlation Coefficient. (In most human studies children are matched for age and sex, because these variables are often found to be important. The results will indicate how far this is also true in the present instance.)

Comparison of frequencies of behaviours

One of the simplest questions which could be investigated concerned the relative quantities of behaviours being directed to others by the children. My impression was that the Problem children were involved in far fewer interactions with other children than is normal for their age; and that they spent most of their time close to their mothers, and interacted rather more with their mothers than is normal. The younger Normal children likewise seemed to be involved in fewer interactions with other children than the older Normals, although they spent much of their time *near* other children. Another impression was that younger Normals engaged in more Actions, and less Speech with their mothers than older Normals. This first series of tests was designed to check these impressions.

PROCEDURE

Table 10·4 will be used to demonstrate the procedure which was devised. In this table the children's use of Actions to other children (with mothers

TABLE 10·4. *Average behavioural output of Actions directed by each child to other children* (*with mothers present*)

N.B. The four Problem children are in italics

Pseudonym of child	Total number of Actions (T.A)	Number of 6-minute observations on child (T.O)	Average number of Actions (T.A/T.O)	Rank order	Ranked names
Boys
Kenneth	55	17	3.2	1	Kenneth
Peter	31	40	0.8	9	⌠ *Karl*
James	33	15	2.2	4	⌡ Doris
Samuel	13	34	0.4	10	Annabel
Kevin	13	16	0.8	9	James
Karl	38	15	2.5	2	⌠ Stewart
Stewart	35	17	2.1	5	⌡ Katherine
Girls
Katherine	44	21	2.1	5	Susanna
Theresa	30	21	1.4	7	Theresa
Lesley	19	19	1.0	8	Lesley
Susanna	27	15	1.8	6	⌠ Peter
Annabel	48	21	2.3	3	⌡ *Kevin*
Lorna	4	14	0.3	11	*Samuel*
Doris	52	21	2.5	2	*Lorna*

present) is being tested. There were four steps involved in the construction of this table.

(1) The total number of Actions which each child directed to other children was obtained from the interaction table in which he was *Initiator* to other children, by adding all the rows containing Actions, viz. rows 1, 4, 5, and 7 (ref. Table 10·3). This total was placed in column 2 of Table 10·4.

(2) The Action total for each child was divided by his number of observation bouts to give an Average Actions number, which was placed in column 4 of Table 10·4.

(3) The Average Actions of all the children were ranked, and the children's names were listed in ranked order in column 6.

(4) The three significance tests were calculated on these rankings.

The four children italicised in Table 10·4 were Problem children. However, as has already been mentioned, Karl did not in fact behave as a 'bad separator' in the nursery. Therefore, for this series of tests he was not included in either group. But he was included in the tables out of interest, to see where he would come. He emerged as quite distinct from the Bad Separators. Table 10·4 gives a striking instance of this divergence. In the significance tests for this table the Bad Separators were found to be different from the Normals ($p < 0.01$), but there were no significant age or sex differences in the Normals.

Twenty-four such tables were calculated in this first series. Table 10·5 gives a summary of the names of these tables, and the significant results for each. There were four groups of tables:

(1) Average output of *all* behaviours; for these six tables *all* the cells from each 'Initiator's' table were summed, and then the averages and rankings were calculated in the way described for the Average Actions table. Table 10·5 shows that there were four significant results from these six tables. These will be discussed in conjunction with the rest below.

(2) Average output of Actions: the computations for these six tables have already been described.

(3) Average output of Speech: for these six tables all the rows containing Speech (viz. 3, 5, 6, and 7) from each 'Initiator' table were summed; then the averages and rankings were calculated as described above.

(4) Average output of Faces: for these six tables all the rows containing Faces (viz. 2, 4, 6, and 7) from each 'Initiator' table were summed; then the averages and rankings were calculated as described above.

RESULTS

Table 10·5 shows that nine Bad Separator, seven age and one sex comparisons are significant. Of these, in *all* the rankings of Bad Separators versus Normals the Bad Separators come at the bottom; and in *all*

TABLE 10·5. *Summary of significant results for a series of twenty-four tables concerned with average 'behavioural output'*

N.B. (i) Children = all other children, with mother present
         Peers   = all other children, with mother absent
     (ii) See text for explanation of behaviour categories
     (iii) B.S.   = Bad Separators

Names of Tables for Average 'behavioural output'	Results			
(1) Average output of all behaviours $(A+F+S)$				
Mother to child				
Child to mother				
Children to child	B.S. low	$p=$ 0.01	Young low	$p=0.05$
Child to children	B.S. low	$p=<0.05$		
Peers to child			Young low	$p=0.05$
Child to peers				
(2) Average output of Actions (A)				
Mother to child				
Child to mother			Young high	$p=0.01$
Children to child	B.S. low	$p=<0.01$		
Child to children	B.S. low	$p=<0.01$		
Peers to child				
Child to peers				
(3) Average output of Speech (S)				
Mother to child				
Child to mother				
Children to child	B.S. low	$p=<0.01$	Young low	$p=0.05$
Child to children	B.S. low	$p=<0.01$	Young low	$p=0.01$
Peers to child	B.S. low	$p=$ 0.05	Young low	$p=0.05$
Child to peers	B.S. low	$p=$ 0.025	Young low	$p=0.05$
(4) Average output of Faces (F)				
Mother to child				
Child to mother	B.S. low	$p=<0.05$	Girls high	$p=0.005$
Children to child				
Child to children				
Peers to child				
Child to peers				

the age rankings, except one, the Young Normals likewise come near the bottom. For five of the significant rankings the Bad Separators and the Young Normals coincide in their positioning. Five out of a possible twenty-four is not a large proportion but it does suggest that the Bad Separators are much more similar to the Young Normals than to the Older Normals, in the amount of behaviour they are directing to others. A further point to notice is that these five rankings which coincide are all concerned with child–children interactions, not mother–child interactions.

In this series of tests there was only one significant difference between Bad Separators and Normals for mother-child interactions: the Bad Separators directed fewer Faces to their mothers than did the Normals ($p < 0.05$). This was probably mainly a difference in the amount of *looking* at the mother. Argyle and Dean (1965) have shown that, for adults, *looking* is less common from short range than from far off. Since the Bad Separators spent more time near their mothers than the Normals did, this may account for the difference. (This possibility can be examined with the film data.) An alternative explanation, more difficult to verify, is that the Bad Separators were actually *avoiding looking* at their mother – a form of ' gaze-aversion ' which would tally with the impression that the relationships between these mothers and children were disturbed. My guess is that both explanations will be found to play a part.

Returning now to the general impressions mentioned at the beginning of this section, it can be seen how well the results confirm or refute these impressions. The results confirm that the Bad Separators are involved in fewer interactions with other children than is normal for their age; and they confirm that the Young Normals direct more Actions to their mothers than Older Normals do. But the idea that Bad Separators have more interactions with their mothers than the Normals is *not* confirmed.

Comparison of responsiveness

The series of tests described above was designed to test the *quantity* of social behaviour that the children and their mothers were using. This next series, which was done in a very similar way, was designed to test the *quality* of the interactions.

My impression was that the Bad Separators did not seem able to ' sustain ' their interactions. For example, if another child *grabbed* a Bad Separator's toy, instead of protesting, or trying to regain the object, as a Normal child would, he would just stare at the thief, or retreat to his mother. Conversely, if another child approached and offered help with, say, a puzzle, the Bad Separator seemed not to know how to cope with this help. Also, Bad Separators seemed unable to join in laughing and joking, or mock-fighting, etc.

Bad Separators tended not to direct what I would call ' constructive ' behaviour to their mothers, for example, giving her a puzzle and asking to be helped with it. More typical were: sitting beside mother with one hand resting on her knee, whilst trying to play with a puzzle with the other hand; or asking mother what to do, or to get something which the child could easily get himself. The responsiveness series of tests was designed to investigate these impressions.

Table 10.6 will be used to demonstrate how responsiveness was calculated. In this table overall responsiveness is being considered, of the children to their mothers. There were six steps involved in the construction of this table.

TABLE 10·6. *'Overall' responsiveness of each child to its mother*

1. Name of child	2. Sum of *AFS* responses to mother (*RR*)	3. Sum of occasions when no response to mother (*NR*)	4. *RR+NR*	5. % response $\dfrac{RR \times 100}{(NR+RR)}$	6. Rank	7. Ranked names
Kenneth	31	36	67	46	4	Stewart
Peter	196	258	454	43	5	Katherine
James	46	63	109	42	6	Annabel
Samuel	98	185	283	35	10	⎰Theresa
Kevin	11	22	33	33	11	⎱Kenneth
Karl	67	92	159	42	6	⎰Peter
Stewart	17	13	30	57	1	⎱Lesley
Katherine	59	62	121	49	2	⎰James
Theresa	91	108	199	46	4	⎱*Karl*
Lesley	90	118	208	43	5	Doris
Susanna	20	30	50	40	8	Susanna
Annabel	46	51	97	47	3	*Lorna*
Lorna	64	102	166	39	9	*Samuel*
Doris	77	112	189	41	7	*Kevin*

(1) The total number of Responses which each child directed to his mother was obtained from the interaction table in which he was *Reactor* to his mother, by adding all the columns except the first, the 'no response' column. This total was placed in column 2 of Table 10·6.

(2) From the same interaction table, the sum of the 'no response' column was placed in column 3.

(3) The sum of these two totals (responses + no responses) was placed in the fourth column.

(4) The % 'responsiveness' of each child was then calculated thus:

$$\frac{\text{(total responses)}}{\text{(total responses + no responses)}} \times 100$$

and placed in column 5.

(5) These % responsiveness results were then ranked.

(6) Lastly the three significance tests were done on them, as explained above, for the previous series.

In this particular table (Table 10·6) only the Bad Separator result is significant ($p<0.01$), i.e. the Bad Separators are *less* responsive to their mothers than Normals are. The comparative responsiveness of the children for the separate categories of A, F and S were calculated in a similar way.

RESULTS

Table 10·7 lists the twenty-four tables which were drawn up for this series of tests, and gives the significant results. As in the previous series, it can be

TABLE 10·7. *Summary of significant results for a series of twenty-four tables concerned with 'responsiveness'*

N.B.   (i) Children = all other children, with mother present
        Peers   = all other children, with mother absent
  (ii) See text for explanation of behaviour categories
  (iii) B.S.   = Bad Separators

Names of tables for 'responsiveness'	Results			
(1) Overall ($A+F+S$) responsiveness				
Mother to child				
Child to mother	B.S. low	$p=<0.01$	Young low	$p=0.01$
Children to child	B.S. low	$p=<0.01$	Young low	$p=0.05$
Child to children	B.S. low	$p=0.05$		
Peers to child	B.S. low	$p=0.025$		
Child to peers	B.S. low	$p=0.025$		
(2) Action (A) responsiveness				
Mother to child				
Child to mother	B.S. low	$p=0.05$		
Children to child			Young low	$p=0.01$
Child to children	B.S. low	$p=<0.05$		
Peers to child				
Child to peers	B.S. low	$p=0.025$		
(3) Speech (S) responsiveness				
Mother to child				
Child to mother	B.S. low	$p=<0.025$		
Children to child				
Child to children				
Peers to child			Young high	$p=0.05$
Child to peers	B.S. low	$p=0.025$		
(4) Faces (F) responsiveness				
Mother to child				
Child to mother				
Children to child			Girls high	$p=0.033$
Child to children	B.S. low	$p=0.01$		
Peers to child			Girls high	$p=0.01$
Child to peers				

seen that the Bad Separators emerge with the largest number of significant differences (eleven in all), compared with four for age and two for sex. And in *all* the significant results, the Bad Separators are again at the lower end of the rankings. Eight results are concerned with child–children interactions. The table demonstrates that not only do the Bad Separators tend to be unresponsive to other children (six significant results), but also, for overall responsiveness, the other children tend to be unresponsive to them too. These results confirmed my impressions that the Bad Separators had difficulty in *sustaining* interactions with other children.

In the mother–child tables there are three significant results: the Bad Separators show less 'overall responsiveness' to their mothers than Normals do (p<0.01). They also show less Action and Speech responsiveness to their mothers than Normals do (*p*=0.05 and 0.025). This presents an interesting paradox. These Bad Separators are unwilling to let their mothers leave them in the nursery, and yet when the mothers stay, their children are unresponsive to them.

To summarise the results so far discussed: the Bad Separators appear in the rankings as different from the Normal children in twenty tests (out of a possible forty-eight); there are eleven age-significant results, and only three sex-significant results, for the Normals. In seven of the tests Bad Separators emerge as similar to Young Normals, but these similarities are all concerned with child–children interactions. There does not appear to be a resemblance in their mother–child interactions. For the Bad Separators, moreover, only four significant results are concerned with mother–child interactions, and these all show differences in the *children*, rather than the mothers. (This surprised us.)

Comparison of the use of Actions, Speech and Faces

The two previous series of tests were concerned with Actions, Speech and Faces in isolation from each other. This next series was designed to examine the relationship between the three categories. Table 10·8 lists three ways in which this relationship was tested, for the mother–child pairs only.

ACTION RESPONSES V. SPEECH AND FACE RESPONSES

For this table there were five steps. In each Reactor's table *all* the columns containing an Action response were summed (columns 1, 4, 5 and 7). The three remaining columns were summed (columns 2, 3 and 6). The ratio between these two sums was calculated. And finally, the ratios were ranked and tested as before. There was one significant result: the mothers of the Young Normals responded to them with more Actions than Speech and Faces, compared with the Mothers of Older Normals (*p*=0.01).

In this table, all the columns containing an Action were summed, even

though three of them also contained a Speech or a Face. Another way
to compare them, which may seem more valid, was also tried: the 'pure'
Action response column (column 1) was compared with the 'pure' Speech
column (column 3). These different techniques for comparison were found
to affect the level of significance, but not the direction. For simplicity's
sake only the one method is presented here.

TABLE 10·8. *Summary of significant results for six tables concerned with the
use of actions*

See tables 10·5 and 10·7 for Key

Names of tables for Actions	Results		
(1) Action response *v.* Speech and Face response Mother to child Child to mother		Young high $p=0.01$	
(2) Action initiation *v.* Speech initiation Mother to child Child to mother	B.S. high	$p=<0.05$	Young high $p=0.05$
(3) Action response to Action *v.* Speech response Mother to child Child to mother	B.S. low	$p=0.01$	

ACTION INITIATIONS V. SPEECH INITIATIONS

For this table the Action columns from each person's Initiator table were
summed; and the Action response rows from his Reactor table were also
summed. Then Action Initiations were calculated by subtracting the
Response total from the Initiator total. The same procedure was used to
obtain Speech Initiations. Then the ratios of Actions *v.* Speech were
ranked and compared as before.

There were two significant results: the Bad Separators and Young
Normals both directed more Action than Speech Initiations to their mothers
compared with the others ($p<0.05$, $p=0.05$).

ACTIONS AS RESPONSE TO ACTIONS V. SPEECH AS RESPONSE TO ACTIONS

The two previous tests suggested to us that we had located one of the
sources of disturbance in the relationship of the Bad Separators and their
mothers, following the reasoning set out in these next two paragraphs.

The significant results showed that the Young Normals initiated more
Actions than Speech to their mothers, compared with the Older Normals.

Correspondingly, the mothers of the Young Normals *responded* to them with more actions than Speech. One would expect these two results, if the interactants were behaving in a 'synchronous' manner to each other.

The Bad Separators resembled the Young Normals in that they also initiated more Actions than Speech to their mothers. But there was no corresponding Action response from their mothers. This suggested that their mothers might be doing fewer Actions as responses to *Actions* producing a 'desynchronised' interaction. So a third table was constructed to test the mothers' responses to their children's Actions.

This table was constructed in a similar manner to the previous ones. And, sure enough, there was one significant result: the mothers of the Bad Separators responded to their children's Actions with fewer Actions than Speech compared with the Normals ($p=0.01$).

ANALYSIS OF ACTIONS, FOR
SAMUEL AND PETER AND THEIR MOTHERS

Two possible reasons why the mothers of the Bad Separators might be giving fewer Action responses to Actions were (1) the Bad Separators might be directing the kind of Actions to their mothers that *required* fewer Action responses, or, (2) their mothers might be trying to *avoid* giving Action responses (e.g. they might be trying to 'encourage' their children to be less dependent on them, by avoiding physical contact; or they might dislike doing Actions to their children).

In order to test these two possibilities the Action category had to be split into its component verbs, to discover (1) whether the Bad Separators were directing proportionately more of one particular kind of Action to their mothers, and (2) whether their mothers responded differently to different Actions. This analysis has so far only been done on a few of the children. Data will be presented here for just one Bad Separator, Samuel, and one control Normal, Peter (who had equivalent nursery experience).

TABLE 10·9. *Totals for the nine most frequent Actions directed by Samuel and Peter to their mothers, and vice versa*

Name of Action	Samuel	Peter	Samuel's mother	Peter's mother
Approach	49	57	0	13
Touch	49	51	14	18
Play on lap of	8	3	0	0
Point	9	9	12	15
Leave	40	45	3	10
Give	4	23	6	10
Play with	3	5	18	38
Show	4	18	8	6
Lean on	2	9	0	0

Table 10·9 gives the ten most frequent Actions which Samuel, Peter and their mothers directed to each other. Using these frequencies a 2×2 contingency table was calculated (Table 10·10), to compare the amounts of *touch v. give* and *show* which the children directed to their mothers. The result showed that Samuel did significantly more *touch* than *give* and *show*, compared with Peter ($x^2 = 15.47$). (This confirmed my impression, mentioned in an earlier section.)

TABLE 10·10. *2×2 table comparing the amounts of touch v. give + show, for Samuel and Peter*

N.B. (38) gives expected value of *touch* for Samuel
$$x^2 = 15.47$$

	Give+Show	Touch	
Samuel	49 (38)	8	57
Peter	51	41	92
Total	100	49	149

It could be argued that *touch* is not so likely to ' require ' an Action response as *give* or *show*. This would favour the first explanation suggested to account for the fact that Samuel's mother responded to his Actions with fewer Actions than Speech, compared with Peter's mother. But since it was also possible that Samuel's mother might dislike being *touched* by him (the psychiatrist had suggested this), the problem was not resolved, and the mothers' responses to these two types of Action had next to be tested.

TABLE 10·11. *2×2 table comparing the mother's Action responses to their children's touch*

	Action response to touch	Speech response to touch	
Samuel's mother	4	16	20
Peter's mother	11	10	21
Total	15	26	41

Tables 10·11 and 10·12 show the numbers of Action and Speech responses which the mothers gave to *touch*, or to *give* and *show*. A test for partial association on these two tables shows a significant difference between the mothers ($x^2 = 6.05$ with one degree of freedom; $p < 0.25 > 0.01$) but no effect of the difference in the child's actions ($x^2 = 0.01$ with 1 d.f.

$p > 0.10$). Samuel's mother thus gave fewer Action than Speech responses to either kind of Action, compared with Peter's mother. There is no difference between the effect that the two kinds of action have on her.

TABLE 10·12. 2×2 *table comparing the mother's Action responses to their children's give + show*

	Action response to give + show	Speech response to give + show	
Samuel's mother	2	12	14
Peter's mother	13	20	33
Total	15	32	47

These results are compatible with the theory that Samuel's mother is, in fact, avoiding responding to his Actions with Actions herself: that her internal 'motivation' is more important than what he is doing to her. This analysis thus goes some way to answering the difficult question of who influences who which is more extensively discussed in some other studies of mother–child behaviour; for example, Blurton Jones and Leach's greetings study (Ch. 9), Hinde and Spencer-Booth (1968), Hinde and Atkinson (1970), David and Appell (1969) and the summary in Bowlby (1969).

Conclusions

The results I have described so far illustrate the dilemma in which the Bad Separator finds himself. In his relationship with other children he finds himself in a vicious circle: he directs less behaviour to, and is less responsive to, other children (and correspondingly they to him), than is normal. So it is clearly difficult for him to become integrated into the social group. This in itself would be sufficient reason for clinging to mother. But in addition, there is the paradoxical situation that, although he stays close to his mother much of the time, the Bad Separator is not interacting with his mother more than is normal; he is in fact less responsive to her than is normal. And she may be trying to avoid interacting with him. So the mother–child relationship seems not to be very rewarding for him either; and the possibility of becoming socially 'adept' by practising with mother must be rather inhibited. The experiments of Harlow and Harlow (1965) on the effects of maternal and peer deprivation are relevant in this context; young rhesus monkeys are apparently able to develop normal social behaviour if they have contact with either mother or peers. The Bad Separators have reduced interaction with both.

The analysis and discussion presented above is by no means complete. Within the confines of this paper it is not possible to elaborate on this; but I hope enough has been said to indicate the potential which this kind of 'commentary' data has for the study of human relationships. Theories about the children's behaviour can be formulated and tested, using very simple statistical techniques (although preparation of the data for these tests does require a great deal of work). The results show that fresh insight into children's behaviour can be obtained from this kind of study, in a way that is impossible for much more widely-used techniques like rating, and so the method may be of interest to psychiatrists as a possible diagnostic tool. The major limitation which marred the analysis described here was insufficient data. This was something which could not easily have been remedied in the present study, for the children were only available for a limited period. A study planned on a larger scale would have overcome this problem.

Acknowledgements

I would like to thank N. G. Blurton Jones for help with the statistics and discussion of the results, the Science Research Council for financial support and Professor J. M. Tanner for the facilities of his department.

APPENDIX 1

LIST OF ITEMS OF BEHAVIOUR

ACTIONS

Approach – The child walks toward a person, or object. (If the child runs towards a person, it is recorded as *run*.)

Avoid (or side-step) – The child is moving in one direction, but is confronted by an object, or person, and steps to the side, and may also bend the body away from obstruction.

Bend over to – This action is most often performed by adults to children. The upper body is inclined towards the child, or overhangs it.

Blow nose – This action may be done by the child itself, or by an adult for the child. Young children are not very skilled at it, and usually just wipe the hanky across the nose, without exhaling to expel mucus. More often, the adult grasps the child's head or upper body, places the hanky over its nose and commands: 'Blow', and then wipes the nose. (Most children dislike this operation, and struggle during it.)

Bump – The child is walking near another person, or climbing, running, etc., and collides, usually with the shoulder; the impact is usually very slight, not enough to throw the other person off balance.

Carry – I. The child is lifted and held in the arms, whilst the adult moves around the room, often with the child's legs astride the adult's hip, with one of her arms around it. II. Objects may be carried by the child, usually clasped to the chest.

Climb – The climbing frame is the object most often climbed in the nursery. The child places its hands on a rung, and grips firmly, then places both feet on a rung below, or just one foot; then the hands are placed on a higher rung, and so on; climbing up, the hands pull the body up, and the legs push. The child may also climb onto large chairs, tables, etc. Small children may place the upper part of the body on e.g. a chair seat, and then try to swing the legs round to the side of the body, and onto the seat. Climbing down the frame, the children do not always face the frame. They may grip the rungs to the side of the body, with the hands, and then step down the rungs, with the arms being extended back and up above the head.

Crouch or *squat* – The knees are fully (or almost fully) flexed, so that the buttocks almost touch the ground. The trunk is usually bent well forward, with the chest touching the thighs.

Do up or *undo apron* – Older children can do this for themselves, or another child. If the teacher does it, the child stands beside her, or is pulled close, and the apron is put over the child's head and the straps clipped together. Children often look away from the teacher during this operation (as they do also for buttoning up of coats). For undoing the apron, the procedure is simply reversed.

Dress – This is a general term to cover all alterations to the clothing, such as putting on jerseys, tying up shoes. The teacher usually does these things for the children.

Drop object – I. The object is allowed to fall from the fingers, without any propulsion. The child may release the object, with its hand hanging by its side; or II (as often happens when the child is up on the climbing frame) at a height from the ground, the arm is extended and the object is released away from the body, without force. This action is usually very deliberate, and the child watches the fall of the object.

Dry, or *wipe hands* – This action may be done by the child itself, or by an adult for the child. Young children tend to place the hands briefly on a towel, without a rubbing action, and leave their hands wet. The adult usually grasps the forearm of the child and rubs the towel up and down it and between the fingers.

Fall – The child is usually performing some locomotory action, *walking, running or climbing*: the body pitches forward or backwards suddenly, out of the child's control, and some part of the child's body hits the ground with a force which may cause injury, bruising, abrasions, etc.

Fight – This word is used when the movements made by the child and its opponent are too complex or too quick to describe in simpler terms, such as *hit, pull, scratch,* etc. Essentially the two people (adult and child, or child and child) grasp each other, usually the arms, and *push* and *pull*. If the combatants are on the floor, half-kneeling or lying, then the fight may be called *wrestle. Playfight* would be recorded if the two children were tussling together as described, but also *laughing, smiling,* or in some way signalling that the interaction was friendly.

Flap hands – The arms are raised at the elbows to about the level of the shoulders, and the hands are flapped up and down, usually rather quickly.

Follow – The child *walks* (or *runs*) towards a person who is moving away from it.

Get object – This covers a variety of reaching gestures, to obtain an object.

Give – An object, held in the child's hand or hands, is held out for another person to grasp and is then released; or the object may be placed on the other person's lap (usually mother's).

Grab (or *snatch*) – The child reaches for an object and pulls it abruptly towards itself, often with the body twisted round so that the object is rendered out of reach of another person.

Help – This is a word which I use frequently, but think it should really be split into the component actions. One person (usually an adult) assists another to perform some manipulative game or task, by a complex array of actions: *showing*, taking from and doing for, *giving*, arranging furniture or small objects, etc., often accompanied by verbal instructions as well.

Hit – Blurton Jones (1967) described a hit, or beat, as 'an overarm blow with the palm side of the lightly clenched fist. The arm is sharply bent at the elbow and raised to a vertical position, then brought down with great force on the opponent, hitting any part of him that gets in the way'. (But in our nursery I have seldom seen a powerful hit of this kind.) Sometimes a child may try to hit a person, and miss; or obviously 'aim to miss' – and this I record as *tryhit*.

Hold – I. The arms are stretched out towards a person and his sides, or arms, are gripped firmly, restricting movement. This action is usually done by a mother or teacher to the child. II. *Hold* is also used for objects: the child may be standing still, with an object clasped to its chest, or in one hand. (If the object is being taken from one place to another, I would record *carry*.) *Hold* would not be recorded if the child was actually manipulating the object; it is used more for 'passive' holding.

Hug, embrace – If mother to child: with mother seated, she places her arm round the child's body, in contact with it. Or mother may crouch and place both arms round the child's body. To *hug* the mother, the child may climb onto her lap and throw its arm round her neck. It may try to enclose the upper part of her body, or if she is standing, the child may clasp her round the legs. Or the embrace may be mutual, both parties extending their arms and placing them round the other's neck or upper body. *Hug* is often preceded by the mother (or teacher) lifting the child.

Jump – If the child jumps from above the ground, e.g. from a chair or the frame, one foot may be extended and simultaneously the other pushed against the apparatus, and the body thrust forward landing on the ground on one foot or both, or the child may propel itself forward keeping the feet together, and landing with feet together. The knees flex at the moment of impact with the ground.

Jumps – This describes a rather different action: the child stands on the ground, then flexes the knees and pushes off the ground with both feet together or alternately, thereby bouncing up and down two or three times on the same spot. The hands are often held up about level with the chest and flapped up and down also, whereas in an ordinary *jump* the hands may be extended to aid balance.

Kick – The child flexes one leg and swings it forward, so that the foot makes an impact on an object or person – usually the leg. If the child is sitting, or raised off the ground, both legs may be kicking simultaneously.

Kneel – The child flexes both legs, and goes down on to one or both knees.

Lead – The child or adult may place the hand on the other child's back, and push it gently, as they walk together in one direction; or, the hand is held out to the other person, his hand is grasped, and pulled, so that they both go in the same direction.

Lean on – The child rests its hips against the person (or object). The rest of the body may also be in contact with the person, usually mother.

Leave – The child walks away from a person or object.

Lie – The child's body is horizontal, on the floor, or on some apparatus.

Offer – The child has an object in its hands which it holds out to another person, by extending the arms. The gesture is usually accompanied by *looking* (and eyebrow raising?), and maybe some verbal comment.

Pat – The flat hand is gently tapped once, or two or three times, on some part of the other person – usually on the upper part of the body.

Pinch – The child places its fingers on the body of another person, and squeezes so that his flesh is gripped painfully.

Play – A 'blanket' term, used in a variety of ways. Essentially it refers to the manipulation of play materials of all kinds, and the taking part in imaginative games.

Point – The child extends its arm, and usually also extends one or more of the fingers, in a specific direction. This action may be accompanied by alternating *glances* at the object being pointed to and another person, who is usually also addressed: 'Look at that', or 'What's that?'. A child who is standing close to another person may touch her/him, and simultaneously *point* and *look* towards some object.

Poke – The child extends the arm and one finger, making contact with the body of another person. A *poke* is not usually hard enough to hurt the recipient, if done with the finger (unless e.g. the eye is poked). But the child may use a weapon instead of the finger; the stick (or whatever) is grasped in the child's hand and then directed at the body of the other person.

Pull – The child grasps another person or an object (usually held by the other person), and tries to draw the person/object towards itself. For a hard *pull*, the child will press hard on the ground with its feet, with the knees slightly flexed, and, after the object is grasped, lean away from the other person. The pulling may be reciprocal.

Push – I. To push an object, such as a doll's pram, the child grips the handle and then walks forward, pressing the hands against the rail, and flexing the arms. II. To push a person, the child flexes the arm(s) and then extends it, with the hand flat against the other person's body, in one continuous, rather violent movement; or, the hand is placed on the person's body with the arm slightly flexed, and the arm is then extended. The child does not usually push so hard that the person falls off balance.

Put – This term, like *get object*, tends only to be used when the child has to expend extra effort on the action: it can be done *standing, crouching, bending,* etc., and refers to the extension of an arm, with an object in the hand, and the placing of the object in some specific position.

Reach to (or *stretch to*) – The child extends its arm, and may also bend or extend the body towards an object or more usually a person, and grasps it.

Receive – This word describes the holding out of the hands so as to grasp an object, which is being given by someone. It involves co-ordinated movements with the giver.

Rock – I. The child transfers its weight from one foot to the other in an oscillatory motion, without moving around the room. The motion may be sideways or forwards and backwards. II. *Rock* can also be done with the body whilst seated, swaying the trunk to and fro.

Run – The child moves forward rapidly, using the legs alternately, both off the ground simultaneously, and the body is usually tilted slightly forward. (With young children I doubt whether the feet are always off the ground together.)

Show – The child holds out an object in its hands, orientating it towards another person, so that it can be seen. Often accompanied by a remark, e.g. 'Look at this'. May be preceded by *approach*, if the child is at a distance from the person to whom the object is to be shown. The distinction between this behaviour and *offer* is on some occasions based on intuitive impressions using cues which I have not yet defined.

Sits – The child sits on a chair, or some other object, or the floor. The upper trunk is usually more or less vertical and the upper leg protruded out in front, with the knee flexed.

Slide – The child sits at the top of the slide and propels itself down, by pushing off with the hands. Can be done in various other positions, but the most usual is sitting upright, with the feet stretched out in front.

Slip – The child loses its balance, whilst *walking* or *climbing*, but manages to regain balance without falling and hitting itself on the ground.

Stamp – One leg is flexed and then the foot is brought down hard upon the ground, usually once; or the feet may be alternately stamped, slowly or quickly and repeatedly.

Stand – This is usually recorded as *stand by*, when a child moves to the side of another person, and stays standing close to them, either inactive or busy with some task. (More consistently recorded for a child who is *inactive* besides someone, I think.)

Stretch arms to – The child extends the arms towards a person (as an invitation to *lift*). If the person is seated, the child's arm may be directed horizontally, but the gesture is more often oriented towards a standing adult, and then the arms are held up obliquely, or above the head, towards the adult. The child may already be beside the adult, but if not, the gesture is made as the child *walks* or *runs* towards the adult. (Same as *arms up* in Blurton Jones and Leach, Ch. 9.)

Take – The child extends its hand and grasps an object that is held by another child, or that the other child was about to grasp itself. This action is similar to *grab* or *snatch*, but is a less vigorous and quick movement. *Take* usually means theft, i.e. the other person did not offer the object, before it was taken; but I have sometimes used it where the other person has been passive, i.e. not trying to prevent the removal of the object.

Tantrum – A vague term to cover the struggling, kicking and writhing movements that a child does, which accompany loud screaming, red face and tears. The actions may be performed writhing on the floor, or restrained by an adult.

Throw – The child has an object in its grasp; the arm is flexed and then abruptly extended, and the object is released. Small children are not able to throw an object in a specific direction: the gesture is uncontrolled, and the object may travel in any direction. Young children usually throw objects overarm; but for an underarm throw the action is different: with the object firmly grasped, the arm is extended downwards and backwards, or slightly sideways, and then the arm is swung forwards, and the object is released towards the end of the swing.

Tickle – The fingers are placed on the other person's body, and then wiggled and squeezed gently, with the person's flesh or clothes between the fingers; or the fingers may caress the person's bare flesh (legs, arms, tummy); both actions usually resulting in the person convulsing his body, and trying to push away the tickler's fingers.

Touch – This word was originally used to cover many different kinds of hand contact to another person. (And is still used as a general category for some analyses.) Now I use it when the child or adult places one hand on another person's body, without grasping it. The hand may be placed just for a moment, or it may be rested on the person for a long period (up to a minute).

Trytake – This is recorded when the child attempts to *take* an object, but fails.

Walk, step – The body is moved forward, with the feet placed alternately in front, and the trunk is usually upright. *Step* is one unit of *walk*. Subdivided also into *approach, leave* and *follow*.

Ward off – The child raises its elbow, with the forearm more or less horizontal, and bends its head so that it is hidden behind the arm. The body may also be *bent away* from the other person – who is usually standing close to the child, with an arm raised to strike it, with or without a weapon.

Wash – This usually refers to the child washing its hands in the basin. The younger children are not able to wash their hands properly (rubbing on soap and chafing the hands together to make a lather to clean them, and then rinsing them under the tap). *Wash* also refers to washing dolls. (Sometimes this was done in the water trough, as part of water play; sometimes it was a more elaborate procedure, prepared by the teacher, with a special bowl of warm water, soap and towel.)

Wave – The child raises a hand to about shoulder height, and moves it to and fro, whilst looking at a person (or object). Small children may do a modified wave, which consists of the hand being raised, and then opened and closed towards the person.

FACES

Avert – The eyes are cast down or sideways, and the head is usually tilted down and to the side, thus avoiding eye-contact with another person.

Bite – The upper and lower rows of teeth are brought rapidly and forcefully together, usually with the lips retracted. When directed to other individuals, it is usually oriented to arms, neck or upper trunk, and is rarely severe enough to break the skin (McGrew's definition).

Blush or *red face* – Sudden reddening of face.

Compress lips – Lips pressed together, and sometimes rolled in between teeth. Corners of mouth may be retracted horizontally. Often present with *fixate*.

Fixate – The child's eyes are directed to the eyes of another person for a prolonged unblinking (?) stare of about three seconds; and the head is usually slightly lowered and thrust toward the person, suddenly, and held still; and the brows are drawn down in a frown.

Frown – Brows are drawn down at centre, making vertical creases in forehead. Eyes usually well open. (There is a range of frowns described by Blurton Jones (in press), e.g. *weak frown* and *strong frown, low frown* – but these were not differentiated by me.)

Glance – The eyes only may be flicked briefly in some direction, or the head may be flicked rapidly, orienting the eyes and face towards something or somebody, and then turned away again. (Not used much by me. I tended to lump *glance*, *look* and *watch*.) Shorter than McGrew's *glance*, which lasts less than three seconds. My *glance* lasts for less than a second.

Grimace – Essentially, the lips are retracted; the teeth may be visible, clenched; and the mouth corners may be turned down. The eyes may be screwed up. (But I use this as another rather vague ' blanket ' term, to cover various contortions of the face which I cannot place elsewhere.) It is *not* used for ' protective ' faces (see *wince*).

Look – The eyes are directed towards a person or object, or the whole head may be re-oriented so that the face is directed to the object. I did not differentiate various lengths of *look*; it could range from less than one second to several seconds. A long look might be called *watch*, but I seldom distinguished this, because one could not usually tell at the beginning of a look whether it was going to be long or short.

Kiss – The slightly protruded lips are brought into contact with another person's body surface, or an object, by moving the head forward (and often leaning forward). The most common targets are lips, face, head and hands. May produce sucking sound.

Nod head – The head is moved up and down, once or several times, fast or slowly. Movement ranges from a barely perceptible single inclination of the head, to vigorous action.

Playful face – A ' blanket ' term, to describe the various contortions of the face seen in a playful context. The eyes are usually wide open and may be directed towards a person whilst the head is tilted sideways at an angle. The mouth is usually open wide, with the mouth corners contracted up (as in McGrew's (in press) *play face*), or pursed to look like an O, so that the expression simulates surprise (this face was commonly used by the teacher).

Pout – Lower lip, or both lips, pushed forward; the lower lip curling down; mouth slightly open or closed and mouth corners pulled down.

Pucker – The forehead is wrinkled both vertically and horizontally, the brows being drawn together with the inner ends raised (as in Blurton Jones' (in press) *oblique* frown). The eyes may be closed, or partly closed. The mouth corners are drawn down, and the lower lip is usually *squared*. The mouth may be open. The face is usually red.

Raised brows – The brows are raised, usually looking rather arched, and the forehead is wrinkled horizontally. The eyelids are usually widely separated.

Shake head – The head is rotated from side to side, at least once, and maybe several times. The movements can vary from very slight to extended swing, and can be a quick flick or slow swing.

Smile – A ' blanket ' term used to cover a wide range including (1) slight raising of the mouth corners, with lips closed; (2) wide-open mouth, with mouth corners retracted horizontally and both rows of teeth visible (McGrew's *grin face*?); and (3) mouth wide open, with mouth corners up, and teeth covered by lips or only partly visible (McGrew's and Blurton Jones' *play face*?). (I recognised but did not differentiate the *grin face* and *play face*.) With this expression particularly, there are considerable individual differences, in e.g. characteristic width of smile.

Sneeze – Short, sharp intake of breath, and explosive exhalation through mouth and/or nose, usually with mucus or saliva. (In adults, the noise may be stylised as e.g. ' atishoo '.)

Spit – Lips pursed, and saliva, ejected by pushing the tongue between the teeth. Or lips pursed open, and tongue placed between them and air let out slowly, producing spray of saliva.

Suck – Object or digit placed in contact with lips and tongue, or poked into mouth, and licked by tongue.

Tongue out – The tongue is protruded between the lips. The tip only may project, between closed lips; or the tongue may be maximally extruded, usually with the mouth wide open. The tongue may point down or up, or horizontally.

Wince – Protective screwing up of eyes with, maybe, mouth corners drawn up and lids blinking rapidly.

SPEECH

Grunt – Gruff, non-verbal sound, e.g. humph!

Laugh – The sound is variable, but is produced by a series of short, repeated expirations + long inspiration of breath, accompanied by some characteristic noise: hee, hee, etc. The mouth is usually wide open, and the head thrown back. In a giggle (not differentiated by me) the mouth might be held shut, or a hand put across it.

Playnoise – A ' blanket ' term, to cover a range of noises used by the child during play, usually imitations of machines: shooting, trains, car. Stereotyped chants, such as ' I am a dalek, I am a dalek ', also come under this heading, but may be recorded as *chant*.

Scream – High-pitched wail, of piercing quality.

Shout – Either a single loud, monosyllabic noise – but without the high-pitch ' urgency ' of a *scream*, or more usually, a sentence, spoken loudly and emphatically, e.g. a command ' Don't do that! '

Sing – Musical utterance, with or without words, usually lasting more than three seconds.

Talk – The lips are moved and air expelled through them, and tongue so placed, to form words, or ' pseudo-words ' (the jumble of sounds produced by younger children when they are trying to talk). *Talk* has subdivisions *ask* and *command*. *Ask* is a string of words, usually with a rising inflection, i.e. asking a question. *Command* is usually a string of words conveying an order, and tends to be spoken emphatically and rather loudly.

Weep – The eyes usually become watery and express tears; young children tend to make the *pucker* face with *weep*. The weeping is usually accompanied by short intake and long outletting of breath, with a moaning sound. The more intense the *weep*, the louder the sound produced. My impression is that the vowel sound changes from ' e ' to a long ' a '. McGrew observes that *weep* can also occur with a *laugh* or a cough.

APPENDIX 2

PRIMATE

Primate is a set of computer programs which operate together as a package. It was designed in an attempt to overcome some of the problems arising in the observation and analysis of child behaviour, animal behaviour, or, for that matter, any situation in which there are a number of animals, people or things, performing actions sequentially and interacting with each other.

Prior attempts to analyse such situations with the aid of a computer have run into many problems, such as the following:

(1) Experimenters are not familiar with computer programming languages and techniques, and do not wish to become so.

(2) In order to use – or write – some sort of standard analysis program, some complex numerical coding system which is appropriate for that analysis has to be devised for recording the data.

(3) Even if such a code is successfully devised, after the first analysis it usually turns out that some other (uncoded) data referant to the situation have been omitted, and new observations, recorded in a new, more appropriate coding scheme, have to be included.

(4) Such coding systems presume that the experimenter/coder is 'perfect' in following the coding rules, whereas errors in coding can wreck the results.

(5) Usually when an experimenter is observing, say, some children in a nursery, he writes down what they are doing *sequentially*, for example: ' Steve and Kit and Terry are sitting in the train and driving it; Steve looks at Paul; looks at Karen; looks at Karen again, looks and smiles at Terry, looks at and talks to his mother while approaching her; looks and smiles at Terry; Terry talks to, and looks at, and points to Steven . . .'

Now, how does one devise a code to find out, for instance, if there are any patterns in the behaviour Steven uses in situations like these, and how these might differ from those of Terry, etc.?

The idea of Primate is that it does all this for you, and not only that, it makes sure that you have recorded the situation reasonably well, as it constantly checks what you have written for bad syntax and ambiguity of description. Observations can be written in free format in a language which has some close relations with English. This language is a shorthand which uses English words for the main parts of speech and connects these by special characters or signs, which indicate the way in which the parts of speech are to *build up* into phrases describing ongoing activity. A Primate translation of the above example would be as follows:

ST + KIT + T, SIT IN + DRIVE-TRAIN, ST, LOOK = P,
LOOK = KA, LOOK = KA, LOOK + SMILE = T, LOOK +
TALK + APPROACH = SM, LOOK + SMILE = T, T * ST,
TALK + LOOK + POINT = ST.

Primate makes its own translation of this input language, and stores it in binary code on a magnetic disk ready for whatever analyses might be specified for it.

In general, it can be said that the types of analyses experimenters may require can be classified under general headings, with additional parameters distinguishing exactly what is required within the general class of the heading.

For instance, one may require frequency counts of

(*Class*)   actions (verbs)   for different people, under ⎫ (*Parameters*)
                                   different conditions   ⎭

or, one may wish to scale patterns sequentially in time:

| (*Class*) | made up of certain actions (verbs), and the way in which they are qualified | for different people, under different conditions | } (*Parameters*) |

or, one may wish to look at:

| (*Class*) | interactions | between different people, under different conditions | } (*Parameters*) |

or one may wish to have combinations of all these types of analyses, plus others as well.

In Primate the general 'classes' of analyses are handled by one-word 'instructions', qualified by lists of parameters which define how these general analyses are to be applied in each particular case. One such qualified instruction is sufficient for Primate to execute a complete analysis and to print out the results. Instructions may be combined in any variety and order and each instruction may be executed for more than one set of parameters within the same Primate run. Primate will work out the correct order in which to execute these instructions so that all the computation required prior to each step is performed before that step is attempted.

In this way someone who has little or no experience of computers can quickly put together his own analyses for his own data, and obtain the results.

Special emphasis has been laid on the provision of a fully comprehensive and fully diagnostic error finding system. If a user errs in his instructions or with his data Primate will identify the error as it occurs and write out a diagnostic message.

One warning should however be made. Primate *will not make decisions for users*. If a user does not know which analyses he requires or has some 'bad data' (e.g. erratic coding), then Primate will prove to be of no advantage to him. Indeed Primate is no more expert than its user when it comes to interpreting the question of 'behaviour', and should be viewed as a tool.

Primate is at present in a state of development, and this development has now reached the stage where:

(i) It is capable of doing immediate useful work on data.

(ii) The rules for writing instructions and coding input data from observations have now been finalised. This is important in so far as it means that any data now prepared will be compatible with future versions of Primate. A users' manual exists which will be extended rather than replaced as Primate becomes more flexible and grows in scope.

(iii) A package of subroutines exists for linking user-written analyses (written in Fortran) onto the Primate system without complicated input–output problems. Instructions to handle new analyses problems can thus be developed reasonably easily.

(iv) A basic set of instructions is now operative, and more are under development. In the long run, the nature of the analysis which will be developed within the Primate system will be governed by users' demands.

BRIEF TECHNICAL SPECIFICATION OF PRIMATE

In its present version Primate requires an IBM 360 series computer with at least 155,000 bytes storage capacity, a linkage editor which permits overlays, and five disk drives.

Primate can be made to fit into less storage space (down to a minimum of about 60,000 bytes), and use fewer disk drives (but needs a minimum of two). However the penalty for such compression is severe loss of execution speed.

Primate is written in 360 Fortran and 360 Assembler. Some of the Fortran subroutines will only work on 360 computers, but it is hoped that future versions of Primate will be developed which will run on IBM 7090/94 and ICL 1900 series computers, although in each case with some inevitable loss of efficiency.

Special features of Primate's mode of operation are dynamic allocation of storage within core, and sharing of translated data between core and disk. Analyses are stored in a library on magnetic disk and are overlayed in core when the instruction specifying a new analysis is encountered. In this way flexibility is gained in two important ways:

(i) The amount of data which can be handled in one run is limited only by the amount of disk storage reserved by the user.

(ii) Primate can 'grow', as new analyses can be added to the analysis library *without* the need for any increase in the core storage required.

An outline of the flow of control for the Primate system is as in the table:

Core storage (155,000 bytes)

Executive	Current analysis being executed	Block of data currently being analysed
Disk 1 List of instructions for this analysis (Scratch disk)	Disk 2 Library of analyses (object code) (Primate disk)	Disks 3 and 4 2 work data sets (Scratch disks)	Disk 5 Data block (semi-permanent) (User's disk)

The Primate system operates in two modes. The first is for the case where fresh data are supplied to be inputed to Primate, and a Translate instruction is specified. Here the translator section of Primate first scans the input phrases which are input in free format from either 80-column cards or papertape, to check them exhaustively for (i) correct syntax, and (ii) to ensure that they can represent an unambiguous description of a 'real' world. The translator then takes this sequential description (of the behaviour of up to thirty interaction subjects in an environment), and converts it into numerical sequences for each subject, with extensive cross referencing, so that no information is lost in the translation.

Verbs (behaviour), adverbs (qualifying the behaviour), objects and places, may all be coded. The words in the description are user supplied (or 'learned' during the actual process of translation) and are independent of the translation system. Distinctions between parallel and sequential acts are made, as well as between causality and contingency. A variety of special features such as time markers and environmental parameters may also be specified.

The translation speed is approximately 12,000 'words' of input data per minute, but can vary greatly according to the complexity of the material being translated.

If the translation is successful, Primate then proceeds to the second mode of operation, where the analyses are implemented corresponding to the instructions specified by the user. These analyses are performed on the translated data, stored on the user's disk (or space hired by a user on a computer centre's disk). The fact that the translation is stored on disk in a form suited to the requirements of the analysis program allows rapid scanning and rescanning of the data under a series of hypotheses.

If the Translate instruction is not specified, Primate expects to find a translation already on the user's disk, and proceeds directly to the second mode of operation.*

REFERENCES

Altmann, S. A. (1965). Sociobiology of rhesus monkeys. II. Stochastics of social communication. *J. theor. Biol.* **8**, 490–522.

Argyle, M. and Dean, J. (1965). Eye contact, distance and affiliation. *Sociometry* **28**, 289–304.

Blurton Jones, N. G. (1967). An ethological study of some aspects of social behaviour of children in nursery school. In *Primate Ethology.* Ed. D. Morris, London: Weidenfeld and Nicolson.

Blurton Jones, N. G. (in press). Criteria for use in describing facial expressions of children. *Human Biology.*

Bobbitt, R. A., Jensen, G. D. and Kuehn, R. E. (1964). Development and application of an observational method: a pilot study of the mother–infant relationship in pigtail monkeys. *J. Genet. Psychol.* **105**, 257.

Bowlby, J. (1960). Separation anxiety. *Int. J. Psychoanal.* **41**, 89–113.

Bowlby, J. (1969). *Attachment and Loss.* Vol. 1. *Attachment.* London: Hogarth Press.

David, M. and Appell, G. (1969). Mother–child relations. In *Modern Perspectives in International Child Psychiatry.* Ed. J. G. Howells, Edinburgh: Oliver and Boyd.

Harlow, H. F. and Harlow, M. K. (1965). The affectional systems. In *Behavior of non-human primates,* vol. 2. Eds. A. M. Schrier, H. F. Harlow and F. Stollnitz, New York: Academic Press.

Hinde, R. A. and Atkinson, S. (1970). Assessing the role of social partners in maintaining mutual proximity, as exemplified by mother–infant relations in rhesus monkeys. *Anim. Behav.* **18**, 169–76.

Hinde, R. A. and Spencer-Booth, Y. (1968). Review lecture. The study of mother–infant interactions in captive group-living rhesus monkeys. *Proc. Roy. Soc. B.* **169**, 177–201.

McGrew (in press). *An Ethological Study of Children's Behaviour.* New York: Academic Press.

* Since the time of writing, Primate has been developed to give counts of frequencies and sequences of behaviour and to produce tables such as those in this paper. Inquiries concerning the Primate manual and source decks for Primate should be sent to Patrick Humphreys, at Department of Psychology, Brunel University, Kingston Lane, Uxbridge, Middx, or at Bartlett School of Architecture, University College London, Gower Street, London, W.C.1.

COMPARATIVE STUDIES

11

ASPECTS OF THE DEVELOPMENTAL ETHOLOGY OF A FORAGING PEOPLE

M. J. KONNER *

SUMMARY

This paper is a preliminary report of the first few months of a study of infancy and early childhood in hunter–gatherer people in north-western Botswana. Neonatal reflexes, developmental tests and direct observation of mother and baby are used to give a detailed picture of Bushman infancy. The data are interpreted with the perspective provided by the theory of natural selection.

The paper describes birth, family planning and eugenics, the reflexive capacity and feeding of the newborn and early maternal behaviour and the circumstances of the infant's first year of life. Special attention is paid to the development of the very intense fear of strangers (both Bushman and European strangers) and the very close attachment of child to mother and the eventual development of independence. Some cross-cultural comparisons both at the level of motor patterns and higher levels are made. It is argued that the role of suckling in the development of attachment should not be underemphasized, and that attachment functions not only for protection from predators but also by ensuring exposure and attention to adult technology.

Introduction

Along the northern half of the border between Botswana and South West Africa, extending east and west for about a hundred miles and ranging north into Angola, lives a nomadic people most of whom hunt and gather for a living, and have always done so. They refer to themselves as 'Zhun/ twasi ',† which may be sensibly glossed as 'the real people.' In recent years they have been the subject of meticulous and stimulating research in social anthropology (Marshall, 1960, 1961, 1965) and of less intensive research in physical anthropology (Tobias, 1966) and health and nutrition (Bronte-Stewart et al., 1960).

They live in an ecozone classed as semidesert, in villages or camps of roughly thirty people in which each nuclear family has its own small, temporary grass dwelling. Their subsistence ecology is complex and flexible in strategy and technique, but their technology, by Western standards, is extremely simple. There is much inter-band variation, but average diet

---

* Department of Anthropology, Harvard University.

† In recent literature they are usually referred to as !Kung Bushmen, or simply, !Kung.

consists of about half vegetable foods. They worry about meat and the gamble involved in going after it, but vegetable foods are always available within a few miles' walk. They are nowhere near the edge of starvation, their diet is well balanced, and they have at least as much leisure time as the average middle-class American (Lee, 1968). Nevertheless, the natural elements and the vagaries of water and food availability have a patent and extensive influence over their lives.

The research in infancy and early childhood to be described is part of a five-year multidisciplinary study of the Botswana part of the population which extends previous research, emphasizing subsistence ecology (Lee, 1968), health and nutrition (Trusswell and Hansen, 1968), population genetics, demography, child training and archaeology. The theoretical perspective of the project is that of the evolution of human behaviour and its goal is the discovery of selective forces that may have acted during the Pleistocene, and their possible effect on behaviour evolution.

The present research in developmental ethology aims at a general description of infancy and early childhood among the Zhun/twasi. The necessarily small sample size makes it possible to examine very diverse aspects of early behaviour, the growth of primary attachment and separation, cognitive and motor development in the first eighteen months, and the growth of peer-directed social behaviour during what corresponds to our American 'pre-school period.' The methods used include cognitive testing, simple experimentation, neuromotor assessment, physical measurement and, most important, systematic and casual observation of mother–infant pairs and groups of 2- to 5-year-olds in their natural setting. Such observation is easy and rewarding in a society in which everyone is outdoors most of the time and the inside of the small houses open and accessible.

While many different theories have provoked the various aspects of the research, the theory we are using to make sense of them together is natural selection. This perspective has organized the research along two major lines of inquiry. First, what items and patterns of early behaviour and development can be said to be present in a sample of infants very disparate in culture, physical characteristics and subsistence ecology from the one in which they were first observed? The answers to this question will help to establish a species-specific ontogeny and early behaviour catalogue for man, so that he can be assigned a place in a phylogeny of such catalogues. Second, what is it about the hunting and gathering way of life, which dominated more than 95% of our species' history, that has given the observed developmental patterns and behaviours adaptive value? What evidence can be found of selective forces which may have acted on maternal behaviour, infant behaviour and developmental patterns during man's long foraging experience during the Pleistocene?

The results of the first few months of this research, reported below, are preliminary and non-quantitative. They consist of the impressions we have gained from our first efforts to apply instruments and codes for assessing behaviour which were designed to describe infants and children in Western societies. They deal only with the most coarse similarities and differences. Except for the data on fear of strangers, the descriptions are based on observations of eight newborns, eighteen infants in the first year and a half, and ten children between ages $1\frac{1}{2}$ and 5, living in four small villages distributed over about one hundred miles.

Perinatal selective effects: Birth, family planning, and eugenics *

Zhun/twa women are remarkable for the equanimity and independence with which they approach pregnancy and childbirth. There is no medical supervision of pregnancy or delivery, and there are no midwives or other expert native persons traditionally concerned with birth. A woman is very much on her own. When the first uterine contractions begin, she simply leaves the village alone or with one or more other women. The delivery is completed in the bush a short distance away. If the infant lives, she returns with it to the village.

She may resume her normal activities at once, or rest for a few days, depending on her inclination and condition. There is no ritual lying-in period before or after delivery. The infant is not put to the breast until the colostrum has run out, and he may be nursed by another lactating woman or simply wait for two or three days until his mother's breasts engorge with milk.

The Zhun/twasi believe that the foetus is formed by the union of semen with menstrual blood, and they abstain from sexual intercourse during menstruation in an effort to avoid pregnancy, and also because it may 'make a man sick'. In addition to this unfortunate error, two successful methods of population control have been reported by Zhun/twa informants.

The first is post-partum abstention from sexual intercourse for periods varying from two to fifteen months. Here also, the conscious effort to avoid another pregnancy is supported by the belief that sexual relations during this period are injurious to the man.

The second method, which many Zhun/twasi report to have been practised commonly until recent years, is infanticide. This was accomplished by burial of the infant within seconds after birth, probably before it breathed. Infants reported to have been abandoned in this way include those born too soon after a sibling (provided the latter was still alive), one of a pair of twins, and certain instances of malpresentation and malformation, such as breech birth, or agenesis of limbs or ears.

* The statements in this section are based on casual interviewing of the Zhun/twa adults undertaken in connection with the present research.

With the exception of the last-mentioned use of infanticide, all these population control measures have the same rationale in the folk-view: a woman cannot nurse more than one infant at a time, and in order to grow strong and healthy an infant should nurse for at least two to three years. A mother's only responsibility is to the infant alive and growing, and therefore births must be well spaced.

Another possible source of pressure for birth spacing is that a woman out gathering cannot routinely carry two infants in addition to sometimes half her own weight in bush foods. Therefore an infant should be able to walk some distance without tiring or fussing before his mother bears another child. As Bowlby citing personal communication from J. W. Anderson has pointed out (Bowlby, 1969: 254–5), an apparently well-coordinated 2-year-old can decline into neuromotor chaos as soon as mother is up and moving. One Zhun/twa 3-year-old with a 3-month-old brother pestered his mother and her gathering companions incessantly with his begging to be carried. One morning his mother decided to leave him at the village with his father and grandfather and go gathering with the baby only. Before she had walked a hundred yards his wailing brought her back again, and she didn't go gathering that day.

In addition to these deliberate efforts there is some evidence that lactation itself may reduce the likelihood of conception (Birdsell, 1968). Thus the Zhun/twa prolongation of it for reasons of health and growth may inadvertently help space births.

The practice of abandoning breech presentations was eugenic in purpose. When we asked what would happen if such a baby were kept, one man said, ' People would talk about it and say it had no sense because it was born backwards '. Research on infants delivered after a breech presentation has demonstrated large departures from the normal pattern in intensity of certain leg reflexes during the first ten days (Prechtl 1961). Sequelae of these signs are as yet unknown, but breech birth is generally considered dangerous by obstetricians. According to a basic obstetrics text, ' In breech delivery possible trauma is fracture of the thigh, ruptured spleen or liver, fracture of ribs, fracture of the humerus, rupture of the cords of the brachial plexus, as well as serious cerebral damage ' (Rhodes, 1967: 228).

Whether the Zhun/twa belief about breech presentations is a matter of coincidence or of quasi-scientific tradition is open to speculation, but the latter seems not beyond the capacities of people who have discovered the two genera of indigenous beetles that make effective arrow poison. Malformed infants were abandoned because they were ' not good ' and because ' people wouldn't like them '. Zhun/twa informants say the practice of infanticide has died out as a result of the threats and advice of Bantu and Europeans.

Normal infants of either sex born thirty months or more after their siblings are as desired and precious to men and women as anything in their lives. A new infant born at an opportune time does not restrict a woman's life, it expands it, drawing attention and help to her from everyone around. A woman of child-bearing age without an infant on her hip or toddling behind her most of the time is an unusual and somehow awkward sight. Barren women are profoundly sad and ill-adjusted, from the Zhun/twa point of view as well as ours. They seem always to be looking for something to do.

The biological background of development

THE REFLEXIVE CAPACITY OF THE NEWBORN

One aspect of the research involves the administration of an instrument for the neurological assessment of newborns * (Prechtl and Beintema, 1964) in connection with naturalistic observation and follow-up studies. To date, examinations have been made of only eight newborns and observations of three more, but it seems worthwhile to make some very general remarks about this admittedly tiny sample.

Of some forty-five scorable responses in the examination, we have failed to elicit only two (biceps reflex and magnet response), and these are among the most subtle and difficult to elicit in European newborns (Beintema, 1968). Two others (pupillary reflex and corneal reflex) have not been administered. All the remaining responses are present in form and degree very reminiscent of infants we saw in Massachusetts and Holland. Specifically, the findings of Geber and Dean (1967, orig. 1957) for African neonates in Uganda – absence of the Moro reflex after four days, absence of ' snapback ' in the arms, absence of the ' doll's eye reflex ', absence of the stepping reflex, and extreme control of the head and spine in pulling to sit, sitting and prone suspension – none of these departures from the European pattern has been observed in these few infants.

It is our initial impression, then, that they begin life with the same basic reflex repertoire as do their European counterparts.† Only a few items in this repertoire have evident survival value for European infants: rooting, sucking and stripping actions of the mouth; staring, following and blinking of the eyes; crying and ' smiling.' Naturalistic observations of Zhun/twa infants have begun to suggest possible survival functions of other patterns, usually thought of simply as signs of an immature nervous system.

---

* I am grateful to Dr T. B. Brazelton, Dr B. Touwen and Dr Y. Akiyama for familiarizing me with procedures for examining newborns, though my imperfections in applying them are no fault of theirs.
† We have by no means ruled out the possibility of more subtle differences, such as differences in activity level, response strength, muscle tonus, etc., and we are examining these and similar variables as the sample expands.

For example, most newborns (East African, European, or Zhun/twa), after the first few days, when placed in the prone position, exhibit some effort to lift the head and move it from side to side, and show supportive 'crawling' movements in the legs. Most, also, when held in the upright position, will exhibit 'placing' and 'stepping' responses to appropriate stimulation of the feet (Beintema, 1968). Infants supine in cribs have little use for these patterns, except to enlighten neurologists. Zhun/twa newborns, however, are carried in a sling which keeps them upright and pressed against the mother's side. No clothing separates the infant's skin from his mother's, and one typically sees sleeping babies with faces pressed into the mother's flesh. From time to time, either spontaneously or in response to postural changes of the mother, the newborn will press his arms against her and twist his head from side to side, or, using his legs as well, twist his entire body. These movements, the components of which appear to be the same as the elicited movements mentioned above, may function to reduce the necessity for the mother to readjust him, and may even prevent him from smothering in her skin.

Bowlby has remarked (discussion of Prechtl's paper in Foss, 1963) that, in connection with the presumed late appearance of clinging in human infants (cf. Bowlby, 1969: 279), it would be interesting to observe an infant raised by a mother who continuously wore a fur coat. While a study of Eskimo infants would be more to the point, Zhun/twa infants fulfil this condition to some extent by virtue of the mothers' beads. Almost all Zhun/twa women wear many long strands of small beads which are ideal for grasping in the same way that hair is. Zhun/twa infants may be seen on occasion to grasp and cling to these masses of beads for brief periods, and with one or both hands, from the first few days of life, usually during a feed. While beads are the most common target for this behaviour at first, infants also cling to clothing and to the skin of the breasts, and later in the first year these targets take precedence.

It is necessary to distinguish this behaviour from the clinging of monkey infants on several grounds. First, it occurs much less frequently and for much shorter periods of time. It never functions to support all of the infant's weight, and it doesn't occur at all in transport contexts during the first few months. Its function in the early months is probably only to stabilize the hold of the infant's mouth on the breast, thus reducing the need for constant vigilance on the part of the mother.

Some light may be thrown on the origin of this behaviour by the fact that spontaneous Moro reflexes during feeds sometimes terminate in one- or two-handed grasping and clinging, and, also, that when a Moro occurs during a one-handed cling, the extension-adduction phase engages only the free arm, while the other continues to cling. This is in keeping with the findings of recent electro-myographic research on the Moro reflex (Prechtl, 1965; Prechtl and Lenard, 1968) demonstrating that if the infant is grasping with both hands at the onset of the reflex, only the flexion–adduction phase occurs. These authors argue that this finding returns the reflex to the phylogenetic status Moro originally assigned to it, that of a vestige of the embracing reflex of infant monkeys – an abrupt, strong flexion–adduction of the limbs, and clinging elicited by the mother's rising and walking off while the infant is holding loosely onto her belly-fur. Our research suggests that Moro was wrong only in considering the reflex in humans completely vestigial.

VEGETATIVE ACTIVITIES

'Demand' feeding in America means feeding the infant when he cries, and this conception of it developed because crying is the only signal that can be perceived at the distance mothers in western society often maintain from their infants. Zhun/twa infants are certainly fed when they cry, but more often long before they cry. The mother, with the infant against her skin, or in her arms, can literally feel his state changes. She makes every effort to anticipate hunger. Waking up, moving, gurgling, the pucker face, the slightest fret, a change in the rate of breathing – any of these may result in nursing. No strict diaries have as yet been kept, but infants through at least the first year are nursed many times a day (twice an hour would be a conservative estimate), for from thirty seconds to ten minutes each time. It would be most sensible to describe Zhun/twa infants as 'continual feeders' (cf. Blurton Jones, Ch. 12).

Maintenance of temperature and state is facilitated through skin-to-skin contact with the mother's body. Whenever it is cool, or when there is a breeze, mothers are very reluctant to break this contact. They are also fairly careful about keeping infants out of the sun for the first two or three months, but since they are often in light shade, or part of the infant's body is exposed to direct sun at times, there is no sunlight 'deprivation'. Babies asleep on the mother's side are constantly rocked by her walking and by the movements of her ordinary activities. When the baby is small enough his body is rocked by her very breathing.

Elimination has no social consequences for Zhun/twa infants (though it does for problem 'bedwetters' in later childhood). Before he can crawl easily the infant routinely urinates and defecates in someone's lap. Usually he is not even moved until it is finished, and it is cleaned up with no comment whatever. Gradually, as he acquires control and mobility, he is told to leave the house and, after he is walking well, to leave the village. In many observed episodes no infant or child has ever been in the least upset in connection with elimination (except infants in the first two or three months upset by the change in position required for cleaning), nor, for that matter, has any adult.

M. J. KONNER

The milieu of development in the first year

From the first weeks of life Zhun/twa infants, when awake, are carried not on the back, but on the hip or side in a sling contoured to support the back, buttocks and thighs, leaving the head, arms and, in older infants, the lower legs, free. The kind of support it gives is very much like that of one device designed to make reaching easier for young infants in an experimental situation (Bruner, 1968). In connection with this posture, it is worth noting some remarks of Gesell and Amatruda concerning the 6-month-old sitting up: 'His eyes widen, pulse strengthens, breathing quickens and he smiles when he is translated from the supine horizontal to the seated perpendicular. This . . . is more than a postural triumph. It is a widening of horizon, a new social orientation' (1947: 42). Zhun/twa infants are held in this position virtually from birth. The horizontal is almost unknown to them during their waking life. From their position on the mother's hip they have available to them her entire social world, the world of objects (particularly work in the mother's hands) and the breast, and the mother has immediate easy access to the infant. When the mother is standing, the infant's face is just at the eye-level of desperately maternal 10- to 12-year-old girls who frequently approach and initiate brief, intense, face-to-face interactions, including mutual smiling and vocalization. When not in the sling they are passed from hand to hand around a fire for similar interactions with one adult or child after another. They are kissed on their faces, bellies, genitals, sung to, bounced, entertained, encouraged, even addressed at length in conversational tones long before they can understand words. Throughout the first year there is rarely any dearth of such attention and love.

Nor is access to the world of objects in any way restricted, although there are no infant toys. Infants are always swiping at, grasping and manipulating beads and other objects hanging around the mother's neck, or playing with, or just staring fixedly at some object or work in the mother's hands. When they can sit alone and begin to crawl the entire natural world is open to them – sticks, grass, rocks, nutshells, insects, dung and the ubiquitous sand – and they exploit it just as Western infants use toys, with the difference that nature never gets boring, and yet is somehow orderable. Furthermore, because all objects and work belonging to adults exist on the ground, infants are never restrained from exploring them, or separated from them by tables, cupboards, or other barriers. Exploration is actively encouraged by adults and such objects are often used to distract fretting babies. They become regular targets for the phrase 'look at that' by the second week.

INFANT SIGNALLING AND ADULT RESPONSES

Crying, the pucker face, and sub-cry vocalizations are the infant's most powerful survival weapons. They appear on the first day of life and remain prominent items in the behaviour repertoire throughout early childhood. While sound spectrographic analysis might conceivably reveal differences between Zhun/twa infants' and Western infants' crying, the naked ear does not. It is the same intensely unpleasant sound, the one one wants to hear stopped immediately. The rhythmical cry and the pain cry, described for infants in Boston (Wolff, 1969), are easily differentiated, the latter being much longer for the first few cries, higher in pitch, and arhythmical. They also produce different responses. While rhythmical crying in infants over a year old produces no response in anyone but the mother or caretaker, one observed instance of a pain cry in a 4-year-old (the boy had burned himself) elicited orientating reactions from everyone in the village and approach responses from a dozen adults. It is not the case, however, as Wolff found for American infants (1969), that mothers are very variable in their responsiveness to rhythmical crying, either in speed or style. Zhun/twa mothers never ignore rhythmical crying during the first year, whereas Wolff's mothers often did, at least temporarily. This is partly because one or more walls routinely separate infant and caretaker in Boston, while here infants are never alone in a distant room. The crying is much more disturbing to the caretaker and to everyone else.

If the infant is with a caretaker other than the mother, the caretaker will make a brief attempt at quieting and then carry the infant to the mother. Unless the infant is completely satiated the mother almost always responds by trying to nurse him. Mothers never use objects other than the breast as pacifiers. If nursing is ineffective or partially effective, rocking and singing are the next responses, often with the infant pressed, front-to-front, against her chest and shoulder. Often the singing is done loudly into his ear in an effort to drown out other stimulation. Sometimes, when he first begins to fret, she will say ' Uhn-uhn, uhn-uhn ' (meaning ' no ') repeatedly and rhythmically, or talk loudly but pleasantly into the infant's face in an effort to distract him. During the course of these efforts she will try nursing several times, and often the infant must be partially quieted through rocking and singing before he will nurse. If he does not quiet in a few seconds, she will rise and walk him while rocking, singing and nursing, and maintain a distance of at least twenty feet from the group she was sitting with when the crying began.

Some common causes of crying are hunger, over-stimulation (including being played with too much), frustration in pursuit of a goal and ' wind '. Since infants are unclothed and soiling attended to immediately, wetness is never a cause of crying. At about five months offering an interesting object emerges as an effective way to stop crying.

Smiling appears in the first few days of life, though not quite in its mature form. But people recognize and respond to it as smiling, with announcements to each other, laughing and increased social and physical stimulation of the infant. By at least the second month people try repeatedly, with some success, to elicit social smiles by bouncing the infant or stroking his cheeks with simultaneous face-to-face interaction. Positive vocalizations are treated with similar, though not as intense, interest.

The growth of mother–infant interaction

By the time an infant can crawl away from his mother (around 8 months) and begin to explore the world alone, he has developed two important patterns of social behaviour: first, a strong attachment to his mother as a specific person; second, an, at least incipient, fear of strangers. He is born with the basis of social behaviour. His crying draws his mother to him and produces responses in her that relieve his distress. His hunger and oral reflexes result in interaction with her breast, and his skin-to-skin contact with her gives him warmth and tactile comfort. His interest in complex, changing, noisy things makes him look at his mother's face. By smiling he can make her smile and vocalize, or even make his surroundings explode with human sounds. By dint of these powers he is a social animal at birth. But he is not capable of attachment, which takes several months to develop. From the point of view of selection, attachment must be fully developed by the time independent locomotion begins, so that following and flight to the mother will develop simultaneously with crawling and walking. A young child lost in the bush would be subject to thirst, hunger, freezing temperatures in winter, and the predation of leopards, lions, hyenas and other carnivores, which even adults are afraid of. Attachment is top priority adaptive behaviour from the time the first exploratory creep is taken. By European standards, as indicated by all proximity-maintaining behaviours, Zhun/twa infants are strongly attached to their mothers, and it may be this very attachment that makes possible the exploration of so hostile an environment.

Considerable attention has been given in recent years to describing the behaviour patterns that make up attachment (Ainsworth, 1963; Bowlby, 1969). These patterns, covering a broad span of levels of development and levels of behaviour description, include the following: visual–postural orientation; rooting and sucking; crying and stopping of crying; smiling; non-cry vocalization; grasping and reaching; separation anxiety; approach; following; greeting; climbing and exploring; burying of face; use of the mother as a base for exploration; flight to the mother; and clinging. When these behaviours occur more often in relation to the mother than anyone else, attachment, by Ainsworth's definition, has begun.

All these patterns have been observed in Zhun/twa infants during the second half-year. But listing all these behaviours and giving them a label does not make an explanation of the growth of attachment. While Bowlby's (1969) 'ethological' formulation – which greatly de-emphasizes the role of feeding and reinforcement learning – is very helpful in terms of what to look for, it is somewhat confusing in terms of the etiology of attachment behaviour, at least in Zhun/twa babies. This is probably because (in observable, not theoretical, terms) nursing is a manifestly important part of their lives and of their relationship to their mothers. The frequency of nursing and freedom of access to the breast from birth to weaning are very high. The first instance of the use of the mother as a base for exploration occurs when, by the second month, the infant stares at interesting sights while relaxed by suckling. At 5 months he may vocalize continually while nursing and from time to time be answered by his mother. By 8 or 9 months he begins to fondle the free breast while nursing, and though this behaviour is persistent and not entirely gentle, most women in no way discourage it. It continues until weaning, which, if the mother does not conceive again, may be as late as 6 or 8 years. Nursing is an experience engaging the whole body, associated with extension-flexion movements in the legs and pelvis, moving skin-to-skin contact with the mother, sometimes dramatic state changes, the pleasure of sucking and the assuagement of hunger. As the infant passes through the second year, it gradually becomes the one reason for approaching the mother's body for which the approach is never refused. Finally, all attachments of any kind between Zhun/twa *adults* involve continual giving and receiving of food. Perhaps feeding is an unimportant aspect of attachment in England, or even in Uganda, but here it emphatically is not.

In assigning an important role to feeding I do not mean to rule out other factors already mentioned; merely to stress one factor that has been de-emphasized in recent theorizing. It is suggested that both the innate features of social behaviour – crying, interest in faces, smiling – *and* reinforcement learning, with not only feeding but also warmth and tactile stimulation as reinforcers, contribute to the growth of attachment during the first half-year.

The growth of responses to strangers

Between 7 and 9 months of age, Zhun/twa infants (like their Western counterparts) who formerly played happily with anyone, develop a discriminating uneasiness in the presence of people they don't know. With a kind of Hebbian perspicacity, Zhun/twa mothers see it as a sign of wisdom. The fear of strangers (also called ' stranger anxiety ' and ' 8-months anxiety ') has been a popular subject for research in developmental psychology (e.g. Ainsworth and Wittig, 1969; Morgan and Ricciuti, 1969), and its etiology a subject for extensive theoretical controversy (e.g. Bowlby, 1969). It is of interest to ethologists because it is the earliest instance of agonistic behaviour, and because it has the apparent adaptive function of removing the infant from a potentially dangerous, or at least unknown, individual.

In order to examine cross-sectionally the development of fear of strangers, responses to the standard approach of a female stranger were observed in 36 infants and young children (20 girls and 16 boys). The stranger approached the infant slowly, smiling and repeating the infant's name with high inflection while the infant was seated or standing within a few feet of the mother. Then the stranger touched or picked up the infant. (Only the oldest subjects were not picked up, and they were held firmly in both arms.)

The responses scored by the observer and the weights assigned them are listed in Table 11·1. Higher weights were assigned to those responses which only appeared when lower-weighted responses also appeared (for example, laugh was weighted more than smile, because laugh never occurred unless smile occurred, whereas the reverse was not true). Weights of all responses observed in a subject during the episode were summed algebraically to yield a 'fear of stranger' score. Each possible response was scored only once, however frequently it occurred.

TABLE 11·1. *Responses to strangers according to weights assigned them*

−3	−2	−1	0	+1	+2	+3
Laugh	Smile	Stare at	Mouth	Gaze avert	Approach	Cling
Touch	Non-fret	stranger's	hand	(within	mother	Nurse
stranger	vocaliza-	face		2 sec)	Touch	Cry
	tion	(more		Look at	mother	
		than		mother	Fret	
		10 sec)		Withdraw		
				from		
				stranger		
				Pucker		
				face		

Eighteen infants were tested by both European and Zhun/twa female strangers, and the remainder by the European stranger only. (It is often impossible to find a woman who is unknown to an infant.) Since the more foreign a stranger is, the more dangerous he should be, it was reasoned that there would be a clearly more fearful response to the European, but this expectation was not confirmed. In twelve cases the scores for the two were identical. Three were more fearful of the European, and three more fearful of the Zhun/twa. The only difference was that in the ones more fearful of the European the difference in scores was larger. There were too many ties for non-parametric procedures to be applied to discrimination between the groups.

Where different, the European and Zhun/twa scores were averaged, and the scores for all subjects were ordinally ranked. The results of this ranking, in relation to age, are displayed in Fig. 11·1. The first unequivocally fearful response was in an 8-month-old, and the strength of response was greatest in the second half of the second year. The oldest child showing a clearly fearful response was 40 months old, but fearful responses were absent in a number of children between 24 and 40 months. Although squirming and reaching toward the mother in younger infants were counted as 'withdraw' or 'approach mother', and touch, cling and nurse were coded even if the mother approached the infant first, the curve for at least the first year is steepened by simple neuromotor maturation. However, even if the locomotor responses are subtracted there is no decline in fear scores before the end of the second year.

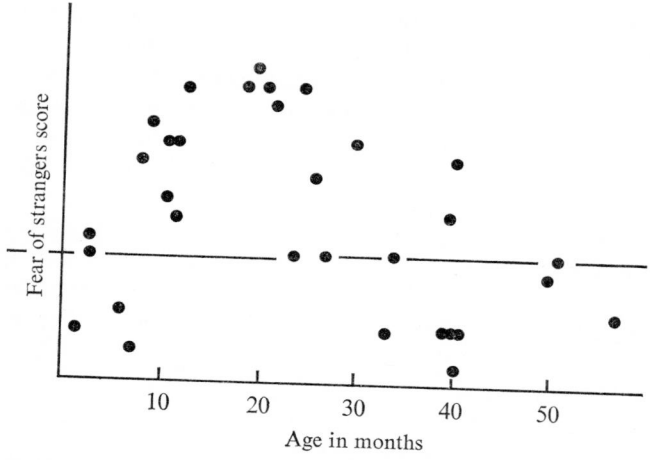

Fig. 11.1. Responses to strangers. The ordinal ranking of subjects by fear of strangers scores (y-axis, increasing fearfulness) is shown in relation to age in calendar months. The broken line indicates the rank of individuals whose algebraically summed responses were equal to zero (neither fearful nor positive). Each dot represents a child.

The reaction is markedly more extreme than what we are familiar with in Western infants, often characterized by immediate loud screams, headlong flight to the mother, clinging and nursing, even though she is only a few feet away. Clinging and nursing may be maintained for as long as the stranger is close by (compare the mild responses of 1-year-olds to a similar test in America by Ainsworth and Wittig, 1969). The fear is more difficult to overcome, sometimes requiring days of familiarity, giving of food, entertaining, and so on, with the active co-operation of the parents. It also persists much later in development. The response to strangers reported for British pre-school children by Blurton Jones (1967) and by Connolly and Smith (Ch. 6) of presenting the stranger with an object has never been observed among Zhun/twa children of a comparable age in any context. There is no approach at all until familiarity has been established.

There are several possible explanations for these differences, but the simplest is that Zhun/twa infants have much less experience with strangers. Western infants, or at least the urban ones that have been the subjects of most studies, see or meet strangers many times a day, and so their fearful responses to strangers in general and to any given stranger habituate more quickly. Though Zhun/twa infants do see some strangers, as people move from camp to camp, it is only a tiny fraction of the number Western infants see. To Zhun/twa infants the class of strangers, as well as the individual stranger, is strange.

From an adaptive viewpoint it is worth noting that Zhun/twa children between 18 months and 5 years old spend considerable time playing together on the outskirts of a sedentary camp, though never out of earshot of adults. This pattern of social behaviour may produce a selective advantage for fearful responses to strangers beyond the first 18 months. (This is a different order of explanation. It does not remove the problem of etiology, i.e. the developmental mechanism through which natural selection gets translated into child behaviour.)

The distribution of several specific fearful responses may be of interest. The flight response appears as soon as the motor capacity for flight exists, and it invariably carries the infant not only away from the stranger, but *to* the mother. Like the crying response, which emerges earlier, it functions to bring the infant and mother together, and not merely to separate the infant from the stranger.

Clinging to the mother is a common component after 9 months. It is also a component of non-fearful attachment appearing during nursing and in other attachment contexts from the first few days, and a component of the infant's posture during certain kinds of transport by around 8 months.

Nursing is commonly associated with visual fixation of the stranger's face in infants who, when not nursing, immediately avert. This is an instance of the use of the mother as a base for exploration.

Mouthing of the hand is a very common response in older infants who show no other scored behaviour, fearful or positive, but seem to be trying to make up their minds, or perhaps just ' waiting it out '. This may have a function similar to nursing at a lower level of arousal, but it is in no sense derived from nursing, since hand-to-mouth activity resulting in self-quieting can be seen from the first few days of life.

Attachment, imitation and subsistence play

While attachment has important immediate adaptive dividends, it has some long-range ones as well, because it functions to maintain proximity with effective models of subsistence and reproductive behaviour. By the end of the first year (within a few months after attachment itself develops), well-differentiated, deferred imitation (Piaget, 1962) of the elementary components of adult subsistence activities appears (pounding with a mortar and pestle, digging with a digging stick, and others), as does the imitation of singing, clapping and dancing. Adults delight in these early accomplishments, and spend much time trying to encourage and re-elicit them. Infants under a year of age may be encouraged to inspect and chase after, and even bite, large insects, which they gladly do.

By the second half of the second year autonomous exploration is well-established, two-word phrases are replacing baby noises and infants engage in social play with slightly older children, usually in imaginative imitation of adults. The interest of both boys and girls in animals continues to expand, and by the age of 5 they take interest and pleasure in bothering and killing them. It is very striking that most of the component behaviours in rough and tumble play – chasing, fleeing, laughing, jumping, play-noise and play-face (Blurton Jones, 1967) along with completed 'object beats' (striking with an object) can be seen in Zhun/twa children annoying large animals (dogs, or cows belonging to neighbouring herding people) or trying to kill small ones.

All these activities take place within earshot, if not within sight, of adults, and the activities themselves are obviously child versions of adult life. Such imitation is characteristic of British children as well, but there it is not often something the child will eventually do for a living that is imitated, but rather things like astronaut, cowboy and soldier. Girls in both societies, though, occupy themselves with 'playing house' – cooking and serving food, going to bed, and so on.

The continuous acquisition of subsistence behaviours from 1 year of age into adulthood is very evident among the Zhun/twasi, and imitation is a primary mode of learning such behaviours. Attachment, or the maintenance of proximity to models, makes this process possible. Bowlby's emphasis on protection from predators thus accounts for only part of the survival value of attachment behaviour.

Separation and the growth of social behaviour

The attachment which ensures the infant's immediate survival and enables him to learn social interaction patterns and elementary subsistence behaviour must finally decline, to prepare the mother for a new infant and to prepare the child for independent social interaction outside the family. The mother, the infant and attractiveness of the world outside the mother all contribute to the development of separation.

Exploration, using the mother as a base, begins by 7 or 8 months, at the same time that flight behaviours and the more advanced components of attachment – approach, clinging, following and flight to the mother – are emerging. During the first half of the second year, these components combine with several earlier components of attachment – smiling, laughing, positive vocalizations – to form a new social interaction pattern between mothers or other adults and infants, usually initiated by the adult. The adult runs slowly away from the infant, eliciting the following response, then turns and makes a frightening face or noise, eliciting the flight response, and gives chase, only to turn and repeat the pattern again. The presence of smiles, laughing and especially of clinging when the infant catches the adult before he turns around, makes the roots of this pattern in attachment very plain. At the same time, the flight response derives from earliest agonistic behaviour seen in relation to strangers.

This pattern, an elementary adult–child form of rough and tumble play, thus derives its components from both attachment and agonistic patterns and is in an objective sense what psychoanalysts call *ambivalent* behaviour. It is the first tiny dent in the unequivocal indulgence of infants by adults that is characteristic of the first year. Its adult–child form continues into middle childhood, but shortly after it emerges it gives rise to several child–child variations.

By 18 months to 2 years the child spends considerable lengths of time playing with children of 2, 3, 4 and 5. At any time a village may have five such children, or three, or only one or two. They may play among themselves or with older children, who play an important part in their lives. For much of the time, though, their world is a kind of large playground in which adults and older children are going about their business. It differs structurally from the nursery schools of England and America in several important respects. First, there is unlimited space, and most objects of interest – sticks or grass – are available in unlimited quantity. Second, there are often no peers, strictly speaking, because village populations are too small for there to be, say, several 3-year-olds. Differences of a year or less at this age are large and obvious to the children. They are enjoined by adults to look on older children as models and objects of dependence, and on younger ones as responsibilities. For these reasons there is comparatively very little real or play fighting among children in this age group here. Rough and tumble play is usually either stylized, as when one child pretends to be an animal that the others are attacking, or else it takes a mild form that consists, in spite of the available space, of laughing, hugging and rolling around on the ground together. In this mild form it grades into another kind of social play discussed below. However, when five or six children of roughly the same age *do* have the opportunity to play together (as when two formerly separate camps merge), rough and tumble play appears prominently, and in the same form as in British children. As in the animal-directed variety, completed object beats are included in the pattern.

Children are not lacking, however, in real aggressive behaviours (or, by inference, aggressive feelings). They do snatch food or objects from one another, but this is mediated by the age difference. The older child either nurtures the younger one, or overpowers him; in either case there is no struggle. More elaborate fighting behaviour can be seen, however, in relation to parents. Unlike the passive tantrums we are familiar with, a Zhun/twa tantrum is often characterized by beating, object beating and throwing of objects, all directed at the mother, in addition to frowning, grimacing and crying. Mothers are quite serene as the tantrum progresses, often laughing and talking to other adults while they ward off the tiny blows. They do not respond with the immediate anger characteristic of Western mothers hit by their children, but usually allow the episode to run its course. The Western tantrum, characterized by aimless thrashing and flailing of limbs with the same facial expressions and vocalizations, may be the result of parental 'training out' of real aggressive acts. If aggression *is* something that can be *displaced* or *redirected*, then this difference in the acceptability of real aggression against parents may help to account for the relative lack of fighting among young children in Zhun/ twa society.

Similarly, the aggressive feelings expressed in rough and tumble play, may, among Zhun/twa children, find an adaptively appropriate 'outlet' in relation to animals. In evolutionary terms, the basic primate pattern of rough and tumble play has become, in part, specialized in man to serve the acquisition of hunting behaviour.

One further pattern of social play is common among 1- to 5-year-olds. Its components are mutual touching, tangling of legs, clinging and rolling while lying on the ground. The absence of laughing, the slowness of movement and the unlikelihood of standing up are what distinguish it from the mild form of rough and tumble play. Unless it includes explicitly genital activity (which also occurs during this age period) this behaviour, which might be called 'gentle and tumble' play, is ignored by adults. Its derivation from parental attachment behaviour is very apparent, both from the shared behaviour components and from the fact that this play may take an imaginative form in which the older child takes the role of parent. The influence of parents as models is all-pervasive.

In later childhood gentle and tumble play is never publicly seen (although grooming shares several of its components). Rough and tumble play very much like that of British nursery school children becomes increasingly common until late adolescence. In contrast, the attitude toward animals at first becomes more serious and restrained, but the final adult pattern, with respect to game animals, at least, is reminiscent of the excitement of 4-year-olds chasing butterflies.

Discussion

Many psychologists now recognize the importance of evolutionary perspective in theorizing, but this is often limited to the view of an infant as developing *into* an adapted organism. While this is certainly true, it is sometimes allowed to obscure the fact that an infant is first of all, and at every point in his development, an adapted organism. He is first of all surviving, and in the meantime developing.

As in most populations, but especially non-technological populations, the mortality rate among the Zhun/twasi in the first five years of life is much higher than in any comparable span before the end of the breeding period. Consequently selection pressures during this period, however obscure, may be very strong. Selection asks, as it were, ' How well is the child surviving *now*? ', and not just ' what will he be when he grows up? '.

To put the case at its strongest, we should be prepared to consider the possibility that the characteristic features of adult human behaviour have evolved not because they are an ideal adaptation, but because they are the result of an ideal adaptation in infancy. Just as blood-group frequencies among adults are, in part, the result of perinatal selection through maternal-foetal incompatibility, some adult behaviour patterns (for example, marriage) may be in part the result of selective forces favouring certain infant behaviours (for example, strong attachment).

The implication for Western urban behaviour and development is that selection pressures, both those affecting adults and those affecting infants, have changed, and we can understand (and perhaps influence) the course of behavioural evolution by understanding the changing factors affecting species-specific human infancy. If such speculation is unconvincing, it is at least provocative, and it is in any case impossible without studies of infancy in hunting and gathering societies.

Conclusion

This report – fragmentary, diffuse, but hopefully emergent – has described what we have learned so far about the first five years of life among a hunting-and-gathering people, and the selective forces that may be affecting it. Certain preliminary conclusions are possible.

First, ethological methods of research developed in animal studies are as appropriate for research on infants and children in primitive societies as they are in Britain.

Second, in the most complex behaviour patterns there are uniformities which extend across the widest cultural gaps, in behavioural capacity at birth, in patterns of attachment and fear of strangers, and in the social behaviour of toddlers. While this will come as no surprise to ethologists, it may to some cultural anthropologists who suppose human behaviour to be malleable almost to the point of being unlawful. On the other hand, there are variations beyond what some ethologists would expect. The differences are due partly to differences in ecological pressures, and partly to the unsystematic cultural variation anthropologists are concerned with.

The way to determine which is which is through studies of infancy and early childhood in other hunting-and-gathering societies. At the same time, hypotheses derived from such studies (such as the proposed relationship among various modes of expressing aggression in early childhood) can be tested on large, variable samples of Western infants and children.*

Acknowledgements

The assistance of Dr I. DeVore, Dr N. G. Blurton Jones, Dr J. Kagan and Mr. S. R. Tulkin in the preparation for and planning of the research is gratefully acknowledged. This research is financed by the people of the United States through the U.S. Public Health Service (5-RO1-MH-13611-03) and the National Science Foundation (GS-2603), and by the Milton Fund of Harvard University.

I am also grateful for the contribution of Marjorie Shostak Konner to the collection and interpretation of the data, and in criticizing two earlier drafts of this paper.

REFERENCES

Ainsworth, M., (1963). The development of infant–mother interaction among the Ganda. In *Determinants of Infant Behaviour*, vol. 2. Ed. B. M. Foss, London: Methuen.

Ainsworth, M. and Wittig, B. A. (1969). Attachment and exploratory behaviour of one-year-olds in a strange situation. In *Determinants of Infant Behaviour*, vol. 4. Ed. B. M. Foss, London: Methuen.

Beintema, D. (1968). *A Neurological Study of Newborn Infants*. London: Heinemann.

Birdsell, J. (1968). Discussion of 'Population control factors'. In *Man the Hunter*, p. 243. Ed. R. Lee and I. DeVore, Chicago: Aldine.

Blurton Jones, N. G. (1967). An ethological study of some aspects of social behaviour of children in nursery school. In *Primate Ethology*. Ed. D. Morris, London: Weidenfeld and Nicolson.

Bowlby, J. (1969). *Attachment and Loss*, vol. 1: *Attachment*. London: Hogarth Press.

Bronte-Stewart, B., Budtz-Olsen, O. E., Hickley, J. M. and Brock, J. F. (1960). The health and nutritional status of the Kung Bushmen of Southwest Africa. *S. Afr. J. Lab. Clin. med.* **6**, no. 4.

Bruner, J. S. (1968). *Processes of Cognitive Growth: Infancy*. Heinz Warner Lectures. Worcester, Mass: Clark University Press.

Foss, B. M. (1963). *Determinants of Infant Behaviour*, vol. 2. London: Methuen.

Foss, B. M. (1969). *Determinants of Infant Behaviour*, vol. 4. London: Methuen.

Geber, M. and Dean, R. F. A. (1967, orig. 1957). Precocious development of newborn African infants. In *Behaviour in Infancy and Early Childhood*. Ed. Y. Brackbill and G. C. Thompson, New York: The Free Press.

* For those convinced that it is worthwhile to do ethological research on man other than at his (for now) most successful, Murdock (1968) provides a comprehensive annotated list of the foraging populations of the world among which behavioural research is still believed to be possible. Those interested are urged to act in haste.

M. J. KONNER

Gesell, A. and Amatruda, C. (1947). *Developmental Diagnosis.* New York: Harper and Row.

Lee, R. B. (1968). What hunter-gatherers do for a living. In *Man the Hunter.* Ed. R. B. Lee and I. DeVore, Chicago: Aldine.

Lee, R. B. and DeVore, I. (eds.). (1968). *Man the Hunter.* Chicago: Aldine.

Marshall, L. (1960). Kung Bushman bands. *Africa* **30**, no. 4.

Marshall, L. (1961). Sharing, talking and giving: relief of social tensions among Kung Bushmen. *Africa* **31**, no. 13.

Marshall, L. (1965). The Kung Bushmen of the Kalahari Desert. In *Peoples of Africa.* Ed. J. Gibbs, New York: Holt Rinehart and Winston.

Morgan, G. A. and Ricciuti, H. N. (1969). Infants' responses to strangers during the first year. In *Determinants of Infant Behaviour*, vol. 4. Ed. B. M. Foss, London: Methuen.

Murdock, G. P. (1968). The distribution of the world's hunting peoples. In *Man the Hunter.* Ed. R. B. Lee and I. DeVore, Chicago: Aldine.

Piaget, J. (1962). *Play, Dreams, and Imitation in Childhood.* New York: W. W. Norton.

Prechtl, H. F. R. (1961). Neurological sequelae of prenatal and paranatal complications. In *Determinants of Infant Behaviour*, vol. 2. Ed. B. M. Foss, London: Methuen.

Prechtl, H. F. R. (1965). Problems of behavioural studies in the newborn infant. In *Advances in the study of Behaviour*, vol. 1. Ed. D. S. Lehrman, R. A. Hinde and E. Shaw, New York: Academic Press.

Prechtl, H. and Beintema, D. (1964). *The Neurological Examination of the Full-Term Newborn Infant.* London: S.I.M.P./Heinemann.

Prechtl, H. F. R. and Lenard, H. G. (1968). Verhaltensphysiologie des Neugeborenen. In *Fortschritte der Pädologie.* Berlin: Springer-Verlag.

Rhodes, P. (1967). *An Introduction to Gynaecology and Obstetrics.* London: Lloyd-Luke.

Tobias, P. V. (1966). The peoples of Africa south of the *Sahara.* In *The Biology of Human Adaptability.* Ed. P. T. Baker and J. S. Weiner, London: Oxford University Press.

Trusswell, A. S. and Hansen, J. D. L. (1968). Medical and nutritional studies of Kung Bushmen in Northwest Botswana: a preliminary report. *S. Afr. Med. J.* **42**, 1338–9.

Wolff, P. (1969). The natural history of crying and other vocalizations in early infancy. In *Determinants of Infant Behaviour,* vol. 4. Ed. B. M. Foss, London: Methuen.

12

COMPARATIVE ASPECTS OF
MOTHER—CHILD CONTACT

N. BLURTON JONES *

SUMMARY

The methods of comparative studies are illustrated with the amount of mother–child contact as an example. The assumption that human mothers and infants are adapted to remain continuously together is tested by comparison with evidence that they are adapted to sporadic contact. Correlations between various features, including milk composition, sucking rates and spacing of feeds are described for mammals, and milk composition and sucking rate in man are used to extrapolate spacing of feeds. Man shows features in both mother and baby which are typical of those mammals in which the young feeds almost continuously. But it is argued that generally comparative studies are more use for providing 'ultimate', evolutionary, explanations of such human behaviour as is disclosed by direct study than for determining indirectly what this behaviour is.

Introduction

In recent years several popular books, and one or two serious works (e.g. Bowlby, 1969) have made much use of the resemblances between human and animal behaviour. These comparisons have engendered much controversy. But the truth must lie somewhere between the certainty of zoologists that valid comparisons can be made, and the certainty of sociologists that no valid comparisons can be made. Eventually it may be possible to evaluate the use of comparative studies in studying human behaviour, provided that one remains relatively free of commitment to either predominance of species-specific behaviour, or to predominance of 'social facts' independent of biological facts (see Freeman (1966) for a useful discussion of the difficulties of this dichotomy). Ambrose (1968) has already described a different use of animal studies, for advancing the concepts and the methodology of studies of behaviour development. Animal data may also be used to suggest hypotheses about behaviour, or to suggest phenomena or mechanisms to look for in man. Another advantage in the comparative viewpoint, or at least in the interest in the effects and survival value of behaviour which must go with it, is that one gets an idea of the tasks that the machine one is studying has to perform.

* Department of Growth and Development, Institute of Child Health, University of London.

The development of a child's behaviour is a vast and unwieldy subject, a huge system to analyse. But if one knows what functions it has to fulfil, the task of finding out how it does it may be very much easier. It has been argued (e.g. Freedman, 1967; Fox and Tiger, 1966) that the evolutionary perspective also has other important contributions to make.

As a zoologist who is involved in direct studies of human behaviour (and to this extent sees things from a psychologist's viewpoint) I hope that I can illustrate, with one small comparative study, the principles behind comparative studies. These principles have not always been evident in the recent popular books. I have investigated, and describe and discuss here, one particular example which may be of importance to studies of mother–infant attachment. I must emphasise that this chapter concerns an entirely different part of ethological method from that employed in most other chapters in this book.

It is commonly assumed by those of us who are interested both in human and non-human primates that children are meant to be carried constantly on their mother, and that it is an aberrancy of our modern culture that our children are seldom carried. To explore and illustrate the comparative method I have been seeking evidence for the opposite theory, that human babies are meant to be 'cached', left safely parked away from their mother, much as we do in present-day England. How do we investigate such a proposition?

First of all, what do I mean when I say that a baby is 'meant to be' either cached or carried? The popular meaning is that babies will be unhappy, or grow up peculiar if they are not (for example) carried. Unhappiness may mean that they cry a lot, and it is often said (e.g. Erikson, 1965) (but with no quantitative data which distinguishes readiness to cry from the abundance of situations which tend to evoke crying, or from speed of quieting) that babies seldom cry in cultures where they are in constant contact with the mother. But some people say it is good for babies to cry, either for exercise, or because they should learn early that they don't get everything they want. Whether they grow up peculiar (or any other more 'scientific' sounding word which means the same) is nearly undefinable. Traditionally we meant 'ill-fitted to our culture' but we now realise this may mean 'fitted to some other culture'. A carried baby may not fit well in our culture, as Erikson (1965) suggests. Thus, both these arguments about what babies are meant to undergo seem to be purely ethnocentric. Different patterns of child-rearing are likely to suit children to living in different cultures.

What I actually imply by 'meant to' is whether human babies show any of the typical adaptations to particular kinds of mammalian child-rearing practices, either nesting or caching on the one hand, with relatively discontinuous contact between mother and child, or following or carrying on the other hand, with relatively continuous contact. The presence of adaptations to one kind of rearing need not imply that things will go wrong with subsequent development if the rearing practice is changed (though we know that this does often happen, e.g. Harlow and Harlow, 1965), but it will imply that a child raised the 'wrong' way will be ill-adapted to the environment in which this behaviour evolved (for instance by failing to survive while a baby). The presence of adaptations to a certain kind of rearing does imply that this is the developmental context in which the whole system of development of behaviour is adapted to function. The effects on development could (as has often been shown in direct studies) therefore be wide-ranging, but they need not be. They may be much more restricted than psychoanalytic theory for example, or learning theory, would imply.

In his book *Attachment and Loss* Bowlby (1969) briefly argues that a long period of constant contact between mother and child is a characteristic of higher primates particularly, but also of many other animals. He suggests that its major survival value has been as an anti-predator device, and that there were plenty of potential predators on human infants, such as leopards, until very recent times. By this he is enabled to take a fresh look at attachment, able to examine the possibility that its development is relatively independent from reinforcers such as food and warmth. But he also follows the implication that, on the comparative evidence, human children and mothers must have evolved some characteristics which ensured that, in the range of circumstances in which most of man's evolution occurred, a close attachment would develop reliably. This statement is sophisticated as regards development but lacks one important step in the zoological argument. The way of life of man has for a long time differed from that of all other higher primates in that a substantial proportion of his food has been gained by hunting and killing other animals. An animal's way of life has profound effects on many aspects of its behaviour and structure. It is therefore necessary to consider, and this is what most modern studies of the evolution of man are doing, what modification of general primate patterns this might have brought about. In the particular case of attachment, it is significant that many other carnivorous mammals keep their young in nests. Many carnivorous mammals, or even most (as Morris (1967) points out too), do not carry their young with them. They usually leave young in a hidden nest, in some cases guarded by a parent or baby-sitter (Ewer, 1968; Murie, 1961; Kühme, 1965).

The question for Bowlby's comparative argument is whether man's partly carnivorous way of life has modified the general higher primate pattern of child care, which involves a long period in which the infant rides on the mother, leaving only to go short distances away from her, and accompanying her wherever she goes. One must seek more evidence than just the implications of the ecology. The ecological implications are anyway complicated by the marked division of labour in man; in general men hunt and women gather, and probably have done so for a very long time (Watanabe, 1968; Binford and Binford, 1969).

Background information

Some introductory notes must be included at this point before I attempt to outline the methods employed in this paper.

THE ECOLOGICAL NICHE OF EVOLVING MAN

Lee and DeVore (1968) argue that at least 99% of human generations have lived in a hunter–gatherer economy. The evidence for the very earliest-claimed hunting behaviour of the human line concerns bone tools with Australopithecine remains in South Africa (the evidence about these is very equivocal) and stone tools, which have been found with Australopithecine remains in other areas. The importance of the latter evidence depends on the adequacy of the archaeological evidence mustered by the palaeonto-logists concerned but this is abundant and is generally regarded as accept-able. This also concerns a time nearly two million years ago, and the evidence for the datings seems to be generally accepted by palaeoanthropologists. Abundant unequivocal evidence dates back nearly half a million years to hominids more certainly on the *Homo sapiens* line. This is still a duration of evolutionary significance; it is the time in which the major changes in size of the human brain occurred, in marked contrast to the earlier long period of seed-eating life in open country proposed by Jolly (1970) to account for aspects of face and jaw structure. The time since the invention of agriculture, at the most 10,000 years, is insignificant beside this, and apparently produced no major physical changes. An up-to-date discussion of many facets of the hunting and gathering way of life can be found in Lee and DeVore (1968) and for anyone remotely interested in the evolution of man this is essential reading. It is also required reading for those who feel that the reconstruction of human evolution is so unreliable as to be scientifically idle. A very good account of work in this field for the general reader is that of Pfeiffer (1969).

Since my interest in baby care is defined in terms of evolutionary adaptations, to argue from the present-day practices of industrial man may be misleading. Very many people alive today apparently carry their babies with them most of the time. Non-anthropologists classify such people as primitive on purely personal grounds with no bearing on evolution. From the evolutionary point of view any people who use agriculture, however strange they are to us, are living in a very recent way. So to argue that because Chinese or Central Americans carry their babies about, there-fore primitive man has always done so, is at best innocent ethnocentrism. People who grow no food and have no domesticated animals can be con-sidered primitive in their way of life, even though some of them may have reverted to this way of life in almost historical times. People living in this ecological niche, in which man is deduced to have evolved, are therefore the relevant ones. Most surviving hunter–gatherers are reported to carry their children much of the time. The position in which they carry them varies, as do the devices in which they carry them. However, the larger, more sedentary groups of hunting people who might have existed in several places may not have done things this way. Also, if one's interest in comparative studies is to reconstruct information about man's evolution then it makes the argument partly circular to use contemporary hunter–gatherers as part of the evidence in this way. It would be better to keep contemporary human data and comparative data as two separate lines of evidence.

ECOLOGY AND ENVIRONMENT

The phrase ' way of life ' is used by zoologists as nearly synonymous with ' ecological niche '. The former stresses what the animal does for a living, the latter stresses how this differentiates it from other species in the same area and how its ecology interrelates with that of all the other species in the area. This latter aspect tends to be ignored in current studies of human evolution so I should refer readers to Elton's original founder work (1927), and to his recent detailed demonstration of the total involvement of any species with all the other species in its neighbourhood (1966). Niche should not be confused with ' environment ' in its popular sense of climate, geology, flora and fauna. Archaeological data shows that man has lived in a wide range of environments in the popular sense but until very recently he lived in only one ecological niche (one could argue on the basis of Lee's (1968) figures that there has been a quantitative trend from a bear-like niche in the tropics to a big-cat-like niche in the temperate and arctic regions). Meat eating is traditionally regarded as a completely new departure of man's ancestors from the primate pattern but evidence enough has been accumulating for Lattin (1969) to argue that it is a quantitative exaggeration of a rather general primate habit. However, the present-day great apes predominantly eat plant food, including fruit (see Schaller, 1963; Goodall, 1968; Suzuki, 1969).

The uniqueness of the human niche among higher primates (as well as the interwoven nature of the ecology of various species – precisely how was early man ecologically differentiated from other predators?) implies that there has been a mistake in the research strategy, in emphasising studies of primates as opposed to the mammals as a whole (see also Eisenberg, 1966).

MAMMALIAN CHILD-REARING PRACTICES

Ewer (1968) and Ben Shaul (1962b) give a useful summary of the child-rearing practices of mammals, classifying them into four types: nesting, caching, carrying, following.

309

(1) Nesting. The young stay in a prepared, protected or concealed place, usually where they were born. The mother often leaves them there for long periods (e.g. rabbits, *Tupaia*) but may stay continuously with them, e.g. some bears which hibernate while the young are small. There are usually, but not always, more young per litter than in non-nesting mammals.

(2) Carrying. The young ride on the mother, except for brief excursions, and go with her wherever she goes. There are often few young but e.g. opossums have large numbers. Nest-building animals transport their young occasionally, for example if a nest is disturbed, or to retrieve their young and return them to the nest. Usually the nesting mother carries her young in her mouth whereas the 'carrying' young normally support themselves on their mother (e.g. most monkeys) except for instance in many marsupials where the young are protected and later supported in the pouch.

(3) Following. The young also stay in almost constant proximity to their mother but by walking, following her wherever she goes. Common in ungulates.

(4) Caching. The young stay in a hiding place, which is varied and not excavated or similarly protected, and are left for long periods by the mother whom they meet briefly for wide-spaced feeds. Walther (1969) gives useful information on this behaviour in one species.

Methods

It has lately been fashionable to compare man with other primates, or less reputably even with any animal picked at random or to suit a particular theory, but both these procedures ignore the rules for making comparisons between different kinds of animal. This is particularly important when, as is usually the case in comparisons involving man, man is taken as an 'unknown' whose attributes are to be predicted from comparison. There is great variation of some features within any taxonomic group of animals, so the simple assumption that man must resemble other primates in all features is most unreliable. This variation results from the tendency of any major taxonomic group to 'radiate' into a variety of ecological niches which exert different selection pressures and produce appropriate modifications of the basic characteristics of the group. In this process some members of the group may come to resemble in certain respects members of other groups who have a similar way of life. A simple example is the presence of wings in both birds and bats. While birds and bats both have wings there are many features of bats (e.g. fur and teeth) which are features of mammals and not of birds. Features such as wings are called 'convergent' characters, conveying the 'visual' model of this argument: that in respect to the character under discussion the two animals have evolved towards each other, on converging paths. The degree of adaptive radiation and convergence in the animal kingdom is so great that comparative studies are best done over a wide range of animals, and must involve studies of the ecology of these animals. In our particular exercise, filling in 'missing' data about man, wide-ranging comparison allows one to develop a picture of (a) what adaptations to expect for a particular way of life, e.g. the long partly carnivorous period of human evolution, and (b) what way of life normally goes along with what adaptive features of an animal. In the present paper I confine myself to a limited use of the second picture (b) in considering one or two aspects of parent–child relationship in mammals. But there might eventually be much to gain from a closer quantitative comparative study of commonplace statements about the animal kingdom as a whole; for instance the negative correlation between amount of parental care and number of young born.

The methods employed in comparative zoology are well-established but seldom explicitly described. (Perhaps this is why comparative anatomy takes so long to teach.) In this paper I have relied on three methods for discovering the relationship between survival value and anatomy or behaviour.

Method 1

The direct experimental test of the effects of variation in certain features upon the survival of the adults or young. I use data from this only a little, and it is the most recently developed method. An example is the study by Tinbergen *et al.* (1967) (see also Tinbergen, 1965) on the differential predation on eggs placed inside, on the edge, and outside a Black-headed Gull (*Larus ridibundus*) colony. This showed that predation is reduced by the density of adult birds, and subsequent studies showed this was partly due to the communal mass attacks on predators.

Method 2

Consideration of the basic physical requirements of an animal and its situation, e.g. warmth, food, invisibility to predators, inaudibility to predators, the fact that accumulations of faeces may produce a smell which can attract predators, etc. I use this method a little more but despite its seemingly firm basis in simple physiology and physics it is the most speculative of the three methods. This is for two reasons. First, it is very hard to tell which features are relevant to the ecology and selection pressures on the particular animal. Second, it is hard to tell which physical features will be relevant in a particular environment. For example scent may be unimportant in a completely windless environment, and the species may rest or nest in windless parts of a windswept locality. A recent example can be found in the interesting paper by Newman (1970) where discussion and experiments on human thermoregulation ignored the effects on cooling of air movement during locomotion, with a radical effect on the conclusions about the evolution of human ' nakedness '.

Method 3

This is the most traditional but least explicit method. It is best described as a search for correlations, using data from a wide variety of animals, between structure or behaviour on the one hand and ecology or way of life on the other hand (Tinbergen, 1967). In this particular paper I look for correlations of anatomy, physiology, behaviour with ways of rearing young, particularly with the amount of time that mother and young spend together. This method can be extended, using multivariate statistics, to cover more features of the animals and their way of life, and then to show to what features of the way of life the different amounts of mother–child contact, etc., relate. In this paper, the amount of contact between the human baby and its mother (during a significant part of human evolution) is taken as an unknown or ' missing observation ' to be filled in by applying the correlations found in mammals as a whole to the anatomy and physiology of mother and child (and to a lesser extent to their behaviour, because to include behaviour would weaken subsequent arguments that this or that feature of infant behaviour is adapted to this or that feature of its way of life).

This is an unusual way in which to describe this aspect of comparative zoology but it makes the method explicit and therefore less easily charged with being merely speculative. If required, an actual figure could be derived from this formulation for the probability of the human infant having evolved in a certain system of baby care. The aim of this analysis is very different from analyses aimed at discovering evolutionary relationships. For an explicit description of these the reader is referred to Martin (1968b) or to the literature, in for example the *Journal of Systematic Zoology*, where multivariate techniques, usually cluster analysis, are used to work out evolutionary ' trees '.

Method 3 should ideally be able to use data from method 1, and from studies of population control which show at what points and on what features selection actually does act. Added to the findings of method 1 on the effects of variation in various features upon mortality this allows a very direct assessment of the adaptive value of features of the animal. However, since both detailed studies of population and experiments on effects of variation in characteristics on survival have only started very recently it is perhaps better to use method 3 more modestly. By showing correlations between features of an animal and various known but rather general features of its way of life one can, beside the quantitative extrapolation of missing data, perhaps suggest realistic hypotheses about selection pressures which may be tested by method 1 and by population studies.

Evidence for caching

The question is: do human babies show any divergences from the general higher primate pattern towards the intermittent-contact caching system of some mammals, which most closely resembles the British and American system of child care? The evidence that babies are adapted to being cached turns out to be far less convincing than the evidence that they are adapted to being in constant contact with their mother. The difference between constant contact and sporadic contact is the most easily studied. Possible adaptations to nesting as opposed to carrying will require separate treatment in another paper.

Ewer (1968) summarised the differences between cached and following ungulates as being a difference in the balance of the tendency to sleep after a meal as against the tendency to follow the mother, which increases at a later stage in development in a caching species. (The late onset of visually directed smiling by babies might be taken as a similar adaptation.) But Ewer, while accounting for the intermediate position of sheep and goats, may have oversimplified the position in caching ungulates. Observations by Walther (1965) and Bubenik (1965) and Jewell (pers. comm.) of young ungulates walking away from the mother to their hiding place, suggest that there is more to this behaviour than simply falling asleep straight after a meal.

Some major problems facing a cached baby mammal are thermoregulation, protection from predators, return of the mother for feeding. Young animals that are cached often do not urinate or defaecate unless stimulated (e.g. antelopes, Ben Shaul, 1962a). This is presumably important for not attracting predators by scent. It seems very clear that human babies will defaecate and urinate when unstimulated by the mother, although no one has systematically tried normal mammalian techniques to stimulate these responses so that we cannot say that they cannot be evoked, only that as far as we know they often seem to occur without maternal stimulation.

Other anti-predator devices of cached infants suggest nothing in this direction about human babies. Human babies are not obviously cryptic, but then nest-dwelling babies are not cryptic either. They make a lot of noise in the absence of the mother (between two and four hours after a large feed in the U.K. and U.S.A.). The possibility that babies were cached in ' nests ' or home sites protected by adult ' baby-sitters ' could remove the need for anti-predator adaptations of the baby.

Thermoregulation is a problem to most young mammals. A baby which is in contact with its mother may almost become part of her thermoregulatory system and be relieved of the problem. The ability to maintain a constant temperature is poor in newborn humans, although some of the component responses are present (see Jonxis, Visser and Troelstra, 1964). Rowell, Din and Omar (1968) have shown that baboon babies are on their mothers more during rain. But Harlow and Harlow (1965) have shown that heat is a much less powerful proximate stimulus to contact than is tactile stimulation. Both a cached and a following baby would have roughly equal problems with thermoregulation, both are in the open, not in contact with the mother, and effects of exercise on thermoregulation are variable. Nest-living babies may be sheltered and in some cases have been shown to thermoregulate by dispersing and clumping (Ewer, 1968), which is not possible for the human neonate or other higher primates which are usually born singly. Young lagomorphs also appear to benefit from brown adipose tissue, which generates heat (Dawkins and Hull, 1964, and others). This is also present in newborn humans but its contribution to the overall thermoregulation and energy balance seems not to have been worked out. The amount of this tissue in a human baby is a much smaller proportion of body weight than it is in rabbits (Dawkins and Hull, 1964). The taxonomic distribution of brown adipose tissue does not seem to be very well known. Should it be absent in other primates this would be the only powerful argument for adaptation to caching in human babies that has come to light.

Ambrose (1966) in one of the few papers taking a comparative approach to behaviour of human newborns has stressed the loss of the human baby's ability to cling to the mother (because of her hairlessness) as a major selection pressure behind the evolution of smiling and crying, which becomes necesssary to make the mother maintain or resume contact with the baby.

Smiling has been considered by most authors (on very indirect evidence) to be a vital part of the development of the attachment between babies and their mothers, and this fits well with Ambrose's suggestion as to its adaptive value. However, the context in which it has this value may be either: contact initiated by the mother in the early months, or by assisting the development, resulting from the mother's responses, of a tendency in the child to remain near the mother after it is able to move about at the end of its first year (see Bowlby, 1969; Anderson, Ch. 8; Konner, Ch. 13). The findings of Blurton Jones and Leach (Ch. 9) suggest that smiling has little to do with immediate proximity-gaining behaviour in children over 2 years old, it may instead have to do with development of interactions with people generally. If smiling functions in the first context this would argue for either caching (by reinforcing maternal visits) or constant contact (by reinforcing maternal carrying). The late development of actual following behaviour (long after the ability to walk, see Anderson, Ch. 8, and as quoted in Bowlby, 1969) or of smiling to visual stimuli might argue for an early caching phase but does not seem a strong argument for this.

Crying appears to be effective in recalling mothers and making them pick their child up. But this can equally well work to maintain a constant carrying relationship as it can work to recall the mother from afar. In fact cached young remain silent, any sound recall of the mother (except when already found by a predator, and except by ultrasound, if the predator is unable to hear ultrasound, which is absent by definition in humans but widespread among mammals as an infant distress call) could lead predators to the youngster sooner than the mother. It seems that cached young are adapted to sit it out until their mother returns, although how long and how far the initiative remains with the mother seems to have been little studied. Current views on the human mother–child relationship have stressed the amount of initiative by the child even in the early stages (e.g. Bowlby, 1969; Ainsworth, 1969). But studies of rhesus monkey interactions (e.g. Hinde and Spencer-Booth, 1968), demonstrate a relative change from proportionally more initiative by the mother to more by the infant as time goes by (this may follow the course of a slowly developing attachment but, even so, there are indications like the response to tactile stimuli documented by Harlow and Harlow (1965) that the newborn rhesus monkey will make unprovoked initiatives in contacting the mother). The age differences reported in Blurton Jones and Leach (Ch. 9) also indicate a relative decrease in maternal initiatives with time in humans.

Evidence for carrying

Arguments against caching and for continuous contact are more convincing. Several of the above points work tentatively against caching but further anatomical–physiological features strongly favour constant contact. In discussing this it will become clear that, as every modern comparative anatomist knows, anatomy and behaviour are scarcely separable. Behaviour is the immediate link to the environment through which selection pressures are exerted on anatomy. Anatomical and physiological changes occur to render the behavioural adaptations more effective. (It is at least as true to say that we are built the way we are because we walk, as that we walk because we are built the way we are.)

The main argument concerns the composition of milk. Ben Shaul (1962b) has surveyed the composition of milk in many species of mammal from many groups. She finds that there is little orderly relationship to major taxonomic groups. The correlations are to some extent with growth rate and activity of the young, and most clearly with the schedule of feeding. A major dimension is between wide-spaced 'scheduled' feeders and almost continuous 'demand' feeders. (Ben Shaul uses these terms as shorthand for wide-spaced and short-spaced. Whether the other connotations of these terms apply is a topic for investigation but in the way discussed above, where cached infants must passively await the mother's return, there may be some relationship.) Within the ungulates for example, milk composition relates closely to whether the species has cached young or following young (with cattle being intermediate). Extremes are found in other groups. For instance in the lagomorphs (rabbits and hares), feeding occurs every twenty-four hours (Zarrow, Denenberg and Anderson, 1965) and they have milk with very high protein and fat content. *Tupaia belangeri* goes even further (Martin, 1968*a*), feeding every forty-eight hours and having still higher protein and fat content. Higher primates feed nearly continuously, having constant access to the nipple, and they have very low protein and fat content. Human milk is almost identical to that of the other apes, and typical of a continuous feeder in any taxonomic group.

The importance of growth rate and activity of young seems to be secondary, growth rate is not correlated with the spacing of meals, milk contents are adjusted to fit any of these to whatever schedule is present. The growth rate of human infants is very high but is falling fast at birth and falls slightly faster than that of chimpanzees (see Tanner, 1962). Human babies are usually assumed to be less active than other ape infants (although young ape infants are very inactive), which should require milk with lower sugar content. This they do not have. Milk composition may change as lactation proceeds so that the argument may be confined to the neonatal period until more data is available. But Underwood, Hepner and Abdullah (1970) show that protein content of human milk does not change in two years of lactation though lipid content increases slightly. It seems unlikely that any such changes are going to mask the immense differences between for instance higher primates and *Tupaia*.

So man has this adaptation in the mother for continuous feeding by the baby. Feeding at this frequency implies that the mother cannot leave the baby for long, so that she must either, like some bears, live permanently in a nest with the baby, on food that is stored in the body, or the nest, or brought by another individual, or else carry the baby (either by its efforts or hers) with her wherever she goes. To match this there is an increasing amount of indirect evidence, summarised by MacKeith (1969) and Richards and Bernal (1970), that human infants have rather sensitive physiological adaptations to the milk content of their species. The above authors review literature that suggests that there are slight physical ill-effects of feeding babies on cows' milk and that this is due to the higher protein content (and not simply to presence of alien proteins or to higher incidence of infections caught from poorly-cleaned bottles). The studies on which this is based were on small samples which one might have expected to produce differences due only to the different distribution of feeding human or cows' milk in different social classes (Meyer, 1968; Newson and Newson, 1963) which would then associate cows' milk with low birthweight babies who are anyway prone to illness. The data presented by Hooper (1965) shows no relationship between kind of milk and birthweight or between birthweight and illness (her study included no very low birthweight babies). Several papers report favourably on the use of human milk in feeding premature babies (e.g. Davies and Russel, 1968; Hambreus and Wranne, 1968).

Ill-effects of too spaced and too large meals are suggested by Boelkins' (1962) description of hand-rearing rhesus monkeys. Fed on a two-hour schedule (stretched for the experimenters' convenience) they frequently vomited and this was a major problem for the technique. Monkey babies with their mothers never vomit, nor do they burp noisily (though they do hiccup, particularly after hurriedly eating oranges). Possibly the frequent vomiting and ' posseting ' of human babies is a result of our insistence on the very early development of a four-hourly schedule rather than the quarter-hour to two-hour interval suggested by comparative data on milk composition, and by the rapid cessation of suckling early in a 'meal' (some authors describe the successful attempts by English mothers to re-elicit suckling in their babies and prolong and increase the size of the meal, e.g. Richards and Bernal, Ch. 7).

Wolff (1968) has published measures of the sucking frequency of various mammals. Their relationship to feeding frequency and to the closely related protein and fat content of the milk of these species in Ben Shaul's table (1962b) is very evident. These measures correlate closely with Wolff's figures. Using Spearman's ranked correlation coefficient, sucking frequency correlates with feeding frequency for the twelve animals for which both figures are available ($r=0.76$, $p<0.01$). Sucking frequency for the seventeen animals for which milk content is also available correlates to the same extent with protein ($r=0.76$, $p<0.01$) and slightly less with fat ($r=0.58$, $p<0.01$). Thus the animals which feed least often suck fastest. This would be expected if sucking rate was related to time since last meal, because Wolff tested each animal one hour or less before a scheduled feed. It is not clear whether they were fed according to a natural schedule or with milk of a composition typical of the species (many zoos would do this after Ben Shaul's paper appeared), but Wolff appears to discount any effect of food deprivation on sucking rate. Wolff's measure is of sucking rate within bouts of sucking; Kron, Stein, Goddard and Phoenix (1967, and elsewhere) use a measure of sucks per minute which embraces both within-bout and between-bout rates. They find differences in this measure according to nutrient used (so did Wolff, who specifies that the difference was a change in bout frequency), and according to time since last meal, which they show to be due mostly to increased rate rather than pressure, although they do not say whether this too resulted from increased frequency or length of bouts. If Wolff's measure really is independent of hunger, the rate would appear to be preadapted to ingesting different amounts of food at each meal, and perhaps even more effectively to shortening the total feeding time in the cached, spaced feeders (see below). The rate varies inversely to the assumed viscosity of the milk (faster sucking when lower proportion of water) which suggests that Wolff's result is not due to the variations in the kind of milk fed to the animals (as he confirmed with human infants). The very slow rate of human sucking (which was excluded from the above correlations) can thus be taken as highly suggestive support for adaptations in the baby, to match those in the mother, to continuous contact between them.

Data on duration of feeds tend to confirm that spaced feeders feed very quickly. Rabbit feeds, once every twenty-four hours, last four to five minutes (Findlay, 1969). *Tupaia belangeri* feeds, once every forty-eight hours, last five minutes (Martin, 1968a). In observations in our laboratory, stump-tailed macaque (*Macaca arctoides*) feeds last ten to thirty minutes and occur with about half-hourly intervals, though much time is spent with the nipple in the mouth without sucking.

There may also be related differences in the stimuli which elicit suckling behaviour in the mother. Cross (1952) and Findlay (1969) have shown that pressure of milk is one important short-term stimulus to the rabbit mother. Findlay quotes Lehrman (1961) as summarising evidence that other stimuli predominate in the elicitation of suckling in the laboratory rat. A spaced feeder requires stimuli which are not provided by the young to ensure its return to the young. In an animal with constant contact between mother and young (perhaps ensured by other stimuli) stimuli from the young would be adequate to elicit suckling. Further work on comparative lactation is obviously needed but would clearly benefit from consideration of Ben Shaul's findings.

Since human babies and their mothers are evidently adapted for the baby to stay with the mother and so perhaps to ride around on her, it would be tempting to use the largely dorsal distribution of what brown adipose tissue there is to determine the position in which they have ridden and upon which selection pressure has acted most strongly. Local heating effects are described by Silverman, Zamelis, Sinclair and Agate (1967) for the interscapular deposits of brown adipose tissue. This could be taken to mean that ventral contact is normal as in other primates but it says nothing about where on the mother the baby is carried. Brown adipose tissue occurs in the interscapular region of many animals, so that its significance here may not be very great. It could for example relate to the ancestral carrying habit of the mammalian stock which Martin (1969) proposes. However, it might be worth comparing the soothing effects on human infants of ventral and dorsal contact. I would predict a much greater effect of ventral contact (as, also, would most experienced mothers).

Vestigial behaviour and further points about carrying

A striking omission from my evidence for babies having been carried for a significant portion of human evolution raises an interesting inconsistency in the comparative method which is worth clarifying. We have all been

318

taught to regard the neonatal grasping reflexes as being vestigial (function-less remnants of primate characters). Why do I not regard the features associated with continuous feeding as vestigial? And does it affect the importance we attach to these behaviour patterns? One crucial point is the amount of time during which we regard the character as having been functionless. Traditionally we have regarded clinging as unimportant because the mother has no hair to cling to, and is assumed to have had none for a very long time.

Related to this is the classification of clinging as a reflex which mysteri-ously dies away quite early in life. Classification as a reflex, at a behavioural level, is mainly based on assumed unrelatedness to other behaviour. An isolated reflex is assumed to be of no importance to other developing behaviour.

Prechtl *et al.* (1967) and others have shown that many neonatal reflexes including grasping are influenced by many stimuli and vary with state and kind of response. There is just as much evidence to say that sucking is independent of other behaviour. It is probably only because of Freud's theories that sucking has attracted the attention that grasping has missed. Sucking is often described and has been demonstrated by Kessen and Leutzendorff (1963), Birns, Blank and Bridger (1966), Wolff and Simmons (1967), as having a calming effect. Sucking also appears to calm young monkeys, but Harlow and Harlow (1965) have shown that grasping calms them more (stops them fleeing, and permits them to look at a stimulus that evoked fleeing, and also reinforces fleeing from strange objects to a towelling mother rather than to a nippled mother). That grasping may be functionless for carriage in humans does not necessarily imply that grasping or contact no longer have some such function as reducing arousal or stabilising state.

The classical criterion for deciding whether a character is vestigial is whether its counterparts in the animal or its social partners, or its survival value, have disappeared. Thus the relative hairlessness of the human mother is held to render grasping vestigial. However, as Konner (Ch. 11) describes, babies may be carried in a way that enables them to grasp with their hands as well and as long as any other primate. The experiments of Kovach and Kling (1967) on kittens, which showed that the sucking 'reflex' atrophies and can no longer be elicited if not used in the first twenty days, raises the question of whether the same may be true of human neonate grasping. It is not established whether hairlessness evolved along with the change from clinging to being carried, or whether it followed it much later. Chimpanzee mothers often assist their infant by supporting it with one hand (Goodall, 1968) and the bipedal habit which was present very early in human history would permit this very extensively and might also necessitate it (see below). The persistence of long female head hair and of axillary hair must also be taken into account in any discussion of infant carriage.

The grasp response of the toes is a better candidate for the vestigial label. Man (both infant and adult) has lost the opposable big toe which is sometimes held to be a vital part of the clinging mechanism (Martin, 1969). *Australopithecus* had also lost much of the opposability of the big toe (Zihlman, in press). So possibly self-support by the infant and certainly the ability to move about on the mother was lost at least one and a half million years ago. In contrast to the grasping complex, the milk composition–feeding schedule–infant sucking and metabolism complex has most of its components still present. Only if it was argued that the mother–infant relationship was obsolete could the milk complex be classed as vestigial (except for the physiological components and probable physical ill-effects of deviating from it).

Many babies (see Spitz, 1957; Gunther, 1965) develop after the first few weeks a rhythmical clasping and unclasping hand movement directed at breast or bottle. This superficially resembles the ' milk tread ' of many mammals. Ewer (1968) reports that even in the cat this behaviour takes some time to develop. She also points out that a milk tread is typical of those young mammals that feed lying down whereas those that feed standing use a butting movement of the snout. Baby stump-tailed macaques (Blurton Jones, Trollope and Dick, pers. obs.) grip their mother (as do human neonates, Richards and Bernal, pers. comm. and Wortis, pers. comm.) while feeding but subsequently they do not develop any rhythmical movements before or during feeding even though in our conditions they seldom need to hold the mother for support, as illustrated by Bertrand (1969). I can find no descriptions of such movements for any non-human primate. It therefore seems very possible that human infants have a higher propensity to develop such rhythmic movements than do monkey babies. The evolution of this propensity would take time, and may imply that human babies have not had to support themselves by clinging to the mother for a significant portion of human evolution and may therefore have been supported by their mother. This infant ' milk tread ' appears to be the same movement and therefore perhaps the precursor in ontogeny of the ' ear flipping ' (described by Anderson, Ch. 8) and other similar habits which often accompany digit sucking in older children. Whether the ineffectual-looking ' milk tread ' actually affects the milk supply is quite unknown. Some mothers report it as being very pleasant. Gentle stroking can be used by mothers in manually expressing milk but some of them describe their baby's cry as having a much greater effect. It would be worth investigating whether any feature of the elicitation of the mother's feeding behaviour or of the sucking adaptive complex can explain the enlargement of human breasts which is not found in other primates. Morris (1967) has suggested that this is a sexual signal not related to lactation.

But Abercrombie (1971) has made the extremely interesting suggestion that it is an arrangement to bring about a face to face position during suckling.

Why carry babies?

The question now arises as to why man or any other animal should evolve a frequent-feeding schedule and close mother–infant relationship. Because it seems possible for evolution to deal with different growth and energy requirements on any feeding schedule, one might argue that the more frequent types of feeding schedule could have a predominantly social function, such as developing a close bond between mother and infant. But it seems unlikely that the feeding schedule relates closely to adult sociality in the sense of herd size, or time spent alone or in company. Whether a mother–child attachment occurs depends on which kind of anti-predator system is present. Each of the four main kinds of mammal child-care system includes adequate protection against predators, and also requires different kinds of feeding schedule. But what determines which of these systems is used? The answer is not easy to see and is not examined in any detail here.

If frequent feeding is an adaptation to developing some kind of social relationship, particularly an early tie between mother and child, this would be support from comparative studies for Bowlby's suggestion that suckling does in some way contribute to the child's attachment to its mother. However, it is not going to be possible to be sure about the comparative argument until far more information on non-primate mammals is available. It seems clear that the degree of association between mother and young is not related to sociability of the adults alone. For instance grizzly bears (*Ursus arctos horribilis*) are notably solitary animals as adults, but the young stay with their mother, sometimes still suckling, for as long as two and a half years (Murie, 1961). The initial phase of child-rearing in foxes and wolves seems to be similar yet they differ markedly in adult sociability. The number of different kinds of food taken by the species would seem to be as good a candidate as sociability for a correlation with the duration of the association between mother and offspring (if not with other aspects of the association). That mother–child contact is not an indispensable way of developing even minimal species recognition is shown by the successful survival of those cuckoos (e.g. *Cuculus canorus*) who mate despite having never seen their parents. There are many ways of solving any particular problem of survival. But the ways that are open to a particular animal are restricted by the ways in which it solves or its ancestors had solved other problems of survival.

In summary, I feel that the comparative evidence makes it highly probable, although the evidence is very incomplete, that Bowlby is right in saying that suckling is in some ways an adaptation for developing a close mother–child attachment. The association in the mammals between frequent feeding and a following or carrying system of child care is not nutritionally necessary, but rapid onset of hunger and satiation in the baby would be a simple mechanism for ensuring that it stays with the mother.

Discussion

It now remains to discuss any general conclusion from this exercise in comparative ethology. Renewed interest in aspects of the functional anatomy of man may have interesting implications for behaviour work. For instance the present study suggests to me that we should look for effects of individual variation in attachment on responses to stress, rather than on acquisition of social behaviour, because of the calming effects of suckling, and the gross deviation from the evolved suckling frequency which most individuals in industrialised society undergo. And, to take a different aspect of suckling adaptations, the function of the buccal pad in children requires work on its effectiveness (a) on sucking, and (b) on cheek shape, and of this on adult responses. The age at which it disappears, when children become lean-faced around 4 years old, may indicate some major change in their situation and in their behaviour or in the behaviour of adults to them. It may have to do with the end of suckling and the changes in relationship to the mother which might go with this, or with other changes in behaviour towards the mother and a change in mother behaviour which accompanies them. The taxonomic distribution of the buccal pad is interesting. It appears to be absent from most mammals including monkeys, but if it functions to increase pressure during sucking this will depend partly on the shape of the mouth. However, Cowie and Folley (1961) argue that suction is only of secondary importance in suckling, but the unusual form of human mammaries may again be relevant here, especially to the difficulty of retaining the short nipple in the mouth rather than extracting milk, and this may in turn account for Wolff's (1968) finding that human babies were unique in their pattern of non-nutritive sucking, as they are also when compared to the non-nutritive nipple-holding of baby monkeys.

In zoology there is often an interaction between comparative studies and studies of physiology or development. The interaction seems to involve at first comparative surveys, which assemble data from anatomy, physiology and ontogeny into a pattern of historical events. Gaps are then noticed within this pattern which suggest further work on anatomy, etc., which will usually then be of direct relevance to comparative studies. Thus, in the example in this paper, the need for studies of the 'calming' (cry-stopping) effect of grasping, ventral versus dorsal contact, as well as the well-studied sucking and rocking, became evident. It is also evident that, at some stage in an analysis of the role of different kinds of infant care, one will need this data from other species as well – for instance, is there also a calming effect of sucking or rocking in spaced feeders, what is the effect of licking of young of cached species? The main value to psychology of this kind of comparative study may be in allowing us to challenge, or simply notice, accepted viewpoints. The use Bowlby has made of the idea that attachment is predominantly an anti-predator device, a special adaptation to life as a baby (like larval adaptations in zoologists' terms), is a good example. One can then no longer assume that it is simply the way we start acquiring social behaviour, or that it is bound to be related to food. But equally one cannot assume that this function implies any more about the method of development of the attachment than that it must develop reliably in the context in which it evolved. There is no implication that it must be ' innate ' in the sense used in early ethology; indeed if the implications of my comparative study are correct then the situation in which babies develop has been exceptionally constant throughout our evolution, right back into our earliest hominoid phase some twenty-five million years ago and beyond throughout our higher primate ancestry of some forty million years. This implies that there has been very little need for rigid genetic canalisation of behaviour to produce developmental systems that give the same result in a wide range of environments.

An important factor in assessing the value of comparative studies which include man is one's standpoint and ultimate interest. To the zoologist the comparative story is the endpoint, it comes after the psychologist and social anthropologist have done their work. For a zoologist those features of human behaviour which are common to other animals, and those that are specific to man both have to be explained in terms of how they came about. To many but not all zoologists this is *the* explanation of human behaviour, psychologists and sociologists always seem to stop short of the real answer.

It is quite possible that much of the controversy about the popular ' ethology ' book depends on which interest is uppermost: (1) reconstruction of the course of human evolution, or (2) finding out how behaviour is controlled and develops. If these books are taken as saying things about our evolutionary history they are only rather incomplete and in places erroneous, in places ingenious and stimulating. If they are working in other directions and saying that this implies things about the way in which our behaviour develops and is evoked (as Lorenz (1966) certainly is) they are doing something which simply does not follow from their method. The usefulness of comparative studies for studying the evolution of man is far greater than their usefulness for determining or describing causation and development of behaviour. This conclusion could have been logically derived from Tinbergen's (1951) classification of the four main questions about behaviour. The evolutionary story is the ultimate explanation of causation and ontogeny, it provides the last link in the causal chain, but it does not give us the data about how behaviour develops or is caused and therefore it is not giving us any verdict on the practical problems of developmental or social psychology.

Comparative studies of behaviour have usually concerned either the relatively fixed motor patterns involved in bird displays, for example Lorenz's classical study of the displays of *Anatinae* (1941, 1953) or the occurrence and adaptive value of large-scale aspects like territory, or flocking. There have been very few studies which cover the whole of this range (e.g. Crook, 1964) but these suggest that there are relationships between the large scale and the small scale. However, these studies are too few to allow prediction from the large-scale aspects of behaviour of a 'new' species to the detailed aspects, and certainly not to the kind of causation or kind of development required to bring them about. Yet this is what Lorenz is doing in his book *On Aggression* (Lorenz, 1966). He is in effect arguing that because man must have had a spacing-out mechanism it must consist of aggression which is caused spontaneously and which develops regardless of the circumstances. He may or may not be right, but he has not produced the evidence. The most powerful evidence would be direct data on causation and development of aggression in man. Comparative evidence would have to come from comparative studies of the taxonomic distribution and adaptive value of various causal systems for aggression (spontaneous, frustration, proximity of conspecifics, with or without effects of food deprivation, hormonal state, etc.). The data on which to do this are simply not available, this sort of detail is available for very few species indeed. Likewise comparative studies of developmental systems scarcely exist and are as yet hardly feasible. Even if they were feasible they could only do one of two things, either predict and guide investigation to test the predictions about development, or explain how a developmental system described by direct investigation has come about. From the point of view of practical applied social psychology or sociology the only gain from comparative study is a certain perspective and framework for research. But from the point of view of academic explanations of human behaviour the evolutionary story is the endpoint.

Acknowledgements

This paper owes the largest part of its existence to helpful, encouraging and frequent discussion with R. D. Martin of the Department of Anthropology, University College London. The guidance of a full-time comparative zoologist was invaluable for this excursion back into my zoological youth. I am also indebted to John Bareham, Royal Veterinary College, University of London, and to M. P. M. Richards, University of Cambridge, M. J. Konner, Harvard University, for discussion and references and to M. F.

Hall, Department of Psychiatry, The London Hospital Medical School, for a critical reading of an earlier draft of this paper.

REFERENCES

Abercrombie, J. (1971). Face to face: proximity and distance. *J. psychosom. Res.* **15**, 395–402.

Ainsworth, M. D. S. (1969). Object relations, dependency, and attachment: a theoretical review of the infant–mother relationship. *Child Develop.* **40**, 969–1027.

Ambrose, J. A. (1966). Ritualization in the human infant–mother bond. *Phil. Trans. Roy. Soc.* B **251**, 359–62.

Ambrose, J. A. (1968). The comparative approach to early child development: the data of ethology. In *Foundations of Child Psychiatry*. Ed. E. Miller, London: Pergamon.

Ben Shaul, D. M. (1962a). Notes on hand-rearing various species of mammals. *Int. Zoo Year Book* **4**, 300–32.

Ben Shaul, D. M. (1962b). The composition of the milk of wild animals. *Int. Zoo Year Book* **4**, 333–42.

Bertrand, M. (1969). The behavioural repertoire of the stump-tailed macaque. *Bibliotheca Primatologia*, no. 11.

Binford, S. R. and Binford, L. R. (1969). Stone tools and human behaviour. *Sci. Amer.* **220**, 70–84.

Birns, B., Blank, M. and Bridger, Wagner H. (1966). The effectiveness of various soothing techniques on human neonates. *Psychosom. Med.* **28**, 316–22.

Boelkins, R. C. (1962). Large-scale rearing of infant rhesus monkeys (*M. mulatta*) in the laboratory. *Int. Zoo Year Book* **4**, 285–9.

Bowlby, J. (1969). *Attachment and loss*, vol. 1: *Attachment*. London: Hogarth Press.

Bubenik, A. B. (1965). Beitrag zur Geburtskunde und zur den Mutter–Kind-Beziehungen des Reh- (*Capreolus capreolus* L.) und Rotwildes (*Cervus elaphus* L.) *Z. Saugetierk* **30**, 65–128.

Cowie, A. T. and Folley, S. J. (1961). The mammary gland and lactation. In *Sex and Internal Secretions*. Ed. W. C. Young, Baltimore: Williams and Wilkins.

Crook, J. H. (1964). The evolution of social organisation and visual communication in weaver birds (Ploceinae). *Behaviour, Suppl.* **10**, 1–178.

Cross, B. A. (1952). Nursing behaviour and the milk-ejection reflex in rabbits. *J. Endoc.* **8**, 13.

Davies, P. A. and Russel, H. (1968). Later progress of 100 infants weighing 1000–2000 g at birth fed immediately with breast milk. *Devel. Med. Child Neurol.* **10**, 725–35.

Dawkins, M. J. R. and Hull, D. (1964). Brown adipose tissue and non-shivering thermogenesis in newborn animals. In *The Adaptation of the Newborn Infant to Extra-Uterine Life*. Ed. J. H. P. Jonxis *et al.* Leiden: Stenfert Kroese.

Eisenberg, J. (1966). The social organisation of mammals. *Handbuch der Zoologie*, VIII (10/7), *Liefering* **39**.

Elton, C. S. (1927). *Animal Ecology*. London: Sidgwick and Jackson.

Elton, C. S. (1966). *The Pattern of Animal Communities*. London: Methuen.

Erikson, E. H. (1965). *Childhood and Society* (Norton. U.S.A. 1950). Harmondsworth: Penguin Books.

Ewer, R. F. (1968). *Ethology of Mammals*. London: Logos Press.

Findlay, A. L. R. (1969). Nursing behaviour and the condition of the mammary gland in the rabbit. *J. comp. physiol. Psychol.* **69**, 115–18.

Fox, J. R. and Tiger, L. (1966). The zoological perspective in social science. *Man* **1**, 75–81.

Freeman, Derek (1966). Social anthropology and the scientific study of human behaviour. *Man* **1**, 330–42.

Freedman, D. G. (1967). A biological view of man's social behaviour. In *Social Behaviour from Fish to Man*. Ed. W. Etkin, Chicago and London: Univ. of Chicago Press.

Goodall, Jane van Lawick (1968). The behaviour of free-living chimpanzees in the Gombe Stream Reserve. *Anim. Behav. Monog.* **1**, 165–311.

Gunther, M. (1965). Discussion of Rheingold, H. L. and Keen, G. C. 'Transport of the Human Young'. In *Determinants of Infant Behaviour*, vol. 3. Ed. B. M. Foss, London: Methuen.

Hambreus, L. and Wranne, L. (1968). The plasma phenylalanine level in newborn infants of normal and low birth weights fed on human milk. *Biolog. Neonat.* **13**, 315–24.

Harlow, H. F. and Harlow, M. K. (1965). The affectional systems. In *Behavior of non-human Primates*, vol. 2. Ed. A. M. Schrier, H. F. Harlow and F. Stollnitz, New York: Academic Press.

Hinde, R. A. and Spencer-Booth, Y. (1968). Review lecture. The study of mother–infant interactions in captive group-living rhesus monkeys. *Proc. Roy. Soc.* B **169**, 177–201.

Hooper, P. D. (1965). Infant feeding and its relation to weight gain and illness. *Practitioner* **194**, 391–5.

Jolly, C. (1970). The seed-eaters: a new model of hominid differentiation based on a baboon analogy. *Man* (n.s.) **5**, 1–26.

Jonxis, J. H. P., Visser, H. K. A. and Troelstra, J. A. (eds.) (1964). *The Adaptation of the Newborn Infant to Extra-Uterine life*. Nutricia Symposium 1964. Leiden: Stenfert Kroese.

Kessen, W. and Leutzendorff, A. M. (1963). The effect of non-nutritive sucking on movement in the human newborn. *J. comp. physiol. Psychol.* **56**, 69–72.

Kovach, J. K. and Kling, A. (1967). Mechanism of neonate sucking behaviour in the kitten. *Anim. Behav.* **15**, 91–101.

Kron, R. E., Stein, M., Goddard, K. E. and Phoenix, M. D. (1967). Effect of nutrient upon the sucking behaviour of newborn infants. *Psychosom. Med.* **24**, 24–32.

Kühme, W. (1965). Communal food distribution and division of labour in African hunting dogs. *Nature, Lond.* **205**, 443–4.

Lattin, P. R. (1969). A consideration of some aspects of the behaviour and ecology of the early hominids. M.A. thesis, University of Durham.

Lee, R. B. (1968). What hunters do for a living, or, how to make out on scarce resources. In *Man the Hunter*. Ed. R. B. Lee and I. DeVore, Chicago: Aldine.

Lee, R. B. and DeVore, I. (eds.). (1968). *Man the Hunter*. Chicago: Aldine.

Lehrman, D. (1961). Hormonal regulation of parental behaviour in birds and infrahuman mammals. In *Sex and Internal Secretions*. Ed. W. C. Young, Baltimore: Williams and Wilkins.

Lorenz, K. (1941). Vergleichende Bewegungsstudien an Anatinen *Suppl. J. Ornith.* **89**, 194–294.

Lorenz, K. (1953). Comparative studies on the behaviour of the *Anatinae*. Reprinted from the *Avicultural Magazine*, London.

Lorenz, K. (1966). *On Aggression*. London: Methuen.

MacKeith, R. C. (1969). Breast feed for the first two months. Editorial in *Develop. Med. Child Neurol.* **11**, 277.

Martin, R. D. (1968*a*). Reproduction and ontogeny in tree-shrews (*Tupaia belangeri*), with reference to their general behaviour and taxonomic relationship. *Z. Tierpsychol.* **25**, 409–95 and 505–32.

Martin, R. D. (1968*b*). Towards a new definition of primates. *Man* (n.s.) **3**, 377–401.

Martin, R. D. (1969). The evolution of reproductive mechanisms in primates. *J. Reprod. Fert. Suppl.* **6**, 49–66.

Meyer, H. F. (1968). Breast feeding in the United States. Report of a 1966 national survey with comparable 1946 and 1956 data. *Clin. Paediat.* **7**, 708–15.

Morris, D. (1967). *The Naked Ape.* London: Jonathan Cape.

Murie, Adolph. (1961). *A Naturalist in Alaska.* (Devin–Adais Co. New York.) New York: Doubleday.

Newman, R. W. (1970). Why man is such a sweaty and thirsty naked animal: a speculative review. *Hum. Biol.* **42**, 12–27.

Newson J. and Newson, E. (1963). *Infant Care in an Urban Community.* London: Allen and Unwin.

Pfeiffer, John E. (1969). *The Emergence of Man.* New York: Harper and Row; London: Nelson.

Prechtl, H. F., Vlach, V., Lenard, H. G. and Kerr Grant, D. (1967). Exteroceptive and tendon reflexes in various behavioural states in newborn infants. *Biol. Neonat.* **11**, 159–75.

Richards, M. P. and Bernal, Judith (1970). The effects of bottle and breast feeding on infant development. *J. Psychosom. Res.* **14**, 247–52.

Rowell, T. E., Din, N. A. and Omar, A. (1968). The social development of baboons in their first three months. *J. Zool.* **155**, 461–83.

Schaller, G. B. (1963). *The Mountain Gorilla: Ecology and Behaviour.* Chicago: University of Chicago Press.

Silverman, W. A., Zamelis, A., Sinclair, J. C. and Agate, F. J. (1964). Warm nape of the newborn. *Pediatrics* **33**, 984–7.

Spitz, R. A. (1957). *No and Yes; on the beginning of human Communication.* New York: Internat. Univ. Press.

Suzuki, A. (1969). An ecological study of chimpanzees in a savanna woodland. *Primates* **10**, 103–48.

Tanner, J. M. (1962). *Growth at Adolescence.* Oxford and Edinburgh: Blackwell.

Tinbergen, N. (1951). *The Study of Instinct.* London: Oxford University Press.

Tinbergen, N. (1965). Behaviour and natural selection: In *Ideas in Modern Biology.* Ed. J. A. Moore, New York: Doubleday.

Tinbergen, N. (1967). Adaptive features of the black-headed gull. *Proc. 14th Internat. ornith. Congr.* Ed. D. W. Snow, Oxford and Edinburgh: Blackwell.

Tinbergen, N., Impekoven, M. and Frank, D. (1967). An experiment on spacing-out as a defence against predation. *Behaviour* **28**, 307–21.

Underwood, B. A., Hepner R. and Abdullah, H. (1970). Protein, lipid and fatty acids of human milk from Pakistani women during prolonged periods of lactation. *Amer. J. Clin. Nutrition* **23**, 400–407.

Walther, F. (1965). Verhaltensstudien an der Grantgazelle (*Gazella granti* Brooke, 1872) in Ngorongoro-Krater. *Z. Tierpsychol.* **22**, 167–208.

Walther, F. (1969). Flight behaviour and avoidance of predators in Thomson's gazelle. *Behaviour* **34**, 184–221.

Watanabe, Hitoshi (1968). Subsistence and ecology of northern food gatherers with special reference to the Ainu. In *Man the Hunter*. Ed. R. B. Lee and I. DeVore, Chicago: Aldine.

Wolff, P. H. (1968). Sucking patterns of infant mammals. *Brain, Behaviour and Evolution* **1**, 354–67.

Wolff, P. H. and Simmons, M. A. (1967). Non-nutritive sucking and response thresholds in young infants. *Child Develop.* **38**, 631–8.

Zarrow, M. X., Denenberg, V. H. and Anderson, C. O. (1965). Rabbit: frequency of suckling in the pup. *Science, N.Y.* **150**, 1835–6.

Zihlman, A. (in press). The question of locomotor differences in *Australopithecus*. *Proc. Internat. Primatol. Congr.*, Zurich, 1970.

13

THE EVOLUTION AND ONTOGENY OF
HAND FUNCTION

KEVIN CONNOLLY AND JOHN ELLIOTT *

SUMMARY

A hand similar to that of man is a feature of almost all primates. The prehensile specialisation of the hand permits it to perform a wide range of functions. Prehensility is achieved by varying means in different primate genera and a consideration of the details of the grasping ability of various primates reveals that both the anatomy of the hand and its repertoire of movement represent a substantial specialisation appropriate to the species. The wide range of manual ability shown by man is a consequence of the use of remarkably few prehensile patterns by a hand particularly suited to undertake manipulative work of both a fine and coarse character. The chapter reviews the range of primate hand function and the terminology used in describing it. It considers also the development of hand usage in man and the little that is known of its development in infra-human primates. There is work of substance on the development of prehension during the first year of life in humans but little on the emergence of tool using ability which constitutes one of the main distinguishing features of human manual skill. Observations on spontaneous tool using (a paint brush) by children aged between 3 and 5 are reported. A range of grasps and movements is described and data on their frequency of occurrence reported. An increasing tendency to use the right hand with increasing age was found. The results are discussed in terms of Napier's power/precision grip dichotomy. It is concluded that in several important respects the use of the hand is not fully developed in children within this age range.

1. Introduction

Bell, in his monograph on the hand, saw man, ' by the power of the hand (as the ready instrument of the mind) accommodated to every condition through which his destinies promise to be accomplished ' (1833: 231–2). Buettner-Janusch (1966) describes the human hand as ' probably the most elegant and skilful organ that has been developed through natural selection ' (1966: 322).

The importance of the hand to man is not in question, and a hand similar to that of man is a feature of almost all primates. As a mammalian order, the primates are not defined by one unique characteristic, but by a cluster of characteristics, not all of which need occur within a given

* Department of Psychology, University of Sheffield.

genus. One of the most universally occurring primate characteristics is the differentiation of the hand and foot as manipulative organs. Over and above the general primate hand have been superimposed modifications specific to the various primate groups. The great apes, for example, show peculiarities related to their mode of locomotion (modified brachiation,

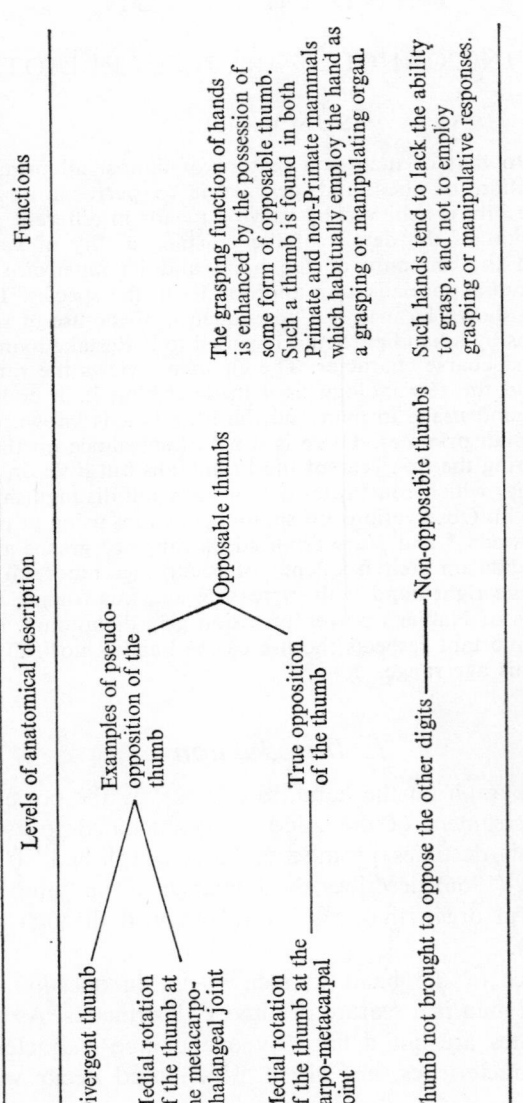

Fig. 13·1. Relation between structure and function illustrated by reference to the nature of opposition of the thumb in Primates.

knuckle walking), despite their close relation to man in primate phylogeny (Erikson, 1963; Napier, 1960, 1963; Tuttle, 1967, 1969).

The terms used in discussing the hand should observe a distinction between functional and anatomical description. Anatomy is concerned with both the structure of organs and the operations of which they are capable. In so far as these operations involve movement, however, there is a distinction between movement and function. Function refers to effects, to the operation of the organ in terms of consequences, and thus entails reference to other organs or to the environment. It is possible, for example, to have a functional anatomy of the brain (Ranson and Clark, 1947), in which, clearly, the functioning parts do not move. The construction of an artificial hand would involve an attempt at replicating function by means of parts differing 'anatomically' from those in the living organ. Prehension is a function which such a prosthesis might be expected to perform, and it is one which the different primate hands accomplish through various anatomical routes (Fig. 13·1). The anatomy of their hands limits but does not define their functions. In this way the distinction between structure, movement and function may be maintained.

The human hand may be used in non-locomotor and non-prehensile ways, as in pushing or clubbing objects. Fingers may be used for poking, scratching, etc. Primarily, however, the hand is adapted to serve the requirements of prehension. The skeletal elements consist of three groups of bones, the phalanges or finger bones; the metacarpals or bones of the hand; and the carpals or bones of the wrist. The carpals serve to provide a firm yet elastic link between the bones of the arm and those of the hand. The metacarpals articulate with the phalangeal bones in a way which is closely related to the efficiency and mobility of the digits. In man, the thumb obtains a mobility greater than that available to the fingers by virtue of the nature of the articulation between the carpal and metacarpal bones. The volar (palmar) surface of the thumb faces across the palm of the hand; this combined with the nature of the carpo-metacarpal articulation renders the thumb opposable to the fingers. This opposition is the basis of the mobility and dexterity in use shown by the human hand.

The operation of the human hand in terms of the discrete movements of the joints and the action of the individual muscles is well understood. Study of the action of the hand as a whole has further to go. In analysing the work of the hand at this level, a number of concepts have been widely used (Napier, 1961, 1966).

CONVERGENCE AND DIVERGENCE

These terms refer to the opposite extremes of movements occurring at the metacarpo-phalangeal joints. Divergence is the fanning out of the digits by means of extension and abduction. Convergence is the approximation of the finger tips by a movement of flexion and adduction, Fig. 13·2.

Although defined as referring to the position of the digits at the conclusion of certain movements the terms have come also to refer to properties of the hand. Primate hands are said to be convergent because of the convergence of the digits in flexion and adduction. In almost all primates the thumb is said to be divergent, since, when the digits are in the divergent position, the thumb shows a greater separation from the fingers than these do from each other.

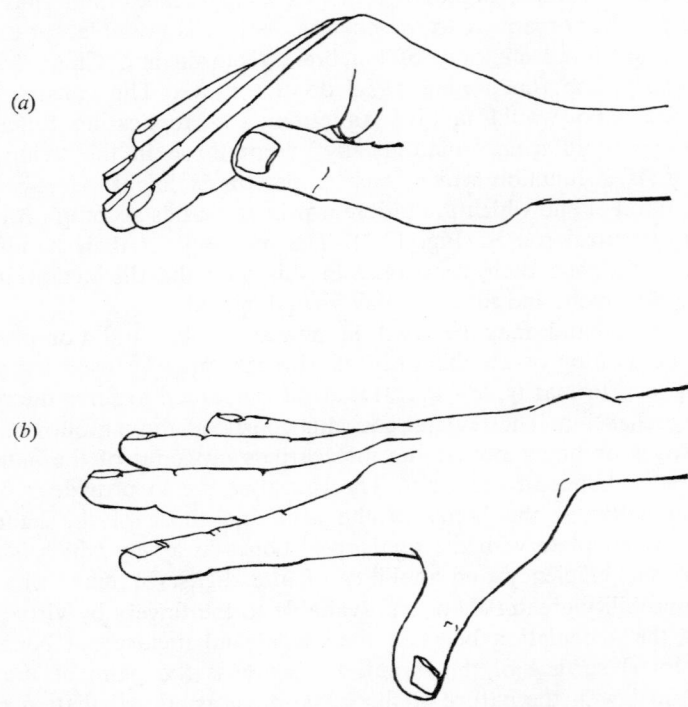

Fig. 13·2. Convergence and divergence of the human hand (a) convergence (b) divergence.

OPPOSITION OF THE THUMB

Napier (1956) defines opposition as a movement which results in the pulp of the thumb being placed squarely in contact with, or diametrically opposite, the pulp of one of the other fingers. Opposition is a property of the thumb found in many primates, and is achieved by a variety of mechanisms. Opposition in man, the great apes and many Old World monkeys ('true opposition', Napier, 1961), is achieved by the peculiar structure of the carpo-metacarpal joint, such that abduction of the thumb automatically causes an inward (medial) rotation, bringing the pulp round to face that of the finger, Fig. 13·3. Opposition is thus achieved by flexion and abduction plus rotation of the thumb. Opposition achieved in other ways is known as 'pseudo-opposition' (Napier, 1961), for example when the thumb is divergent enough to oppose the fingers on flexion without rotation. Extreme examples of this can be seen in hands of Lorisiformes.

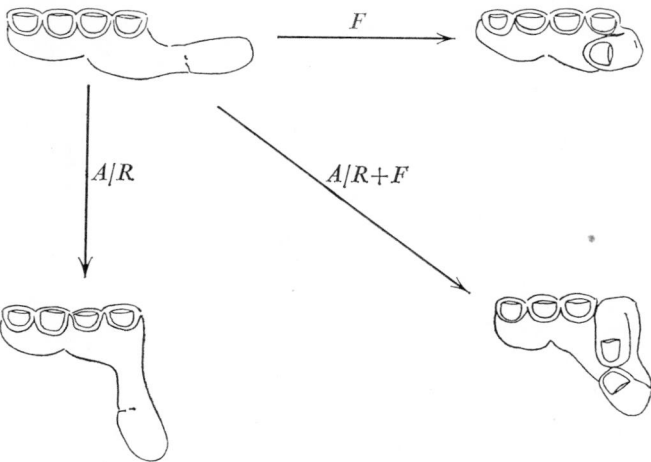

Fig. 13·3. Diagrammatic representation of human thumb opposition. Opposition occurs only when abduction and rotation are combined with flexion. Abduction and rotation, or flexion alone, do not achieve opposition. (A/R, abduction and rotation; F, flexion).

PREHENSION

Prehensile movements are those involved in grasping an object. Our operational definition of prehension is the ability to pick up an object in one hand. Bishop (1964) distinguishes a prehensive pattern as 'the changing positions of the hand as it reaches to take hold of an object', and a prehensive grip as a configuration of the hand while actually grasping. Despite the great range of prehensile activity exhibited by man, Napier (1956) classifies grips into two types only, power and precision. These are illustrated in Fig. 13·4. In the power grip the object is held in a clamp formed by the partially flexed fingers and the palm of the hand, counter pressure being applied by the thumb roughly in the plane of the palm. In the precision grip the object is held pinched between the flexor aspect of the finger(s) and opposing thumb. In this latter case the palm of the hand is not involved. Napier (1956) claims that it is invariably the nature of the task which is to be performed and not the shape of the object which determines the grip employed. The power grip lends added force to the grip at the expense of the mobility allowed by the independent use of digits in the precision grip. However, the size of the object does exert some influence upon the grip at the extremes of the range, and the shape of the object has an effect on the developmental sequences of grasping (Halverson, 1931; see below). In certain activities the two grips are combined at the same time. When this occurs the precision element is usually dominant. Tying a knot in a piece of string is the example given by Napier (1956).

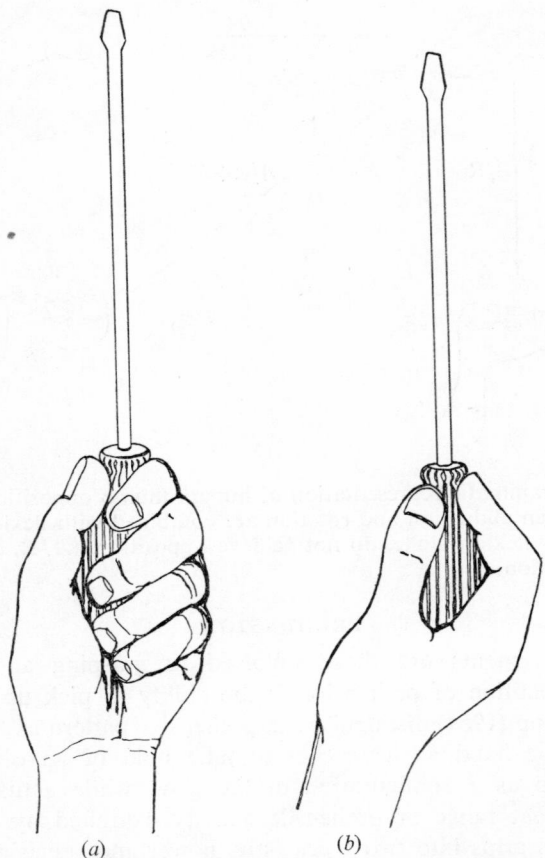

(a)   (b)

Fig. 13·4. Basic grip configurations of the hand
(a) power grip, (b) precision grip.

Power and precision grips are strictly speaking defined only for the human hand. As the hands of other primates differ more and more from those of man, anatomically homologous grips are less likely to be seen. However, powerful and precise grips are certainly to be found (Bishop, 1964; Napier, 1960) in other species, though not definable in anatomical universals.

Convergence, divergence, opposition and prehension are basic properties of the hand. The subsequent sections of this paper review briefly what is known of hand function in infra-human primates and the development of primate hand function, which has been studied almost exclusively in humans below the age of 24 months. The result of a series of observations which we have made on tool using by pre-school children are reported in some detail. Our interest in this subject stemmed from a concern with the development of skilled behaviour and the way in which the hand indicates the shaping and expression of human intelligence and ability.

2. Hand use in primates

The five digits in the pentadactyl limb represent an ancient condition, that of the earliest, ancestral mammals (Jones, 1941). Many groups of living mammals lost varying numbers of this original complement of digits, generally in the evolution of specialised locomotor apparatus. It has been argued by several authors that the primitive pentadactyl condition has been preserved more tenaciously in primates than many other mammalian features. Jones (1941) expressed it in this way: '. . . The human condition of complete pentadactylism is therefore a very note-worthy feature, a feature that stamps this part of man's anatomy with the hall-mark of primitiveness and a feature that a great host of other mammals has lost by specialisation leading to a reduction of their digital series.' Such a view should not, however, be allowed to obscure the fact that contemporary primate hands are in many other respects highly evolved organs.

The prehensile hand is one of the most typical characteristics of the primates * (Clark, 1959; Buettner-Janusch, 1963, 1966). The manipulative ability of a hand allows it to be put to a variety of uses, which may be represented as:

   (i) arboreal locomotion;

   (ii) feeding;

   (iii) grooming;

   (iv) tool-using, in a few species, and in man also tool making; and

   (v) infants clinging to mother's fur.

Evidently the specialisation of the hand as a prehensile organ has not resulted in the loss of flexibility and adaptability to changing circumstances that are often seen as a consequence of structural specialisation, where increased efficiency in dealing with a particular environment is obtained at the expense of future adaptability. The arboreal sloths (*Choloepus* and *Bradypus*) offer an example of a locomotor specialisation

---

* Martin (1968) suggests that the opposability of the thumb is a primitive feature of placental mammals, secondarily lost by most mammalian groups. He also concurs with other authors (Van Valen, 1965; Campbell, 1966) in separating the Tupaiidae from the primates on the basis of many characteristics, thus further removing support from the view that the ancestral primate hand was a tupaiid-like non-prehensile organ with clawed digits.

severely restricting the non-locomotor use of the manus. It is noticeable also that the primates show prehensile action of the basic pentadactyl hand by several different structural mechanisms. 'The impressive thing about the primate grasping organ is the variety of special anatomical forms in which it exists, yet its specialisation does not seem to have led to an evolutionary dead end. The behavioural consequences of the basic grasping adaptation have apparently such a wide range of applications to varying ecological sites that specialisation has not yet proved to be maladaptive'

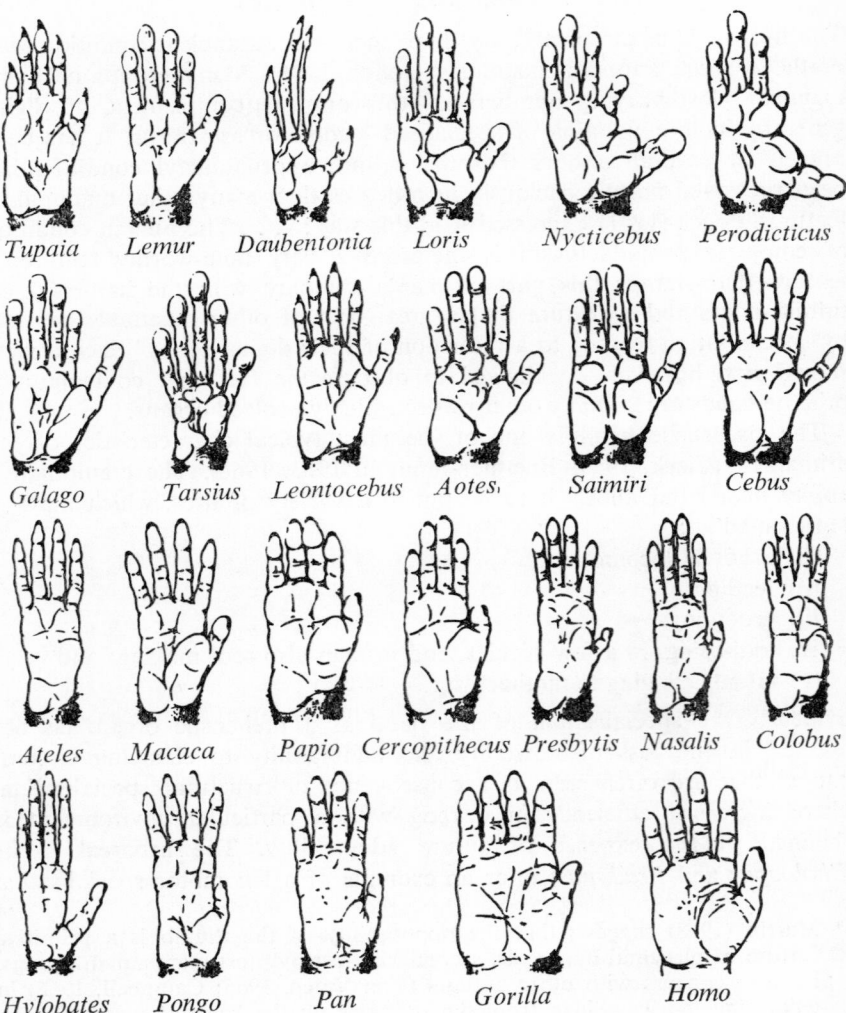

Fig. 13·5. Range of primate hand form. (From Schultz, 1956.)

(Buettner-Janusch, 1963: 2). The distinct types of prehensile mechanisms in different genera can be examined for relationships of function to structure without implying a phylogenetic relationship. The range of hand structure exhibited by the primates is shown in Fig. 13·5.

Comparisons of primate hands reveal adaptive trends independently of the phylogenetic relationships of the genera involved. Reviewing these comparisons, hands are grouped according to the nature of their structure and prehensive mechanisms, rather than following the phylogenetic relationships of the various primates. A more detailed perspective is provided by Bishop (1962, 1964), Schultz (1968) and Napier and Napier (1967).

In addition, however, to this variety of bone and muscle anatomy, neuroanatomy has evolved to meet the demands of prehension. The motor and tactile capacities of the primate hand are accompanied by a special enlargement and differentiation of the precentral motor and postcentral sensory regions of the cortex, along with their mutual interconnections. The evolution of the hand was concomitant with the evolution of the brain (Biegert, 1964), and as greater manual dexterity was achieved, additional neurological advances occurred. In the human hand this has resulted in a high level of independence and sensitivity of the digits.

Appendix 1 gives a summary by genera of hand function in the infrahuman primates. The hand least adapted for grasping is that of the Tupaiidae (tree shrews), squirrel-like arboreal Asian animals, which have often been regarded as primitive primates. *Urogale* (Philippine tree shrew) has been known to catch flies one-handed (Polyak, 1957), but the most widely studied genus, *Tupaia*, seldom if ever shows one-handed prehension. The hand has short digits relative to the length of the palm, the digits are convergent and bear claws, not nails. The thumb is divergent but non-opposable. The single grip involves simple flexion of all digits together, and the hand is not oriented to the object. Bishop (1964) found that the orientation of the hand on a dowel was the most variable of any of the primates she studied. In reaching for an object the hand is flexed over it, and the forearm is flexed, raking the object back. This hand thus shows little differentiation of the digits and minimal adaptation to grasping requirements.

The Callithricidae (marmosets) display a hand closely similar to that of the tree shrews in both structure and function, but differing in being prehensile. They habitually hold food in one hand, and show a trend to orienting the hand transversely on branches. The similarity of the hands in Tupaiidae and Callithricidae is particularly interesting in that the latter are New World monkeys.

Two distinct, more complex hand types are those of the Lemuriformes (lemurs) and Lorisiformes (lorises). The hands of the lorises and lemurs are distinguished by the pattern of palmar pads, the tendency for the loris thumb to diverge to extremes, with concomitant reduction of the index fingers, and the relatively higher length/breadth ratio of lemurs. Apart from these differences of structure, the prehensive patterns of the two groups differ. Lemurs reach for an object with the digits slightly flexed, leading with the tips of the digits. Lorises open the hand widely (digits extended) prior to contact, and close the hand by flexion of the digits when the palm touches the target.

Both these hands have pseudo-opposable thumbs, and the range of hand orientations in respect to a dowel shows less variability than in the Tupaii-formes, especially in the lorises (Bishop, 1964).

Some lemuriform genera (*Microcebus, Cheirogaleus*) have a hand similar to that of Lorisiformes, with shortened digits and enhanced thumb divergence, though retaining the lemuriform palmar pad pattern. The prehensive pattern of these genera, however, remains that of the lemurs, not the lorises. This retention of the lemur prehensive style despite variations in hand structure suggests that the loris-like hands of *Microcebus* and *Cheirogaleus* have developed from a lemur-like ancestor. Although the two superfamilies show the differences outlined, they share the relatively simple grip involved in simply flexing all the digits. Due to the convergence of the digits and the pseudo-opposition of the thumb, this results in a prehensile grasp. There is no individual control of the digits, except in some lemurs (e.g. *Hapalemur*) in which the thumb may be flexed with all the fingers, or opposing them. The size of the object grasped appears to determine the grip in such cases, but it is also true that smaller objects may be grasped for a different end than large ones.

The single genus, *Tarsius*, occupies an infra-order of its own. Its hand shows some similarities to that of Lorisiformes, as does its prehensive pattern, and it shares the general stereotype of prehension seen in the Prosimians as a whole. It possesses, however, its own prehensive mechanism involving a rotation of the thumb at the metacarpo-phalangeal joint. This thus differs from the rotation of the human thumb, and constitutes an example of a unique prehensive adaptation. Napier (1961), describing this mechanism, classifies it as an instance of pseudo-opposition. Napier and Napier (1967) reclassify it as non-opposable without comment.

It is generally correct to say that the various Prosimian hands, though revealing several different prehensile mechanisms, are relatively simple devices, lacking in fine motor control, and handling objects regardless of size or shape in a single stereotyped hand flexion. In the Anthropoidea or higher primates, including man, three superfamilies are distinguished (Simpson, 1945), the Ceboidea, Cercopithecoidea and Hominoidea. The Ceboidea comprise all the living New World primates, including the marmosets. The Cercopithecoidea include all the Old World monkeys and baboons. The Hominoidea include the gibbons and great apes (Pongidae), and man (Hominidae). Among the higher primates two main hand types occur, apart from that of the Callithricidae.

(i) An elongation of the palm and the digits, with or without a reduction in the thumb, resulting in a hook grip involving the fingers only, operating in unison, and employed in the arm-swinging or brachiating locomotion associated with this trend. Examples from the Ceboidea include *Ateles* and *Brachyteles* (spider monkeys), from the Cercopithecoidea the single example of *Colobus*, and from the Hominoidea, *Hylobates* (gibbons).

A precision grip is seen in some of these hands in which small objects are grasped between the adjacent surfaces of the second and third digits, by adduction of the fingers. This is not the case in *Hylobates*, which has a well-developed thumb and its own unique mechanism of opposition (Jouffroy and Lessertisseur, 1960), but it is seen in many ceboid genera, which may lack thumb opposition altogether.

(ii) A relatively short hand, with thumb opposition well developed by various mechanisms. This is combined with independence of the index finger from the other fingers in some cases, notably the baboons (*Papio*), which are terrestrial. This hand is associated with quadrupedal locomotion. *Pan* and *Gorilla* show quadrupedal locomotion a great deal more than any form of brachiation, walking on the knuckles of the flexed hand, i.e. on the dorsal surface of the middle phalanges of the fingers. *Pongo* does not show knuckle walking, but moves almost entirely by means of laborious and cautious suspension by all four limbs. Normal quadrupedal monkeys such as baboons rest the weight on the ventral surface of the digits (digitigrade), or the palm (plantigrade). Although this type of hand is typical of the Cercopithecoidea, a parallel development of manipulative ability and locomotor style is found in *Cebus*, alone among the Ceboidea with a record of tool-using (Hill, 1960).

The geographical location of the New World primates is indicative of an early separation from those of the Old World and the fact that New and Old World primates both show a functionally equivalent radiation of kinds of prehensile mechanism is an instance of the parallel differentiation of functionally similar apparatus.

These two hand types represent evolutionary trends which are not mutually exclusive. Although all the Hominoidea except man and *Gorilla* show elongation of the hand, and all except man show a greater or lesser degree of much modified brachiation, they have an opposable thumb and certainly great manipulative dexterity.* The trend to elongation of the hand and reduction of the thumb, however, has resulted in manipulative techniques which, while displaying the trend to individuation of the digits seen in higher primates, tend to reduce the importance of the thumb. Consequently the scissors-like grip in Ceboids is paralleled by a similar inter-digital grip in the orang-utan (Napier, 1960), though not in *Colobus*. Even where the thumb is capable of true opposition, as in all the great

---

* For discussion of locomotion in primates see Napier, 1963; Erikson, 1963.

apes, its shortness relative to the long fingers prevents pulp to pulp opposition. In this context the gibbons (*Hylobates*, *Symphalangus*) present another instance of a unique specialisation. Though true brachiators, they retain a long and fully opposable thumb. The rotation of the thumb in opposition occurs by means of a ball and socket carpo-metacarpal joint. This opposable thumb is not used in brachiating locomotion, but serves in grasping vertical branches and probably has a manipulative function in feeding and grooming.

With the exception of *Colobus* all the Cercopithecoidea possess a truly opposable thumb. Two kinds of fine hand control are found in this group. The first is the precision grip of the arboreal members of this superfamily, the thumb being flexed against the lateral (outer) side of the index finger or hand. The second is more typical of the terrestrial monkeys such as the baboons, which are able to control the second digit in conjunction with the thumb and independently of the other digits.

The Hominoidea possess the ability to control each of the digits separately and all have a truly opposable thumb, except the gibbons which achieve opposition with their unique ball and socket joint. There are clearly distinguishable power and precision grips The power grip is closely similar to that described for man. The precision grip involves the opposition of the thumb to the lateral surface of the index finger, as with some Cercopithecoidea. Sometimes small objects are caught up in the flexed digits two and three or between the phalanges by finger adduction. The absence of pulp-to-pulp thumb–index opposition is due to the long fingers and short thumb, relating to the partial brachiation of the group.

In summary, therefore, it appears that among the Prosimii and the New World Callithricidae, the hand is either very primitive and barely prehensile (Tupaiids, marmosets) or else quite distinctive group patterns of reaching and grasping have been evolved. These are stereotyped and show an emphasis on whole-arm and whole-hand control (lemurs, lorises, Tarsier). Among the Anthropoidea the use of grasps involving a greater degree of independence of the digits is found, allowing a greater variety of grips. This culminates in man and involves several patterns of thumb opposition and 'power/precision' grip divisions. The prosimian grips more often involve specialisation of structure used in fixed and stereotyped ways. Except for the Callithricidae, anthropoid grips display superior mobility due to facilitating structures and concomitant neural development. Thus in the Cercopithecoidea and Hominoidea the structural specialisation involved in true opposition of the thumb clearly facilitates their manipulative ability.

In her excellent paper on the use of the hand in lower primates, Bishop (1964) considers the factors that might have influenced the development of the fine control seen in higher primates. She suggests that grooming, as an important activity of primates, might operate a selective pressure for independent thumb mobility, as an aid to parting the hair, on the basis of observations of grooming in lemurs and lorises. It is also possible that variability in locomotor play may lead to variation in motor patterns.

The development of an enlarged brain operating a finely controlled set of at least partially independent, sensitive digits provides the necessary substrate for the highly developed motor skills exhibited by man. We might expect that in the higher primates and man evidence of this skill can be found in the developmental patterns of prehension and skilled hand use. The use of tools and certain of the complex artifacts found in human culture involve a great deal of learning, for example, playing the piano. Underlying the sensory-motor integration involved in piano playing there is in addition a gradually acquired facility of general hand use which is fundamental to almost all manual activity. The next section of this paper is concerned with the development of prehension and other aspects of hand use, which has been studied almost exclusively in man.

3. Ontogeny of hand use

Studies on the development of hand function in human infants are sparse, and in infra-human primates almost non-existent. Reports vary both in quality and in scope, and gaps in the literature will become evident to the reader.

Hooker (1938) described the earliest response of the human hand to stimulation as being incomplete finger closure, without any movements of the thumb, at $10\frac{1}{2}$ weeks' gestation. In response to stimulation (stroking the palm lightly with a hair), all four fingers move together, and there is a flexion of the hand. By about the twelfth week of gestation the thumb participates in this response, by moving across the palm of the hand (flexion). At 13 weeks there is greater flexion of digits 3, 4 and 5 than of 2. This crude prehensile pattern slowly wanes, but is usually still present in a weakened form by $18\frac{1}{2}$ weeks gestational age (Hooker, 1958).

Reflex mechanisms play some role in the development of voluntary behaviour in the human infant; prehension therefore is based on the reflex substrates which develop and change during the first months after birth. Twitchell (1965) investigating in greater detail the grasp reflex (as described by Prechtl and Beintema, 1964; and Beintema, 1968) has distinguished three kinds of automatic grasping response in infants during the first four months post-partum. The first of these, the *traction response,* a flexor synergy of the upper limb elicited by stretching the shoulder flexor and adductor muscles, occurs in neonates. The second, the *grasp reflex,* consisting of a flexion–adduction of the fingers, and elicited by a contact stimulus to the palm, emerges between 1 and 3 months of age. The third, the *instinctive grasp* reaction, is a complex exploratory and prehensile response, also elicited by a contact stimulus to the hand and developing between the fourth and tenth month. During the period when the traction response is dominant no ' voluntary ' prehension occurs at all, though an object placed in the infant's hand may be ' held ' momentarily. More effective prehension involving visually directed reaching for the first time, occurs after about four months in normal development, and is preceded by the maturation of the grasp reflex. At this stage the whole hand is involved in a ' palmar grasp ', even when the infant is trying to pick up small objects for which such a grasp is very inefficient. The precision grasp begins to emerge at about 8 months; true finger-thumb opposition occurs, giving rise to what Twitchell (1965) calls a ' pincer grasp '.

The problem of how the hand is projected into the visual field is discussed in a later paper by Twitchell (1970). Well-coordinated projections of the limb into space occur only following the development of the instinctive grasp reaction. Most studies on the development of prehension have emphasised the importance of visual guidance, but Twitchell's work shows that the appearance and integration of the grasping, and also the avoiding automatisms, are essential for the emergence of normal voluntary prehension. During development these avoiding and grasping reactions to a contact stimulus emerge in an overlapping fashion, and in an orderly sequence. In the early stages of visually directed reaching an object is approached from above and grasped only when the palm of the hand comes in contact with it. Following the emergence of the orientation phase of the instinctive grasp reaction, and the acquisition of individual reflex responses to contact on individual digits, the hand adapts to the object. The radial (lateral) aspect of the hand is directed at the object, and dexterity is improved.

The growth of visually directed reaching has been studied by a number of writers (Halverson, 1931; McGraw, 1943; Piaget, 1952; White, Castle and Held, 1964). Piaget, and White et al., concentrated their attention largely on the period between the first and fourth months, whereas Halverson's study commenced when the subjects were $4\frac{1}{2}$ months old and extended until the end of the first year. Halverson's investigations were concerned to produce a normative picture of the infant's voluntary manual ability, and were founded on the maturational theory of development formulated by Gesell (1929). The maturation hypothesis itself is open to a number of questions (Connolly, 1970). More recent research has investigated the importance and nature of the interaction with the environment in the development of voluntary motor control (Held and Hein, 1963; Connolly, 1969).

White, Castle and Held (1964) have described in detail the emergence of visually directed reaching. They give a ten-step analysis, culminating in visually directed reaching at around 5 months. At 1 or 2 months a stimulus moving in the periphery of vision will produce uncertain, jerky head pursuit movements. At about 2 months the infant, tested whilst lying in his cot, will swipe with a closed fist in response to an object about twelve inches away. Subsequent items of behaviour include bringing the hands to the mid-line and clasping them, and hand regard, slowly giving way to what White *et al.* call the top-level reach – a rapid and direct reach from out of the visual field, with anticipatory grasping. This behaviour is much less explosive and more controlled in character than that which preceded it, the wide open hand reaches slowly towards the object and upon contact grasps it. The object is then usually carried to the mouth. Bruner (1969), in discussing the role of vision in the ' sophisticated ' 7-month-old infant, points out that a reaching response is likely to be launched in response to a visual stimulus, but is executed without it, since the visual component of the act takes the form of fixating the object (the goal), and not the moving hand. (This assumes that visual stimulation from the periphery is of little importance.) On the basis of observations of cup use in infants, Bruner argues that the growth of skill occurs by a reduction in ' degrees of freedom ' following the development of ' programmes ': ' Where there is failure of reduction, then we see athetoid behaviour, disruption in crying, or immobilisation. With growth there are longer and more variable sequences of directed activity, involving a more complex integrative task.' ' Degrees of freedom ' may be affected by the range of variation in movements available to the child, or by the efficacy of central processing mechanisms, or by the perceptual capacities of the child. Thus the means suggested as available to the infant to reduce the degrees of freedom are many: a restriction of the movement of the joints, the use of the power rather than the precision grip in manipulating objects, the importance of midline position. Bruner (1969) also suggests that gaze aversion (abolishing visual information) is important as a means of reducing complexity in the interest of exercising a limited skill.

Halverson's (1931, 1932, 1937) detailed studies on the components and development of voluntary manual activity described both the reaching response and the prehensive grip. In the course of the observations the infants were in a sitting position, and the stimulus used was a one-inch cube placed at a specified distance in front of the subject. The movements were analysed from cine films.

Halverson's findings may be summarised as follows. At 16 weeks reaching, if present, is achieved by a very circuitous approach of the hand to the object, and this remains noticeable until 36–40 weeks, when the trend to a more direct approach is pronounced. Between 16 and 24 weeks hand movements described as incipient approaches were noted during cube regard, taking such forms as a raising of the hand or movements of the fingers. The circuitous approach favoured by the younger groups of subjects consisted of side to side movements of the forearm with a sufficient arm extension in the case of successful hand-cube apposition, and too little or too much in less successful cases. Until 36 weeks there persisted a declining tendency to place the hand behind the cube, drawing it towards the body by arm flexion. By 36 weeks the approach is much straighter (Fig. 13·6), and by 52 weeks it is almost perfectly straight. The straightening of the route of the hand to the cube is accomplished by the elimination of medial deviation prior to lateral deviation. Halverson suggests that this improves the visual control over reaching since medial deviation obscures the sight of the cube. However, Bruner's (1969) observation that the eyes are sometimes closed during reaching movements, and also observations made by Alt (cited in Bruner, 1969) that a screen to occlude the sight of the hand but not of the object does not impair reaching, suggest that the elimination of lateral deviation later in the developmental sequence may have an anatomical basis.

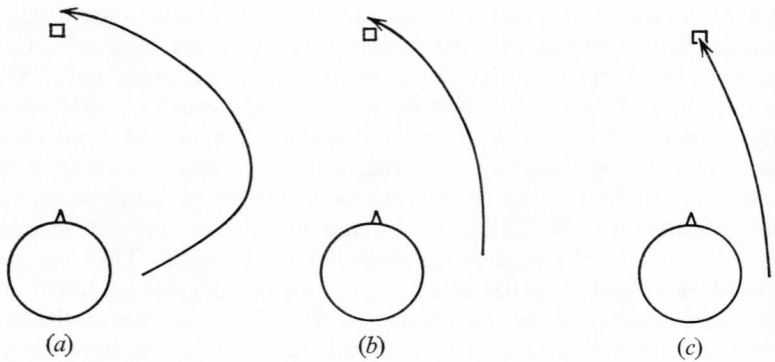

(a)   (b)   (c)

Fig. 13·6. Diagrammatic representation of progressive reduction in lateral deviation of hand of human infant reaching for a cube. (a) at 28 weeks, (b) at 36 weeks, (c) at 52 weeks. (After Halverson, 1943)

In addition to deviations in the horizontal there is deviation in the vertical which is also eliminated during the course of development. At 16 weeks Halverson found that there is a substantial upward and downward hand travel at the start and finish of the movement. These movements give the impression of being discrete sections organised successively. This vertical 'loop' movement is replaced in the majority of 24–28-week-old subjects by a slide along the table top. From 36–52 weeks a 'planing' response was observed, in which there was in effect no deviation, the hand planing out towards the cube in a long arc. By 40 weeks the impression of of a series of discrete acts is removed by the observation of a single fluent movement.

Halverson's findings on the hand configuration employed indicate that prior to 28 weeks the grip does not appear to involve thumb opposition at all in most subjects. The object is held in a power grip, a clamp of the flexed fingers into the palm. The thumb itself flexes, but not in opposition, thus apparently lacking independent abduction. Opposition appears around 28 weeks, and for the next 8 weeks it is most frequently found in association with a palmar (power) grip. From about 36 weeks onwards Halverson claims that finger-tip grasping is progressively the preferred method. It is important to remember, as Halverson himself observed, that different objects may somewhat affect the time sequence outlined. Thumb opposition is delayed, for example, in the case of a rod, which is not held in the fingers until about 36 weeks. The same grip is seen on the cube at 28 weeks. Our own incidental observations indicate that with smaller objects, such as a pellet, a flexing of the fingers in an attempt to drag it into the palm may still be seen around 40 weeks.

There is a trend in the development of grasping for the object to move distally and radially with respect to the palm; in the earlier stages, at around 12 weeks, the object is often in contact with the ulnar border of the hand (Fig. 13·7). This trend involves the progressive differentiation of the thumb and index finger in the grip, and a progressive use of the digits

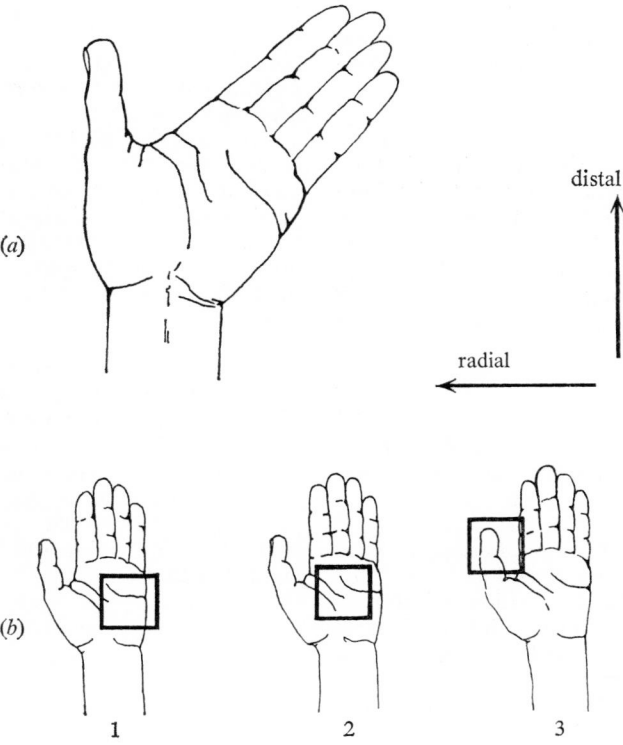

Fig. 13·7. (a) The human hand, showing ulnar deviation. (b) The position of a grasped cube relative to the palm, showing radial and distal shift in position with increasing age, 1, 12 weeks; 2, 24 weeks; 3, 36 weeks.

done without the involvement of the palm. The progressive use of the radial part of the hand goes together with an increased ulnar flexion of the wrist during reaching. This ulnar flexion is one of the indications that the hand is now responding in anticipation of its goal. Although no measure is given Halverson suggests that the degree of force employed in the grip declines with increasing age and use of the digits in grasping.

Unfortunately there has been little work on the development of prehension in the infra-human primates. Held and Bauer (1967) have shown that a rhesus monkey reared without the opportunity of seeing its hands during its first month does not then reach accurately for an object when its hand is first exposed. The young monkey reared under these conditions

TABLE 13·1. *Comparison of the development of prehension in Macaca nemestrina and man*

Infant *M. nemestrina* handling a raisin (after Jensen, 1961)	Human infant, handling a cube (after Halverson, 1931)
25–34 days. Inadequate reaching and abortive grasping with one hand. Definite visual regard of raisin.	*ca.* 16th week. Inadequate reaching or 'incipient reaching' hand movement. Lateral movements of forearm. Definite regard of cube.
34–36 days. Radial aspect of hand brought into contact with object by means of raking movement with forelimb starting beyond the raisin, the hand is brought back towards the animal by limb flexion. The raisin is scraped along, all fingers flexing around the object in an inefficient grasp.	20–24 weeks. The hand is brought behind the cube by means of an awkward arm movement involving vertical and lateral displacement of the hand. The cube is scraped back by arm flexion. If grasped, it is by all digits flexing, without thumb opposition.
	24–32 weeks. Progressive emphasis on the use of the radial aspect of the hand. Some thumb opposition.
36–46 days. Digits 2 and 3 flexed over raisin. Thumb adducts to meet them.	34–60 weeks. Continuing shift to the use of the radial aspect of hand. The 2nd and 3rd digits, or the 2nd alone, are employed now, with true opposition, ultimately giving a precision grip similar to that of adults.
46–51 days. Thumb adducted to meet 2nd digit, with opposition.	
51–185 days. Opposition of thumb, first to the distal interphalangeal junction of the 2nd digit *then* to the tip of the index.	
N.B. The mother showed a preference for opposition to the interphalangeal joint. This is likely to be more compatible with the thumb–index ratio for this species.	

fixes its gaze upon its hand as it enters the visual field, and watches it in a manner reminiscent of the early period of reaching in human infants (Piaget, 1952; White, Castle and Held, 1964). Accurate visual guidance of reaching and grasping is gradually achieved in the course of the next few days. Held and Bauer suggest that visually guided reaching requires an integration of the visuo-motor control of head movement and the non-visual control of limb movement, and that such integration requires the viewing of the moving hand.

Jensen (1961) has reported observations on the development of hand usage in an infant pigtailed macaque (*Macaca nemestrina*). He recorded the behaviour of the animal in response to raisins placed before it every few days from 25 to 185 days of age. Allowance having been made for the disparity in time scales, there is a remarkable similarity in the sequence of prehensive grip development shown by human and monkey infants. A detailed comparison is shown in Table 13·1. The anatomical difference between the hands of man and the hands of the monkey may account for some of the differences. Man's thumb is approximately two-thirds the length of the index finger, whereas the monkey's thumb is only about half the length.* The thumb is opposed to the distal part of the index finger in the first stage of opposition in the monkey. In the human infant thumb–finger opposition is pulp-to-pulp as soon as it occurs. The long index finger of the macaque may be curled around a small object, and this may be effectively used for grasping small objects. It is a pity that the single macaque in question appears to be the only non-human individual on which observations of this sort have been carried out.

Outside the context of developmental diagnosis by the establishment of developmental norms (Gesell and Amatruda, 1947) little work has been done on the ontogeny of hand usage in man. Moreover, as indicated in the foregoing review, the main components of smooth, accurate prehension are regarded as well established. The use of the hand, however, is not confined to the prehension of encountered objects, for the use of tools involves the grasping of objects for some further purpose. Tools in fact, are functional objects, as implied in the term ' implement '. This aspect of hand function, though not the subject of any of the studies so far mentioned, clearly requires skills other than those involved in casual prehension, as will be apparent to anyone who observes a 3-year-old with a spoon.

A battery of tests for assessing children's hand function in a clinical context has been developed by Holt (1965). These tests form part of a larger assessment procedure designed for work with cerebral palsied children, and whilst they provide means of estimating the degree of deficit in hand function suffered by these children, they do not tell us very much

* Thumb–finger ratios are from adults of both species. Anatomical data from a representative sample of infants is not available (Napier and Napier, 1967).

about the development of normal hand usage. Work has been done on children's painting and drawing, but this has concentrated on indexing the intellectual development of the child through the study of his representational ability (Bühler, 1933; Eng, 1954). Such work has therefore dealt with the content of the picture, and has hardly been concerned at all with the means of its production. Other studies have dealt with copying ability. Some of these have also been concerned with ascertaining the level of intellectual ability (Goodenough, 1926), others with the development of visual–motor or cognitive abilities (Townsend, 1951; Piaget and Inhelder, 1956; Vereecken, 1961; Birch and Lefford, 1963, 1967; Connolly, 1968). Very few of these studies have been in any way concerned with the details of what the child is doing while carrying out its task, either in the way of describing the motor activity, or analysing the finished drawing into its component lines. Gesell and Ames (1946), Rice (1930) and Abercrombie, Lindon and Tyson (1968) have carried out experiments and made observations on the direction in which lines of various orientations are drawn by normal, and in the latter case brain-injured children. In almost all studies of copying, geometrical figures have been used. Kellogg (1955) has analysed the structural components of a vast number of unsolicited drawings, and this appears to be the only study of its kind which has not involved constraining the children in certain ways.

The remaining portion of this chapter reports aspects of hand function as revealed in the use of the paint brush as a tool, data being collected under conditions which imposed no constraints on the children, in an effort to gain information on the development of tool-using ability in a period later in life than the first 18 months.

4. The use of a tool by pre-school children

Halverson's (1943) conclusion, that the most significant development in the mechanism of prehension occurred in the course of the first year, is legitimate to the extent that he found the 60-week-old infant capable of grasping an object with almost the delicacy and digital configuration of the adult. Napier (1956) has shown that in the adult the use made of tools dictated which of the grip complexes, power or precision, was to be used; and that the shape of the tool was less relevant in determining the grip. Since Halverson's work was restricted to observations on the reaching for and examination of objects no conclusions may be drawn, on the basis of these observations, about the development of hand usage in other situations.

The purpose of the study described below was to examine the ways in which young children used a tool in performing a skilled task when no constraints were imposed on them by the observer. The primary interest was in the prehensive pattern adopted by the children but other parameters important in the skilled activity were also recorded and analysed. Most of the studies on the development of skill in children have been of an experimental nature inasmuch as the investigator has manipulated certain variables (Connolly, 1968). Such studies restrict the possible range of responses shown by the child because they can often only be carried out in a particular manner. Our aim, therefore, was to impose the minimum restriction on the child and in no way to interfere with or direct his behaviour. Bearing in mind the basic purpose of the study, certain practical requirements had to be met. The activity on which the child engaged had to be one which allowed of accurate observation without any interference from the observer directly or via recording equipment such as a cine camera or video tape recorder. It had also to be an activity which the children willingly and frequently engaged in, to permit the collection of an adequate amount of data. Painting is thus a convenient activity by which to study hand usage. The subjects are motivated and may be observed for periods of up to ten minutes at a stretch. Whilst painting, the child remains in one location; the observer therefore does not have to move around in order to make his observations. In addition, a permanent record is left behind.

The present study investigated unrestricted painting, and specifically excluded from consideration all representational paintings. This was done to avoid the influence of content on the orientation of lines in the picture, since orientation of line was one of the measures taken. However, it is impossible to assume that a young child's pictures can be sorted reliably into content and non-content categories. A rule of thumb was adopted, that if no recognisable thing was seen to be depicted, then the data from that painting were included. The child's intentions could not be ascertained in order to aid this decision. A question to a child almost inevitably carries the implication that the picture in question is intended to represent something, and *post hoc* naming of content might occur.* Inquiry in advance has similar hazards. No rule of thumb, therefore, was adopted to eliminate obviously representational material.

Methods

SUBJECTS

Forty-nine nursery school children, twenty-three boys and twenty-six girls, made up the sample. The median age of the children was 4 years, and the age range 2 years 10 months to 4 years 10 months (Fig. 13·8). Forty-three

---

* This is the subject of a disagreement between Eng (1954) and Bühler (1933). Bühler believes that children imitate adults in naming their paintings, but that the pictures were not constructed to symbolise the object they are said to represent. Eng believes the pictures actually stand for what they are stated to represent.

of the children attended a single school, the catchment area of which was a single block of municipal flats. These children were therefore drawn from a very homogeneous socio-economic background. The remaining children who made up the sample were from another nursery school. The children in this second school came from a much greater diversity of home background. Since upon observation there were no apparent differences between the two sub-groups the material from the two was pooled for analysis.

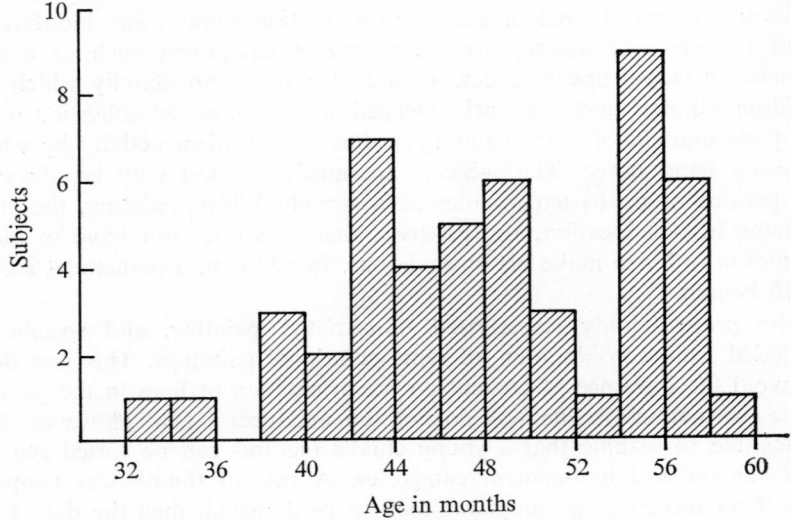

Fig. 13·8. Distribution of subjects by age in sample.

PROCEDURE

The children painted on paper clipped to a near vertical easel (Fig. 13·9). Each easel accommodated two children on opposite faces and was permanently available for two children to use between certain hours every day. The observer assumed a position approximately 5 feet behind the subject and to the side of the dominant hand. Teachers frequently suggested painting to children in the classroom, but never obliged them to paint, nor were they encouraged to attempt representational painting.

The pots of paint were located on a tray fixed to the easel at the foot of the paper, except in the case of the six children from the second nursery. For these children the paint pots stood on a table placed to one side of the easel. All six of these subjects showed a marked hand preference (98% of each subject's actions were right-handed) when per cent right- and left-handed acts were calculated, despite the fact that the paint pots could be on either side of the subject. It was concluded therefore that choice of right or left hand was not materially affected by the location of the paint pots to one side or the other.

Each subject was observed on a minimum of four separate occasions, and for each painting up to twenty-five successive observations were made. A minimum of a hundred observations per subject was required. Ideally a set of twenty-five observations per day for four days would have been collected. This was not possible because the subjects were not painting to order, and the time and duration of the painting sessions were therefore entirely unpredictable.

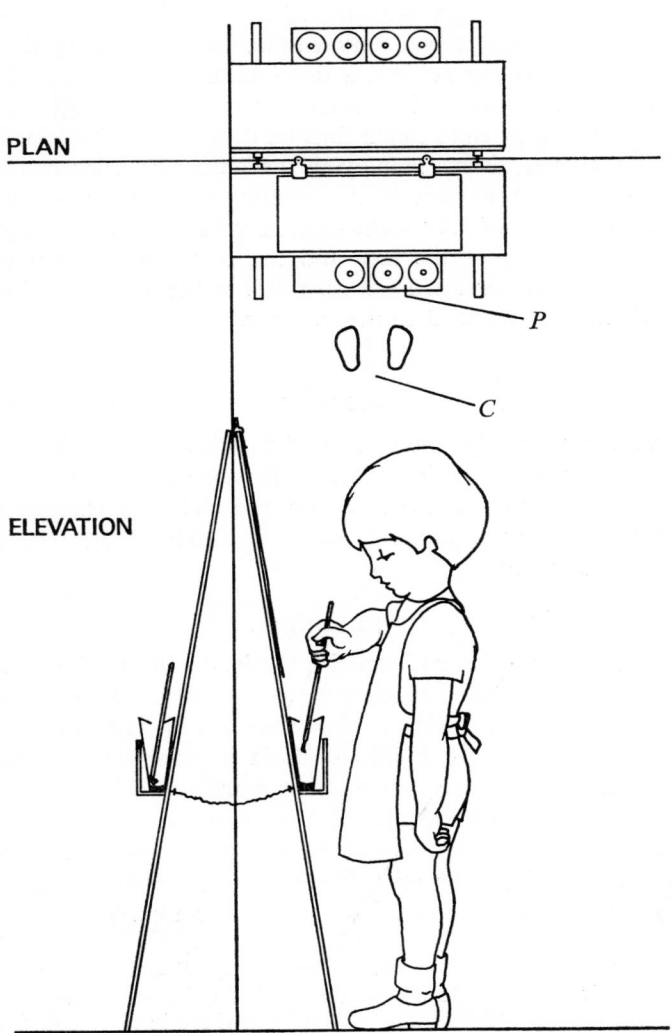

Fig. 13·9. Plan and elevation of easel, *P* paint pots, *C* position of child.

351

On the basis of a large number of preliminary observations, four para-meters or categories of observation were selected for careful study in the investigation. These were:

1. Hand employed to hold the paint brush
2. Grip employed to hold the brush
3. Movement of the arm and body
4. The stroke produced on paper.

The various responses described within each parameter are mutually exclusive. Each observation thus recorded four simultaneous events, or responses,* one in each response dimension. On the basis of the hundred or more observations per subject, a distribution of responses within each dimension could be calculated as percentages, totalling 100% within each response dimension. A child might thus be described as 80% right-handed (parameter 1 above) always employing the adult grip (parameter 2), and so on. These four parameters of the painting activity are not exhaustive. The vigour and speed of movement vary, as does the size of line produced. Associated movements of the face and the contralateral limb were seen from time to time. Observation was restricted to the four defined categories to avoid information overload on the observer.

Results

The results of the investigation consist of the classification and description of the various prehensive grips, types of movement, etc., and quantitative data relating to their frequency of occurrence and their changes with age. The results are reported under a series of sub-headings related to the response dimensions studied.

HANDEDNESS

Several paint brushes of a uniform size (12 in. × ½ in. maximum diameter) were available to each child along with two or more pots of paint. There are basically four possibilities; the child may use his right or left hand, or grasp the brush with both hands, or hold a brush in each hand. For quantitative purposes, three observations were recognised, namely right hand, left hand, and both hands. The latter category included both the independent use of two brushes at once and the two-handed use of a single brush. Summing over all subjects, the frequency in the sample of each of the three observations is shown in Table 13·2. There is a marked

---

* The term ' response ' does not here carry the implication of a response to a stimulus. It is used only to define the smallest units of behaviour described. The use of the term ' behaviour ' as used elsewhere in this book, involves an aggregate of smaller units. The level of analysis employed in this study made the use of a different label for units advisable.

tendency to use only one hand at a time, usually the right. Table 13·3 shows the distribution of the preferred response. This gives the distribution of right-handed, left-handed and ‘ both-handed ’ (*not* ambidextrous) children in the sample based on the most frequently occurring response for each

TABLE 13·2. *Frequency of occurrence of right, left and both hand responses in the sample. The column on the right gives % frequency when both hands responses are excluded*

Hand	Frequency	(%)
Right	83.9	88.2
Left	11.2	11.8
Both	4.9	

child. Considering one-handed responses only, there is a marked tendency in favour of right-handedness, only 10% (5/49) of the population exhibiting a >50% preference for using the left hand. Considering one-handed and both-handed responses, few children show a both-hand response on more than 10% of occasions. The distribution of both-handed responses is independent of the distribution of right- and left-handed responses.

TABLE 13·3. *Distribution of subjects' modal responses with respect to hand preference*

Hand used	Subjects showing it as modal response
Right	42
Left	5
Both	2

Ambidextrous children can be defined as making less than 80% of their one-handed reponses with a particular hand. There are four such children. They cannot be thought of as representing a stable subset of the sample because there is a trend in the data for hand preference to become increasingly pronounced with age. Of the subjects whose responses were either all right- or all left-handed, the proportion occurring in the older half of the population is much greater than in the younger half (χ^2 $p<0.01$). Older children thus show more pronounced preferences for a particular hand. This trend has been widely reported in children of this age group (Hildreth, 1949).

PREHENSIVE GRIP PATTERNS

Grips and grasps may be described and classified in terms of the power and precision grip complexes defined by Napier (1956). Within the sample studied, a number of distinct grips were shown by the children in using a paint brush. These were defined by the anatomical configuration of the hand. Each grip was described in terms of four dimensions.

1. Grips may involve holding the brush in the palm of the hand, when the grip may be described as palmar; or the digits only may be involved. when the grip is digital (see Halverson, 1943).

2. Grips may or may not involve opposition of the thumb, the term opposition being used here in the manner defined by Napier (1961), and thus involving medial rotation of the thumb at the carpo-metacarpal joint, together with flexion and abduction (Fig. 13·3). Flexion alone does not qualify as opposing the thumb.

3. The digits in a grasp may be tightly clenched or only loosely flexed, the dividing point is not exact. Functionally, clenched digits lack mobility, unlike in light flexion. If the degree of flexion appears to preclude independent finger movement, then the term clenched is applied.

4. The orientation of the brush to the hand varies from grip to grip and carries with it certain minor changes in the anatomy of the hand in most cases. The brush may project medially (Fig. 13·12), laterally (Fig. 13·12) or distally (Fig. 13·10) in the plane of the hand, or ventrally, being perpendicular to the hand palm (Fig. 13·11).

Details of the different prehensive patterns actually observed are given below, and the grip is described as being a power or precision one according to Napier's definition. A power grasp involves a clamping action of the

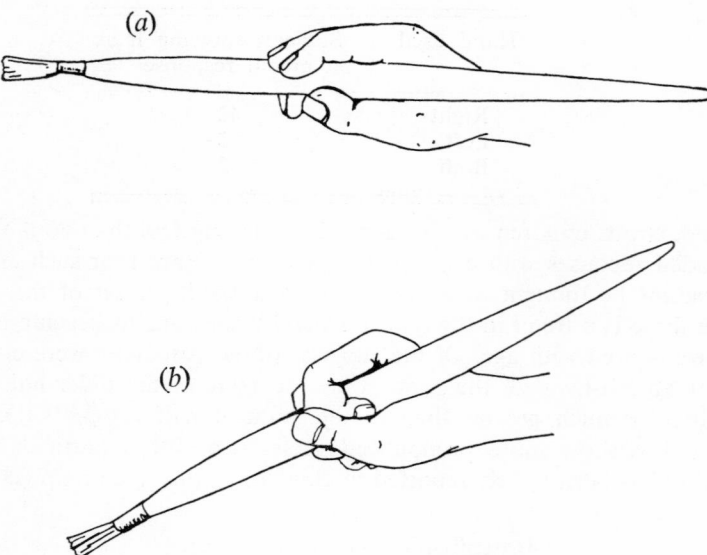

(a)

(b)

Fig. 13·10. Grip configuration observed (a) adult,
(b) adult clenched. See text for details.

fingers into the palm without thumb opposition. A precision grip involves opposition of the thumb, and a spreading (abduction) of the fingers.

Adult grip

This is a precision grip. The handle of the brush lies dorsally on or near the metacarpus of the thumb, passing distally between the thumb and index finger. Occasionally the brush may pass between the index finger and the third digit (Fig. 13·10).

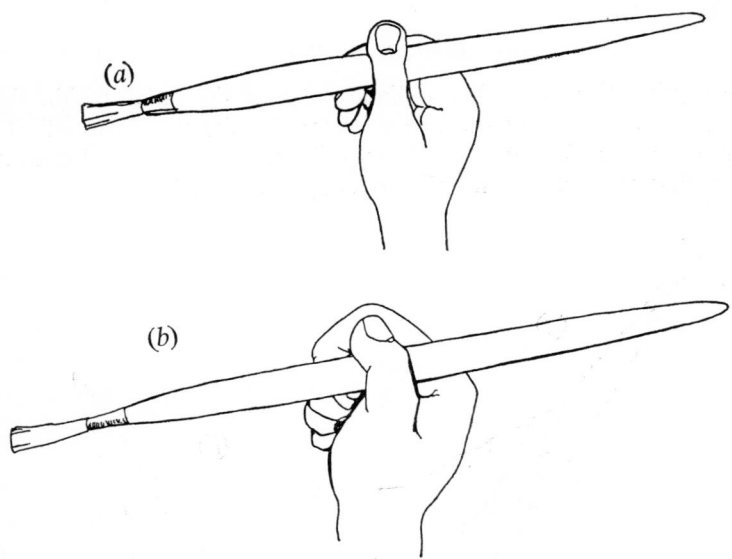

Fig. 13·11. Grip configurations observed (*a*) ventral, (*b*) ventral clenched. See text for details.

Adult clenched

This is a power grip. The brush passes between the flexed thumb and index finger. A certain degree of thumb opposition may be present, but this is difficult to judge. The brush may also pass between the index finger and the third digit or between the third and fourth digits; in such cases the thumb may be tucked into the fist (Fig. 13·10).

Ventral

This also is a power grip. The rotation of the brush to point ventrally brings it to lie between the ball of the flexed thumb and the lateral surface of the middle finger. The index is more flexed than is usual in the adult grip and the thumb is not opposed; in other respects these two grip patterns are similar (Fig. 13·11).

Ventral clenched

Again a power grip. The ventral orientation of the brush prevents it from passing between thumb and index finger and then between the index finger and the third digit. It is thus always seen between thumb and index when the hand configuration closely resembles certain forms of the adult clenched grip (Fig. 13·11).

Oblique palmar

A power grip. The brush lies obliquely across the palm within the fist and projects with the bristles directed laterally; the thumb usually lies in the axis of the brush and on it. It may lie ventral to it, flexing onto the lateral surface of the index. It is thus not opposed (Fig. 13·12).

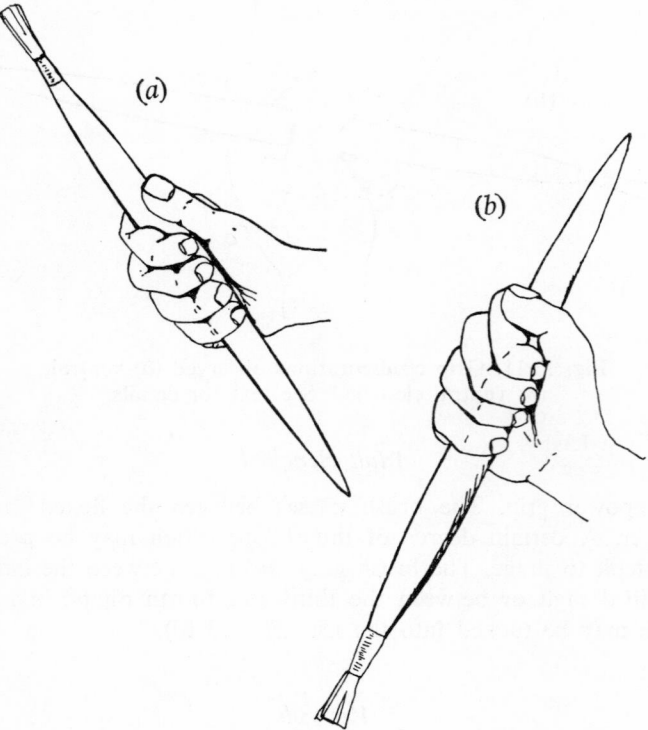

Fig. 13·12. Grip configurations observed (a) oblique palmar, (b) transverse palmar. See text for details.

Transverse palmar

A power grip. The brush runs straight through the fist at right angles to the fingers and projects with the bristles directed medially. The thumb may be opposed onto the clenched fingers (Fig. 13·12).

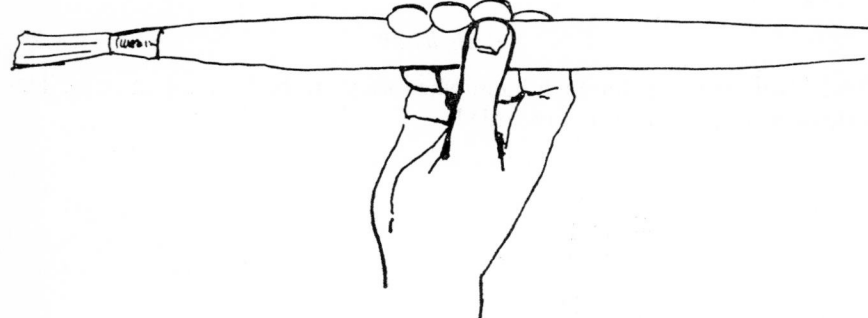

Fig. 13·13. Transverse digital grip. See text for details.

TABLE 13·4. *Frequency of occurrence of various grips in sample, two-handed grip having been excluded*

Grip	Frequency (%)
Adult	
Digital, thumb opposed, digits extended not clenched, brush pointing distally	74.8
Adult clenched	
Digital, thumb not opposed, digits clenched, brush pointing distally	6.1
Ventral	
Digital, thumb not opposed, digits extended, brush pointing ventrally	4.2
Ventral clenched	
Digital, thumb not opposed, digits clenched, brush pointing ventrally	1.7
Oblique palmar	
Palmar, thumb not opposed, digits clenched, brush points laterally and distally	6.9
Transverse palmar	
Palmar, thumb not opposed, digits clenched, brush pointing medially	6.2
Transverse digital	
Digital, thumb opposed, digits extended, brush pointing medially	0.1

Transverse digital

This is a precision grip. The brush lies across the finger tips and is held there by the opposed thumb. This grip was observed very rarely; it shows with particular clarity the digital-palmar and opposed–non-opposed distinctions when contrasted with the transverse palmar grip (Fig. 13·13).

Both hands

This involves a grip for each hand when they are both in use at once. The details of the grips were not recorded.

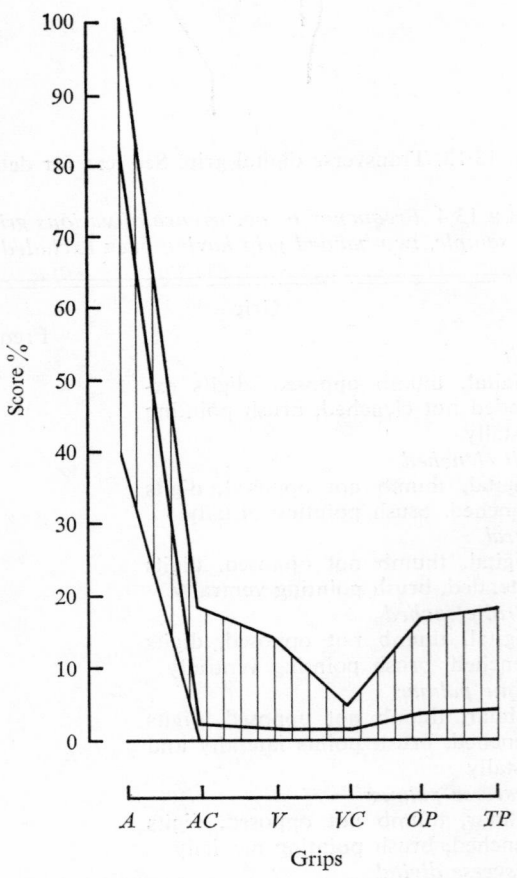

Fig. 13·14. Median and 80% limits for scores on each grip (*A*, adult; *AC*, adult clenched; *V*, ventral; *VC*, ventral clenched; *OP*, oblique palmar; *TP*, transverse palmar).

Both hand responses occur with a frequency of 4.9% in the sample. Table 13·4 summarises the various grips described and shows their frequency of occurrence when ' both hand ' responses are excluded. The adult grip is by far the most common accounting for 74.8% of all the prehensive patterns observed. Although the variability of grip scores is considerable, the broad trends are consistent across almost all the children. The mean frequency of each grip response for all subjects is shown in Fig. 13·14.

MOVEMENTS

The movements observed were divided into five classes on the basis of the most proximal joint involved in the movement, beginning with body joints and going distally to the wrist. Anatomical and kinaesiological terminology is based on Wells (1966).

Body movements

Movements in which the brush stroke is produced as a result of movements of the trunk. The trunk may be rotated at the hips, or moved sideways in the frontal plane (lateral flexion), in which case horizontal brush strokes result. Flexion of the trunk in the saggital plane was also seen and this results in vertical strokes. The body movements were not differentiated into these various types in the data collected.

Movements of the shoulder

(a) Arm circumduction. Whether flexed or not, the whole arm performs a circular movement as a result of a more or less smooth succession of flexion, abduction, extension and adduction at the shoulder.

(b) Extended arm movement. Movements of the fully extended arm in one single direction as a result of shoulder control.

(c) Lateral arm sweep. Rotation of the upper arm with a degree of tonic elbow flexion, so that the forearm moves in a plane about the axis of the upper arm. Some adduction and abduction of the upper arm may occur.

Shoulder and elbow joint movements

(a) Vertical arm sweep. Flexion and extension of the upper arm at the shoulder, with simultaneous extension and flexion at the elbow. The hand travels in the plane of elbow flexion.

(b) Vertical and lateral arm sweep. A compound movement in which the movements of the vertical arm sweep occur, plus a rotation of the upper arm, or a degree of abduction and adduction of the upper arm, such that the hand travels at an oblique angle to the plane of elbow flexion.

Elbow joint movements

(a) Forearm stab. Extension and flexion at the elbow only. No wrist movement is usual in this pattern. This form of movement almost always results in dots rather than lines, except when the child orients to face along the easel so that the hand moves almost in the plane of the paper.

Wrist joint movements

(a) Forearm and wrist. To a movement of the forearm (for example a vertical arm sweep) is added pronounced flexion and extension of the wrist; this is added at the end of the forearm stroke and greatly lengthens and emphasises it. This is a very striking motor pattern.

(b) Wrist movements. Other movements of the hand due primarily to the wrist joint. The wrist is an extremely versatile joint and it is not in practice easy to break down observed movement into flexion, extension, circumduction, etc.

Summed over all subjects, the frequency of occurrence of the different classes of movements is shown in Table 13·5. Movements at the shoulder and elbow joints account for a little over half of all the movements observed, 52.1%. Of the shoulder joint movements the lateral arm sweep itself accounts for 18.9% of all movements. Together the vertical arm sweep, vertical and lateral arm sweep and the lateral arm sweep account

TABLE 13·5. *Frequency of occurrence of movement responses in the sample*

Movements	Frequency	(%)
Body movements		2.4
Shoulder joint movements		28.5
Arm circumduction	6.6	
Extended arm movement	3.0	
Lateral arm sweep	18.9	
Shoulder and elbow joint movements		52.1
Vertical arm sweep	26.6	
Vertical and lateral arm sweep	25.5	
Elbow joint movements		2.2
Forearm stab	2.2	
Wrist joint movements		14.8
Forearm and wrist	2.4	
Wrist movements	12.4	

for 71% of all movements. The vertical and lateral arm sweep, as the name implies, comprises elements from the other two.

Wrist movements, which are the next most frequent movements (accounting for 12.4% of all movements) are essential for delicate or deliberate work; the hand itself is the predominant moving part. The data, however, do not show any significant trend towards a greater use of wrist movements with increasing age. As with grips, there is a consistency in movement frequencies across children as shown in Fig. 13·15.

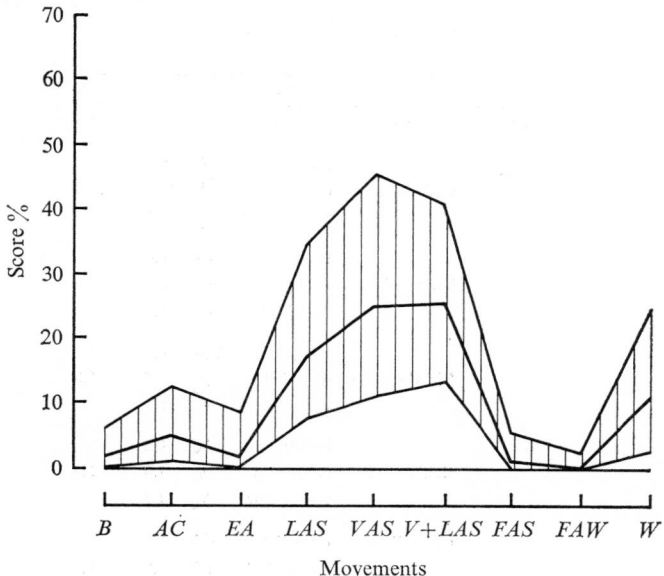

Movements

Fig. 13·15. Median and 80% limits for scores on each movement (*B*, body; *AC*, arm circumduction; *EA*, extended arm; *LAS*, lateral arm sweep; *VAS*, vertical arm sweep; *V+LAS*, vertical and lateral arm sweep; *FAS*, forearm sweep; *FAW*, forearm and wrist; *W*, wrist).

THE PRODUCTION OF STROKES AND DOTS

Painting with a brush involves the production of lines or dots. The data collected included the orientation (to within 45°) of straight lines and the direction of production for both straight and curved lines. Dots of course lack orientation and direction. The strokes may be one-directional, i.e. from one end of the line to the other, or two-directional, the line being produced by a to-and-fro movement in both directions. The criterion adopted to determine a two-directional painting of a line was whether or not the brush left the paper between movements. To-and-fro repetitive movements or scribble were common, and on this basis readily distinguishable. Oblique lines were classified as ' right obliques ' (/) or ' left obliques ' (\ ), depending on which end of the oblique was higher on the paper.

Table 13·6 shows the frequency in the sample of lines and dots in the various orientations and directions. The most frequent orientation of the straight lines was the vertical (50.9% of all responses). Vertical and horizontal lines together made up 73.4% of all strokes or 88.4% of all straight lines produced. There were three times the number of right obliques as left obliques, but obliques accounted for only 11.5% of straight lines or 9.5% of all strokes.

TABLE 13·6. *Frequency of occurrence of the various strokes (direction and orientation) in the sample*

Stroke	Orientation	Direction		(%)	(%)
Dots (9.7%)	—	—			9.7
Lines (90.3%)		up	↑	2.9	
	vertical	down	↓	19.4	50.9
		up and down	↕	28.6	
		to right	→	4.6	
	horizontal	to left	←	2.8	22.5
		to and fro	↔	15.1	
		up right	↗	0.6	
	'right' oblique	down left	↙	1.4	7.3
		up and down	⤢	5.3	
		up left	↖	0.2	
	'left' oblique	down right	↘	1.0	2.2
		up and down	⤡	1.0	
	curved lines	clockwise	↻	2.6	
		anti-clockwise	↺	4.8	7.4
100.0					100.0

Excepting in the case of left obliques and curves there is a strong tendency to use a to-and-fro movement. Strokes which rise relative to the horizontal were less common than those which fall. To some extent, however, this may be an artifact since the paper tends to ride up on an upwards stroke, because it is secured only at the top of the easel. Strokes travelling to the right (dextrad) rather than to the left (sinistrad) were found to occur more frequently.

An examination of the data from individual subjects shows that the response preferences broadly parallel the response frequencies in the sample as a whole with a fair degree of reliability (Fig. 13·16). Individual differences, however, were observed. For forty-six of the subjects the modal response was found to be a vertical line, whilst for three of them it was a horizontal line. Considering oblique lines forty out of forty-eight subjects produced more right obliques (/) than left obliques (\).

Left-handed subjects' preferences for direction of drawing lines in the various orientations were contrasted with preferences for right-handers (Table 13·7). Fisher's exact probability test was used and it was found that:

(i) Left-handers tend to draw right oblique lines with an up- or with a down-going stroke, whereas right-handers tend to draw them with an up-and-down stroke ($p=0.03$).

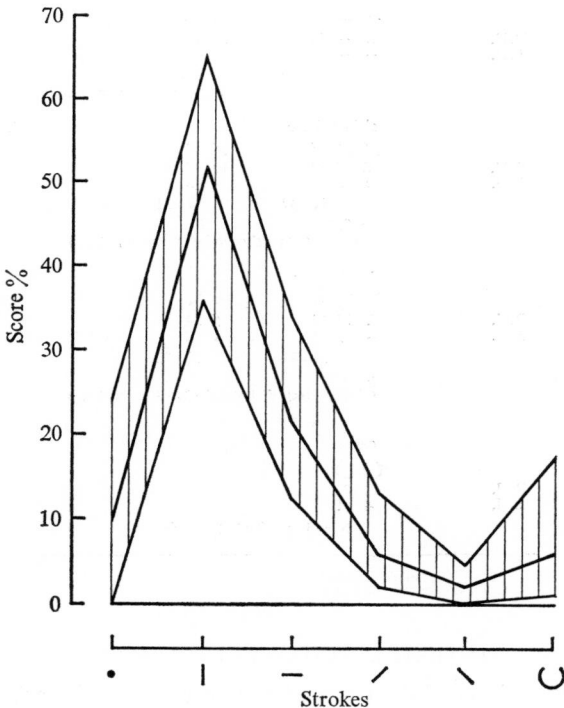

Fig. 13·16. Median and 80% limits for scores on each stroke.

(ii) Left-handers tend to draw left oblique lines with an up-and-down stroke, right-handers using up- or down-going strokes ($p=0.08$). Right- and left-handers thus show opposite trends on the two obliques.

(iii) Left-handers tend to draw horizontal lines sinistrad, right-handers to draw them dextrad ($p=0.01$), and

(iv) Left-handers tend to draw curved lines clockwise, right-handers to draw them anticlockwise ($p=0.07$). To-and-fro strokes were not seen in the drawing of curved lines.

TABLE 13·7. *Comparing right- and left-handed subjects' directional preferences in drawing various orientations of line*

(*Matrices in the right-hand column of the table were calculated after to-and-fro responses had been excluded*)

Subjects	Modal directional response for lines of various orientations			
	vertical			
	↑ ↓ ↕		↑ ↓	
R.H.	− 16 28		− 44	
L.H.	− 2 3		− 5	
	N=49		N=49	
	horizontal			
	→ ← ↔		→ ←	
R.H.	2 − 42		30 13	
L.H.	− − 5		− 5	
	N=49		N=48	
			p=0.01 (Fisher's test)	
	right oblique			
	↗ ↙ ↗↙		↗ ↙	
R.H.	2 7 33		10 17	
L.H.	1 3 1		1 3	
	N=47		N=31	
	p=0.03			
	(Fisher's test: dichotomise ↗↙ versus ↗ + ↙)			
	left oblique			
	↖ ↘ ↖↘		↖ ↘	
R.H.	2 23 10		5 24	
L.H.	− 1 4		1 2	
	N=40		N=32	
	p=0.08			
	(Fisher's test: dichotomise ↘ versus ↖ + ↘)			
	curves			
	⋃ ⋂			
R.H.	11 29			
L.H.	4 1			
	N=45 p=0.07 (Fisher's test)			

INTER-CATEGORY RELATIONS

The analysis by subjects of their modal response within the *grip, movement* and *stroke* categories is shown in Table 13·8. It is clear that few subjects show unusual modal response within any particular category, although there is a considerable range of individual variation on the various responses (Figs. 13·14, 13·15 and 13·16).

Within the *movement* category, subjects tend to score similarly, and highly, on both vertical, and vertical and lateral arm sweeps. These two movements contain common elements, and they were therefore combined, and the distribution of subjects' modal responses recalculated as follows:

vertical plus vertical and lateral arm sweeps – 45 subjects

lateral arm sweeps – 3 subjects

forearm and wrist – 1 subject.

TABLE 13·8. *Distribution of subjects' modal responses within the grip, movement and stroke response categories*

Response	Subjects showing it as modal response
Grips	
Adult	44
Oblique palmar	3
Transverse palmar	1
Ventral	1
Movement	
Vertical and lateral arm sweep	19
Vertical arm sweep	18
Lateral arm sweep	7
Wrist movements	2
Forearm and wrist	2
Arm circumduction	1
Stroke	
Vertical lines	46
Horizontal lines	3

χ^2 measures of association applied to subjects' (vertical plus vertical and lateral) arm sweep scores, their adult grip scores and their horizontal and vertical stroke scores, revealed the following results:

(i) Subjects above the median in adult grip scores tend to fall below the median on (vertical plus vertical and lateral) arm sweep scores ($p < 0.05$). There is a non-significant tendency for them to have lateral arm sweep scores above the median.

(ii) There is no significant association between subjects' scores on adult grip, and either horizontal or vertical strokes, although high scores on either of these strokes tend to be found in individuals with high adult grip scores.

(iii) Subjects scoring highly on lateral arm sweeps also tend to score highly on horizontal strokes ($p < 0.02$) but no other significant association between strokes and movements tested was found.

The subjects with unusual modal preferences were examined further and it was found that different subjects were involved in the different categories. That is, subjects whose modal response was unusual in a particular category had the usual modal response in the other two. Consequently it is not possible to say, with a sample of only forty-nine subjects, whether there were sub-groups of subjects differing consistently across more than one category of observation.

AGE EFFECTS

The distribution of age through the sample is shown in Fig. 13·8. The age of each child was taken as the mean of his ages on the various dates on which data was collected. In order to investigate age effects the sample was dichotomised into a young (below the median) and an old (above the median) age group. Relating age to the principal dimensions investigated the following findings emerged:

1. The exclusive (100%) use of one hand, either the right or the left, was more frequent in the older group ($p<0.01$, χ^2).

2. The older children drew more horizontal lines than did the younger children; there was no evidence of any age related effect in the case of the vertical lines ($p<0.02$, χ^2).

3. The use of the adult grasp was greater in the older group ($p<0.02$, χ^2). Since the adult grasp was almost the only precision grip observed in the sample, it is clear that the precision grip becomes more evident with increasing age. If the ventral grip is classed as a precision grip * then the age effect is more pronounced ($p<0.001$, χ^2).

4. There are no age-dependent trends in the movement category.

SUMMARY OF RESULTS

The findings from the study are summarised under the different dimensions of response.

Handedness

(*a*) 92% of the children made more than 80% of their responses with the right hand or with the left hand, 8% were thus ambidextrous.

(*b*) By the criterion $(R-L)/(R+L)$ is a positive number, 91% of the subjects were right-handed, 9% left-handed in the particular situation observed (Durost, 1934).

(*c*) The preference for a particular hand increases with age.

(*d*) Some subjects occasionally employ both hands simultaneously on one or more brushes.

Grips

(*a*) Seven distinct types of grip were described.

(*b*) The commonest grip pattern involved true opposition of the thumb, and only moderate finger flexion, allowing relative mobility of the finger.

(*c*) The incidence of this grip pattern increases with age.

Movement

(*a*) Nine movement patterns of the hand and arm were described and classified according to the joint proximally involved.

---

* The ventral grip may be regarded as either power or precision, see discussion. It is regarded here as a precision grip because it permits finger movements in controlling the thumb.

Discussion

Laterality and hand preference have been the subject of many investigations. Darwin, in reporting observations on one of his own infants, wrote in 1877, ' When 77 days old, he took the sucking bottle (with which he was partly fed) in his right hand, whether he was held on the left or right arm of his nurse, and he would not take it in his left hand until a week later although I tried to make him do so ' (1877: 286–7). The infant subsequently proved to be left-handed and Darwin says that this was no doubt inherited.

Gesell and Ames (1947) found evidence of a clear-cut dominance by the end of the second year, the majority of their sample being right-handed and most of the remainder being left-handed. Tests which place a premium on precision of movements, rather than on frequency irrespective of the activity, may be most revealing for the early detection of handedness. The nature of the activity in question must be considered in evaluating claims such as those made by Gesell and Ames regarding the emergence of clear-cut hand preferences by the end of the second year.

In keeping with all of the previous findings regarding the incidence of right-handedness, left-handedness and ambidexterity, the results show that most of the sample (by the criterion of 80% of the responses being made with one particular hand) are right-handed and very few show evidence of ambidexterity. Painting involves manipulative skills, and the hand frequencies observed might be rather different from the frequencies seen in casual manual activity. This may well account for the difference between the two halves of the sample, when it is divided on the basis of age, and for the apparent inconsistencies with the findings of Gesell and Ames (1947) mentioned above.

Schaller (1963) on the basis of his observations of gorillas in the wild suggests that there may be some laterality of function. In 90 out of 110 observations of chest beating the display was begun with the right hand. Finch (1941) has reported on a careful study of handedness in thirty chimpanzees. He used four test situations which demanded precise, skilful manipulations and based his results on 800 observations on each animal. Using a criterion of 80% responses with one hand as an index of preference he found both left- and right-handed animals in approximately equal numbers in his sample.

The results regarding the production of strokes by the children are broadly in line with those of other investigations which have analysed children's drawings in this way. Gesell (1929) provides a genetic sequence of what he calls crayon and paper behaviour in children. Between 2 and $2\frac{1}{2}$ he observed that children would imitate a vertical stroke; the imitation of a horizontal stroke, however, did not occur until approximately twelve months later. In the painting situation, whilst all the children produced both vertical and horizontal lines, there was nevertheless a much greater incidence of horizontal line painting in the older half of the sample with no corresponding increase in the frequency of vertical lines. Gesell and Ames (1946) studied the direction of drawing movements and found that the movements were downwards in drawing a vertical, from left to right for a horizontal and predominantly anticlockwise for a circle. These findings correspond to our own for the right-handed subset of the sample. The left-handed children in our sample drew horizontal lines going from the right to the left and curves were drawn in a predominantly clockwise direction; they were in fact the opposite of right-handers in these respects and conform with Gesell and Ames' observations.

Abercrombie, Lindon and Tyson (1968) studied the direction of drawing movements in a sample of normal and cerebral palsied children under rather different experimental conditions. The children 'drew' simple line figures with their fingertips whilst being unable to see their hands. Each subject was shown a card with a line drawing on it and asked to pretend to draw it with his fingertip. Although these conditions differed from those of the present study in several important ways, their results are very similar to those reported above. In addition to asking a child to copy a figure with one hand they examined the situation where the child was required to 'draw' with both hands simultaneously. Under these conditions they report that in producing horizontal lines the hands moved either towards each other or away from each other but rarely in the same direction. A similar pattern was found when the vertical and horizontal components were considered separately in drawing a circle. On the basis of their comparison between single and simultaneous movements of the hands they conclude that the latter case evokes more primitive or infantile movements associated with the acquisition of dominance. In the case of the brain injured children they similarly suggest that the differences between them and the normal sample may result from a comparative weakness of lateralisation.

Kellogg (1955) has reported the analysis into stroke components of a very large number of children's drawings and paintings. She describes a more elaborate set of strokes but these are reducible with some simplifications to the set reported here. Kellogg points out that she has gained the impression that children deliberately exercise their skill in the arrangement and production of their repertoire of strokes, as a stage in the development of drawing. She does not offer quantitative analyses.

Morris (1962) analysed some of the works of art produced by a chimpanzee, Congo, and reports three phases. These involve initially one-directional simple lines, then a multiple (to-and-fro) scribble and finally simpler lines again but now with more variety in the shape of the diagrams inasmuch as he claimed recognisable patterns of lines. Horizontal lines were less common than vertical lines as is the case with young children. These findings do imply that for some reason (perhaps biomechanical) horizontal lines are more difficult. However, a single orang-utan examined by Morris showed a predominance of horizontal lines.

Napier (1956) has argued that there are three types of grip; the power grip, the precision grip and a composite grip which is essentially a mixture of the two basic hand configurations. Napier has further argued that the shape of the object is less important in determining the grip than the purpose for which the object is grasped. The power grip ensures greater strength at the expense of independent finger movement whereas the precision grip permits precise manipulation of the object. A further distinction between the grasps is that the power grip involves lateral rotation (towards the thumb) of the fingers, with ulnar inclination of the hand (away from the thumb), whereas in the precision grip the fingers are abducted and axially rotated. Ulnar deviation of the hand is shown in the power grip but not the precision grip. Halverson's (1931) observations indicate that ulnar deviation occurs during reaching before the end of the first year when the object is being held in a precision grip; however, he does not say whether the deviation is maintained during retrieval.

If the grasps described in this study are considered in the light of Napier's criteria difficulties in exact classification arise. The *transverse digital* grasp shows thumb opposition, digital separation and axial rotation, and an exactly similar configuration is used by Napier (1956) to illustrate the precision grasp. The *adult* grip shows the opposition but usually only the first two or three digits are employed actually to hold the brush. The remaining digits show the characteristics of the power grip, thus this is a composite grip. The *ventral* grip is like the *adult* grip but lacks the opposition. The grasp itself is similar to that sometimes employed by the great apes (Napier 1961) to grasp small objects – the brush in this grip is pressed against the lateral surface of the first finger by thumb flexion without adduction or rotation. The overall anatomical configuration of the hand is that of a power grip.

These three grips, the *transverse digital*, the *adult* and the *ventral* all allow a relatively high degree of finger control over the manipulanda, though our observations do not actually establish that this control was asserted in the subjects studied. By comparison the two palmar grasps (*oblique* and *transverse palmar*) and the two clenched grasps (*adult clenched* and *ventral clenched*) lack this possibility of control. The division reflects the degree of finger flexion involved; the palmar grasps are both illustrated by Napier (1956) using various sizes of hammer, as examples of the power grip complex. In the case of the paint brush it should be noted that there is a perfect correspondence between the direction in which the brush lies relative to the hand, and the palmar grip involved. The *oblique palmar* grip always involves the head (bristles) of the brush being to the lateral (thumb) aspect of the hand, whereas the *transverse palmar* grip involves a medial projection of the brush.

The clenched grasps cannot be easily allocated to the power or precision categories. In these cases the anatomical configuration of the hand is that of a power grip. The brush, however, is held in position by adduction of the fingers and flexion, but not opposition, of the thumb.

It is true that the anatomical configuration of the hand does fall into a power or precision dichotomy. However, in the case of the grasps just described it is not true that the anatomical division necessarily reflects the uses (power or precision) which the grasp will serve, as Napier implies. Bishop (1964) in discussing prehensive grasps in Ceboid monkeys, refers to a precision grasp in which the object is held between the knuckles of the second and third digits. Napier (1961) offers a similar example in a juvenile orang-utan. Morris (1962) distinguished 'primitive' and 'advanced' grips in his study of simian painting, these two patterns corresponding to the *palmar* grips and the *ventral* grip respectively. The advanced grip involved the thumb flexing against the lateral surface of the index finger, and opposition is not evident in the photographs published by Morris, but he states that the advanced grip was accompanied by 'an advance in calligraphic variety', and describes it as 'sophisticated'. Precision is used in these examples as a functional term, implying delicacy and fine manipulation, although it is not explicitly defined as such. It is our opinion that the concepts of precision and power grasps are appropriately defined independently of the anatomical configuration of the hand by reference to the skill and force employed in the particular purpose to which the hand is put: and that, while such definitions are not yet available it is unlikely that they would correspond exactly to the anatomical division of hand configuration described by Napier (1956).

The fact that the incidence of the *adult* grasp increases with age in our sample, coupled with the range of grasps actually employed indicates that while the 60-week-old infant may be able to grasp an object in an essentially adult manner, the development of hand function is by no means complete even by the fourth year.

The examination of an object appears to elicit different responses from the hand in comparison with those involved in the use of a tool. Because man enjoys a degree of fine hand control unique amongst the primates, control which permits him to perform such highly skilled actions as writing, Jones (1941) has suggested that the range of human hand function is a reflection of brain specialisation and not hand specialisation. Painting may well represent a form of sensory–motor exploration, especially when (as in the present case) it is non-representational. Presumably then, hand control is being learned as a skill during the stage of painting in which non-representational strokes are being produced. This may be one of the ways in which the child learns to coordinate the activity of the brain and hand – a process of making the hand do what the brain 'sees'.

Halverson's (1931) study emphasised the decline in the use of unnecessary force in the progressive prehensive response during the first year. There is in this case an implied gain in precision at the expense of power. A similar effect appears to accompany the decline in frequency of grips which involve the clenched fingers with increasing age which we observed in the present sample. The elimination of unnecessary movements and unnecessary force is a recognised features in the acquisition of skill and is particularly striking in the case of skill acquisition by children.

If it is true that man, having freed his hands from the demands of loco-motor activity by the assumption of a bipedal gait, developed thereby an unrivalled manual dexterity, it is not surprising that the hand should be a late developer, showing adult skill as a result of a prolonged period of juvenile experimentation and sensory–motor integration.

Acknowledgements

The authors are grateful to the children and teachers at the nursery schools visited and in particular to Mrs D. Gabbertas, Headmistress of the Grace Owen Nursery School and Miss J. O. Packer, Headmistress of the Broomhall Nursery School. The cooperation of the Director of Education for the City of Sheffield is also gratefully acknowledged. Some of the work reported in this paper was supported by a research grant from the Spastics Society. The authors are grateful to Professor A. H. Schultz for permission to use Fig. 13·5.

APPENDIX

Summary by genus of primate hand usage. (Taxon – the term used to describe a principal grouping, Buettner-Janusch, 1963; 2.) Since all infra-human primates use the hands in locomotion this function is only listed where further information is given. The absence of data cannot be taken to imply the absence of a function

Taxon	Genus	Thumb	Hand	Functions	References
Tupaiiformes	*Tupaia*	divergent, non-opposable	non-prehensile, single prehensive pattern and grip	*feeding* both hands, food occasionally raked in under flexed digits; *grooming* slight hand use; *locomotion* quadrupedal plantigrade, single grip	Andrew, 1964 Bishop, 1964 Jolly, 1964 Napier and Napier, 1967
	Anathana				
	Urogale		barely prehensile	*feeding* capable of one-handed grasping, not always accurately; *locomotion* quadrupedal, plantigrade	Napier and Napier, 1967 Polyak, 1957
	Dendrogale	divergent, non-opposable, mobile			
	Ptilocercus		barely prehensile	*feeding* insects may be grasped with one hand	Clark, 1926
Lemuriformes	*Lemur*	pseudo-opposable	prehensile, object grasped between fingers and proximal palmar pads	*feeding; grooming; agonistic behaviour; scent marking*	Bishop, 1964 Jolly, 1964
	Hapalemur	pseudo-opposable	prehensile, fingers, flex against palm, thumb not always opposed	*feeding; grooming*	Bishop, 1964

Lepilemur	pseudo-opposable	prehensile, grasp simple no fine movements	*agonistic behaviour*; *locomotion* grasping large vertical branches; small objects held between digits and palm	Napier and Napier, 1967 Petter, 1965
Cheirogaleus	pseudo-opposable	prehensile	infrequently for *feeding* and *grooming*; *locomotion*, principal axis of grasp between digits 2 and 3	Bishop, 1964 Napier and Napier, 1967 Petter, 1965
Microcebus	pseudo-opposable	prehensile, *Loris*-like grip, *Lemur*-like reaching pattern	*feeding* hands used to manipulate food; *cleaning* face with both hands; *scent marking*; *grooming*; *locomotion* principal axis of grasp between digits 1 and 2	Bishop, 1964 Jolly, 1964 Petter, 1962 Petter, 1965
Phaner	pseudo-opposable	prehensile	*feeding*	Napier and Napier, 1967
Indri	pseudo-opposable	prehensile	*locomotion* grasps large vertical branches	Napier and Napier, 1967
Avahi	pseudo-opposable	prehensile	*locomotion* only coarse grasping; ulnar border of hand provides dominant grip	Napier and Napier, 1967
Propithecus	pseudo-opposable	prehensile, objects grasped against distal palmar pads, all digits flexed towards palm	*feeding*; *locomotion* only coarse grasping	Bishop, 1964 Napier and Napier, 1967
Daubentonia			*feeding* specialised digit 3 to percuss bark, holds food stable against substrate while eating. Functional axis of hand between digits 1 and 2	Napier and Napier, 1967 Petter, 1965

APPENDIX—*continued*

Taxon	Genus	Thumb	Hand	Functions	References
Lorisiformes	*Loris*	widely divergent pseudo-opposable	prehensile, thumb and fingers operate as clamp, single grip, hand closes on palmar contact	*locomotion* always involving prehension; *feeding* not observed to manipulate objects other than food; *grooming*; *agonistic behaviour*	Bishop, 1964 Jolly, 1964
	Nycticebus	widely divergent pseudo-opposable	prehensile, as *Loris*	*feeding*; *grooming*; *locomotion*, as *Loris*	Bishop, 1964
	Arctocebus	widely divergent pseudo-opposable	prehensile, as *Loris*	*feeding*; *locomotion*, as *Loris*	Napier and Napier, 1967
	Perodicticus	widely divergent (180° to digit 3) pseudo-opposable	prehensile, as *Loris*	*locomotion*, as *Loris*; *feeding* manipulates objects to obtain food *grooming*	Bishop, 1964 Jolly, 1964
	Galago	pseudo-opposable	prehensile, object grasped between proximal phalanges and palmar pads, reaches like *Loris*	*feeding* manipulates objects to obtain food; *grooming*; *scent marking*	Bishop, 1964 Andrew, 1964 Napier and Napier, 1967 Jolly, 1964
Tarsiiformes	*Tarsius*	divergent, pseudo-opposable shows some mobility at metacarpo-phalangeal joint	prehensile, similar to *Loris*	*locomotion* clasps vertical branches; *feeding* uses single hand	Polyak, 1957 Napier, 1961

Ceboidea	*Callithrix*	non-opposable	prehensile, otherwise similar to *Tupaia* objects gripped between flexed digits and proximal palm	*feeding* single handed; *locomotion* hand placed transversely on branches	Bishop, 1964 Napier and Napier, 1967
	Cebuella				
	Saguinus	non-opposable	prehensile	*locomotion* as *Callithrix*; *feeding* single handed	Napier and Napier, 1967
	Leontideus	non-opposable	prehensile	*feeding* food clasped between flexed digits and palm; *social grooming* thumb not differentiated	Bishop, 1964
	Callimico	non-opposable	prehensile		Bishop, 1962
	Aotus	non-opposable	prehensile, single prehensive pattern, finger tips used for sensory discrimination	*grooming*	Bishop, 1964
	Callicebus	non-opposable barely differentiated functionally	prehensile, single prehensive pattern, finger tips used for manipulation	*grooming*	Bishop, 1964
	Pithecia	pseudo-opposable	prehensile	functional axis of hand between digits 2 and 3	Napier and Napier, 1967
	Chiropotes	pseudo-opposable	prehensile		Napier and Napier, 1967

APPENDIX—*continued*

Taxon	Genus	Thumb	Hand	Functions	References
Ceboidea	*Cacajao*	non-opposable	prehensile, precision grip involving thumb only	*feeding* manipulates food between supinated wrists. Functional axis of hand between digits 2 and 3	Bishop, 1964 Hill, 1960
	Alouatta	pseudo-opposable	prehensile, effective grasp between thumb and other digits	*locomotion* semi-brachiation using a hook grip	Carpenter, 1934 Erikson, 1963 Napier and Napier, 1967
	Cebus	pseudo-opposable	prehensile	*tool using;* *agonistic behaviour;* *throwing*	Hill, 1960 Kortlandt and Kooij, 1963 Napier, 1962 Vevers and Weiner, 1963
	Saimiri	pseudo-opposable	prehensile, whole hand used in manipulation finger tips used in sensory discrimination	*grooming*	Bishop, 1964 Hill, 1960
	Ateles	absent	prehensile, hook grip, precision grip, 'scissors' grip between digits alternatively first digit folds around small object	*locomotion* semi-brachiation	Bishop, 1964 Napier and Napier, 1967

		thumb	grip	function / locomotion	references
	Brachyteles	absent	prehensile, as *Ateles*	as *Ateles*	Napier and Napier, 1967
Cercopithecoidea	*Macaca*	opposable	prehensile, precision grip, thumb and index finger	*feeding; grooming; locomotion* quadrupedal, digitigrade or plantigrade	Jensen, 1961 Napier and Napier, 1967
	Cynopithecus		prehensile		Napier and Napier, 1967
	Cercocebus	opposable	prehensile, precision grip, thumb and index finger	*locomotion* quadrupedal, digitigrade or plantigrade	Napier and Napier, 1967
	Papio	opposable	prehensile, precision grip, thumb and index finger independent of other digits	*feeding; grooming; exploratory manipulation; locomotion* quadrupedal, digitigrade	Hall, 1963 Napier and Napier, 1967 Trevarthen, 1971
	Mandrillus	opposable	prehensile, precision and power grips well differentiated	*locomotion* quadrupedal, digitigrade	Napier and Napier, 1967
	Theropithecus	opposable	prehensile		Napier and Napier, 1967
	Cercopithecus	opposable	prehensile	*feeding* manipulates fruit	Gartlan and Brain, 1968
	Erythrocebus	opposable	prehensile, fully separate precision and power grips	*feeding; locomotion* quadrupedal, occasionally bipedal	Bishop, 1964 Hall and Meyer, 1966 Napier and Napier, 1967

APPENDIX—*continued*

Taxon	Genus	Thumb	Hand	Functions	References
Cercopithecoidea	*Presbytis*	opposable	prehensile, fine manipulative movements not observed, poor precision grip	*locomotion* quadrupedal, leaves plucked by thumb acting against side of hand; *feeding; grooming*	Jay, 1965 Napier and Napier, 1967
	Rhinopithecus				
	Nasalis	opposable	prehensile	*feeding; locomotion* semi-brachiation	Napier and Napier, 1967
	Simias				
	Colobus	vestigial	prehensile, power/ precision grip distinction maintained, index finger flexes back against vestigial thumb hook grip	*locomotion* semi-brachiation involving hook grip	Bishop, 1964 Napier and Napier, 1967
Anthropoidea	*Hylobates*	opposable, ball and socket carpometacarpal joint	prehensile, precision grip of thumb against lateral surface of index, hook grip	*feeding* and *grooming* both involving thumb; *locomotion* brachiation using hook grip thumb involved in gripping vertical branches	Carpenter, 1940 Joufroy and Lessertisseur, 1960 Tuttle, 1969
	Symphalangus	as *Hylobates*	as *Hylobates*	as *Hylobates*	Joufroy and Lessertisseur, 1960 Napier and Napier, 1967 Tuttle, 1969

Pongo	opposable	prehensile, hook grip including 'double locked' mechanism, two precision grips (a) thumb against lateral surface of index (b) inter-digital grip	*feeding; tool using; locomotion* modified brachiation involving hook grip	Davenport, 1967 Napier, 1960 Napier, 1963 Tuttle, 1967 Tuttle, 1969
Pan	opposable	prehensile, hook grip including 'double locked' mechanism precision grip thumb against lateral surface of index finger	*feeding; self grooming nest building; agonistic behaviour; tool using; locomotion* quadrupedal knuckle walking. Some brachiation with hook grip	Goodall, 1968 Morris, 1962 Napier, 1960 Napier, 1963 Tuttle, 1967, 1969
Gorilla	opposable	prehensile, precision and power grips differentiated	*feeding; nest building; grooming; agonistic behaviour; locomotion* quadrupedal knuckle walking, some modified brachiation	Morris, 1962 Napier, 1963 Schaller, 1965 Tuttle, 1967, 1969

379

K. CONNOLLY AND J. ELLIOTT
REFERENCES

Abercrombie, M. L. J., Lindon, R. L. and Tyson, M. C. (1968). Direction of drawing movements. *Devel. Med. Child Neurol.* **10**, 93–7.

Andrew, R. J. (1964). Displays of the primates. In *Evolutionary and Genetic Biology of Primates*, vol. 2. Ed. J. Buettner-Janusch, London: Academic Press.

Beintema, D. J. (1968). *A Neurological Study of Newborn Infants.* London: Heinemann.

Bell, Sir C. (1833). The Bridgewater treatises: IV. *The Hand.* Second edition. London: William Pickering.

Biegert, J. (1964). The evaluation of characteristics of the skull, hands, and feet for primate taxonomy. In *Classification and Human Evolution.* Ed. S. L. Washburn, London: Methuen.

Birch, H. G. and Lefford, A. (1963). Intersensory development in children. *Monog. Soc. Res. Child Develop.* **28** (set no. 89).

Birch, H. G. and Lefford, A. (1967). Visual differentiation, intersensory integration, and voluntary motor control. *Monog. Soc. Res. Child Develop.* **32** (ser. no. 110).

Bishop, A. (1962). Control of the hand in lower primates. *Ann. N.Y. Acad. Sci.* **102**, 316–17.

Bishop, A. (1964). Use of the hand in lower primates. In *Evolutionary and Genetic Biology of Primates*, vol. 2. Ed. J. Buettner-Janusch, London: Academic Press.

Bruner, J. S. (1969). *Processes of Cognitive Growth: Infancy.* Heinz Werner Lectures. Massachusetts: Clark University Press.

Buettner-Janusch, J. (1963). An introduction to the primates. In *Evolutionary and Genetic Biology of Primates*, vol. 1. Ed. J. Buettner-Janusch, London: Academic Press.

Buettner-Janusch, J. (1966). *Origins of man.* London: Wiley.

Bühler, K. (1933). *The Mental Development of the Child.* London: Kegan Paul.

Campbell, C. B. G. (1966). Taxonomic status of treeshrews. *Science, N.Y.* **153**, 436.

Carpenter, C. R. (1934). A field study of the behavior and social relations of the howling monkey (*Alouatta palliata*). *Comp. Psychol. Monog.* **10**. Also in Carpenter, C. R., *Naturalistic Behavior of Nonhuman Primates.* Pennsylvania: Pennsylvania State University Press.

Carpenter, C. R. (1940). Field study in Siam of the behavior and social relations of the gibbon (*Hylobates lar*). *Comp. Psychol. Monog.* **16**. Also in Carpenter, C. R., *Naturalistic Behavior of Nonhuman Primates.* Pennsylvania: Pennsylvania State University Press.

Clark, W. E. Le Gros (1926). The anatomy of the pen-tailed treeshrew. *Proc. zool. soc. Lond.* **46**, 1179–309.

Clark, W. E. Le Gros (1959). *The Antecedents of Man.* Edinburgh: Edinburgh University Press.

Connolly, K. J. (1968). Some mechanisms involved in the development of motor skills. *Aspects of Education* **7**, 82–100.

Connolly, K. J. (1969). Sensory–motor co-ordination: mechanisms and plans. In *Planning for Better Learning.* Ed. P. H. Wolff and R. MacKeith, London: S.I.M.P./Heinemann.

Connolly, K. J. (1970). Skill development: problems and plans. In *Mechanisms of Motor Skill Development.* Ed. K. J. Connolly, London: Academic Press.

Darwin, C. (1877). A biographical sketch of an infant. *Mind* **2**, 285–94.

Davenport, R. K. (1967). The orang-utan in Sabah. *Folia Primat.* **5**, 247–63.

Durost, W. N. (1934). The development of a battery of objective group tests of manual laterality, with the results of their application to 1300 children. *Genet. Psychol. Monog.* **16**, 225–335.

Eng, H. (1954). *The psychology of children's drawings.* Second edition. London: Routledge and Kegan Paul.

Erikson, G. E. (1963). Brachiation in the New World monkeys. In *The Primates, Symp. Zool. Soc. Lond.* **10**, 135–64.

Finch, G. (1941). Chimpanzee handedness. *Science, N.Y.* **94**, 117–18.

Gartlan, J. S. and Brain, C. K. (1968). Ecology and social variability in *Cercopithecus aethiops.* In *Primates : Studies in Adaptation and Variability.* Ed. P. C. Jay, London: Holt Rinehart and Winston.

Gesell, A. (1929). Maturation and infant behavior patterns. *Psychol. Rev.* **36**, 307–19.

Gesell, A. and Amatruda, C. S. (1947). *Developmental Diagnosis.* London: Harper and Row.

Gesell, A. and Ames, L. B. (1946). The development of directionality in drawing. *J. genet. Psychol.* **68**, 45–61.

Gesell, A. and Ames, L. B. (1947). The development of handedness. *J. genet. Psychol.* **70**, 155–75.

Goodall, J. van Lawick (1968). The behaviour of free-living chimpanzees in the Gombe Stream Reserve. *Anim. Behav. Monog.* **1**, 161–311.

Goodenough, F. L. (1926). *The measurement of intelligence by drawings.* New York: World Book Co.

Hall, K. R. L. (1963). Tool-using performance as indicators of behavioral adaptability. *Current Anthropology* **4**, no. 5, 479–94.

Hall, K. R. L. and Meyer, Barbara (1966). Hand preference and dexterities of captive Patas monkeys. *Folia Primat.* **4**, 169–85.

Halverson, H. M. (1931). An experimental study of prehension in infants by means of systematic cinema records. *Genet. Psychol. Monog.* **10**, nos. 2, 3, 110–286.

Halverson, H. M. (1932). A further study of grasping. *J. Gen. Psychol.* **7**, 34–63.

Halverson, H. M. (1937). Studies of the grasping responses of early infancy. I, II, III. *J. genet. Psychol.* **51**, 371–449.

Halverson, H. M. (1943). The development of prehension in infants. In *Child Development and Behaviour.* Ed. R. G. Barker, J. S. Kounin and H. F. Wright, London: McGraw-Hill.

Held, R. and Bauer, J. (1967). Visually guided reaching in infant monkeys after restricted rearing. *Science, N.Y.* **155**, 718–20.

Held, R. and Hein, A. (1963). Movement produced stimulation in the development of visually guided behavior. *J. comp. physiol. Psychol.* **56**, 872–6.

Hildreth, G. (1949). The development and training of hand dominance. II: Developmental tendencies in handedness. *J. genet. Psychol.* **75**, 221–54.

Hill, W. C. O. (1960). *Primates,* vol. 4: Cebidae, Part A. Edinburgh: Edinburgh University Press.

Holt, K. S. (1965). *Assessment of Cerebral Palsy. 1. Muscle Function, Locomotion and Hand Function.* London: Lloyd-Luke.

Hooker, D. (1938). Origin of the grasping movement in man. *Proc. Amer. Phil. Soc.* **79**, 597–606.

Hooker, D. (1958). Evidence of prenatal function of CNS in man. James Arthur Lecture. *Amer. Mus. Nat. Hist. N.Y.*

Jay, P. C. (1965). The common langur of North India. In *Primate behavior.* Ed. I. DeVore, London: Holt Rinehart and Winston.

Jensen, G. D. (1961). The development of prehension in a macaque. *J. comp. physiol. Psychol.* **54**, 11–12.

Jolly, A. (1964). Prosimians' manipulation of simple object problems. *Anim. Behav.* **12**, 560–70.

Jones, F. W. (1941). *The Hand.* Second edition. London: Bailliere, Tindall and Cox.

Jouffroy, F. K. and Lessertisseur, J. (1960). Les spécialisations anatomiques de la main chez les singes à progression suspendue. *Mammalia* **24**, 93–151.

Kellogg, R. (1955). *What Children Scribble and Why.* Palo Alto, California: N-P Publications.

Kortlandt, A. and Kooij, M. (1963). Protohominid behaviour in primates (preliminary communication). In *The Primates. Symp. Zool. Soc. Lond.* **10**, 61–88.

Martin, R. D. (1968). Towards a new definition of primates. *Man* (n.s.) **3**, 378–401.

McGraw, M. B. (1943). *The Neuromuscular Maturation of the Human Infant.* New York: Columbia University Press.

Morris, D. (1962). *The Biology of Art.* London: Methuen.

Napier, J. R. (1956). The prehensile movements of the human hand. *J. Bone Jt. Surgery* **38B**, 902–13.

Napier, J. R. (1960). Studies of the hands of living primates. *Proc. zool. Soc. Lond.* **134**, 647–57.

Napier, J. R. (1961). Prehensility and opposability in the hands of primates. In *Vertebrate Locomotion. Symp. zool. Soc. Lond.* **5**, 115–32.

Napier, J. R. (1963). Brachiation and brachiators. In *The Primates. Symp. zool. Soc. Lond.* **10**, 183–95.

Napier, J. R. (1966). Functional aspects of the anatomy of the hand. In *The Hand: Clinical Surgery* 7. Ed. R. G. Pulvertaft, London: Butterworths.

Napier, J. R. and Napier, P. H. (1967). *A Handbook of Living Primates.* London: Academic Press.

Petter, J. J. (1962). Ecological and behavioral studies of Madagascar lemurs in the field. *Ann. N.Y. Acad. Sci.* **102**, 267–81.

Petter, J. J. (1965). The lemurs of Madagascar. In *Primate Behavior.* Ed. I. DeVore, London: Holt Rinehart and Winston.

Piaget, J. (1952). *Origins of Intelligence in the Child.* London: Routledge and Kegan Paul.

Piaget, J. and Inhelder, B. (1956). *The Child's Conception of Space.* London: Routledge and Kegan Paul.

Polyak, S. (1957). *The Vertebrate Visual System.* Chicago: Chicago Univ. Press.

Prechtl, H. R. F. and Beintema, D. (1964). *The Neurological Examination of the Full-Term Newborn Infant.* London: S.I.M.P./Heinemann.

Ranson, S. W. and Clark, S. L. (1947). *The Anatomy of the Nervous System.* Eighth edition. Philadelphia: Saunders.

Rice, C. (1930). Excellence of production and types of movement in drawing. *Child Develop.* **1**, 1–14.

Schaller, G. B. (1963). *The Mountain Gorilla: Ecology and Behavior.* Chicago: Chicago Univ. Press.

Schaller, G. B. (1965). The behavior of the mountain gorilla. In *Primate Behavior.* Ed. I. DeVore, London: Holt Rinehart and Winston.

Schultz, A. H. (1956). Post-embryonic age changes. In *Primatologia* 1. Ed. H. Hofer, A. H. Schultz and D. Starck, Basel: Karger.

Schultz, A. H. (1968). Form und Function der Primatehände. In *Handgebrauch und Verständigung bei Affen und Frühmenschen*. Bern and Stuttgart: Huber.

Simpson, G. G. (1945). The principles of classification and a classification of the mammals. *Bull. Amer. Mus. Nat. Hist.* **85**, 1–350.

Townsend, E. A. (1951). A study of copying ability in children. *Genet. Psychol. Monog.* **43**, 3–51.

Trevarthen, C. B. (1971). Manipulative strategies of baboons and the origin of cerebral assymetry. In *Hemispheric Assymetry of Function*. Ed. M. Kinsbourne, London: Tavistock.

Tuttle, R. H. (1967). Knuckle-walking and the evolution of hominoid hands. *Amer. J. Phys. Anthrop.* **26**, 171–206.

Tuttle, R. H. (1969). Quantitative and functional studies on the hands of the Anthropoidea. 1: The Hominoidea. *J. Morph.* **128**, 309–64.

Twitchell, T. E. (1965). The automatic grasping responses of infants. *Neuropsychologia* **3**, 247–59.

Twitchell, T. E. (1970). Reflex mechanisms and the development of prehension. In *Mechanisms of Motor Skill Development*. Ed. K. J. Connolly, London: Academic Press.

Van Valen, L. (1965). Treeshrews, primates and fossils. *Evolution* **19**, 137–51.

Vereecken, P. (1961). *Spatial Development*. Groningen: J. B. Wolters.

Vevers, G. M. and Weiner, J. S. (1963). Use of a tool by a captive capuchin monkey (*Cebus apella*). In *The Primates. Symp. zool. Soc. Lond.* **10**, 115–17.

Wells, K. F. (1966). *Kinesiology*. Fourth edition. Philadelphia: Saunders.

White, B., Castle, P. and Held, R. (1964). Observations on the development of visually-directed reaching. *Child Develop.* **35**, 349–64.

AUTHOR INDEX

Note : page numbers in **bold** type refer to lists of references

SUBJECT INDEX

actions
 behaviour units involving, 270–5
 classification of behaviour units into
  those involving face, speech, and,
  254, 256–8, 259–70
adipose tissue, brown, heat-generating,
 314, 318
adult behaviour
 applicability of studies on children to,
  25–6
 facial expressions of, 52, 54–5
 imitation of, by children, 21–2, 298–9
 see also mothers
' affiliativeness ', 13
age
 and aggression, 112
 in factor analysis of behaviour, 81, 82,
  86, 88, 99, 107, 116–19
 and handedness, 353
 and interactions of children with
  mothers and other children, 259, 261,
  262, 265, 266–7, 299–301
 of mothers, and method of feeding
  baby, 188
 and painting grasps and strokes, 365–6,
  367–8
 and 'permeability' of primate groups,
  150
 and responses to strangers, 151, 171,
  296–7
 and rough and tumble play, 83, 109
 and selection pressure, 302
 and separation behaviour, 224, 229
 and social behaviour, 113, 118
 and vocalisations, 81, 82
aggression, 13, 17, 18, 19, 324
 behaviour associated with, 42, 48
 eyebrow movements accompanying,
  40–1
 in factor analysis of behaviour, 107,
  110–13, 120, 121, 123–4
 imitation of, 123
 by new members of group, 140–1,
  142–3
 towards new members of group: not
  shown by children, 149; shown by
  primates, 149–50, 151
 posture showing balance between
  escape and, 49
 relation between adults' ratings of, and
  dominance, 144
 rough and tumble play and, 108–9,
  113, 121, 123, 301
 by Zhun/twa children, 300–1

agonistic behaviours, 49, 69, 79, 142–3
Alouatta, hand of, 376
ambivalence, behaviour in situations of,
 152, 211, 300
Anathana, hand of, 372
anatomy
 and behaviour, 315
 concerned with both structure and
  function, 331
animals
 communication between, 38, 47
 comparative studies of humans and,
  6, 8, 9–10, 305, 310, 323–4
 development of independence from
  mother in, 230
 interactions, between, 7, 14, 15
 psychology of, 66
 studies of behaviour of, vii; as source
  of hypotheses, 3, 41, and of methods,
  4
anthropology, and ethology, 4, 6, 9, 28,
 302–3
anti-predator behaviour, 313, 321
 attachment of mother and baby as,
  238, 294, 307, 323
anxiety-producing situations, responses
 to, 152, 212
 sex differences in, 85
Aotus, hand of, 375
appeasement, signals aiming at, 48, 150
approaches by children
 to mothers, at greeting, 223, 225, 232,
  233
 to strangers: analysis of behaviour in,
  43; behaviour of stranger and, 164–
  71; extra frequency of, by sociable
  and isolated types of child, 171–2;
  type of institution and, 158–64
aptitude tests, 23
archaeology, and ethology, 6, 9, 308
Arctocebus, hand of, 374
arms
 behaviour units involving, 60–2
 gestures with, by toddlers out of doors,
  205–8, 213
 movements of (shoulder, elbow, wrist),
  in painting, 359–61, 366
 raising of (asking to be picked up), 207;
  associated with touching by mother,
  231; immature behaviour, 228;
  mother-specific, 213, 226, 227
 traction response of, in new-born
  babies, 341
arousal, inhibition or reduction of, 85,
 212, 319